Luminos is the Open Access monograph publishing program from UC Press. Luminos provides a framework for preserving and reinvigorating monograph publishing for the future and increases the reach and visibility of important scholarly work. Titles published in the UC Press Luminos model are published with the same high standards for selection, peer review, production, and marketing as those in our traditional program. www.luminosoa.org

D1571844

This publication is openly available online thanks to generous support from Arcadia, a charitable fund of Lisbet Rausing and Peter Baldwin.

# Archipelago of Resettlement

AMERICAN CROSSROADS

Edited by Earl Lewis, George Lipsitz, George Sánchez, Dana Takagi, Laura Briggs, and Nikhil Pal Singh

# Archipelago of Resettlement

*Vietnamese Refugee Settlers and Decolonization
across Guam and Israel-Palestine*

———

Evyn Lê Espiritu Gandhi

UNIVERSITY OF CALIFORNIA PRESS

University of California Press
Oakland, California

Suggested citation: Gandhi, E. L. E. *Archipelago of Resettlement:
Vietnamese Refugee Settlers and Decolonization across Guam and
Israel-Palestine*. Oakland: University of California Press, 2022.
DOI: https://doi.org/10.1525/luminos.123

Names: Gandhi, Evyn Lê Espiritu, author.
Title: Archipelago of resettlement : Vietnamese refugee settlers and
    decolonization across Guam and Israel-Palestine / Evyn Lê Espiritu Gandhi.
Description: Oakland, California : University of California Press, [2022] |
    Includes bibliographical references and index.
Identifiers: LCCN 2021042119 (print) | LCCN 2021042120 (ebook) |
    ISBN 9780520379657 (paperback) | ISBN 9780520976832 (ebook)
Subjects: LCSH: Refugees—Guam--20th century. | Vietnamese—
    Guam—20th century. | Refugees—Israel—20th century. |
    Vietnamese—Israel—20th century. | Settler colonialism—Political aspects.
Classification: LCC HV640.5.V5 E87 2022 (print) | LCC HV640.5.V5
    (ebook) | DDC 325/.210959709967—dc23/eng/20211005
LC record available at https://lccn.loc.gov/2021042119
LC ebook record available at https://lccn.loc.gov/2021042120

28  27  26  25  24  23  22
10  9  8  7  6  5  4  3  2  1

# CONTENTS

# LIST OF ILLUSTRATIONS

## MAP

## FIGURES

# ACKNOWLEDGMENTS

This book has two beginnings. I first wrote about Vietnamese refugee resettlement in Israel-Palestine as a Rhetoric PhD student in Daniel Boyarin's "Rhetoric and History: Comparative Diasporas" class at University of California, Berkeley, during fall 2013. This paper became the kernel of my dissertation. The deadly airstrikes on Gaza during summer 2014 further clarified the stakes of this research. Writing became a way to situate my support for the contemporary Palestinian liberation struggle as a second-generation Vietnamese-Filipina.

The second beginning of this book is rooted in family history. In April 1975, my mother and grandmother left Vietnam as refugees and were processed on the Chamorro island of Guam during Operation New Life. After moving around Southern California, they eventually resettled in Oceanside, California, near Camp Pendleton on Luiseño, Juaneño, and Kumeyaay lands, where I grew up. I am forever indebted to my Bà Ngoại, Hồ Ngọc Hoa, who helped raise me and who loves me unconditionally, and my mother, Yến Lê Espiritu, who initiated the field of critical refugee studies and who inspires me every day, both personally and professionally. Their courage and refugee resilience have profoundly shaped who I am today.

This project developed in conversation with scholars across three institutions. At UC Berkeley, on Ohlone lands, I am grateful for the friendship and intellectual camaraderie of Lilith Acadia, Andrew Cheng, Natalia Duong, Will Gow, Kuan Hwa, Ryan Ikeda, Anooj Kansara, Chris Waldo, and Camila Yadeau, among others. Trinh T. Minh-ha taught me that writing can be beautiful and theory should arise from context. Colleen Lye helped me develop a strong foundation in Asian American literature, and her tough love approach prepared me for the challenges of this profession. Daniel Boyarin's class on diaspora theory informs my critique of the nation-state. Keith Feldman's work on Palestine as well as his insightful feedback on the dissertation deeply shapes this book. Ryan Rhadigan first introduced me to Indigenous and settler colonial studies. Rachel Lim remains one of my sharpest interlocutors and dearest friends. At College of the Holy Cross, on Nimpuc tribal lands, I thank Ann Marie Leshkowich and Tat-Siong Benny Liew for their postdoctoral mentorship. Pau Cañigueral Batllosera, Ernest Hartwell, and Rebecca Castleman provided invaluable friendship during our carpool commutes to and from Cambridge, Massachusetts. Now at University of California, Los Angeles, on the traditional homelands of the Gabrielino/Tongva people, I thank my amazing department: Victor Bascara, Lucy Mae San Pablo Burns, Jennifer Chun, Grace Kyugwon Hong, Jinqi Ling, Purnima Mankekar, Valerie Masumoto, Natalie Masuoka, Kyeyong Park, Renee Tajima-Peña, Karen Umemoto, David Yoo, Min Zhou, Kelly Fong, Lily Anne Welty Tamai, Wendy Fujinami, Kylin Sakamoto, and Greg Pancho. Both Nguyễn-võ Thu-hương and Keith L. Camacho provided crucial feedback on the manuscript and supported my research even before I came to UCLA. I couldn't have asked for a more incredible and supportive cohort of fellow junior colleagues: Loubna Qutami, Lee Ann Wang, Cindy Sangalan, and Jolie Chea. Lastly, I thank all the students I have taught across multiple institutions, who have pushed my thinking in important ways.

This research has also benefited from conversations and friendships across many different fields. In Vietnamese refugee studies, I thank Vinh Nguyen, Trung PQ Nguyen, Timothy K. August, Lan Duong, Viet Thanh Nguyen, Catherine H. Nguyen, Long Bui, Cindy Nguyen, Quyên Nguyen-Le, Ly Thuy Nguyen, Thy Phu, and Thuy Vo Dang, among others. I am inspired by scholars of Asian settler colonial studies and Asian-Indigenous relations, including Candace Fujikane, Dean Saranillio, Iyko Day, Yu-ting Huang, Juliana Hu Pegues, Quynh Nhu Le, Demiliza Saramosing, and Tiffany Wang-Su Tran. Presenting my research on a panel with Palestinian and Palestine studies feminists Lila Sharif, Sarah Ihmoud, Maryam Griffin, and Jennifer Lynn Kelly at the 2017 National Women's Studies Association conference was pivotal. Lila Sharif also offered invaluable feedback on chapter 6. In Chamorro and Guåhan studies, I have learned deeply from Craig Santos Perez, Kristin Obierno, Tiara Na'puti, Josephine Faith Ong, Antoinette Charfauros McDaniel, Alfred Flores, and Michael Lujan Bevacqua. In Asian American and American studies more broadly, I thank Cathy Schlund-Vials, Chad Shomura, Quinn Lester, Douglas Ishii, Heidi Amin-Hong, and Terry Park. Huan He, Christina Juhasz-Wood, and Rachel Lim have been an incredibly supportive writing group, particularly during the final stages of this manuscript. I also thank the University of California, Irvine, Global Studies Conference, especially Sharad Chari, Briana Nichols, and Eman Ghanayem, for the opportunity to workshop chapter 1; and the University of Southern California Migration and Refugee Studies working group, particularly Lillian Ngan, who invited me, for their helpful feedback on chapter 2.

I appreciate all the interlocutors, transcribers, translators, and archivists across multiple archipelagic geographies who made this book possible. Thank you to everyone who trusted me with their stories and oral histories in Vietnam, Guam, and Israel-Palestine, including those who chose to remain unnamed. I especially thank Vaan Nguyen for answering all my questions and her father, Hoài Mỹ Nguyễn, for connecting me to other Vietnamese Israelis. Vivian Dames hosted me in Talofofo, Guam, and connected me to key folks across the island, and Sophia Ritchie hosted me in Ramallah, Palestine, and helped me navigate the West Bank. Ishwanzya D. Rivers of PhD Transcribing, Ken Saw, and Jenny Lu helped with English-language transcriptions, and Diem Ramakrishnan, Justin Vu, and Angela Dang assisted with Vietnamese-language transcriptions. Adriana X. Jacobs graciously shared early translations of Vaan Nguyen's Hebrew-language poetry even prior to the 2021 publication of *The Truffle Eye* in English. Kobi Fischer scanned and translated documents from the Israel State Archives. Tom Pessah answered my Hebrew inquiries. Shireen Hamza helped transcribe the Arabic quotes from Mourid Barghouti's *I Saw Ramallah*, discussed in chapter 6. Archivists at the Institute of Palestine Studies in Ramallah, the Richard F. Taitano Micronesian Area Research Center at the University of Guam, and the Nieves M. Flores Memorial Library in Hagåtña provided crucial research support.

I am honored to publish my book with the University of California Press, which released a powerful statement in solidarity with Palestine in May 2021. I thank Niels Hooper for nurturing this project into publication and George Sánchez for including the book in the American Crossroads series. Naja Pulliam Collins, Robin Manley, and Cindy Fulton all helped with the publication process. PJ Heim created the index. Jana K. Lipman and the anonymous reviewer's incisive feedback strengthened the manuscript in countless ways. Ajean Lee Ryan's cover art perfectly encapsulates the archipelagic.

This research was supported by the Ford Foundation Predoctoral Fellowship, a Berkeley Institute for Jewish Law and Israel Studies Research Grant, a UC Berkeley Center for Race and Gender Travel Grant, a UCLA Asian American Studies Center Grant, and a UCLA Institute of American Cultures Research Grant. This book is freely available in an open access edition thanks to TOME (Toward an Open Monograph Ecosystem)—a collaboration of the Association of American Universities, the Association of University Presses, and the Association of Research Libraries—and the generous support of Arcadia, a charitable fund of Lisbet Rausing and Peter Baldwin, and the UCLA Library. Learn more at the TOME website, openmonographs.org. An earlier version of chapter 1 was published as Evyn Lê Espiritu, "Cold War Entanglements, Third World Solidarities: Vietnam and Palestine, 1967–75," *Canadian Review of American Studies* 48, no. 3 (2018): 352–86, reprinted by permission of University of Toronto Press. An earlier version of chapter 6 was published as Evyn Lê Espiritu, "Vexed Solidarities: Vietnamese Israelis and the Question of Palestine," *LIT: Literature Interpretation Theory* 29,

no. 1 (2018): 8–28, reprinted by permission of Taylor & Francis Ltd (http://www
.tandfonline.com). I also thank Tony Azios for the opportunity to share research
from chapter 3 as a *Memoirs Pasifika* podcast episode.

I am incredibly grateful to all my family, especially my Bà Ngoại, my parents,
and my siblings, Maya and Gabriel, whose commitment to education in all its
forms inspires me. My best friend and husband, Ashvin Gandhi, believed in me
even before I started this project and has been a much-needed anchor through the
ups and downs of the research and writing process. Thank you as well to the entire
Gandhi family, who have warmly embraced me as their own.

This book is for all the activists, academics, cultural producers, and movement
makers fighting for decolonization, liberation, and refuge for all peoples. As I write
this in spring 2021, the numbers of refugees seeking asylum is at an all-time high.
Guam is yet again being considered as a processing center for refugees displaced
by US military intervention, this time from Afghanistan, and people around the
world are raising their voices in solidarity with Palestine. It is my hope that this
book can offer guidance for thinking through refugee-Indigenous solidarities during this time of ongoing struggle.

# Introduction

## Nước: *Archipelogics and Land/Water Politics*

In Vietnamese, the word for *water* and the word for *a nation, a country,* and *a homeland* are one and the same: *nước.*
—LÊ THI DIEM THÚY[1]

Beirut was the birthplace for thousands of Palestinians who knew no other cradle. Beirut was an island upon which Arab immigrants dreaming of a new world landed.
—MAHMOUD DARWISH[2]

. . . Remember:
home is not simply a house, village, or island; home
is an archipelago of belonging.
—CRAIG SANTOS PEREZ[3]

~ ~ ~

Vietnam is *nước*: water, country, homeland. Land and water. Water is land.
A duality without division; a contrast without contradiction.
*Nước Việt Nam:* a home, a cradle, a point of departure.
One island in an archipelago of diasporic collectivity.

~ ~ ~

According to Vietnamese mythology, Vietnam was born out of the consummation of water and land. Âu Cơ, the mountain fairy, fell in love with Lạc Long Quân, the sea dragon king. Together they produced a hundred human children, *Bách Việt*. But Âu Cơ longed for the mountains, and Lạc Long Quân longed for the sea, and so they separated, dividing their children across the lands and waters of Vietnam.

Perhaps this originary division of a mother's children prefigured future cleavages: the division of North from South Vietnam along the 17th parallel in 1954, followed by two decades of civil war and US military intervention, and then the division of a unified Vietnam from its post-1975 refugee diaspora, who fled war's aftermath by air and by sea, who touched down on new lands and were washed in saltwater.

Vietnamese refugees resettled around the world, forging new islands of belonging in their respective countries of asylum. Collectively, these islands make up an archipelago of resettlement: a postwar diaspora connected by the fluid memory of a beloved homeland, lost to war. As the Pacific Ocean links what Tongan writer Epeli Hauʻofa famously termed a "sea of islands," so too does *nước* connect the archipelago of Vietnamese refugee resettlement.[4]

But resettlement is vexed when refugees resettle in settler colonial states. Resettlement is unsettling when predicated on the systemic dispossession of Indigenous peoples. This book asks: What are the political implications of refugees claiming refuge on stolen land? Do archipelagos of refugee resettlement reinforce ongoing structures of settler colonialism? Or can they be refracted through *nước*—a land/water dialectic—to call forth decolonial solidarities? These questions challenge us to think through distinct yet overlapping modalities of refugee and Indigenous displacement, shaped by entangled histories of war, imperialism, settler colonialism, and US military violence. They invite us to imagine new forms of ethical relationality.

~ ~ ~

*Yêu nước*: to love one's country, "[t]he highest virtue demanded of a Vietnamese"[5]
*Mất nước*: to lose one's country, "to be without the life source of water"[6]
*Làm nước*: to make water/land, to quench the thirst of a parched heart

~ ~ ~

This book puts Indigenous and settler colonial studies in conversation with critical refugee studies in order to theorize the *refugee settler condition*: the vexed positionality of refugee subjects whose citizenship in a settler colonial state is predicated upon the unjust dispossession of an Indigenous population. Settler colonialism is a distinct form of colonial violence defined by the expropriation of Indigenous lands and waters for colonial settlement. As a reiterative "structure" rather than a singular "event," settler colonialism incessantly seeks to overwrite Indigenous relationships to place.[7] In other words, settlers attempt the "elimination"—or what Palestinian American scholar Lila Sharif calls "vanishment"—of Indigenous subjects from the lands and waters that have shaped their cosmologies, in order to establish a myth of colonial nativity.[8] But settler colonial projects are never totalizing. Indigenous survivance persists, via place-based acts of resistance, resurgence, and decolonization.[9]

Critical refugee studies, meanwhile, intervenes in dominant representations of the refugee as a victim of persecution or an object of humanitarianism, to instead conceptualize the refugee as a paradigmatic figure of geopolitical critique.[10] In "We Refugees," Giorgio Agamben, building on the work of Jewish political theorist Hannah Arendt, posits the refugee as "nothing less than a border concept that radically calls into question the principles of the nation-state."[11] Nation-states, with their conflation of one nation or people with one sovereign state, territorialize land and erect borders to delineate inclusion and exclusion. Refugees render visible the fiction that a nation-state order can guarantee human rights for stateless peoples.[12] Refugeehood thus calls forth "a no-longer-delayable renewal of categories," a push to reimagine more multiplicitous forms of collective organization.[13] Refugees are not, however, mere abstract figures of political philosophy but complex subjects with individual stories. According to Yến Lê Espiritu, the "refugee" is a "critical idea but also . . . a social actor whose life, when traced, illuminates the interconnections of colonization, war, and global social change."[14] Refugee movement marks overlapping structures of forced displacement; to trace an archipelago of refugee resettlement, therefore, is to illuminate the entanglement of these seemingly disconnected structures.

Critical analyses of settler colonial states necessitate an engagement with Indigenous and settler colonial studies in addition to critical refugee studies, insofar as these states' "jurisdiction is predicated upon the ability to settle certain people and unsettle others."[15] Reconfiguring Indigenous lands and waters as colonial property, settlers mark not only stateless refugees but also Indigenous subjects as external threats to the national body politic. Indeed, one could argue that Indigenous subjects are even more disruptive to the settler colonial state than stateless refugees, given that the ongoing presence of Indigenous subjects challenges the myth of colonial nativity, while stateless refugees can be absorbed and granted citizenship in the settler colonial state. Contra Agamben and Arendt, Espiritu argues that refugees can "constitute a *solution*, rather than a *problem*" for nation-states.[16] For example, following defeat at the end of the Vietnam War, the United States elided accusations of imperial intervention by reframing itself as the humanitarian rescuer of anticommunist Vietnamese refugees: what Espiritu identifies as the "we-win-even-when-we-lose" syndrome.[17] By extension, this book argues that refugees are often positioned as a solution for settler colonial states seeking to counter critiques of colonial violence: the humanitarian resettlement of refugees not only projects an image of multicultural inclusion but also pointedly occludes ongoing structures of Indigenous dispossession.

I propose that we name these refugees, resettled in settler colonial states, *refugee settlers*, and that we grapple with the colonial implications of the *refugee settler condition*. Previous scholarship has identified the ways in which settler colonialism intersects with white supremacy, heteronormativity, and racial capitalism, necessitating an analysis of the power dynamics structuring different non-native settler positions. Lorenzo Veracini, for example, distinguishes settlers from migrants, "a category encompassing all forms of nonsovereign displacement."[18]

More specifically, Jodi Byrd (Chickasaw Nation of Oklahoma) borrows Carib-bean poet Kamau Brathwaite's term "arrivant" to describe nonsovereign slaves and coolies forcefully brought to the Americas, thus calling attention to "arriv-ant colonialism."[19] Byrd's work echoes that of Haunani-Kay Trask (Kanaka Maoli), who critiques the ways "settlers of color" have undermined Native Hawaiian sovereignty via civil rights struggles for inclusion into the settler colonial state.[20] Inspired by Trask, Asian Americanists such as Candace Fujikane, Jonathan Y. Okamura, and Dean Saranillio have developed the field of "Asian settler colonial-ism," which includes scholarship on Chinese "railroad colonialism" across Native American lands; Japanese American internment on Native American reserva-tions; Asian-Indigenous cross-representations throughout the Américas; colonial entanglements between Alaska Native peoples and Asian immigrants in the "last frontier" of Alaska; aesthetics of ocean passage across Oceania; and "settler allies" and "settler aloha ʻāina" in Hawaiʻi.[21] Iyko Day proposes the term "alien" to index the particular racialization of Asian laborers simultaneously rendered perpetual foreigners in North American settler colonial states, while Yu-ting Huang pre-fers "co-colonizer" and "minor settler" to identify Chinese labor migration to the Pacific Islands.[22] None of these studies, however, adequately address the distinct positionality of *the refugee* in settler colonial states.[23]

Although this is the first book to theorize the refugee settler condition, the term "refugee settler" itself is not new. An analysis of American newspapers from the late nineteenth century reveals that the term was once used to describe white working-class settlers who braved the so-called "frontier" in pursuit of private property, and who were subsequently chased out of their settlements by Indige-nous nations defending their lands.[24] This white settler narrative of refugeehood—which depicts white settler colonists as innocent victims of Native violence, rather than aggressive intruders onto sovereign land—is foundational to American national identity, since it morally absolves the US of settler imperial violence.[25] In the words of one high school valedictorian in 1924: "Once we were a handful of refugee settlers; today we are 110 million strong."[26] Indigenous and settler colo-nial studies scholars meanwhile have argued that the term "refugee settlers" may apply to Indigenous "refugee" subjects, forcibly displaced from their traditional homelands by American expansion, who end up resettling on another Indigenous nation's territory.[27] Alternatively, historian Ikuko Asaka has used the term "refugee settler" in reference to fugitive Black subjects fleeing slavery during the late eigh-teenth and nineteenth centuries who aspired to inclusion in the white settler body politic in North America.[28] Lastly, during World War II, many Anglophone news-papers described Palestine as a "homeland for Jewish refugee settlers."[29] Although the term "settlers" here acknowledges the non-native status of Jewish refugees who had fled the Holocaust, the designation of Palestine as a "homeland" for these Jewish subjects undermines Palestinians' Indigenous claims to the land.[30]

The term "refugee settler" is thus contested, alternatively deployed to describe native and non-native peoples displaced onto Indigenous lands. In this book, I use the term "refugee settlers" to describe non-Indigenous refugees who, due to resettlement following forced displacement, become settlers in settler colonial states. Refugee settlers are not directly responsible for the settler colonial policies of the state into which they are both interpolated and interpellated. However, their processes of home-making—of creating an island of belonging in their new country of resettlement—do take place on contested land, rendering them what Michael Rothberg calls "implicated subjects."[31] The challenge, then, is to put refugee critiques of the nation-state in conversation with Indigenous critiques of settler colonialism in order to challenge settler colonial states' monopoly over the land and sea. Articulated together, refugee modalities of statelessness and Indigenous epistemologies of human-land-water relations can unsettle settler colonial state violence, pointing us toward more pluralized forms of collective belonging routed through *nước*. To *làm nước* then, to make water/land, is to forge decolonial futurities.

~ ~ ~

*Resettlement:* to settle again, after forced unsettlement
*Re-settlement:* to reproduce the act of producing a settlement
*Reset-tlement:* to settle again, and again and again, to constantly resettle, to
        never settle, to unsettle the settled status of the resettled

~ ~ ~

In this book, I examine Vietnamese refugee settlers in Guam and Israel-Palestine using Espiritu's method of "critical juxtaposing": the "bringing together of seemingly different and disconnected events, communities, histories, and spaces in order to illuminate what would otherwise not be visible about the contours, contents, and afterlives of war and empire."[32] Guam and Israel-Palestine are often relegated to the margins of American studies. Area studies' divisions, furthermore, inhibit discussions of the two in relation. Guam and Israel-Palestine, however, should be *central* to analyses of settler colonialism, US empire, and decolonization. To analyze the two in relation, furthermore, illuminates connections between seemingly distinct forms of settler colonial and imperial violence and attendant forms of Indigenous and refugee critique.

Previous scholarship on Vietnamese refugees has focused primarily on the United States, examining how refugee resettlement reinforces the machinations of liberal empire.[33] Less accounted for is how imperialism is co-constitutive with settler colonialism, manifesting what Byrd has termed the "transit of empire": the usage of "executive, legislative, and judicial means to make 'Indian' those peoples and nations who stand in the way of U.S. military and economic desires."[34]

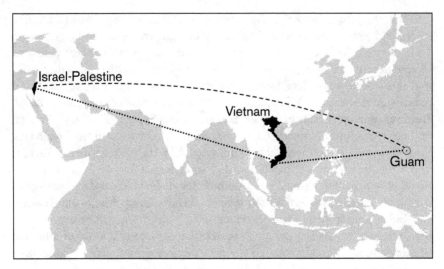

MAP 1. This map illustrates Vietnamese refugee migration to Guam and Israel-Palestine—what this book terms an archipelago of resettlement. This archipelago of Vietnamese refugee resettlement, in turn, illuminates a corresponding archipelago of trans-Indigenous resistance: how Chamorro decolonization efforts and Palestinian liberation struggles are connected through the Vietnamese refugee figure. Map drawn by M. Roy Cartography.

During the Vietnam War, for example, the US military racialized enemy territory as "Indian country," linking settler colonialism across Turtle Island with imperialism in Southeast Asia.[35] Although the continental United States remains an important site for grappling with the refugee settler condition—indeed, chapter 2 of this book examines post-1975 Vietnamese Americans as a point of departure—it is overrepresented in the existing scholarship on Vietnamese refugees. This book therefore centers the overlooked sites of Guam and Israel-Palestine, extending the geographical scope of critical refugee studies. Tracing an archipelago of Vietnamese refugee resettlement to Guam and Israel-Palestine, moreover, illuminates two more forms of critical geography: an archipelago of US empire—how the Vietnam War is linked to US military buildup in Guam and unwavering support of Israel—and a corresponding archipelago of trans-Indigenous resistance—how Chamorro decolonization efforts and Palestinian liberation struggles are connected through the Vietnamese refugee figure. Chickasaw scholar Chadwick Allen coined the term "trans-Indigenous" to explore "new methodologies for a global Indigenous literary studies in English."[36] In conversation with Allen, I invoke "trans-Indigenous" to trace "purposeful Indigenous juxtapositions" between locally situated but interconnected struggles against settler colonialism and refugee displacement.[37] In sum, the figure of the archipelago indexes formations of settler imperial power as well as challenges to it.

Guam, an unincorporated territory of the United States since 1898, served as the first major US processing center for Vietnamese refugees after the Fall of Saigon. Between April and October 1975, more than 112,000 refugees were processed by the US military in Guam. Operation New Life transformed the island, a strategic US military outpost in the Pacific, into a postwar humanitarian refuge. Such humanitarian rhetoric overwrote, however, the US military's continual dispossession of Indigenous Chamorros. Today, Vietnamese Americans who chose to stay in Guam after Operation New Life instead of resettling in the continental United States must grapple with their relationship to Chamorro decolonization struggles.

In June 1977, Israeli prime minister Menachem Begin granted asylum to sixty-six Vietnamese refugees as his first official act in office, citing parallels with the plight of Jewish Holocaust refugees three decades earlier. Two more groups of Vietnamese refugees would follow, bringing the total population of resettled Vietnamese Israelis to 366 by 1979. This was the first time Israel offered asylum and eventual citizenship to non-Jewish subjects. Furthermore, this case remains an exception to Israel's strict asylum policy, which continues to displace and dispossess native Palestinians, as well as turn away asylum seekers from Eritrea, Sudan, and Syria. By virtue of their citizenship, Vietnamese Israelis remain implicated in Israel's settler colonial foundation and ongoing structures of occupation, a situation that marks their fraught positionality in relation to the Palestinian liberation struggle.

In some ways, Guam and Israel-Palestine represent very different case studies in the history of Vietnamese refugee resettlement. While Guam served primarily as a temporary processing center for Vietnamese refugees, Israel-Palestine functioned as a country of permanent resettlement. Furthermore, the socioeconomic and ethnic backgrounds of the refugees in these two cases differ. Vietnamese refugees who were processed in Guam in 1975 were primarily anticommunist politicians of the fallen Republic of Vietnam; high-ranking officials of the Army of the Republic of Vietnam (ARVN); individuals connected to the US government, military, or embassy; and their families—in other words, those most vulnerable to political retribution after the Fall of Saigon. For the most part, this first wave of Vietnamese refugees was highly educated and well connected.

In contrast, Vietnamese refugees who resettled in Israel-Palestine were part of the second wave, who left primarily by boat. From 1977 to 1979, more than a quarter million "boat refugees" fled Vietnam to escape the communist government's radical reorganization of society. Without direct connections to US officials, many of these refugees—farmers, fishermen, former business owners, ethnic Chinese entrepreneurs, and low-level South Vietnamese government workers—drifted aimlessly at sea for days and even weeks, in the hopes of being picked up in international waters and dropped off at a Southeast Asian refugee camp of first asylum.[38] Of the 277,500 people who fled Vietnam, at least 30,000 to 40,000 perished at sea.[39] Images of the boat refugees circulated prominently in the international media, prompting the United Nations High Commission for Refugees (UNHCR) to declare a global crisis. In response, countries around the world, including the State of Israel, offered to resettle the boat refugees.

Vietnamese refugee resettlement in Guam and Israel-Palestine are connected, however, by two interrelated nodes of structural violence. First, both Guam and Israel-Palestine are spaces of settler colonialism. In 1521, Portuguese explorer Ferdinand Magellan stumbled upon the Chamorro island of Guåhan, meaning "we have." In 1668, Spanish missionaries led by Father Diego Luis de Sanvitores formally colonized the island and renamed it "Guam." During the following two centuries, genocide, disease, and forced relocation to Spanish-controlled population centers dramatically reduced the Chamorro population in Guam from approximately 100,000 to 9,000.[40]

In 1898, following defeat in the Spanish-American War, Spain relinquished colonial control of Guam to the settler imperial United States. In the Insular Cases of 1901, the Supreme Court ruled that the United States did not have to extend civil rights to its colonial subjects; in short, the Constitution does not "follow the flag."[41] US military buildup in Guam began in earnest after World War II. In August 1945, Admiral Chester Nimitz requested 55 percent of the land for US naval operations, and in 1946 the Land Acquisition Act authorized the Navy Department to acquire private land with minimal—and sometimes no—compensation to Chamorro residents.[42] By 1947, an estimated 1,350 Chamorro families had lost their homes.[43] Over the following decades, Guam was transformed from "a lonely American outpost surrounded by hostile Japanese islands" into "the center of an American-dominated lake that encompassed the entire western Pacific Ocean," second in military importance only to Hawai'i.[44] Following passage of the Organic Act of 1950, Chamorros were granted US citizenship but denied key constitutional rights, such as the right to congressional representation and the right to vote in presidential elections. According to Governor Ricardo J. Bordallo, who oversaw the processing of Vietnamese refugees during Operation New Life, the Organic Act was "not designed to enhance the dignity of the indigenous people" but rather "designed to enhance the colonial authority of the United States."[45] Today, the US military occupies a third of Guam's land, manifesting "the highest ratio of U.S. military spending and military hardware and land takings from indigenous U.S. populations of any place on Earth."[46] In sum, in Guam, "settler colonialism and militarization have simultaneously perpetuated, legitimated, and concealed one another," a dynamic that historian Juliet Nebolon has termed "settler militarism."[47] Tracing what Setsu Shigematsu and Keith L. Camacho call the "militarized currents" linking Guam, Israel-Palestine, and Vietnam helps to illuminate corresponding connections between settler militarism, settler colonialism, and settler imperialism.[48]

As in Guam, Zionist settlement in Palestine disregarded the land claims of Indigenous Palestinians.[49] In 1892, Austrian Jewish writer Nathan Birnbaum first coined the term "Zionism" to describe the exiled Jewish people's millennia-long aspiration to return to Zion, after their expulsion from Jerusalem following the destruction of their temples in 586 BCE and 70 CE, respectively. It was Theodor Herzl, though, who mobilized Zionism as a nationalist project. In response to the rise of both ethnonationalism and anti-Semitism in Europe during the late nineteenth century, he advocated the establishment of a Jewish nation-state.[50] In 1946, Hồ Chí Minh suggested Hà Nội to David Ben-Gurion as the headquarters of a Jewish government in exile.[51] Zionist organizations eventually decided on Palestine as the ideal location, however, given the land's religious significance.

Zionists' settler colonial disregard for the native Palestinian population is epitomized by the terra nullius belief that Palestine was "a land without a people for a people without a land."[52] Jewish historian Michael Brenner identifies five main waves of Zionist immigration, or *aliyahs*—a term with religious connotations of an accession to Mount Zion—to Palestine, extending from the 1880s to World War II and thus spanning Palestine's status as a subject of the Ottoman Empire to a British mandate following World War I.[53] By 1936, Jewish settlers constituted almost a third of Palestine's population, prompting the "Great Revolt": a three-year nationalist uprising by Palestinians demanding independence from Britain and an end to colonial control over immigration. Increasing tensions between native Palestinians, Jewish settlers, and British administrators culminated in the Zionist foundation of the State of Israel in 1948 as a Jewish settler state. Some 750,000 Palestinians fled their homes in terror: a catastrophe collectively remembered as al-Nakba.[54] Palestinian scholar Edward Said mourns the painful irony of having been "turned into exiles by the proverbial people of exile, the Jews."[55] Palestinians who stayed within Israel's 1948 borders, meanwhile, were rendered third-class citizens. Two decades later, the Israel Defense Forces conquered Gaza and the West Bank during the Six Day War of 1967, initiating Israel's colonial occupation of an ever-shrinking space of Palestinian mobility.[56] Referred to in "wry and subversive understatement" as al-Naksa, or the "setback," the 1967 war displaced an additional 400,000 Palestinians, about half of whom were 1948 refugees displaced yet again.[57] To this day, Israeli laws written to maintain a Jewish majority in Israel forbid Palestinian refugees and exiles the Right of Return.

Guam and Israel-Palestine are sites of not only settler colonialism but also US empire—what Byrd identifies as "U.S. settler imperialism née colonialism."[58] The year 1898 marked a radical shift in US frontier expansion from what Manu Karuka calls "continental imperialism" to overseas imperialism.[59] Following the Spanish-American War, the United States acquired not only Guam but also the Philippines, Cuba, and Puerto Rico from Spain; Hawai'i via illegal annexation; Wake Island via imperial declaration; and eastern Sāmoa through the Tripartite Convention in 1899. As the so-called "Tip of the Spear," Guam has since served as a military stronghold of US imperialism in the Pacific.[60] Indeed, settler militarism in Guam facilitated US imperial intervention in Southeast Asia during the Vietnam War, as well as the subsequent creation of a displaced Vietnamese refugee population fleeing the war's aftermath. Meanwhile the State of Israel, the largest recipient of US foreign aid since World War II, acts as a proxy of US influence in the so-called Middle East. US tax dollars prop up Israel's settler colonial regime, implicating US citizens in the continual dispossession of native Palestinians.[61] Ethnic studies scholars have noted mutually reinforcing parallels between US and Israeli settler colonialisms and, by extension, the Indigenous struggles of Native Americans and Palestinians.[62]

Vietnamese refugees fleeing the debris of the Vietnam War ended up resettling in these spaces of settler colonialism and US imperialism: Guam and Israel-Palestine. Indeed, this book argues that long-standing US influence in Guam and Israel-Palestine *prefigured* the passage of Vietnamese refugees to these very sites. Inserted into a fluid circuit of US settler imperial power, Vietnamese refugees washed ashore on lands similarly caught up in the flow.

~ ~ ~

I believe in the resilience
of our bodies
because our hearts
are 75% hånom
and every pulse is
i napu: *a wave*
accustomed
to breaking
—CRAIG SANTOS PEREZ[63]

~ ~ ~

*al-baḥr*: the sea; the meter, or poetic measure, of Palestinian prosody[64]

~ ~ ~

Like *nước*, an archipelago is made up of both land and water. A duality without division; a contrast without contradiction. Land, understood as a "storied site of human interaction" and a "meaning-making process rather than a claimed object," is a key focus of Indigenous sovereignty movements.[65] Indigenous sovereignty, moreover, is distinct from nation-state sovereignty, in that the former "embraces diversity, and focuses on inclusivity rather than exclusivity."[66] While settler colonial states understand land as property, decolonization promotes "grounded normativity": what Glen Coulthard (Yellowknives Dene First Nation) and Leeane Betasamosake Simpson (Alderville First Nation) define as "practices and procedures, based on deep reciprocity, that are inherently informed by an intimate relationship to place."[67] Simpson elaborates: "Indigenous resurgence, in its most radical form, is nation building, not nation-state building," that works by "centering, amplifying, animating, and actualizing the processes of grounded normativity as flight paths or fugitive escapes from the violences of settler colonialism."[68] Since land is settler colonialism's "specific, irreducible element," it is "at the heart of indigenous peoples' struggles" for sovereignty.[69]

Water, on the other hand, connotes fluidity, fugitivity, movement, and connectivity—the erosion of borders by the constant waves of the sea. Water is a salient medium and metaphor for diaspora and forced displacement, from the Black Atlantic to the transpacific, from Syrian to Vietnamese boat refugees. Water, however, is not in opposition to land.[70] The figure of the archipelago, refracted through Vietnamese epistemologies of *nước*, reminds us of the entanglements between land and water, Indigenous and refugee; that, indeed, Indigenous peoples can be refugees of settler colonial displacement, and refugees can become settlers on Indigenous lands and waters. Indigeneity's "emphasis on the specificities of origin, place, and belonging," in other words, is not in opposition to "movement, dispersal, and diaspora."[71] This duality is most apparent in Pacific Islander scholarship, which theorizes Oceania as a life force connecting Indigenous island nations to one other as well as their respective diasporas.[72]

According to Lanny Thompson, "archipe-logics" emphasize "discontinuous connections rather than physical proximity, fluid movements across porous margins rather than delimited borders, and complex spatial networks rather than the oblique horizons of landscapes—in sum, moving islands rather than fixed geographic formations."[73] Archipelogics call to mind Édouard Glissant's "poetics of relation": a philosophy grounded in the Antilles archipelago, "in which each and every identity is extended through a relationship with the Other."[74] Relational archipelogics mark this book's metaphors and methodology: the practice of tracing an archipelago of Vietnamese refugee resettlement to illuminate an archipelago of US empire and a corresponding archipelago of trans-Indigenous resistance. In this configuration, Guam and Israel-Palestine represent "moving islands" apprehended in relation, rather than fixed geographic formations, calling to mind the Carolinian navigational practice of *etak*: what Filipino-Pohnpeian scholar Vicente M. Diaz theorizes as an "archipelagic way of apprehending self and space."[75]

This book builds on the growing field of archipelagic studies, which includes Michel Foucault's "carceral archipelago" and Paul Amar's "security archipelago," Sylvia Wynter's "archipelago of Human Otherness" and Gleb Raygorodetsky's "archipelago of hope."[76] *Archipelagic American Studies*, edited by Brian Russell Roberts and Michelle Ann Stephens, probes what American studies told from the viewpoint of islands, rather than the continent, entails.[77] Thompson pinpoints the United States' 1898 colonial acquisition of Pacific and Caribbean island nations as the start of an "imperial archipelago," which in turn paved the way in the second half of the twentieth century for what Bruce Cumings calls an "archipelago of empire": a vast network of roughly eight hundred overseas US military installations.[78] Attending to oceanic territories and fractal temporalities, Roberts highlights the terraqueous nature of the "archipelagic States of America" via a

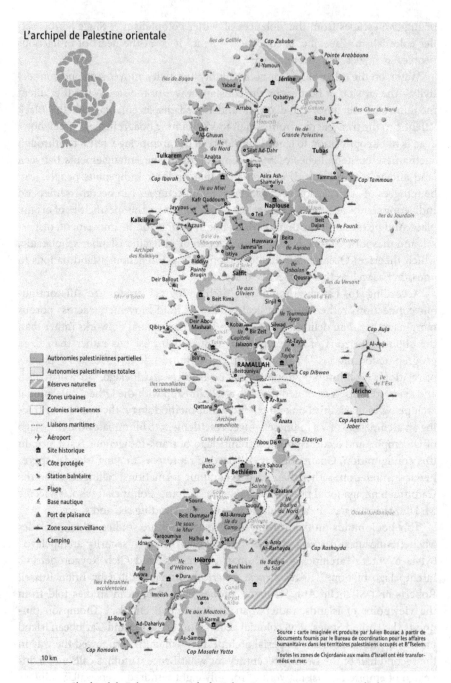

## L'archipel de Palestine orientale

Iles de Galilée
Cap Zububa
Al-Yamoun
Pointe Arabbouna
Yabad
Jénine
Iles de Baqaa
Qabatiya
Arraba
Banque Gakia
Raba
Canal de Hawesh
Iles Ghor du Nord
Deir Al-Ghusun
Ile du Nord
Silat Ad-Dahr
Tubas
Tulkarem
Anabta
Burqa
Asira Ash-Shamaliya
Tammun
Cap Tammoun
Cap Ibarah
Ile au Miel
Kafr Qaddoum
Naplouse
Kalkiliya
Jayyous
Tell
Beit Dajan
Ile Founik
Iles du Jourdain
Azzun
Archipel des Kalkiliya
Baie de Shomron
Huwwara
Jamma'in
Beita
Ile Aqraba
Canal d'Itamar
Deir Istiya
Biddiya
Ile Qabalan
Pointe Brugin
Salfit
Qousra
Iles du Versant
Deir Ballout
Ile aux Oliviers
Canal d'Ariel
Mer d'Israël
Beit Rima
Sinjil
Canal d'Eli
Deir Abou Mashaal
Kobar
Ile Tourmous Ayya
Qibiya
Bir Zeit
Silwad
Cap Auja
Ile Capitale
Jalazon
At-Tayba
Al-Auja
Bili'in
Ile Tayba
RAMALLAH
Beitouniya
Cap Dibwan
Iles ramalliotes occidentales
Ile de l'Est
Jéricho
Qattana
Ar-Ram
Archipel ramalliote
Anata
Cap Agabat Jaber
Canal de Jérusalem
Abou Dis
Cap Elzariya
Iles Battir
Beit Sahour
Bethléem
Ile Sainte
Golfe d'Etzion
Zaatara
Sourif
Touqu'
Ile Badiya du Nord
Océan Jordanique
Beit Oummar
Al-Arroub
Ile du Camp
Falloute Tegoa
Ile sous le Mur
Tarqoumiya
Halhul
Sa'ir
Arab Ar-Rashayda
Cap Rashayda
Idna
Ile d'Hébron
Hébron
Bani Naim
Ile Badiya du Sud
Beit Awwa
Dura
Iles hébronites occidentales
Canal de Kirsat Alba
Imreish
Yatta
Ile aux Moutons
Al-Bourj
Al-Karmil
Ad-Dahariya
As-Samou
Cap Ramadin
Cap Masafer Yatta

Autonomies palestiniennes partielles
Autonomies palestiniennes totales
Réserves naturelles
Zones urbaines
Colonies israéliennes
Liaisons maritimes
Aéroport
Site historique
Côte protégée
Station balnéaire
Plage
Base nautique
Port de plaisance
Zone sous surveillance
Camping

Source : carte imaginée et produite par Julien Bousac à partir de documents fournis par le Bureau de coordination pour les affaires humanitaires dans les territoires palestiniens occupés et B'Tselem.
Toutes les zones de Cisjordanie aux mains d'Israël ont été transformées en mer.

10 km

FIGURE 1. *L'archipel de Palestine orientale*, by Julien Bousac. Image courtesy of Julien Bousac.

focus on "borderwaters."[79] To this scholarship, this book adds an *archipelago of resettlement* routed through *nước*.

The figure of the archipelago emerges from the specificity of this book's sites of analysis. Guam is actually part of a larger archipelago of Indigenous Chamorro land, the Marianas. Centuries of colonization, however, have divided Guam from its fourteen sister islands to the north. After the Spanish-American War, the United States took over Guam, while Germany took over the Northern Marianas. Following Germany's defeat in World War I, Japan ruled the Northern Marianas, until its own defeat in World War II.[80] To this day, the Chamorro people remain divided across two distinct political entities: the unincorporated territory of Guam and the Commonwealth of the Northern Mariana Islands.[81] To retain an archipelagic imaginary, therefore, is to resist what Chamorro scholar Tiara R. Na'puti calls "colonial cartographic violence."[82] *Hånom* charts the fluid connections between Chamorros ,living across the Marianas archipelago as well as dispersed throughout the diaspora.

Palestine, meanwhile, has become increasingly archipelagic as Israeli settlement and occupation disrupt the contiguity of Palestinian life. In *L'archipel de Palestine orientale* (The archipelago of eastern Palestine), French artist Julien Bousac takes the 1995 Oslo Accords' division of the West Bank into A, B, and C zones as a point of departure, illustrating, in Jennifer Lynn Kelly's words, "how settler colonial state practice can create island formations without water."[83] The 1995 Oslo Accords divided the West Bank into three distinct areas of jurisdiction: (1) the Palestinian Authority, which gained limited governing authority following the 1993 Oslo Accords, administers 18 percent of the West Bank designated Area A; (2) the Palestinian Authority and the State of Israel jointly administer 22 percent of the West Bank designated Area B; and (3) the State of Israel exclusively controls the largest and only contiguous portion of the West Bank, Area C, which includes Palestinian villages as well as illegal Israeli settlements. In his map, Bousac submerges Area C in blue water, illuminating an archipelago of noncontiguous Palestinian islands: "Holy Island" (*Ile Sainte*), or Bethlehem; "Capital Island" (*Ile Capitale*) or Palestine's de facto capital of Ramallah, given Jerusalem's occupation; "Isle of the Olive Trees" (*Ile aux Oliviers*), in honor of ancestral Palestinian groves; and "Island beneath the Wall" (*Ile sous le Mur*), for the area south of the Western Wall in Jerusalem and east of the apartheid wall separating the West Bank from the State of Israel.[84]

According to Palestinian American scholars Loubna Qutami and Omar Zahzah, the Oslo Accords ushered in an "oppressive status quo of seemingly perpetual occupation, siege and geographical fragmentation."[85] When Palestinian leaders abandoned "the boundless fervor of a call for liberation—and calls for decolonization are always boundless"—in favor of an aspirational two-state solution with Israel, they ceded 78 percent of Palestine to the Zionist state and sacrificed "Palestinians' legibility as one *peoplehood*."[86] Qutami and Zahzah caution against Indigenous sovereignty movements that articulate their goals within the narrow discourse of nation-state independence. In the case of Palestine, the "quest for statehood prioritized a simultaneously arbitrary and life-shattering distinction of inside and out, of *mwatan* (citizen) and *lajet* (refugee), and left for dead those Palestinians inside 1948 territories, engulfed by the realization of a Zionist state that even enjoined recognition by its victims."[87] Visions of decolonization therefore must not lose sight of *al-baḥr*: the sea, the Mediterranean, cut off from the West Bank and exiled Palestinians, ever since Israel's settler colonial foundation in 1948.

~ ~ ~

In the car, Ma starts to cry. "What about the sea?" she asks. "What about the garden?" Ba says we can come back in the morning and dig up the stalks of lemongrass and fold the sea into a blue square. Ma is sobbing. She is beating the dashboard with her fists. "I want to know," she says, "'I want to know, I want to know . . . who is doing this to us?" Hiccupping she says, "I want to know, why—why there's always a fence."
—LÊ THI DIEM THÚY[88]

~ ~ ~

A note on terms: When referring to Palestinians and Chamorros collectively, I use the term "Indigenous": "a political category that enables solidarity among diverse indigenous peoples and nations," particularly in light of the 2007 United Nations Declaration on the Rights of Indigenous Peoples.[89] According to Māori scholar Linda Tuhiwai Smith (Ngāti Awa and Ngāti Porou), the term "Indigenous peoples" enables "the collective voices of colonized people to be expressed strategically in the international arena."[90] As a collective formation, "Indigenous" is archipelagic in orientation: different communities "come together, transcending their own colonized contexts and experiences, in order to learn, share, plan, organize and struggle collectively for self-determination on the global and local stages."[91] When referring to local contexts, I often substitute "native" for "Indigenous" in order to distinguish natives from settlers under conditions of settler colonialism. "Native," like "Indigenous," is an "analytic of political resistance."[92]

Naming Indigenous land is a political act. At the risk of reproducing colonial cartography, I default to the colonial term "Guam" rather the Indigenous term "Guåhan" in order to index the ongoing structures of US imperialism and settler militarism. I reserve "Guåhan" for references to Chamorro visions of decolonization. Moreover, some self-determination activists have recently begun to identify as "CHamoru," dismissing "Chamorro" as a product of colonial orthography.[93] Although I recognize the decolonial impetus of "CHamoru," this book uses the more standard spelling "Chamorro" to reflect the orthography of the archival documents and the self-identification of the majority of this book's older generation of interview subjects. I also distinguish between "Chamorro" and "Guamanian." Although the meaning of the term "Guamanian" has changed over time, in this book "Guamanian" refers to all residents of Guam, including settlers.[94]

Similarly, the land to which both native Palestinians and Israeli settlers lay claim is contested, and naming this land is therefore a political act. This book uses different terms to refer to the land, depending on context. I use "Israel" when I want to emphasize and implicate Israeli state policies. For example, Vietnamese refugees are citizens of Israel, not Palestine. They are a product of Israeli executive action; Palestinians had no say regarding Vietnamese refugees' resettlement on native Palestinian land. I use "Palestine" when I want to emphasize Palestinians' Indigenous claim to the land and draw attention to Zionist settler colonialism. "Israel-Palestine" refers collectively to the lands known after 1967 as the State of Israel, Gaza, and the West Bank, thus indexing present conditions of colonial occupation.

For consistency with other country names, I use the English spelling "Vietnam" to refer to nước Việt Nam. However, except in direct quotes, this book defaults to the Vietnamese spelling of city names, such as Hà Nội and Sài Gòn. Diacritics, when known, are included for Vietnamese subjects' names unless they have been dropped by the Vietnamese subjects in their countries of resettlement. Family names are placed at the beginning or end depending on the subject's preference. For consistency, I follow the US convention of referring to Vietnamese subjects by their family names instead of their first names.

Throughout the book I refer to the post-1975 displaced Vietnamese as "refugees," though US officials initially tried to distinguish them as "evacuees."[95] As historian Jana K. Lipman notes, this linguistic preference was politically motivated: "Not only did *evacuee* lack the drama and compassion that *refugee* connoted, it also was bereft of international or national rights or obligations; there were no international conventions on evacuees."[96] "Evacuee," however, is not a legal term. According to US law, the first wave of displaced Vietnamese processed in Guam were actually "parolees," "a linguistic invention in the 1952 McCarran-Walter Act, which allowed for 'temporary admission' for foreigners who fell outside U.S. immigration law."[97] This book uses "refugee" to refer to the displaced Vietnamese because it is the term most often referenced in archival documents, and because it includes the multiple waves of escape from Vietnam. Moreover, "refugee" calls to mind the politics of "refugeetude"—what Vinh Nguyen, building on the work of Khatharya Um, defines as a "continued state of being and a mode of relationality."[98] For many refugees, refugee subjectivity did not cease after citizenship in the settler colonial state; indeed, refugeetude is often passed down to subsequent generations via what Marianne Hirsch terms "postmemory."[99] Refugeetude, furthermore, is "crucially tied to relational politics—ways of knowing and being with others."[100] This book explores what decolonial futures are imaginable when refugeetude is understood in relation to Indigeneity.

~ ~ ~

> [R]efuse to take for granted the naming process. To this end, the
> intervals between *refuge* and *refuse*, *refused* and *refuse*, or even more
> importantly, between *refuse* and *refuse* itself, are constantly played out. If,
> despite their relation, noun and verb inhabit the two very different and
> well-located worlds of designated and designator, the space in-between
> them remains a surreptitious site of movement and passage whose open,
> communal character makes exclusive belonging and long-term resi-
> dence undesirable, if not impossible. Passage: the state of metamorpho-
> sis; the conversion of water into steam; the alteration of an entire musical
> framework.
>
> —TRINH T. MINH-HA[101]

~ ~ ~

Re(fugee)settlement flows into Re(fuse)settlement: the conversion of *nước*
into steam.

~ ~ ~

*Archipelago of Resettlement* is organized archipelagically, inviting an archipelagic reading practice. Each of the book's three parts consists of two chapters that
should be read in conjunction, as well as in relation to the other chapter pairs.
As the meaning of *nước* shifts in juxtaposition to *hånom* and *baḥr*, so too does
the story and argument of each chapter unfold in relation to the others, forming individual islands that together make up an archipelago of analysis. Part one,
"Mapping Sources," operates as a preface of sorts for the book's main case studies,
establishing the historical and conceptual framework for making sense of Vietnamese refugee resettlement across Guam and Israel-Palestine. Chapter 1 examines
how, even prior to post-1975 Vietnamese refugee resettlement, the fates of Vietnam, Palestine, and Guam became entangled in the US imperial imaginary: from
the 1967 Six Day War in Israel-Palestine and President Lyndon B. Johnson's "Guam
Conference" on the Vietnam War, to the 1975 Fall of Saigon and commencement of
Operation New Life in Guam. This chapter introduces and exemplifies a method of
archipelagic history that informs how to read the rest of the book. Chapter 2 elaborates the book's terms of engagement—refugee settler, refugee settler condition,
and refugee settler desire—and situates the US War in Vietnam within a longer
frontier history of US settler imperial expansion. Focusing on Turtle Island, this
chapter examines the refugee settler condition in a context perhaps more familiar
to American studies scholars, orienting readers for the following discussions of
Vietnamese refugee resettlement in Guam and Israel-Palestine.

Part two, "Tracing Migrations," analyzes the resettlement of Vietnamese refugees to Guam in 1975 and to Israel-Palestine in 1977 and 1979. Drawing from
oral histories developed with Vietnamese refugees as well as archival research

conducted at the Richard F. Taitano Micronesian Area Research Center (MARC), the Nieves M. Flores Memorial Library in Hagåtña, and the Israel State Archives (ISA), chapters 3 and 4 critique how the US military in Guam and the Zionist government in Israel emphasized the humanitarian aspects of Vietnamese refugee resettlement in order to direct attention away from contemporaneous policies of Indigenous dispossession. Such humanitarian rhetoric positioned Vietnamese refugees in a structurally antagonistic relationship with Indigenous struggles for decolonization, insofar as the refugee figure was used to recuperate the image of the settler colonial state. Both chapters end with examples of refugee refusal to ventriloquize state narratives of benevolence in the face of ongoing settler colonial violence. Read together, these chapters demonstrate how tracing an archipelago of Vietnamese refugee resettlement illuminates the archipelagic nature of US settler colonial empire.

Whereas part two narrates the development of the refugee settler condition in Guam and Israel-Palestine, part three, "Unsettling Resettlements," theorizes decolonial potentials for refugee-Indigenous solidarity. Given the structural antagonisms dividing refugee and Indigenous subjects, no broad coalitions have yet formed in either Guam or Israel-Palestine. I therefore turn to cultural production to probe what Raymond Williams terms emergent "structures of feeling."[102] Chapter 5 examines three representations of Operation New Life and its afterlives: a Chamorro high school student's newspaper article, a Vietnamese refugee repatriate's memoir, and a Chamorro-Vietnamese college student's blog. I posit that given the distinct permanent/transient temporality of settler militarism in Guam—in which the relative transience of individual militarized bodies masks the as-of-yet permanence of the US military as a settler colonial institution—the politics of staying in Guam resonates very differently than in other settler colonial contexts. Unlike the vast majority of Vietnamese refugees who used Guam as a stepping stone for permanent resettlement in the continental United States, Vietnamese Guamanians remain in dialogue with Chamorros' ongoing calls for decolonization. Chapter 6 explores uneven translations between the Law of Return for Jewish immigrants, the Right of Return for Palestinian refugees and exiles, and the journey of return for Vietnamese refugees. Reading the work of Vietnamese Israeli poet Vaan Nguyen alongside Palestinian poet Mourid Barghouti, this chapter considers the implications of understanding home as what Barghouti calls a "shape of time."[103] Via an analysis of the documentary film *The Journey of Vaan Nguyen*, it charts connections between Vietnamese and Palestinian experiences of displacement and land dispossession, marking potentials for a shared struggle.

*Archipelago of Resettlement* concludes with a gesture toward refugee futurities. The afterword juxtaposes two works of speculative fiction—Linh Dinh's short story "A Floating Community" and Tuan Andrew Nguyen's video installation *The Island*—to consider how the refugee histories analyzed in this book promise to shape our collective futures and decolonial horizons.

~ ~ ~

When land meets water and water washes over land
Trace the archipelagos upon which to stand
*Làm nước đi.*

~ ~ ~

# PART ONE

# Mapping Sources

## Archipelagic Histories and Fluid Frontiers

# 1

# Archipelagic History

## *Vietnam, Palestine, Guam, 1967–1975*

On 2 September 1975, Vietnam, Palestine, and Guam were juxtaposed on the front page of Guam's newspaper, the *Pacific Daily News* (*PDN*). The top half of the page featured two articles: one discussing the impending Interim Peace Agreement, brokered by US secretary of state Henry A. Kissinger, which would strengthen diplomatic relations between Israel, Egypt, and the United States; and the other reporting the Palestine Liberation Organization (PLO) leader Yasser Arafat's response "in the name of Palestine that the American solution cannot and will not succeed. We will liberate Palestine with our bodies, blood and soul."[1] The bottom half of *PDN*'s front page, meanwhile, described unruly protests at one of Guam's Operation New Life camps.[2] A group of Vietnamese refugees on Asan Beach demanded that the US government allow them to repatriate to Vietnam, challenging the US military's narrative of humanitarian rescue and unidirectional migration to the West.[3]

This front page of the *PDN* invites an archival reading practice that I call *archipelagic history*: one that traces different forms of US military empire across oceans and continents in order to chart how Vietnam, Palestine, and Guam became entangled in the US imperial imagination between 1967 and 1975. Unlike other models of writing history across multiple locales, such as world history, global history, transnational history, or diasporic history, archipelagic history is not organized around a particular empire, superpower, nation-state, or ethnic diaspora.[4] Rather, it traces connections between spaces on the seeming margins of grand historical narratives in order to draw attention to South-South relations: the exchange of political knowledge, military strategy, solidarity rhetoric, and intimate relations between subjects of the global South who resist aggression from the global North. Archipelagic history upends linear notions of causal temporality and instead attends to the concurrent reverberations of war and imperialism across multiple sites.

Existing historiographies of this time period rarely discuss Vietnam, Palestine, and Guam in relation to one another, if at all. This neglect is due in part to area studies divisions, which posit Vietnam, Palestine, and Guam as "discretely bounded objects" of analysis with "isolated origins and independent progressive development."[5] This proclivity to segregate along continental lines, however, obfuscates the archipelagic nature of US empire: how US military bases, strategic allyships, and sites of imperial intervention in so-called "Communist Asia," the "Middle East," and the "Pacific Rim" are in reality connected. Asian American studies, with its transnational turn, has recently begun to discuss Palestine as part of West Asia and Guam as part of the Pacific Islands; however, scholarship has yet to analyze the two in relation, let alone triangulated with Vietnam.[6] Likewise American studies, though it seeks to "decenter the United States and analyze its centralized imperial power," often limits its study of empire to the continental United States and one "Other."[7] Archipelagic history, in contrast, traces what Françoise Lionnet and Shu-mei Shih call "minor transnationalism" and Lisa Lowe terms "intimacies": "less visible forms of alliance, affinity, and society among variously colonized peoples beyond the metropolitan national center."[8] It charts imperial geographies as well as attendant anti-imperial struggles in order to illuminate contours of power.

Focusing on the 1967–75 period—from the year of the Six Day War in Israel-Palestine and President Lyndon B. Johnson's "Guam Conference" on the Vietnam War, to the year of the Fall of Saigon in Vietnam and the commencement of Operation New Life in Guam—this chapter details how Vietnam, Palestine, and Guam became entangled in an archipelago of US empire even prior to the post-1975 displacement of Vietnamese refugees. Indeed, I argue, Vietnamese refugees ended up resettling in Guam and Israel-Palestine *because of* these prior entanglements, or what Kris Manjapra calls "knotted itineraries."[9] To understand the refugee settler condition in Guam and Israel-Palestine as an archipelagic formation, it is important to first establish an archipelagic history of Vietnam, Palestine, and Guam's connections prior to the advent of refugee resettlement.

Mapping this archipelagic history is challenging because US imperialism manifested differently in Vietnam, Palestine, and Guam during the 1967–75 period: direct military intervention in Vietnam, support for Zionism in Palestine, and settler militarism in Guam. As a result, struggles for self-determination were articulated distinctly at each site: competing communist and anticommunist visions of independence in Vietnam; liberation from Zionist occupation in Palestine; and an end to the indeterminate status as an unincorporated territory, via either statehood, free association, or Indigenous sovereignty, in Guam. During this period, Palestine and Guam were connected via their respective relations to Vietnam, understood alternatively as a war, a divided people, and a revolutionary struggle. US officials' concurrent discussions of Vietnam and Palestine were shaped by Cold

War suspicions of these spaces' shared susceptibility to Soviet Union intervention. In turn, revolutionaries in Vietnam and Palestine articulated a shared struggle against US imperialism via the Third World Liberation rhetoric circulating at the time. Vietnam and Guam's relationship during this period, meanwhile, was largely shaped by the US War in Vietnam. During the war, Andersen Air Force Base and Naval Base Guam functioned as key sites of US military offensive, and more than 6,000 Chamorro soldiers served in Vietnam—a staggering proportion of the island's civilian population of less than 40,000.[10] Although these Indigenous soldiers were positioned in opposition to North Vietnam's anticolonial struggle for independence, unexpected intimacies and "structures of recognition" formed between Chamorro soldiers, South Vietnamese soldiers, and Vietnamese civilians, evidencing ways of relating otherwise.[11]

The first section of this chapter is based on original archival research conducted at the Institute of Palestine Studies (IPS) in Ramallah during summer 2016. I rely primarily on the *International Documents on Palestine* (*IDP*), annual anthologies of reprinted newspaper articles, public speeches, and United Nations documents pertaining to Palestine's international relations with other countries and political leaders. Collated, translated, and published in English by the Institute of Palestine Studies, these anthologies reflect IPS's editorial choices. Indeed, as a narration of Palestine's own internationalist history, the IPS archive functions as a political act of sovereignty—one that enacts state claims to writing history in the facing of ongoing Zionist erasure. Although the IPS archive privileges the PLO's particular viewpoint and, like all state archives, is subject to omissions, it functions as an important assertion of decolonial knowledge production.[12] This chapter privileges IPS's archival choices, cross-referencing and supplementing the anthologies' texts with other sources and interviews.[13]

The second section of this chapter engages both archival research and oral histories. Drawing primarily from Guam's newspaper, entitled *Guam Daily News* (*GDN*) during the late 1960s and later renamed *PDN* in the early 1970s, I first track how Chamorro and non-Chamorro writers represented Guam's relationship to Vietnam during the Vietnam War, as well as concurrent debates about Guam's status as an unincorporated territory with limited constitutional rights. Next, I draw from oral histories conducted with Chamorro Vietnam War veterans during summer 2018 to trace unexpected intimacies between Chamorro soldiers and Vietnamese soldiers and civilians brought together by US militarism, highlighting moments of cross-racial identification across the borders of empire.[14]

In sum, this chapter charts an archipelagic history between Vietnam, Palestine, and Guam, tracing different forms of US empire across distinct colonized spaces, or "islands," in order to illuminate the *nước* that connects them. Throughout this chapter I treat "Vietnam," "Palestine," and "Guam" as fluid rhetorical signifiers whose meanings change in relation to each other and respective political actors. The goals of this chapter are threefold: to map the archipelagic nature of US military empire; to demonstrate how different anti-imperialist subjects enacted solidarities and unexpected intimacies with one another; and to show how the historical connections forged between Vietnam, Palestine, and Guam between 1967 and 1975 prefigured the routes taken by post-1975 Vietnamese refugees displaced in the aftermath of the US War in Vietnam.

## VIETNAM AND PALESTINE

### Cold War Entanglements: US Foreign Policy in Vietnam and the Middle East

According to historian Judith Klinghoffer, the Cold War's "Vietnamese–Middle Eastern connection" has been "effectively buried."[15] Both the United States and the Soviet Union felt embarrassed by their concurrent foreign policies in Vietnam and the so-called "Middle East" and subsequently attempted to reject "any relationship between the two conflicts."[16] Whereas "American policy makers were widely criticized for permitting their preoccupation with Vietnam to lead to the neglect of the Middle East" and later were "constantly accused of being willing to sacrifice Israeli interests on the altar of an advantageous exit from Vietnam," the Soviets "were accused of inciting the Arabs to war, and then 'selling them out.'"[17] Supplementing Klinghoffer's analysis with *IDP* and other archival sources, this first section details the occluded history of Vietnam-Palestine connections during the 1967–75 period. I begin by demonstrating how US foreign policy officials, subscribing to a "Cold War logics and epistemology," used the perceived threat of Soviet expansion into Southeast and West Asia to justify concomitant US imperialist intervention in the two regions.[18]

On 17 May 1948, the Soviet Union became the first country to recognize the newly established state of Israel. However, Moscow's relations with Israel soon deteriorated, and the superpower began to denounce Zionist aggression. Positing itself as the leader of the non-Western world, the Soviet Union pivoted its support to the surrounding Arab nations in the form of weapons and other military resources. During the War of Attrition (1967–70), for example, the Soviet Union stationed fighter pilots in Egypt, which engaged in combat with the Israeli Air Force. At first, US officials were too preoccupied with the Cold War struggle in Southeast Asia to counter growing Soviet Union influence in the Middle East. However, after Israel's "lightning victory" during the Six Day War in 1967—a striking counterpoint to the United States' own quagmire in Vietnam—"Americans en masse fell in love with Israel."[19] Moreover, the 1968 Tết Offensive prompted US officials to begin debating in earnest whether to scale back the unpopular war in Vietnam in order to pivot attention to the Middle East.

In a *New York Times* article entitled "We Should De-escalate the Importance of Vietnam" dated 21 December 1969, former undersecretary of state (1961–66) and US ambassador to the United Nations (1968) George W. Ball dismisses Vietnam as an "area of marginal strategic importance," belittles US commitments to South Vietnam's vision of a democratic state, and instead argues that the United States should bolster its strategic interests in the Middle East.[20] In "Suez Is the Front To Watch," published half a year later, Ball dispenses with the liberal Cold War rhetoric of spreading "democracy" and "freedom" often used to justify foreign intervention during this period. Centering capitalist concerns, he posits that South Vietnam commands little economic or geographical significance and suggests that the United States would be better off securing the Middle East, which in contrast is "an economic prize of extraordinary value," an "area of concentrated American investment," that "*does* lie near the center of world power," which he identifies as Central and Western Europe.[21]

A shift in Cold War foreign policy regarding the Middle East would also appease the increasingly vocal bloc of liberal Jewish American voters who criticized the US War in Vietnam but advocated greater US intervention in defense of Israel following the Six Day War: a seemingly contradictory anti–Vietnam War, pro–Middle East interventionist position held by what Klinghoffer calls "Hoves and Dawks."[22] In his June 1970 article, however, Ball advises the Nixon administration to frame US intervention in the Middle East not as an "action to defend Israel from destruction at Arab hands" but rather as one to "prevent the Soviet Union from using Arab surrogate armies to extend its dominion over the Middle East."[23] In doing so, he suggests, Americans are less interested in shedding blood on behalf of the "liberty" of small nations like South Vietnam or Israel than in combating the perceived threat of Soviet domination. In a television interview conducted a week later, President Richard Nixon echoed Ball's analysis, admitting that the situation in the Middle East was "more dangerous" and, by extension, more important than the situation in Vietnam, given the potential "collision of the superpowers."[24] In sum, Nixon's pivot to the Middle East and subsequent abandonment of the South Vietnamese was driven by the desire to maintain "U.S. interests" and the Cold War "balance of power."[25]

Although US Cold War policy during the 1967–75 period prompted comparisons between Israel and South Vietnam, prior to 1967 many Israeli liberals actually identified more with the North Vietnamese cause. By December 1965, a series of demonstrations critiquing US intervention in Vietnam and supporting the communist-led Vietnamese liberation struggle had erupted across Jerusalem and Tel Aviv.[26] Many Israeli Jews empathized with the North Vietnamese because as survivors and descendants of the Holocaust, they too saw themselves as victims of Western persecution, struggling to maintain their own precarious nation-state. Radical leftist Knesset member Uri Avery, for example, compared the US killing of Vietnamese freedom fighters to the German slaughter of Holocaust Jews.[27] Israel's political elite, raised in the European socialist tradition, "felt closer" to Hồ Chí Minh, the North Vietnamese communist leader, than to Nguyễn Cao Kỳ, the prime minister of South Vietnam from 1965 to 1967.[28] In fact, David

Ben-Gurion had befriended Hồ Chí Minh in 1946, when the two lived in the same Paris hotel. Before the Zionist establishment of Israel in 1948, Hồ had suggested that Ben-Gurion establish a Jewish government in exile headquartered in Hà Nội. Returning the sentiment of solidarity, Ben-Gurion asserted in 1966, "If I were the American President, I would have pulled out the American army from Vietnam, even though such a move might possibly have grave consequences."[29] As a displaced Jew, Ben-Gurion identified with Hồ's aspirations for a liberated nation-state. Once Ben-Gurion's nationalist aspirations manifested as a settler colonial project, however, Hồ distanced his own Vietnamese revolution, aligning instead with the emergent Third World Liberation movement, whose emphasis on decolonial, anti-racist, pro-Indigenous politics necessitated a critique of Zionist theft of Palestinian lands.

Israel's Cold War entanglement with South Vietnam over North Vietnam solidified in 1966, when popular Israeli military leader Moshe Dayan toured South Vietnam to study US counterinsurgency tactics. Israeli leftists, foreign officials, and American antiwar activists interpreted the trip as a deliberate move to align Israel with the United States and, by extension, *against* North Vietnam, Palestine, and the Soviet Union in the Cold War order.[30] The next year, following the Six Day War, Prime Minister Levi Eshkol named Dayan the minister of defense, tasked with maintaining security over the newly occupied territories of the West Bank and Gaza, where Dayan put his newfound counterinsurgency intelligence to use. As US support for Israel increased after 1967, exemplified by the sale of Phantom jets used in the Vietnam War to Israel in 1968, Palestine and other nonaligned nations projected the US war against North Vietnam onto Israel's own politics.[31] By the following decade, this shift had solidified: in a 1974 speech at the United Nations General Assembly's 2282nd meeting, Arafat denounced Israel's "backing of South Viet-Nam against the Viet-Namese revolution."[32] Occluding the Israeli left's prior support of the (North) Vietnamese anticolonial struggle, Palestine and nonaligned nations of the emerging Third World Liberation movement accused Israel of supporting the United States' proxy war in Vietnam.

*Third World Solidarities: Archipelagic Critiques*
*of Western Imperialism*

In Cold War debates regarding the Soviet Union's growing influence in Southeast Asia and the Middle East, US officials drew implicit connections between Vietnam and Palestine during the 1967–75 period. In the texts discussed above, however, neither Ball nor Nixon explicitly name the Palestinian people. Ball refers to "the refugees" as one problem preventing Israel and the Arab states from "reaching a settlement" and Nixon characterizes the "*fedayeen*"—Arabic for "those willing to sacrifice themselves (for God)"—as "superradicals" who make for a "very difficult situation."[33] Neither acknowledges that Palestinians have an independent stake in the conflict, given their forced displacement by Zionist settlement and occupation. Indeed, 1967 constituted a key "moment of opportunity for Palestinians to decouple themselves from pan-Arabism, reconstitute their own particularistic identity and take the lead in their own national liberation."[34]

In contrast to US officials like Ball and Nixon, Third World Liberation leaders used the analytic of Western imperialism to draw connections between Vietnam and Palestine and express anti-imperial solidarity. While some actors, such as the Soviet Union, focused on Egypt's, Syria's, and Jordan's territorial losses at the hand of Israel, others, such as China, explicitly identified Palestinians' distinct grievances. All condemned the United States and Israel as imperialist forces, though how they defined the precise relationship between the two countries differed based on political ideology.

Some non-Western actors characterized the United States and Israel as independent actors who nonetheless coordinated their imperialist attacks. For example, in August 1968 the Ba'ath Party of Syria and the Communist Party of the Soviet Union declared that "the Zionist-imperialist aggression against the Arab countries and the American imperialist aggression against the people of Vietnam arise from an over-all imperialist plan" that "constitute[s] a danger to world peace and the security of all peoples."[35] In making this claim, the parties mapped archipelagic connections not only between Vietnam and Palestine but also between anti-imperialist and anticolonial struggles in Cuba, Cambodia, Laos, South Africa, Rhodesia, and elsewhere. Similarly, following the Israeli attack on Karameh, Jordan, in March 1968, the Soviet government took the opportunity to condemn not only Israel's "continuing aggression against neighboring Arab states" but also US intervention in Vietnam, drawing parallels between the two "aggressive imperialist forces" by identifying their common objective: "to strike a blow at the national liberation movement and its advanced detachments."[36] By identifying a common enemy in Western imperialism, the Soviet Union articulated a global "national liberation movement," short-circuiting the geographic distance between Vietnam and the Middle East. Such declarations were also self-interested: invoking a Cold War framework, the Soviet Union positioned itself as the leader of this anti-imperial movement.

Other political actors argued that Israel was just a proxy for US imperialist interests in the Middle East. For example, a May 1969 appeal by the Executive Secretariat of the Afro-Asian–Latin American Peoples' Solidarity Organization to "Support the Arab and Palestinian Peoples' Struggle against Israel's Aggression" characterized "Israel's acts of aggression and crimes" as part of "a plan drawn up by the imperialist powers which stand behind Israel and goad it on," foremost among those powers being "American imperialism, which uses Israel to protect its economic, military and political interest in this part of the world."[37] For countries outside the Middle East, US imperialism presented a much more immediate threat than Israeli aggression; they thus enfolded their criticism of Israel into a larger Cold War critique of US foreign intervention. Such rhetorical statements denied Israel's own complex history and agency: although the United States has indeed contributed significant amounts of military and financial aid to Israel at the expense of the

Palestinian liberation struggle, and both the United States and Israel function as settler colonial states, Zionists who hoped to create a safe haven for Jews displaced by the Holocaust—even though this haven was predicated upon the displacement and dispossession of native Palestinians—did not consider Israel a mere lackey of some US imperialist "plan."[38] Nonetheless, for many nonaligned countries such as Yugoslavia, the "connection between the Middle East and Far East" was "quite clear: in our opinion the United States is responsible for both these crisis [sic]."[39] In a 1974 interview, President Houari Boumediene of Algeria likewise insisted that "problems" in Vietnam and Palestine "are identical" and questioned how "Zionist propaganda [could] have secured the silence of the world" when this same world "opposed the American presence in Vietnam."[40] Although Zionism echoed some of the postcolonial nonaligned rhetoric of national independence, Israel's sovereignty was built upon settler colonial foundations, aligning Israel more with the United States than with the anticolonial, pro-Indigenous Third World Liberation movement by the late 1960s.

Although a Cold War framework simplistically pits socialism and authoritarianism against capitalism and liberal democracy, socialists' interests were far from homogeneous.[41] Wary of the Soviet Union's unchecked rise to power over the socialist world, in June 1968 Chinese journalists published an article in the *Peking Review* accusing "the Soviet revisionist renegade clique" of "working hand in glove" with US imperialism to push through "a so-called 'political settlement' of the Middle East question in an attempt to force the Arab countries to an all-around capitulation to the US-Israeli aggressors."[42] They critiqued UN resolutions that would "coerc[e] the Arab countries into unilaterally accepting a 'cease-fire,'" which would delegitimize the Palestinian armed uprising led by Arafat.[43] Although this article reveals the interregional competition for power that underwrote Cold War arguments critiquing Western imperialism, it also highlights the specificity of the Palestinian liberation struggle. While countries like Egypt and Jordan might settle for US-brokered peace with Israel in exchange for inclusion in Western capitalist markets, Palestinian liberation fighters could not afford to abandon the struggle for their stolen homeland. The *Peking Review* article, however, credited the ongoing "awakening" of Palestinian consciousness to "Mao Tse-tung's thought."[44] Although some leftist parties under the larger PLO umbrella, such as the Popular Front for the Liberation of Palestine (PFLP), did draw inspiration from Maoism, others engaged different ideologies of Marxism, Indigenous resistance, and national liberation.[45] The *Peking Review*'s claim, furthermore, occluded the longer history of Palestinian struggle against the Ottoman Empire, British colonialists, and Zionist settlers.

Some political statements dispensed with Cold War rhetoric, highlighting instead the racial dimensions of imperialism in order to articulate a more grounded transnational solidarity from below. Prior to the establishment of the State of Israel in 1948, prominent Black leaders such as W. E. B. Du Bois encouraged African

Americans to support Zionism, drawing comparisons between the Black inde-pendence movement and the Jewish fight for a homeland. By the 1960s, however, many radical Black leaders aligned with the Vietnamese and Palestinian libera-tion struggles, drawing connections between the "permanent state of war" against domestic people of color and the United States' intervention in Southeast Asia and the Middle East.[46] The Black Panther Party, for example, critiqued the Israeli government as "an imperialist, expansionist power in Palestine" and foregrounded parallels between the racial oppression and political imprisonment suffered by African Americans and Palestinians.[47] Likewise, in an advertisement featured in the 2 November 1970 issue of the *New York Times*, a prominent group of self-identified "Black Americans" expressed "complete solidarity with our Palestin-ian brothers and sisters, who like us, are struggling for self-determination and an end to racist oppression."[48] This group connected the United States' "support for King Hussein's slaughter of Palestinian refugees and freedom-fighters" with its "support of reactionary dictatorships throughout the world," such as those in "Cambodia and Vietnam." As in the above *Peking Review* article, the group identi-fied both "Zionists and Arab reactionaries" as aiding "American Imperialism."[49] Unlike those previously cited statements, however, this one critiqued not only US support for Israeli settler occupation but also Israeli support for "United States policies of aggression in Southeast Asia, policies that are responsible for the death and wounding of thousands of black youths."[50] By pinpointing how Western impe-rialism impacted multiple communities, this group mapped an archipelago of solidarity between Vietnamese freedom fighters, Palestinian fedayeen, and disen-franchised Black Americans sent off to war.

Leftist student groups and academic activists in the United States also identi-fied Third World solidarities between Vietnam, Palestine, and domestic people of color. Following the Six Day War, the Organization of Arab Students endorsed resolutions not only promoting Palestinian independence and Arab unity but also declaring solidarity with African Americans and the National Liberation Front. Recognizing linkages across struggles, they asserted, "Our battle is an inseparable part of the imperialistic design being executed against the dynamic revolution-ary forces in the Third World."[51] Likewise, the 1969 convention resolution of the Association of Arab American University Graduates (AAUG) drew explicit con-nections between the "Palestinian Revolution" and the "just cause of the people of Asia, Africa, Latin America and the Black Community in the U.S."[52] In his pres-idential address the same year, Ibrahim Abu-Lughold declared that the AAUG stood united with "our Black Brothers in the United States, South Africa, Rhodesia and in Mozambique and Angola," as well as "the gallant fighters of Vietnam."[53] Echoing these sentiments, Naseer Aruri, a founding member of AAUG, recalls in his memoir: "We perceived our own struggle for emancipation in the Arab world in the same context of the anti-colonialist movement in Vietnam and the struggle for equality in the United States. We often considered our movement as part and parcel of the fight for third world liberation."[54] Student groups such as the Arab Student Association, the Tri-Continental Progressive Student Committee, the Liberation Support Movement at the University of California, Berkeley, and the Anti-Imperialist Movement at Columbia University organized film screenings and teach-ins that drew connections between Vietnam and Palestine, and passed out leaflets with slogans such "Vietnam-Palestine One Struggle" and "Southeast Asians Struggle for Independence, Palestinians Struggle for Freedom, G.I.s Struggle for Liberty."[55] In "Communiqué #4," released following the successful jailbreak of Timothy Leary in 1970, the Weather Underground, a militant left-wing organization originally founded at the University of Michigan, Ann Arbor, declared: "With the NLF [National Liberation Front] and the North Vietnamese, with the Democratic Front for the Liberation of Palestine and Al Fatah, with Rap Brown and Angela Davis, with all black and brown revolutionaries, the Soledad brothers and all prisoners of war in Amerikan [sic] concentration camps we know that peace is only possible with the destruction of U.S. imperialism."[56] Like the organizations discussed above, the Weather Underground identified resistance to US imperialism as the common factor linking an archipelago of Third World Liberation struggles across Vietnam, Palestine, and the Americas.

### Direct Addresses: Vietnam to Palestine, Palestine to Vietnam

Archipelagic discourses of solidarity were produced not only about but also by Vietnamese and Palestinian revolutionaries between 1967 and 1975, evidencing Robert J. C. Young's assertion that "anti-colonialism was a diasporic production, a revolutionary mixture of the indigenous and the cosmopolitan, a complex constellation of situated local knowledges combined with radical universal political principles, constructed and facilitated through international networks."[57] In spring 1967, prominent Palestinian resistance poet Samih al-Qasim, who remained in Israel after 1948 as a third-class citizen, translated a half-dozen quatrains of Hồ Chí Minh's *Prison Diary* from English to Arabic for the popular Arabic-language publication *al-Jadid*. Drawing attention to "the parallel fates of political prisoners both at home and around the world," Qasim not only highlighted the routine incarceration of Palestinians in Israeli prisons but also suggested that living under Zionist martial law in Israel (which lasted until 1966) was a form of imprisonment itself.[58] Qasim's poetry also invoked the Vietnamese liberation struggle. In "From a Revolutionary in the East" (1964), for example, he writes:

> From a revolutionary in the East
> to revolutionaries lighting up the darkness
> to fellow revolutionaries, wherever they are
> in the Nile, in the Congo, in Vietnam.
> . . .
> My brothers! With blood you write
> your history—and headlines![59]

FIGURE 2. General Võ Nguyên Giáp shares photos of the establishment of the Vietnam People's Army with PLO leader Yasser Arafat during his visit to Hà Nội, March 1970. Photo courtesy of AFP.

Locating himself squarely in the "East," in this poem Qasim subverts Western colonial distinctions between the "Far" and "Near" East and thus imagines stronger geopolitical connections between Vietnam and Palestine. The poem also posits Third World revolutionaries as historical actors capable of writing their own history and headlines through armed guerrilla warfare, instead of mere reactionaries to US-Soviet Cold War maneuvers.

During the 1967–75 period, Palestinian fedayeen identified with Vietnamese revolutionaries and condemned US imperialism in Vietnam in their public speeches and political platforms.[60] They also, like other decolonization movements around the world, drew inspiration from Vietnam. Following General Võ Nguyên Giáp's unexpected victory in 1954 over the French in the Battle of Điện Biên Phủ, Palestinian soldiers took on the nickname "Giap."[61] General Giáp's writings, translated into Arabic, circulated throughout Palestinian refugee camps, and posters of Hồ Chí Minh decorated camp walls.[62] Based on subsequent Vietnamese successes in holding off American troops, the leftist PFLP concluded that the guerrilla warfare "course adopted by Vietnam and Cuba is the only way in which underdeveloped countries can triumph and overcome the scientific and technological superiority of imperialism and neocolonialism."[63] Recognizing that they could not compete with the superiority of the US-backed Israeli military on its own terms, Palestinian fedayeen declared a people's war, encouraging workers and peasants most vulnerable to "the oppressive exploitation process exercised by world imperialism and its allies in our homeland" to take up arms.[64] Arafat, the iconic PLO leader of militant resistance for many decades, affirmed as well the "firm relationship between the Palestinian revolution and the Vietnam revolution through the experience provided to us by the heroic people of Vietnam and their mighty revolution."[65] In 1966, Khalil al-Wazir of the Fatah party visited Vietnam, and over the following years, Arafat sent several groups of Palestinian soldiers to train in Vietnam and learn Vietnamese guerrilla tactics.[66] Fedayeen in turn invited the

Vietnamese to visit the Palestinian military bases in southern Lebanon.[67] In March 1970, Arafat accompanied a delegation of Palestinian liberation fighters to Hà Nội to visit Hồ Chí Minh and General Võ Nguyên Giáp.[68] During their meeting, the latter told Arafat: "The Vietnamese and Palestinian people have much in common, just like two people suffering the same illness."[69] Giáp thus drew archipelagic connections between the Vietnamese and Palestinian liberation struggles, positioning them against the common enemy of Western imperialism.

The fedayeen imagined turning the Middle East into a "Second Vietnam" and one of the surrounding Arab capitals, such as Amman or Beirut, into an "Arab Hanoi," which would then serve as a center for revolutionary action based on the North Vietnamese model.[70] For example, capitalizing on American anxieties regarding an impending military defeat in Vietnam, the Palestinian Commando Organizations released a statement on 9 August 1970 declaring, "We must make the Middle East a second Vietnam to defeat Zionism and imperialism and to liberate completely the soil of the Palestinian and Arab homeland."[71] This statement emerged from the then solidifying Third World Liberation solidarities, which defined strategic alliances between Vietnam, Palestine, and other Third World nations. At the Tenth World Festival of Youth and Students, held in East Berlin in 1973, the PLO was invited to take up the "banner of the global struggle" from Vietnamese freedom fighters, whose struggle was thought to have concluded after the signing of the 1973 Paris Peace Accords ending US combat in Vietnam.[72] With North Vietnam's victory against US imperialism seemingly secured, the Third World Liberation movement turned its attention to the next major anti-imperialist struggle: Palestine.[73] Reflecting on the event, Palestinian poet Mahmoud Darwish reported: "In the conscience of the peoples of the world, the torch has been passed from Vietnam to us."[74]

Vietnamese freedom fighters in turn expressed support for the Palestinian struggle. North Vietnam and the PLO established ties in 1968. In a message to the International Conference for the Support of Arab Peoples held in Cairo on 24 January 1969, Hồ Chí Minh, who could not attend in person, asserted that the "Vietnamese people vehemently condemn the Israeli aggressors" and "fully support the Palestinian people's liberation movement and the struggle of the Arab people for the liberation of territories occupied by Israeli forces."[75] Vietnam, moreover, was "determined to fight the American aggressors until total victory" and thereby "fulfill its obligations" to both "its own nation" *and* "its friends in the fight against imperialism and colonialism, for independence of liberty."[76] In fighting US imperialist forces in Southeast Asia, Vietnam hoped to weaken US imperialism's capacity to suppress liberation movements in other parts of the world, including Palestine.[77] Conversely, in December 1969 Arafat argued that Palestinians were fighting not only for themselves but for "the freedom of peoples who are fighting for their liberty and existence, the freedom of the people of Vietnam who are suffering like the people of Palestine, the freedom of all humanity from oppression, discrimination and exploitation."[78] Vietnamese and Palestinian revolutionaries thus articulated a larger archipelago of interconnected struggles against Western imperialism, unsubordinated to Soviet expansionism.

The direct impact that Vietnamese pressure on US military forces in Vietnam had on US foreign policy in the Middle East is hard to quantify; however, sometimes US politicians inadvertently admitted that a weakening of US imperialism on one front benefited the national liberation struggle on the other. For example, in a 12 July 1970 television interview, US senator Stuart Symington, chairman of the Foreign Relations Subcommittee on the Middle East, speculated that Nixon's "hand is being forced somewhat in the Middle East as a result of our stalemate, you might say, in the Far East."[79] As much as the US administration tried to compartmentalize its foreign policy initiatives in Vietnam and Palestine, these struggles' respective leaders articulated commonalities and vowed to fight on each other's behalf.

Such Third World Liberation solidarities could also produce unintended results, however. Frustrated by its defeat in Vietnam, the United States would redouble its efforts in the Middle East, anxiously proving its imperial might at the expense of Palestinian liberation. Analyzing American cultural production from this period, Melani McAlister argues that for the United States, "Israel, or a certain image of Israel, came to function as a stage upon which the war in Vietnam was refought—and this time, won."[80] Attributing US defeat in Vietnam to a failure of political will, American conservatives, inspired by Israel's brazen capture of the West Bank and Gaza during the Six Day War, asserted that the United States should act "not only *with* Israel but also *like* Israel on key international issues."[81] In *Peace in the Middle East? Reflections on Justice and Nationhood* (1974), Noam Chomsky—Jewish American intellectual, prominent anti–Vietnam War activist, and stalwart supporter of Palestine—makes a parallel, though critical, observation in suggesting that the United States saw Israel as a "sort of magic slate rewrite of American failure in Vietnam."[82] While Vietnam won independence in 1975, Palestine remains colonized.

These 1967–75 assertions of solidarity between Vietnam and Palestine continue to resonate in the contemporary moment. In a speech celebrating the International Day for Solidarity with the Palestinian People on 28 November 2014, for example, Saadi Salama, ambassador of the State of Palestine in Vietnam, declared that Vietnam's "solidarity and friendship given to Palestine's legitimate struggle over decades has become a strong motivation for the two countries to overcome geographical distances to get closer and further promote special friendship."[83] Indeed, Vietnam's successful struggle for independence continues to inspire Palestine: "When in Palestine, if you say you are a Vietnamese, you will be welcome as a distinguished guest. For those in the land that is still in search of independence, the two words 'Viet Nam' have become a symbol of struggling spirit for the national sacred peace."[84]

Salama's own connection to Vietnam was intimately shaped by the 1967–75 period.[85] Born in 1961, he remembers when Israeli military tanks invaded his Palestinian village on the outskirts of Hebron on 7 June 1967, as part of the Six Day War that initiated the ongoing occupation of the West Bank. Four years later, as ten-year-old Salama sold newspapers in Hebron's bustling city center, he was struck by the visual parallels between the images of the Vietnam War covering the newspapers' front pages and his own life under Israeli occupation: how the white faces of the US soldiers carrying M16s and riding ominous tanks in Vietnam mirrored the fair-skinned faces of the Israeli soldiers carrying M16s and riding M3 half-tracks in Hebron. It was then and there that Salama realized that the Palestinians and Vietnamese, "living under occupation," shared the "same struggle for freedom and national independence" against "foreign invaders."[86] Shaped by these experiences, Salama chose to study abroad in Vietnam during the 1980s, worked at the embassy of the State of Palestine in Hà Nội between 1989 and 1992, and returned in December 2009 to serve as the embassy's ambassador. He asserts that "Vietnam continues to extend its strong support to the Palestinian people's just cause and their struggle to achieve their national rights, including the right of self-determination and the right to establish an independent Palestinian state with East Jerusalem as its capital. This is the unchangeable position of Vietnam toward the question of Palestine."[87]

## VIETNAM AND GUAM

### "Tip of the Spear": US Militarism in Guam during the US War in Vietnam

Unlike Palestinian liberation fighters, Chamorro leaders did not articulate Third World solidarity with Vietnamese revolutionaries such as Hồ Chí Minh during the 1967–75 period. According to Joseph F. Ada, who later served as governor from 1987 to 1995, Guam was largely "shielded" from the Third World Liberation "movement toward independence and decolonization" by US policies seeking to "mold Guam in an American image" and curtail "our understanding of our rights as people."[88] Nonetheless, during this period many Chamorros began to critique Guam's colonial status, pointing out that although the 1950 Organic Act granted them US citizenship, they were still denied a voting member of Congress, the right to vote in the presidential election, and, until 1970, the right to elect their own governor. How Guam's unincorporated status should be resolved, however, was open to debate: although some Chamorros began to advocate for free association or Indigenous sovereignty during this period, many self-determination advocates instead expressed interest in greater democratic rights under the US Constitution. Overall, these struggles highlight the acute irony of the United States' claim to fight on behalf of democracy in Vietnam while simultaneously curtailing the democratic rights of Indigenous Chamorros in Guam.

Given its strategic position as the US territory closest geographically to Southeast Asia, Guam was a key site of US military power during the US War in Vietnam. Naval Air Station Agana provided support for carrier-based aircraft during the war, and Naval Hospital Guam treated many wounded US soldiers.[89] The US military first deployed B-52s to Guam in April 1964, and on 18 June 1964, it launched thirty bombers from Andersen Air Force Base, initiating Operation Arc Light.[90] Over the next eight years, tons of bombs were unloaded at the US naval base at Apra Harbor, stored in Naval Magazine Guam in Santa Rita, on the southern part of the island, and then driven north to Andersen Air Force Base each day to be loaded onto B-52s headed for Vietnam.[91] US militarism disrupted civilian life: large flatbeds transferring the five-hundred-pound bombs shook the island's roads, and loud B-52s pierced the skyline at all hours.[92] Moreover, Chamorros served in the US military in disproportionately high numbers. Of these, seventy-seven Guamanians, most of Chamorro descent, died in Vietnam, the highest per capita casualty rate of any state or territory during the war.[93]

From the US government's standpoint, Guam's entanglement with Vietnam during the 1967–75 period was exemplified by three main events: the Guam Conference of 1967, the Guam Doctrine of 1969, and Operation Linebacker II in 1972. President Lyndon B. Johnson's visit to Guam in March 1967 to discuss Vietnam War policy marked the first time a US sitting president had visited the island. Known as the Guam Conference, following the Honolulu Conference (6–8 February 1966) and the Manila Conference (24–25 October 1966), this meeting came at a critical juncture during the US War in Vietnam. According to American reporter and foreign correspondent George McArthur, 1967 was "the year that will decide the war."[94]

To understand how Guam figured in the US imperial imagination during the Vietnam War, it is illuminating to trace how the island and its people were represented in the days leading up to and during the Guam Conference. US officials often stressed the importance of Guam's strategic location as a bastion of American democracy amidst hostile communist forces, interpolating not only the US military personnel stationed in Guam but the larger civilian population, including native Chamorros. Emphasizing the "significance of Guam to the defense of the free world," Rear Admiral H. V. Bird, commander of the naval forces of the Marianas, for example, invoked the "patriotism and loyalty with which all Guamanians are imbued" and insisted that "wars are not only fought on battlefields but also fought by the patient understanding and faith of every citizen in the cause of freedom."[95] Likewise, in a cable of welcome to President Johnson, Governor Manual Guerrero, who had been appointed by President John F. Kennedy in 1963, claimed to speak on behalf of the entire island when he declared that Guam's "citizens are proud of Guam's role as an important military bastion aiding in the battle for freedom in Vietnam," and that they "are honored you have chosen the island as the site of your conference with the leaders of that struggle."[96] Given

Guam's precarious inclusion in the US body politic as an unincorporated territory, and the conferral of US citizenship only recently, following the 1950 Organic Act, Guerrero was anxious to assert Guam's patriotism during this moment of international visibility. Such rhetoric, however, disavowed concurrent critiques of US settler militarism in Guam, which had displaced many Chamorros from their villages in order to construct the US naval and air force bases.

In an open letter addressed to President Johnson entitled "What, You Ask, Is A Guam?" *GDN* editor Joe Murphy emphasizes Guam's military importance to the US war effort, given the island's "strategic value" as "a gigantic communication center," a "mighty fortress of Democracy in the Far East," the "hub of Micronesia," and an island base "so close to the shore of ominous Red China."[97] He concludes that Guam is "one of the most important pieces of real estate that the U.S. owns by virtue of its strategic location. We may eventually lose our bases in Japan, Okinawa, and the Philippines—but you'll never lose them on Guam, because we are a part of the U.S." Shifting between first person and second person pronouns, Murphy marks his insider-outsider status as a white American settler living in the unincorporated territory of Guam: a colonial possession "own[ed]" by the United States. Using Guam's military importance as collateral, he asks President Johnson for "the right to govern ourselves"—with the caveat that it would be "always in the American way, with a strong tie to the U.S."[98] Murphy's assertion of self-determination raises the question of who is included in such notions of the "self." In assuring continual US tutelage, he denies other, more decolonial visions of self-determination routed through Indigenous sovereignty that were emerging during this period.

Much of the *GDN*'s coverage of the Guam Conference was celebratory. On 20 March 1967, thousands of Guam's residents gathered on the field of Guam International Airport and along the 7.4-mile motorcade route from the airfield to the naval reservation to welcome President Johnson.[99] Children held hand-stenciled signs reading "LBJ, we're with you all the way in Vietnam," "Guam is with you in Vietnam," and "Bomb Hanoi and important seaport of Vietnam."[100] Such signs evidenced Guamanians' interpolation in US war efforts in Vietnam, highlighting the archipelagic nature of US empire. But they also demonstrated the lasting trauma of Japanese occupation during World War II, which conditioned Chamorros' sense of gratitude toward the US military. According to the *GDN*, "Signs everywhere displayed the loyalty of the Guamanians, and their support of the Vietnam war. There was not one single sign that would evidence displeasure, or show anything but good taste throughout [Johnson's] brief stay"—a marked difference from the continental United States, where the antiwar movement was gaining momentum.[101] Indeed, Chamorros who did protest US intervention in Vietnam during this period did so from the continental United States.[102]

To the intense disappointment of those who had waited three hours in the hot sun to catch a glimpse of their nation's leader, however, President Johnson's motorcade rushed by, indexing the ways in which the United States has often bypassed Guam's political desires even as it takes for granted Guam's patriotism.[103] Johnson did not stop until he reached Naval Air Station Agana, where he paused to give a speech positioning the US military commanders and diplomatic officials gathered for the Guam Conference as "those who are helping to wage the peaceful campaign against poverty and want in Vietnam."[104] South Vietnamese leaders, in turn, were represented as weary inheritors of a war "thrust upon them by Communist terror"—a characterization that elided the longer history of anticolonial struggle in Vietnam and denied agency to South Vietnam's democratic struggle.[105]

In his speech, Johnson highlighted Guam's geographical proximity to Vietnam and its history of Japanese occupation during World War II to explain Guam's significance as the site for this important conference: "America, which lost Guam [during World War II] and then freed it again with blood that now stains this ground, has not forgotten that lesson. And so American boys in Vietnam are once again carrying the American commitment to resist aggression, and to make possible the sacred work of peace among men."[106] Positioning the United States as a savior of racialized peoples, Johnson yoked together the fates of Chamorros in Guam and Vietnamese in Vietnam, insisting that the US failure to protect Chamorros from Japanese occupation during World War II only "strengthens our determination to persevere in Vietnam today."[107] In his narrative, Chamorros were thus implicated in US imperialism in Vietnam.

Reports of the Guam Conference itself are contested. Although President Johnson and President Nguyễn Văn Thiệu insisted that the conference decided no new military plans and instead focused on pacification and South Vietnamese state-building efforts, other sources reveal that Prime Minister Nguyễn Cao Kỳ advocated for increased bombing of communist strongholds in North and South Vietnam and the initiation of air warfare in Laos and Cambodia, despite the 1962 Geneva Accord specifying Laos's neutrality; General Cao Văn Viên, minister of national defense, proposed placing armed forces on the Vietnam-Laos border along Route 9 to inhibit North Vietnamese infiltration into South Vietnam; and US admiral Grant Sharp Jr. and his aides outlined an extension of Operation Rolling Thunder, which would entail an estimated 1,715 civilian casualties.[108] Such proposed military escalations worried state and revolutionary leaders around the world.

In their critiques of the Guam Conference, communist and antiwar newspapers implicated Guam in the US War in Vietnam.[109] The *London Morning Star* criticized the conference's optics: "With maximum publicity the leaders of the most powerful and richest western state have gathered to plan the destruction of one of the poorest countries in the world."[110] *Peking People's Daily*, an organ of the Chinese Community Party, asserted that the Guam Conference marked the United States' inevitable failure: "U.S. imperialism has landed itself in the vast ocean of people's war in Vietnam. No matter how desperately it struggles, it cannot escape being submerged."[111] One East German newspaper, *Neue Deutsch Zeitung*, asserted,

"To the Vietnamese, Guam is a symbol of aggression because B-52 planes take off from there to strike at Vietnam. The Guam Conference is a 'war escalation council.'"[112] In effect, this editorial conflated the "Guam Conference" with the entire island of "Guam" and the ideologically specific "Northern Vietnamese forces" with the entire ethnonationalist group of "the Vietnamese." Positing "Guam" and its multiple referents—a military base, yes, but also a Chamorro homeland—as a "symbol of aggression" to the Vietnamese people writ large, this article highlights the structural antagonisms that US militarism erected between self-determination advocates in Guam and anticolonial revolutionaries in Vietnam.

Two years after the Guam Conference, President Nixon presented the Guam Doctrine, precursor to the Nixon Doctrine, which outlined his infamous policy of "Vietnamization." On 25 July 1969, President and First Lady Nixon arrived in Guam en route to Asia as part of Nixon's global goodwill tour. Although Nixon had visited Guam in 1956 as vice president, this was his first visit as president, and thus only Guam's second visit from a sitting president of the United States. In his welcome speech to Nixon, Governor Carlos G. Camacho emphasized Guam's inclusion "in the mainstream of America, although we are thousands of miles removed from the mainland."[113] Like Governor Guerrero before him, he stressed Guam's strategic location "in this remote area of the Pacific" as "the showcase of American democracy to nations in the Far East and Asia, where the spread of Communism is always a threat." Signaling that he understood the ideological importance of Guam for US war efforts in Southeast Asia, he promised that Guam "will do our best, through words and deeds, to project the image of the United States of America as truly the land of the free and the brave."[114] The irony, of course, is that Camacho had been appointed by President Nixon rather than democratically elected, exposing the hypocrisy of the United States' Cold War claims to defending democracy in the region.

At 6:30 p.m. on 25 July 1969, at the Top O' the Mar Officers' Club in Asan, Nixon outlined what would become known as the Guam Doctrine in a series of informal remarks to the press. Four months prior to his televised speech outlining the Nixon Doctrine—in which he famously declared, "In the previous administration, we Americanized the war in Vietnam. In this administration, we are Vietnamizing the search for peace"—Nixon previewed his Vietnamization strategy in the unincorporated territory of Guam, indexing the island's occluded role in US Cold War policy.[115] In this speech, Nixon began by characterizing not only US imperialism in Asia but also settler militarism across the Pacific Islands as inevitable: "Whether we like it or not, geography makes us a Pacific power."[116] Framing the Vietnam War as part of a longer genealogy of transpacific wars, including World War II and the Korean War, Nixon identified Guam as a strategic American stronghold in "the heart of Asia"—a region he in turn characterized as "the greatest threat to peace in the world" as well as "the greatest hope for progress in the world."[117] Nixon thus positioned Guam and Vietnam in the same Cold War frame, marking the region as one in need of US intervention.

The nature of such intervention, however, needed to change. Adopting a paternalistic tone, Nixon argued that the United States should no longer be mired in Asia's battles, sacrificing American lives for Asia's "internal problems." Instead, the United States would shift military "responsibility" to "the Asian nations themselves"—a policy that suggested greater self-determination, even as it merely altered the nature of US militarism in the region.[118] Under Vietnamization, Nixon would withdraw US troops but significantly escalate US bombing campaigns in Southeast Asia, mollifying domestic antiwar protesters who focused on the loss of *American* life while often overlooking the sharp increase in *Southeast Asian* fatalities that such a policy wrought. According to Long T. Bui, Vietnamization functioned as a "subterfuge" that obfuscated "the fact that *most* of the carnage related to the war took place *after* the implementation of this policy."[119]

Perhaps most insidiously, Nixon co-opted the language of decolonization to justify his Guam Doctrine: "Asians will say in every country we visit that they do not want to be dictated to from the outside, Asia for Asians. And that is what we want, and that is the role we should play. We should assist, but we should not dictate."[120] This rhetoric supports Simeon Man's argument that during the Cold War, "decolonization was not antithetical to the spread of U.S. global power but intrinsic to it."[121] Nixon claimed to support decolonization in Asia, but only to the extent that such nations joined the "free world" and rejected competing communist or socialist visions of decolonization. If they did not, the United States would call upon Asian allied nations such as South Korea, Japan, and the Philippines, as well as the unincorporated territory of Guam, to intervene as proxies of US imperial power.

The effects of Nixon's Vietnamization policy were felt intimately in Guam. In February 1972, thirty B-52s were deployed to Guam to reinforce the fleet already stationed at Utapao Air Base in Thailand.[122] The following week, President Nixon spent a night in Guam before continuing on to the People's Republic of China for a landmark trip that would renew US-China diplomatic relations. Nixon's visit prompted *PDN* reporter Charles Denight to observe, "Guam and President Nixon's most historical projects seem to join frequently."[123] In preparation for Nixon's stopover, Governor Camacho—who after his first term as an appointed governor had been democratically elected in 1970 in Guam's first gubernatorial election—urged Guamanians to "come out in full force" and give Nixon "a rousing welcome," explaining that the president was "on an unprecedented search for world peace and we owe it to ourselves, as Americans and freedom-loving people, to give him our full support."[124] He concluded his speech by reemphasizing Guam's entanglement with Vietnam: "We have been witnessing the scaling down of US involvement in Vietnam and the gradual pulling out of our servicemen there. To Guamanians of all colors, this has been one of the most rewarding presidential actions, for we have been making huge contributions to this war effort."[125] The past three Christmases, Camacho had traveled to Vietnam to meet with Chamorro soldiers.[126] Chamorro musician Johnny Sablan, who accompanied Camacho

FIGURE 3. Governor Carlos G. Camacho shakes hands with local villagers during his visit
to Vietnam, December 1969. From the collection of the Richard F. Taitano Micronesian Area
Research Center.

to Vietnam during his first visit in 1969, wrote a song commemorating the event
entitled "Christmas Odyssey in Vietnam." Nixon's visit to China in 1972 sparked
hope for Camacho that "next Christmas there will be no need for me to return
to that embattled nation."[127] In other words, Camacho wished for an end to the
Chamorro death toll in Vietnam.

In an open letter to President Nixon written on behalf of the Eleventh Guam
Legislature and the people of Guam, Speaker Florencio T. Ramirez took a slightly
different tone, combining his welcome of the president with a request for greater
self-representation. Five years earlier, in 1967, Joe Murphy, the *GDN*'s white settler editor, had made a similar request. Now, a Chamorro politician boldly put
forth the case for a nonvoting delegate in Congress and the ability to vote in US
presidential elections. As with Murphy, self-determination in this letter took the
form of greater representation under US democracy; however, Ramirez's comments also prefigured the growing Indigenous rights movement in Guam.

In the letter, Speaker Ramirez critiques settler militarism in Guam, relaying
Chamorros' desire to access their ancestral lands:

> As patriots, we readily agreed to turning over whatever land was needed to bring
> about victory in World War II. Now, as citizens of the U.S. we are well aware of the
> strategic position the military holds here on Guam and we are pleased to be a part of
> America's first line of defense. But we would like to feel that we are welcome on those

non-security recreational lands, such as the beaches and un-spoiled ocean fronts, side by side with our military friends.[128]

Couching his comments in patriotic rhetoric, Ramirez nonetheless insists on "a more equitable re-arrangement of Federal land holdings on this tight little island."[129] This critique of settler militarism laid some of the foundation for a more deliberate Indigenous rights framework in the following decades.

In December 1972, Guam would yet again play a key role in the US War in Vietnam. Throughout the year, Nixon had negotiated with Hà Nội for its assurance of South Vietnam's independence and, by extension, a stronghold of US imperial power in the region. In December, Hà Nội left the negotiation table, prompting Nixon to retaliate with Operation Linebacker II, infamously known as the "Christmas bombing" campaign. From 18 December to 29 December 1972, the United States dispatched 741 B-52 sorties that dropped a total of 15,237 tons of ordnance on eighteen industrial and fourteen military targets.[130] Another 212 B-52 missions targeted sites in South Vietnam.[131] The first four days of the assault alone "delivered the explosive equivalent of a Hiroshima-sized atomic blast."[132]

Many of these B-52s came from Guam: the *PDN* reported that the "runways at Andersen Air Force Base . . . shook with the speeded-up traffic of Stratofortresses."[133] The base population swelled past 15,000, and Andersen Air Force Base hosted more than 150 B-52s.[134] Overall, 1,624 people were killed in North Vietnam during Operation Linebacker II.[135] Succumbing to the military assault, North Vietnamese leaders returned to the negotiation table, and on 23 January 1973, Henry Kissinger and Lê Đức Thọ signed the Paris Peace Accords, effectively ending the United States' direct involvement in the war. The civil war between North and South Vietnam did not abate, however, and on 30 April 1975, Sài Gòn fell to the communist revolutionaries.

What effect did Guam's entanglement in the US War in Vietnam have on Palestine? Although causalities are hard to trace, archipelagic history pinpoints moments of juxtaposition. On 23 December 1972, during the height of Operation Linebacker II, the *PDN* reported on Israeli prime minister Golda Meir's response to the Vietnam War. Speaking to students at Bar-Ilan University, Meir—who infamously claimed Palestinians "did not exist"—chided Israeli newspapers for suggesting that US involvement in the Vietnam War somehow favored Israel because it kept the United States from interfering with Israeli settler colonial policies in Palestine in the name of brokering "peace" in the Middle East.[136] Denouncing the war as a "catastrophe and a tragedy," Meir insisted that Israel's "affair is different from that of Vietnam."[137] The very fact that Meir felt compelled to disavow any archipelagic connection between Vietnam, Palestine, and Guam, however, evidences latent parallels between US intervention in Vietnam and US support for Zionism in Palestine. In a different valence, Ambassador Salama asserts that one of the reasons the United States stayed out of Vietnam in 1973 was that it was focused on supporting Israel during the Arab-Israel War, also known as the Yom

Kippur War, of October 1973—a decision that inadvertently "helped" the Vietnamese communist revolutionaries "a lot" but had devastating and ongoing repercussions for the Palestinian liberation struggle.[138] In sum, writers of archipelagic history must attend to the *nước* linking colonized spaces, bound together by their entanglements with US imperialism in its multiple forms.

*Cross-Racial Intimacies: Vietnamese-Chamorro Relationships*
*Forged during War*

US Cold War policy aligned Guam with US military interests during the Vietnam War. However, it did not foreclose other forms of relationality between Chamorro and Vietnamese subjects during the 1967–75 period. Indeed, the archipelagic nature of US imperial power facilitated intimate encounters between Chamorro and Vietnamese soldiers, doctors, and civilians—two Third World populations who otherwise may not have crossed paths. Such quotidian encounters were not reported in newspapers or archived in government documents. This section therefore turns to oral histories I conducted during summer 2018 with ten Chamorro Vietnam War veterans and two of their partners, supplemented by oral histories conducted by other scholars.

All of the Chamorro soldiers I interviewed had either lived through Japanese occupation during World War II or had family members who did; many said this history influenced their desire to give back to the US military that had "liberated" Guam in 1944.[139] Some interviewees were career soldiers who joined the US military as young men even prior to the Vietnam War; others were drafted. Sergeant Martin Ada Manglona, for example, was drafted into the US Army in January 1962. After being stationed in the Demilitarized Zone in Korea and in Berlin, in 1966 Manglona volunteered to "go to Vietnam to fight for freedom," motivated by his parents and siblings' experiences during World War II before the Marianas were "liberated by the Americans."[140] Juan O. Blaz, a retired sergeant major who served in the army for thirty years, volunteered to go to Vietnam in memory of his cousin James, who had died in battle. Other Chamorros joined the military out of economic necessity.[141] Joseph C. San Nicolas, for example, enlisted to escape the fights that broke out among youth with few other opportunities. His uncle, a police officer who worked for the Hagåtña precinct, had warned San Nicolas, "If you don't join the military, you might be in jail."[142] Settler militarism in Guam constrained Chamorros' economic mobility, pushing Indigenous youth into the military and onto the battlefields of Vietnam.

During the Vietnam War, the newly desegregated military facilitated cross-racial friendships as well as racist encounters. During his training in the continental United States, Manglona recalled being mistaken for a Mexican, being called a "wetback," and, in Alabama, being told to ride at the back of the bus with a Black soldier.[143] Frank Cruz San Nicolas, who voluntarily joined the army in 1970 after high school graduation and accepted an extended eighteen-month tour in Vietnam in order to take a longer leave period in Guam, remembers learning about the Black Power Movement while in Vietnam and being caught in the middle of racial tensions among Black and white soldiers.[144] Blaz, meanwhile, did not recall much outright racial discrimination, though he "might have overheard some kind of discrimination" due to his origin from an unincorporated territory: "because I'm, you know, I'm not from the U.S., I'm from Guam."[145] Some Chamorro veterans were called "gooks" and racialized as the Việt Cộng enemy.[146] Regis Reyes, speaking on behalf of his late father, Vietnam War veteran Cristobal Reyes, attested: "Chamorros looked very similar to 'the enemy' so ["gook"] was loosely thrown around toward Chamorros, and they would get in trouble because they would be getting in fights with soldiers they were supposed to be fighting with."[147] As a result, Chamorros banded together to support one another. Reyes turned the area around his "CONEX" box, which stored military supplies, into a well-known gathering spot known as the "Chamorro Embassy," which "captured the essence" of Chamorro culture: "That environment was a place for Chamorros to relax, it didn't matter what rank you were. All Chamorros knew about the place and they would all go there to hang out."[148]

According to John G. Taitano, racism against Chamorros in the military went back decades. Taitano was the fourth generation of his family to serve in the US military. The oldest of nine children, he decided to follow in his father's footsteps and join the US Navy. As chief steward, in charge of cooking, cleaning, and ordering supplies, his father had faced much racial discrimination. Given his father's experience, Taitano decided he would "do one step better" and join the US Marine Corps as a corpsman, an enlisted medical specialist.[149] After an accelerated eight weeks of training, Taitano was sent to Vietnam in the late 1960s. After just one year, he had received his third Purple Heart.

While on deployment, Taitano was struck by the similarities between Vietnam and Guam, where he had grown up in the 1950s while his father was stationed at Naval Base Guam: "The resemblance of the fruits, the crabs, the climate, everything, just like I was in Guam."[150] Similarly, Frank Cruz San Nicolas said Vietnam's tropical landscape, warm climate, and food reminded him so much of Guam, he thought that if it was not for the war, he might find himself living there.[151] According to Taitano, this parallel in environments "worked real good for me, because I knew a lot of the vegetation and how to, you know, take care of yourself in a hot, humid country. Whereas, the rest of the boys had a lot of proverbial problems in their personal hygiene, their diets, and stuff."[152] Taitano articulated intimate parallels between lived experiences of the landscape in Guam and Vietnam, noting his body's ability to adapt as if it, too, were native to this otherwise foreign landscape. It is perhaps this felt familiarity with the landscape that caused Taitano to empathize with it: he described being moved by one outdoor arena that had "a lot of pockmarks of the war" from bullets. Caught in the crossfire, the built environment also bore the scars of military struggle.

Taitano's recognition of parallels between the landscapes of Guam and Vietnam extended to his feelings of cross-cultural affinities between Chamorros and Vietnamese. Despite the structural antagonisms dividing the two populations, the war also fostered moments of perceived filial intimacy that crossed language, culture, and national borders. Taitano said it "wasn't hard to get along with" the Vietnamese, both the ARVN allies and the civilians whom he met during military patrols.[153] To him, the Vietnamese were similar to "Filipinos, Chamorros, any of the Micronesians. . . . It was always deep seated in my brain that, yeah, there's some resemblance here." He mused, "We could be related."[154]

Raymond T. Baza, who served in Army Psychological Operations from 1969 to 1972, expressed a similar sentiment. During his tour, Baza worked with the Indigenous Highlanders (người Thượng), whom the Việt Cộng targeted for their collaboration with the Americans. He witnessed burning villages, hungry children, beaten men, raped women, and chiefs brutalized for refusing to capitulate to the Vietnamese communists. Amid this violence, Baza became "attached to one of the little kids," who "reminded me of my little sister, so I tried to protect her."[155] Articulating a form of trans-Indigenous solidarity, Baza collapsed geographical distances and racial divergences in positing a familial connection between a Chamorro soldier from Guam and a Highlander child in Vietnam. Overall, he observed, "us Chamorros, when we went to South Vietnam, we all share bonds with the Vietnamese because we look alike."[156] These visual similarities led to observations of cultural similarities: "We [Chamorros] are more knowledgeable of surviving, of taking care of our families because we are all family oriented. Just like in Vietnam they are family oriented. That's what brought us to this world to be together."[157] As subjects of an unincorporated territory, Chamorro soldiers existed in a politically limbo space between the United States and Vietnam: an intermediary positionality that facilitated intimate relationships with Vietnamese subjects.

During the Vietnam War, Chamorros worked closely with the Vietnamese. Taitano's Vietnamese patients called him *bác sĩ*, meaning "doctor"; he recalled instances of pulling out decayed teeth, sans anesthetic or formal training in dentistry. Here, Chamorro-Vietnamese intimacy manifested in these moments of intense bodily pain that were nonetheless facilitated by deep cross-racial trust and vulnerability. Joseph San Nicolas also befriended the ARVN soldiers, whom he relied on in the heat of battle: "the ARVN are saving us."[158] Manglona remembered the ARVN as "good soldiers," just in need of more training. On the other hand, he had a lot of respect for the North Vietnamese army, which he described as "excellent fighters" and "hard-core."[159] Blaz echoed the admiration: he "actually enjoyed going up against the North Vietnamese army, because they were properly equipped and they all got uniforms and they traveled hundreds and hundreds of miles from Hanoi."[160] Once the United States decided to pull out of the war, however, Manglona predicted that the communists would take over South Vietnam because the North Vietnamese were better trained. He expressed sorrow and regret for those who lost their lives—Vietnamese, American, Chamorro—in what at times seemed a needlessly drawn-out conflict: "It was a shame with all the bloodshed over there, and it was just wasted effort as it turned out."[161] Taitano agreed: "It was all for naught. And anybody that says we won the war, we didn't. And any of the soldiers, my buddies, we didn't win that. We didn't do nothing but sacrifice a lot of young boys and a lot of money that could have been used for something else . . . And lives would have been saved."[162] Although he refrained from expressing antiwar sentiments, acknowledging that as a soldier he just followed orders and did as he was told, Taitano critiqued the US military's disregard for lives rendered disposable during the Vietnam War.

Chamorros in Vietnam were also exposed to the violence of US militarism. Although the United States targeted the Vietnamese communists, bombs and chemical defoliants did not differentiate enemy combatants from those deemed collateral damage. Joseph San Nicolas shared a story of being seared by Agent Orange: one night, at three o'clock in the morning, the military sprayed Agent Orange to "slow down the Viet Cong," but then the wind changed direction, and "it took that spray and went over to where we at in our area." The soldiers were told to cover their heads, but San Nicolas only had time to raise his arm in protection, which was exposed to the defoliant. The "chemical reaction on the skin" burned. He described the horror: "The guys that were not doing cover, oh my god, their eyes! You have to take a towel and put it on their eyes and take it down to wipe 'em out. Because it eats up." He pointed to his arm: "You see the elbow here, it's all eaten up."[163] War scarred the body; chemical warfare directed at the Vietnamese communists harmed Chamorro soldiers as well.

But it wasn't all pain and violence. The Vietnam War also facilitated cross-racial attractions and romances. Taitano mourned the war's "destruction of beauty." He recalled, "The most beautiful woman I ever saw in my life was a South Vietnamese soldier," who was "packing a Browning automatic rifle as tall as her" and "had the attitude of a queen, like Joan of Arc."[164] Taitano admired the Vietnamese soldier not only for her looks but also for her strength and the way she commanded respect. When one Vietnamese man "started fooling with her," she "slapped the shit out of him, knocked him out one," asserting a feminist sense of bodily autonomy.[165] Taitano also remembered a friend who claimed that he was dating Saigon Sally, an evening radio show host and anticommunist antithesis to the infamous Hanoi Hannah. The couple would write letters and call each other on the two-way radio. Bridging racial and national differences, the Vietnam War facilitated moments of not only danger and precarity but also attraction and flirting between Chamorros and Vietnamese.

Some Chamorro soldiers fathered children in Vietnam. Most had to leave their Vietnamese lovers and Amerasian children behind. In contrast, Raymond T. Baza was one of a handful of Chamorros who married a Vietnamese woman, Lee T. Baza, and brought her to Guam. Their story is one of contingency and romance: a connection forged during the shared vulnerabilities of war, across differences in language, culture, and background. The couple first met in 1969. One day while flying to Đông Hà, Raymond's chopper came under fire, forcing him and his fellow soldiers to leap out in search of safety:

> Luckily I didn't get shot, but I landed on the bungee stick, you know the bungee stick was standing up, it was not too deep from the hole, right, it went through my boot! That's why I am now suffering from the tendinitis because the tendons in my foot is so sensitive, because they got cut. It was really horrible. And when the guys were leaving, I said "Oh gosh!" I look around to see where my fellow soldiers, couldn't find them! So I heard some forces coming in, speaking Vietnamese, so I took off my shirt, my jungle fatigue shirt, and I just wear my [black] T-shirt.[166]

Raymond was found by an ARVN scouting party that, fortunately, included a nurse named Lee. Motivated by the death of her parents, who had been killed by the Việt Cộng in 1965, Lee had served as an ARVN nurse for eight months before she met Raymond and nursed him back to health. According to Raymond, it was love at first sight:

> When I finally woke up, I met this beautiful nurse and I said, "Who are you?" She said, "Không hiểu." I said, "Oh, okay. You don't understand." We communicated by sign language. The colonel that was with the South Vietnamese Army evaluated me that I can already walk on my own and they already tend to my injuries. They decided to take me back to my company, my unit. I said, "I'm not leaving. She's leaving with me." I said, "I want this girl. She saved my life. I'm going to save her life." Like everybody, how do you say this, love at first sight? That was my first love. It snapped me right then.[167]

After three weeks, however, Raymond had to leave Lee and return to his US army base.

Raymond and Lee did not meet again until five or six months later in Đà Nẵng. However, that first meeting had left an impression. When Lee saw Raymond again, she said she knew then it was love.[168] He recognized her too, and pulled her hair affectionately and asked her to pack a bag and come away with him. Lee had to go back to serve in the field, but when she returned to Đà Nẵng, Raymond was still there, waiting for her.

Lee and Raymond were married in Sài Gòn in the summer of 1971 by a military chaplain and a Vietnamese priest. After their honeymoon, they left Vietnam in February 1972. On the Pan Am jet to Guam, Lee was the sole Vietnamese woman, surrounded by hundreds of US soldiers. Raymond joked that people asked if Lee were his daughter, because she was very small, "only ninety-eight pounds!"[169] His voice brimmed with love.

Asked about her first impression of Guam, Lee noted its similarities to Vietnam. The jungles surrounding Andersen Air Force Base reminded her of the jungles in Vietnam, and initially this caused fearful tears: a too-soon reminder of the war violence she had witnessed in Vietnam as a nurse. Not long after their arrival, Raymond was deployed to Germany, and Lee stayed behind in Guam with Raymond's relatives, forming a cross-racial family brought together by the US War in Vietnam. She got a job at Andersen Air Force Base as a nurse, tending to US soldiers brought back from Vietnam.

Today, Chamorro Vietnam War veterans continue to face inequalities engendered by US settler militarism in Guam. They face discrimination not only in access to Veterans Affairs benefits but also in recognition for their sacrifices to the US military.[170] On 11 June 2018, the Thirty-Fourth Guam Legislature passed resolutions to honor six Chamorro Vietnam War veterans who had earned the Distinguished Service Cross, the nation's second-highest military award: Staff Sergeant Enrique C. Cruz, Specialist Fourth Class Joseph M. Perez, Sergeant First Class Vicente T. Dydasco, Staff Sergeant Tomas G. Reyes, Sergeant Major Juan O. Blaz, and Command Sergeant Major Martin A. Manglona. It is possible, however, that these men instead deserve the Medal of Honor, the nation's highest military award, but suffered "prejudicial attitude on the part of commanders to support or process, to deny or downgrade a recommendation for the Medal of Honor because of race, religion, or ethnicity, or documents perceived to be lost or missing."[171] Retired marine colonel Joaquin "Danny" Santos, who spoke at the legislative ceremony, has been fighting tirelessly for equal recognition for Chamorro Vietnam War veterans. Thanks to his efforts, the service records of these six Chamorro Vietnam War veterans are now being reviewed by the US Army for possible upgrade to the Medal of Honor, in compliance with the 2017 National Defense Authorization Act.[172]

In Guam, Chamorros and Vietnamese continue to interact: in the Vietnamese restaurants run by Vietnamese American families, at the annual Tết celebrations hosted by the Vietnamese American community and well-attended by Chamorro Vietnam War veterans, and in the fishing boats at sea. Nicolas D. Francisco, leader of the Purple Heart group, organizes annual trips to Vietnam for veterans, the majority of whom are Chamorro.[173] Frank Cruz San Nicolas says the trips "reduce some of the emotions": although closure is elusive and forgetting is impossible, returning helps to minimize "the impact of the things that happened."[174] In Vietnam, Chamorro veterans hope to "retrace their steps and pay tribute to the people that are there," replaying old memories and forging new relationships in the aftermath of war.[175]

The militarized intimacies produced during the US War in Vietnam, moreover, continue to influence the political horizons imagined in Guam. During the war, few Chamorros drew comparisons between their own colonial status and that of the Vietnamese. Time in the aftermath of war, however, has revealed new "structures of recognition."[176] Since the mid-1990s, for example, Frank Cruz San Nicolas has advocated for Chamorro land rights. During one direct action, he erected a sign stating, "Vietnam veterans fighting for homeland, only an act of God or

Congress can move me."[177] Similarly, Allan Ramos, who served two tours with the US Marine Corps in Vietnam, pointed out that while resettled Vietnamese refugees in the continental United States have full constitutional rights as US citizens, Chamorros in Guam are still "a possession of the US" fighting for their "liberty and freedom."[178]

I conclude this section with the story of Juan C. Benavente, a Chamorro Vietnam War veteran and one of the key activists currently advocating for Guam's independence. For Benavente, these two identities are not in opposition: "A lot of my peers who served with me in the military cannot understand the dichotomy that on the one hand there is this warrior, a highly American soldier, right? And then, on the other hand, he is also an advocate for Indigenous rights. . . . But with me, I could balance the two of them."[179] As for many Chamorro veterans, Benavente's experience during the Japanese occupation of Guam during World War II influenced his decision to enlist in the US Army in the summer of 1955. As a "professional soldier," Benavente served in the US military until 1982.[180] This tenure encompassed both his tour in Vietnam, during 1968, and his experience with Operation New Life in 1975, when he served as a high school junior ROTC teacher in Guam.

After his retirement, Benavente took classes at the University of Guam, including a course on Vietnamese history. His tour of duty in Vietnam "came to full circle" when he learned about the Vietnamese anticolonial, anti-imperialist struggle: "So when you look at the Vietnamese history, even as a soldier, okay, and you ask, you know, the fundamental question: What were they fighting for? And you would conclude . . . what they want is self-government."[181] Benavente empathized with the Vietnamese revolutionaries, situating US intervention in Vietnam within a longer history of colonial occupation. Interestingly, his career in the US military both occluded and facilitated this later-in-life critique. During the war itself, Benavente did not question what he calls the "political question" of the war's morality. Instead, his first duty was to the men who intimately depended on his leadership. However, after taking the Vietnamese history class, Benavente queried the very US state that administered those duties in the first place, drawing parallels between the "fundamental question" of self-determination in Vietnam and the "fundamental question" of self-governance and independence in Guam: "Because we're being governed from Washington, DC, we have no say on what happens to us. Our citizenship can be taken away as an act of Congress. In 1950, my entire family became citizens of the United States. My grandparents are basically illiterate. But with the snap of a pen, they became citizens of the US."[182] Chamorros' sudden change in political status in 1950 was not the result of a democratic election, and this congressional imposition remains the cornerstone of the self-determination movement today. Appealing to international law protecting Indigenous peoples' rights to self-determination, Chamorro activists like Benavente argue that Chamorros should have the right to hold a plebiscite to determine their political future. Importantly, it was *because* of his experience as a professional soldier who fought in Vietnam, not *despite* it, that Benavente was able to gain this perspective and help lead the ongoing struggle for Guam's independence.

### UNFINISHED REVOLUTIONS: PALESTINE AND GUAM

Via a method of archipelagic history, this chapter has outlined Cold War entanglements, Third World solidarities, and cross-racial intimacies forged between Vietnam, Palestine, and Guam between 1967 and 1975. These archipelagic connections, these currents of *nước*, set the grounds for the post-1975 resettlement of Vietnamese refugees in Guam and Israel-Palestine: spaces entangled in the US imperial imagination. Imperialism, however, is co-constitutive with settler colonialism. While this chapter has examined the imperial dimensions of the US War in Vietnam, the following chapter elaborates the war's settler colonial dynamics: how US intervention in Southeast Asia must be understood within a longer genealogy of westward expansion and Indigenous genocide across Turtle Island. Settler colonialism, in turn, has always been countered by Indigenous resistance.

During the 1967–75 period, Palestine and Guam were connected via the central node of Vietnam, interpellated alternatively as a war, a country, a revolution, or a divided people. Although Vietnamese revolutionaries won independence in 1975, the fight for self-determination in Palestine and Guam continues. The archive contains few traces of the ephemeral threads connecting Palestine to Guam directly, either during the 1967–75 period or today. A turn to poetry, however, can gesture toward what Saidiya Hartman calls "critical fabulation."[183]

In "Between the Pacific and Palestine," Chamorro poet Craig Santos Perez draws connections between settler colonial violence in Guam and Palestine, rendering visible the archipelagic nature of US military empire as well as a corresponding archipelago of trans-Indigenous resistance. This twenty-six-line poem begins by drawing visual parallels between a scene of Perez and his Kanaka Maoli partner walking with their young daughter along Waikīkī Beach and Palestinians marching for the Right of Return in Gaza. This juxtaposition blends into another: Perez and his family building sand castles on the beach while Israel erects illegal settlements across the West Bank. From these parallel images, Perez invokes the first-person plural to articulate shared experiences of Indigenous dispossession, which precipitate a shared struggle:

> . . . Here in the Pacific, we, too, know
> the catastrophe that comes when violent nations
> imagine our sacred lands as their settler paradise.
> Hawai'i, and my ancestral home, Guåhan,
> are still occupied by the United States, who gives
> Israel billions of dollars in weapons each year,
> And who recently relocated its embassy to Jerusalem.[184]

These lines pinpoint the role of the United States in facilitating settler colonialism in both Guåhan and Palestine, through militarized occupation and financial and political support. Yet, despite shared experiences of land dispossession, the following lines of the poem acknowledge that "many sovereign Pacific states" actually supported the controversial relocation of the US embassy to the contested territory of Jerusalem, "because they have diplomatic ties with, / and receive aid from, Israel." Settler colonialism, settler militarism, and racial capitalism threaten to divide contemporaneous Indigenous struggles by pitting colonized peoples against one another in a seeming competition for scarce resources. Perez, however, refuses such divisions, posing questions to prompt recognition of how Chamorro decolonization efforts and Palestinian liberation struggles are indeed entwined:

> . . . How long will we embargo
> our empathy? How long will we blockade flotillas
> of solidarity between the Pacific and
>
> Palestine?[185]

In these final lines, "Palestine" appears distant from "the Pacific," separated as it is by the line break. However, an exaggerated indentation of the last line also suggests a potential linkage: a spatial juxtaposition of these two locales via an archipelagic praxis. This formal juxtaposition is reinforced by the poem's invocation of "empathy": an affective force reminiscent of what Quynh Nhu Le calls "emotional 'excesses' that haunt the peripheries of settler racial hegemonies—nascent, yet-to-be-formed, structures of feelings."[186] A mass movement of solidarity between Chamorro decolonization activists and Palestinian liberation fighters may not yet have been realized, either during the 1967–75 period or today; however, Perez's poem calls forth the promise of trans-Indigenous resistance. It calls forth "flotillas / of solidarity": coordinated patterns of boats cutting across water, across *nước*, *hånom*, *al-baḥr*.

# 2

# The "New Frontier"

*Settler Imperial Prefigurations and Afterlives
of the US War in Vietnam*

In his 2019 free-verse poem "Interwoven," Chamorro poet Craig Santos Perez charts archipelagic connections between Indigenous peoples across Turtle Island (North America) and the Pacific Islands. Moving fluidly between first-person singular and second-person and first-person plural pronouns, the first four stanzas of this seven-stanza poem begin by bridging geographies of difference with parallels in experience: "I come from an island / and you come from a continent, / yet we . . ."[1] Grouped together by the repetition of these opening lines, three stanzas about, respectively, resonant Indigenous epistemologies of land and water, linked histories of European invasion and Christian conversion, and communal memories of boarding schools and cultural genocide are followed by a fourth stanza outlining shared experiences of settler colonial "desecration."[2] Across nine lines, this fourth stanza maps spatial continuities between Turtle Island and Oceania— "We witnessed minerals, trees, wildlife, / and food crops extracted for profit. / We mourn lands stolen and re-named, / waters diverted and damned"—as well as temporal continuities between the past and the present: "We inherit the intergenerational / loss of removal."[3] Such continuities do not preclude important structural differences, however. The fifth stanza, which begins "I come from an island / and migrated to your continent," acknowledges that diasporic Pacific Islanders can become migrant settlers, albeit Indigenous ones, on Turtle Island. But shared histories of dispossession can also lead to a collective struggle for self-determination. While acknowledging geographical and historical specificities, the poem emphasizes trans-Indigenous resonances across multiple sites.

In an untitled poem presented at a rally for Gaza in Saskatoon, Saskatchewan, on 19 July 2014, Nēhiyaw (Cree) poet Erica Violet Lee adds Palestinians to Perez's trans-Indigenous archipelago, similarly noting shared experiences of dispossession. She relates her own, First Nation subjectivity to the experiences of Palestinian women, querying the potential for a common struggle. Whereas Perez's poem marks geographies of difference before expressing parallels in experience—"I come from an island / and you come from a continent, / yet we . . ."—Lee asserts parallels in experiences before acknowledging geographies of difference in stanza two: "We both live in occupied territories / But what can I know about you / Half a world away from me."[4] Stanza three answers this question by indexing how both First Nation and Palestinian "mothers," tasked with protecting the home, hearth, and "memories of the land," are positioned as domestic guardians against the penetration of North American and Israeli colonial state "violence." Stanza four highlights the ongoing and multiplicitous nature of these forced removals, which leave Indigenous subjects "wondering if we'll ever go back."[5] Such enduring connections with home/land exemplify Indigenous "survivance," which Anishinaabe scholar Gerald Vizenor defines as an "active sense of presence" despite centuries of displacement.[6] Like Perez, Lee interweaves parallel histories of Indigenous dispossession in order to articulate what Steven Salaita calls "inter/nationalism": a "commitment to mutual liberation based on the proposition that colonial power must be rendered diffuse across multiple hemispheres through reciprocal struggle."[7]

Together, these two poems interpolate Indigenous subjects on Turtle Island into the Chamorro-Palestinian archipelago of trans-Indigenous resistance discussed at the end of chapter one. While the previous chapter traced connections between Vietnam, Palestine, and Guam between 1967 and 1975 in order to illuminate the archipelagic nature of US military empire, this chapter highlights the *settler colonial* dimensions of the US War in Vietnam. Taking seriously Jodi A. Byrd's coinage "U.S. settler imperialism née colonialism," as well as Jodi Kim's definition of "settler modernity" as "the nexus of US settler colonialism and military empire in Asia and the Pacific," I argue that US intervention in Vietnam should be understood not only as a Cold War phenomenon but as part of a longer genealogy of American westward expansion across the North American continent, across the Pacific Islands (Guam), and into Asia—both Southeast Asia (Vietnam) and West Asia (Palestine).[8] In other words, the US settler imperial project that commenced with the thirteen colonies on Indigenous land—Pequot, Mohegan, Nanticoke, Lenni Lenape, Creek, Cherokee, Conoy, Assateague, Susquehannock, Wampanoag, Nauset, Massachuset, Micmac, Abenaki, Pennacook, Iroquois, Algonquian, Hatteras, Catawba, Shawnee, Seneca, Narragansett, Nipmuc, Yamasee, Powhattan—and extended across Turtle Island via pioneer settlement, "railroad colonialism," and the Mexican-American War (1846–48), paved the way for the overseas imperialism that began in 1898.[9] During the nineteenth and early twentieth century, US settler imperialism disrupted Pacific life-worlds in Guam, the Northern

Mariana Islands, Hawai'i, the Philippines, Wake Island, the Marshall Islands, eastern Sāmoa, Okinawa, and South Korea—spaces that had already been ravaged by European colonialism or Japanese imperialism, or both—in order to establish an archipelago of US military bases directed toward securing US influence in Southeast Asia. In 1954, this archipelago of US military bases rendered possible settler imperial intervention in Vietnam's civil war, which would conclude two decades later with Vietnam's anticolonial unification under communism and the forced displacement of hundreds of thousands of Vietnamese refugees. In short, the "American war story" that culminated in the United States' "frontier war" in Vietnam originated with the "Indian wars that 'cleared' the continent for settlement."[10] Interlocking structures of both imperialism *and* settler colonialism prefigured the post-1975 resettlement of Vietnamese refugee settlers to Turtle Island, Guam, and Israel-Palestine.

This chapter proceeds in three parts. First, I examine how Vietnam became, in the US settler imperial imagination, what President John F. Kennedy called the "New Frontier," extrapolating frontier logics finessed on Turtle Island across Oceania and into Southeast Asia. Kennedy's rhetoric extended the US frontier not only spatially but also temporally, projecting an unending future of US military intervention and occupation abroad. Moreover, as the old frontier had once displaced Native Americans, the "New Frontier" then displaced Vietnamese refugees. Next, I trace Vietnamese refugee resettlement to the so-called "heartland of Empire": the American Midwest on Anishinaabe lands and waters.[11] Analyzing Bich Minh Nguyen's novel *Pioneer Girl* (2014), I examine how settler imperialism circumscribes what I call *refugee settler desire*: Vietnamese refugees' desire to identify with white American narratives of pioneer settlement, over and against ongoing Indigenous dispossession, in order to mitigate the trauma of their own forced displacement due to war. Such refugee identification with white pioneer settlement on Turtle Island, however, can, alternatively, be routed through Indigenous epistemologies of place-making, as a dialogical reading of Louise Erdrich's *The Birchbark House* (1999), an Anishinaabe alternative to Laura Ingalls Wilders' *Little House* books, makes clear. The chapter concludes with a queer Vietnamese American interrogation of refugee settler desire, which relies on heteronormative logics of private property and intergenerational inheritance. Quyên Nguyen-Le's films *Nước (Water/Homeland)* (2016) and *Hoài (Ongoing, Memory)* (2018) gesture toward more ethical forms of refugee home-making on Indigenous lands and waters. In sum, by engaging both historical and cultural analysis, and grappling with the refugee settler condition in a context perhaps more familiar to American studies scholars, this chapter orients readers for the rest of the book. Whereas part two of the book engages archival materials and oral histories to elaborate the refugee settler condition in Guam and Israel-Palestine, part three turns to cultural production to theorize decolonial potentials for relating otherwise.

## THE US WAR IN VIETNAM: "INDIAN" TROPES
## IN A COLD WAR CONTEXT

During settler imperial wars such as the Vietnam War, the US military has often referred to enemy territory as "Indian country," reinforcing Byrd's argument that "the United States deploys a paradigmatic Indianness to facilitate its imperial desires."[12] According to Roxanne Dunbar-Ortiz, the term "Indian Country" and its shortened form "In Country," which originated during the Vietnam War, are not merely "insensitive racial slur[s] . . . tastelessly employed by accident," but rather standard "military terms of trade . . . that appear in military training manuals and are used regularly."[13] This standardization illuminates a longer genealogy of settler imperial violence: how US military tactics used overseas were first developed against Indigenous nations across Turtle Island, in a process Manu Karuka has coined "continental imperialism."[14] But it also facilitates potential solidarities between Native Americans of the original "Indian Country" and the displaced Vietnamese from "In Country"—both targets of settler warfare.

Before these military tactics were deployed in Vietnam but after they originated on Turtle Island, they were finessed across the Pacific. When US Navy admiral George Dewey colonized the Philippines in 1898, following Filipino revolutionaries' declaration of independence from Spain, for example, he described the Filipinos as "Indians," vowing to take over Manila and "keep the Indians out."[15] For some, the comparison felt apt: out of the thirty US generals who served in the Philippines, twenty-six had been officers in the so-called "Indian wars."[16] Before commanding the US army during the Philippine-American War, for example, Major General Nelson A. Miles fought Native American insurgents on Turtle Island.[17] It is unsurprising, then, that the US Army used "counterinsurgency techniques practiced against the Indigenous nations of the North American continent" in the Philippines.[18] And so it continued. Military officers then applied "lessons learned in the Philippines to future imperial ventures," ever expanding the borders of US frontier violence.[19] General Arthur MacArthur, who battled Filipino revolutionary Emilio Aguinaldo, fathered Douglas MacArthur, who served prominently during the Philippine-American War, World War II, and the Korean War—three transpacific ventures that prefigured the US War in Vietnam.[20]

In his Democratic Party presidential nomination acceptance speech on 15 July 1960, John F. Kennedy also articulated continuities between continental imperialism across Turtle Island and overseas imperialism in Vietnam. Marking his spatio-temporal location at the Memorial Coliseum in Los Angeles as an inflection point between the old frontier and what he called the New Frontier, Kennedy updated the rhetoric of Frederick Jackson Turner's 1893 frontier thesis for the Cold War era:

> I stand tonight facing west on what was once the last frontier. From the lands that stretch three thousand miles behind me, the pioneers of old gave up their safety, their comfort and sometimes their lives to build a new world here in the West. . . . Today

some would say that those struggles are all over—that all the horizons have been explored—that all the battles have been won—that there is no longer an American frontier. But . . . the problems are not all solved and the battles are not all won—and we stand today on the edge of a New Frontier—the frontier of the 1960's—a frontier of unknown opportunities and perils, a frontier of unfulfilled hopes and threats.[21]

Refusing to accept that "all the horizons have been explored," Kennedy extended the American frontier imagination westward across the Pacific, identifying "Communist influence" in Southeast Asia and the so-called Middle East as one of the "unknown opportunities and perils" of his New Frontier. Romanticizing the role of continental imperialism in building American character, he advocated a resurgence of frontier energy, calling upon his countrymen to "prove all over again whether this nation . . . can compete with the single-minded advance of the Communist system." In sum, Kennedy asked his audience to be "pioneers on that New Frontier" who would "race for mastery of the sky and the rain, the ocean and the tides, the far side of space and the inside of men's minds."[22] Such a Cold War race pitted the United States against the Soviet Union for settler imperial domination over the very air, land, and sea.

In the decades following Kennedy's "New Frontier" speech, American understandings of the Vietnam War were framed by the "Indian-war metaphor" and the "settlers vs. Indians myth."[23] By 1967, "American troops would be describing Vietnam as 'Indian Country' and search-and-destroy missions as a game of 'Cowboys and Indians'; and Kennedy's ambassador to Vietnam would justify massive military escalation by citing the necessity of moving the 'Indians' away from the 'fort' so that the 'settlers' could plant 'corn.'"[24] The "war room" of Admiral Harry D. Felt, commander in chief of Pacific Command from 1958 to 1964, meanwhile, boasted a notice juxtaposing "Injun Fightin' 1759" and "Counter-Insurgency 1962."[25] During the war, the United States Army Special Forces in Vietnam, also known as the Green Berets, were alternatively characterized as "the shock troops of Kennedy's New Frontier" and compared to the frontier rangers of the French and Indian Wars of the mid-eighteenth century, or described as fighting "like the Indians" themselves—the only effective way to combat the supposedly "savage" Việt Cộng.[26] Attuning to a settler imperial paradigm of white civilizational progress, US leaders interpreted native Vietnamese resistance to US intervention as a rejection of modernity itself.[27]

Reflecting on the temporal origins of the Vietnam War, Vietnam veteran Michael Herr also compared the Vietnam War to the Indian Wars, but in a critical manner. Insisting that neither 1965, following the Gulf of Tonkin Resolution, nor even 1954, the year of Vietnam's division along the 17th parallel following the defeat of the French at Điện Biên Phủ, was an accurate starting point for the war, Herr instead pointed to the forced displacement of Native Americans during the 1830s and 1840s: "Vietnam was where the Trail of Tears was headed all along, the turnaround point where it would touch and come back to form a containing perimeter."[28] According to Herr, the Trail of Tears foreshadowed US intervention in Vietnam, and the US War in Vietnam pointed back toward the United States' fraught history of Indigenous genocide. In other words, the Manifest Destiny rhetoric that underwrote the forced removal of the Choctaw, Chickasaw, Seminole, Creek, and Cherokee nations from what is now the southeastern United States also facilitated US settler imperial intervention in Vietnam during the Cold War. During this period, the borders of the New Frontier—what Herr calls the "containing perimeter"—extended beyond the continental United States and Oceania to penetrate Southeast Asia.

Such archipelagic connections between the Indian Wars and the Vietnam War sometimes prompted moments of recognition between Native American decolonization activists and Vietnamese anticolonial revolutionaries. At the 1971 Winter Soldier Investigations, sponsored by Vietnam Veterans Against the War, for example, veteran Evan Haney (Seminole Nation) testified: "The same massacres happened to the Indians. . . . I got to know the Vietnamese people and I learned they were just like us."[29] Haney's insight was echoed throughout the American Indian Movement of the Long Sixties, which came to fruition alongside roiling anti–Vietnam War protests, thus facilitating connections between continental imperialism on Turtle Island and overseas imperialism in Southeast Asia.[30] The seventy-one-day siege of Wounded Knee in 1973, for example, whose participants protested the federal government's failure to uphold treaty obligations, commemorated the Wounded Knee massacre of 1890, and established the Independent Oglala Nation, was largely sustained by Native Vietnam War veterans, who used guerilla warfare tactics to hold off the US Marshall Service, FBI, and National Guard.[31] Such domestic use of federal military force against civilian protesters prompted the Wounded Knee Legal Defense/Offense Committee to insist that it would defend the protesters against the "legal reign of terror" until "South Dakota begins to look more like America and less like war torn South East Asia."[32] Meanwhile, newspapers reporting on the 1973 siege of Wounded Knee and the 1890 massacre it referenced drew visual parallels with the US military's massacre of racialized people in Vietnam, especially during the fifth anniversary of the Mỹ Lai massacre in March 1973. As these news photos made clear, those who dared to stand in the way of US frontier expansion—whether in Oglala territory or Vietnam—faced being murdered.[33]

Settler imperial rhetoric continues to circulate in twenty-first-century US politics. President Barack Obama's inaugural address in January 2009, for example, echoed some of the "New Frontier" rhetoric of Kennedy's 1960 nomination speech. Praising Americans' frontier ethic, Obama asserted that the "greatness of our nation" had been "earned" by the "risk-takers, the doers, the makers of things" who "traveled across oceans in search of new life" and "toiled in sweatshops and settled the West."[34] Although he includes Black slaves in this national narrative, they are positioned as "arrivants": colonized peoples who are nonetheless implicated in the settler colonial dispossession of Indigenous nations.[35]

In Obama's speech, Native American presence is marked by its stark absence. Consider, for example, the assumptive use of the first-person plural in Obama's description of frontier heroism: "For us, they fought and died in places like Concord and Gettysburg; Normandy and Khe Sanh."[36] Such comments erase the history of the Indian Wars as wars of continental imperialism, highlighting instead, via synecdoche, the United States' more visible military conflicts: the Revolutionary War, World War II, and the Vietnam War. The reference to the 1968 Battle of Khe Sanh here interpolates the US War in Vietnam into this longer history of Indigenous erasure and positions Vietnam as part of the New Frontier upon which American character was tried and tested, to the benefit of those included in Obama's first-person plural "us"—that is, American beneficiaries of settler imperial expansion. In contrast, Native Americans and their allies continue to fight for Indigenous sovereignty, posing an ethical dilemma for refugees unwittingly resettled on stolen land.

## REFUGEE SETTLER DESIRE: NARRATIVES OF HOME-MAKING IN *LITTLE HOUSE* VERSUS *BIRCHBARK HOUSE*

If the US War in Vietnam extended the settler colonial logics of Manifest Destiny across Oceania and into Southeast Asia, then Vietnamese refugees displaced in the aftermath of that war to the continental United States are implicated in the nation's settler imperial genealogy. Vietnamese American literature is well positioned to unpack the interiority of Vietnamese refugees resettled on Indigenous lands and waters—what this book calls the refugee settler condition—as well as to illuminate latent parallels between Indigenous genocide across the US frontier and the mass killing and displacement of Vietnamese subjects across the "New Frontier." Although a growing number of Vietnamese American texts incorporate frontier themes and "cowboys-and-Indians" metaphors to discuss Vietnamese refugee resettlement on Turtle Island, Bich Minh Nguyen's *Pioneer Girl* (2014) is exemplary in its literary depiction of what I call *refugee settler desire*: the urge to mitigate the trauma of forced displacement by rooting oneself in white settler narratives of national belonging.[37] In *Pioneer Girl*, whose title references Laura Ingalls Wilder's autobiography, main character Lee Lien—daughter of Vietnam War refugees, recent PhD in American literature, and aficionado of Wilder's *Little House* books—seeks to "write herself into an American classic, to claim a material connection with the America embodied by the Wilders."[38] In doing so, she eludes other forms of identification, such as with the Anishinaabeg, on whose lands and waters her family finds refuge.

To contextualize the political implications of Lee's identification with the *Little House* books, it is important to understand Wilder's settler status and her books' frontier logics. A descendant of Mayflower immigrants and distant cousin of Franklin Delano Roosevelt, Laura Ingalls was born in a log cabin in western Wisconsin in 1867, nineteen years after statehood.[39] In *Little House on the Prairie* (1935), set in 1869, the Ingalls set off for Montgomery County, Kansas—part of the original "Indian Country," also known as "Indian Territory," which would later be extrapolated across the Pacific and into Vietnam. Indeed, the first chapter of *Little House on the Prairie*, now called "Going West," was originally entitled "Going In" (as in, "into Indian Territory").[40]

In *Little House on the Prairie*, the Ingalls family attempts to settle Osage land. Between 1790 and 1834, Congress had passed six Non-Intercourse Acts, also known as the Indian Intercourse Acts, that forcibly removed federally recognized tribal nations onto government-designated reservations. In 1825, a treaty established the Osage Diminished Reserve in what is now south-central and southeast Kansas. During the 1860s, white settlers began illegally infiltrating the reserve in such great numbers that the Osage appealed to the federal government for military assistance; it promised to relocate the Osage. In 1865, the Osage were pressured into signing the Canville Treaty, which required the United States to sell Osage lands in Kansas on behalf of the tribe at $1.25 per acre and then purchase new lands in Oklahoma using the proceeds from the sale. Crippled by debt incurred during the Civil War, however, the federal government failed to pay the Osage. By 1868, the Osage, facing starvation, were pressured into renegotiating their relocation agreement and signing the unfavorable Sturgis (Drum Creek) Treaty, which dictated the selling of Osage land directly to the Leavenworth, Lawrence & Galveston (LL&G) Railroad at a reduced price of 20 to 25 cents per acre, in exchange for the purchase of Cherokee lands farther south. However, Congress ultimately refused to ratify the Sturgis Treaty, which favored the railroad barons, because they feared a backlash from white settler constituents who desired access to the land under the Homestead Act of 1862.

During the late 1860s, rumors of the impending opening of so-called Indian Territory reached land-hungry settlers like the Ingalls. Buoyed by an unfaltering sense of white entitlement, they rushed to claim land on the Osage Diminished Reserve, undeterred by the illegality of their actions or the genocidal effects on the Osage. As Pa explains to Laura in *Little House on the Prairie*: "When white settlers come into a country, the Indians have to move on. The government is going to move these Indians farther west, any time now. . . . White people are going to settle all this country, and we get the best land because we get here first and take our pick."[41] According to Pa, frontier settlement was preordained by Manifest Destiny.

Almost a century after the Ingalls' venture to claim land on the Osage Diminished Reserve, Rose Wilder Lane, daughter of Laura Ingalls Wilder and ghostwriter of the *Little House on the Prairie* books, traveled to the so-called In Country of Vietnam in August 1965 to write an article about women's experiences during the war.[42] Extending her mother's pioneer movement across the Pacific into Kennedy's

New Frontier, Lane would publish the piece, "August in Vietnam," in *Women's Day* in December 1965. *Pioneer Girl* takes the historical fact of Lane's trip to Vietnam as a point of departure, positing an entanglement of Lane and Wilder's *Little House* books with both US settler imperialism in Vietnam and the post-1975 resettlement of Vietnamese refugees on Turtle Island. In the novel, protagonist Lee Lien seeks to solve the mystery of a gold pin left by an American woman named Rose in the Sài Gòn café owned by her "Ong Hai" (grandfather) in 1965.[43] Lee is struck by the similarities between this gold pin—treasured as a "gift" by Ong Hai and carried to the United States when he fled Vietnam in 1975—and the pin that Almanzo presents to Laura in *These Happy Golden Years*: "On its flat surface was etched a little house, and before it along the bar lay a tiny lake, and a spray of grasses and leaves."[44] Embarking on a research trip that takes her across the Midwest and ultimately westward to the gold rush lands of California, retracing the covered wagon trails followed by the Ingalls a century and a half earlier, Lee asks: What if the Rose in her grandfather's memory was actually Rose Wilder Lane? What if her family's refugee story was intimately entangled with the *Little House* narrative?

Far from an impartial research project, what drives Lee is an obsessive desire to uncover a material linkage between her family's story and that of the *Little House* books: "How many times during the years of my *Little House* obsession had I pretended the pin was Laura's secret gift to me?"[45] Despite the unanswered questions that remain, by the end of the novel, Lee envisions, quite literally, that she has "inherited" the "little house," etched on a gold pin, "from Rose. Whichever Rose that was. Whoever she turns out to be."[46] Indeed, Lee claims to inherit not just the "little house" pin itself, but the larger white settler narrative embodied in the *Little House* series, evidencing the intergenerational private property logics upon which settler colonialism hinges.

The term *refugee settler desire* describes Lee's quest to mitigate the trauma of her own refugee family's displacement and loss of home(land)—indeed, the loss of a "little house"—by tethering their story to Lane and Wilders' quintessential settler narrative of US frontier expansion. Consider this passage from *Pioneer Girl's* second chapter:

> So much immigrant desire in this country could be summed up, quite literally, in gold: as shining as the pin Rose had left behind. A promise taken up, held on to for decades, even while Sam and I were reckless with our own history, searching for things we couldn't yet name. If this Rose was the same Rose of the *Little House* books, the daughter of Laura Ingalls Wilder, then she had defined a part of American desire that my mother understood just as well.[47]

Here Lee articulates a particular "immigrant desire" to claim belonging in the American landscape. What Rose leaves to Lee's family, and what Lee and her brother Sam search for but "couldn't yet name," is a "promise": the promise of multicultural inclusion into the US settler state.

But what if we disaggregate the conflation between "immigrant" and "refugee" that Lee articulates here, and pinpoint more precisely the contours of refugee settler desire? The passage above is preceded by a description of Lee's mother and grandfather's displacement from Vietnam, which can be more accurately characterized not as immigrant mobility but as refugee flight "out of Vietnam, back when the city of Saigon was crumbling around them."[48] Indeed, later in the novel Lee postulates that the reason first her mother and then she "held on" so tightly to "that gold pin" was that their own origins were "lost through language and war."[49] Displaced from little house and homeland, Lee attempts to mitigate her family's refugee loss by interweaving her story with that of white pioneer settlement, holding on to the gold pin as an inherited "promise" of inclusive resettlement in the continental United States.

This project of Vietnamese refugee home-making, which seeks inclusion in the white pioneer myths of the US's foundational national narratives, ultimately risks reproducing the settler colonial violence upon which these myths are built, however. Indeed, by desiring to identify with white pioneer settlement rather than Native American stories of place, Lee unwittingly internalizes the very Manifest Destiny logic that justified US settler imperial expansion across Oceania into Vietnam in the first place—a logic that instigated the very refugee *unsettlement* that she seeks to mitigate throughout the novel.

In *Pioneer Girl*, Lee does acknowledge that the *Little House* series celebrates pioneer resilience and frontier adventure at the expense of Indigenous displacement. For example, she expresses sympathy for the "Osage Indians whose lands are being threatened" and notes that "Ma repeatedly says she hates Indians, while Pa is all about negative capability: he has respect for the leaders, makes a point to learn some of their customs, yet he also believes that their land should be his by right of whiteness."[50] Although *Little House on the Prairie* isolates explicitly genocidal rhetoric like "the only good Indian is a dead Indian" to Pa's character foil of Mr. Scott, the entire book is underwritten by a settler imperial celebration of the pioneering frontier man.[51] Osage writer Dennis McAuliffe further critiques the way Wilder and Lane represent the Osages as "beggars and thieves," compare them to "reptiles, to garbage or scum," and assign them "descriptive adjectives that connote barbarism, brutality, and bloodthirstiness," making "much ado about their odor."[52] Osage loss—of land, lifestyle, and livelihood—only garners cursory mention in *Little House on the Prairie*. By extension, Nguyen's *Pioneer Girl* implicitly posits Indigenous displacement as an unfortunate but unavoidable precondition for refugee resettlement in the settler imperial United States.

Indeed, in the novel Lee's critiques of Manifest Destiny, white settler entitlement, and Indigenous displacement are ultimately eclipsed by the seemingly more pressing issue of racial exclusion. In chapter 14, when Lee finally attempts to explain her research project on Rose Wilder Lane and the mysterious gold pin to her skeptical mother and sympathetic but confused grandfather, she posits that the central violence of white settlement was not the settler colonial displacement of Indigenous peoples such as the Osage but the white supremacist *exclusion* of nonwhite subjects from "the American story." Subsuming the specificity of refugee displacement into a larger immigrant narrative, Lee explains: "I wanted to tell them that my own concept of American history had been unknowingly shaped just by reading those [*Little House*] books, that they had rooted me in a paradox of pride and resentment—a desire to be included in the American story and a knowledge of the limits of such inclusion. Like the Chinese workers who helped build the transcontinental railroad and yet were left out of pictures and edged out of history."[53] Tellingly, the Osage remain excluded, both from "the American story" so desired by Lee, the daughter of Vietnam War refugees, and from Lee's retelling of the limits of inclusion in such a story. Rather than juxtapose refugee and Indigenous displacement, Lee instead reaches for pan-ethnic racial identification with the "Chinese workers" who unwittingly contributed to railroad colonialism during the late nineteenth century.[54] In so doing, Lee attributes her family's exclusion from "the American story" to the failure of multiracial inclusion, rather than to the violence of settler imperialism. By extension, she negates any potential identification with the displaced Osage of *Little House on the Prairie*, positing the two structural positions—refugee and Indigenous—and their attendant structures of domination—US imperialism and settler colonialism—as distinct rather than entangled formations. By inserting her own Vietnamese refugee settler "picture" into the "American story," she inadvertently edges out Indigenous histories and presences.

Lee's privileging of the problem of multiracial inclusion in *Pioneer Girl* is informed by author Bich Minh Nguyen's childhood experiences growing up in the Midwest during the 1980s, as chronicled in her 2007 memoir, *Stealing Buddha's Dinner*. Nguyen details her family's refugee flight from Vietnam in spring 1975 when she was not yet one year old, and their archipelagic passage through refugee camps in Guam, the Philippines, and Fort Chaffee, Arkansas, before eventual resettlement in Grand Rapids, Michigan. Throughout the memoir, Nguyen's central source of anxiety is her racial exclusion from the predominantly white, conservative, Christian communities of Michigan and her desire to assimilate into white American culture via the consumption of American fast foods—Pringles, Toll House cookies, American meat—whose names make up the majority of the memoir's chapter titles. It is only toward the end of the memoir, as Nguyen comes to terms with her Vietnamese heritage and the Mexican culture of her stepmother, Rosa, that more "ethnic" foods are featured as chapter titles: "Holiday Tamales," "Mooncakes," "Cha Gio."

In chapter 11, entitled "Salt Pork" in honor of *Little House on the Prairie*, Nguyen describes her own childhood obsession with the *Little House* books and her identification with the protagonist, Laura Ingalls: "After I read the *Little House* books I began to pretend that bacon was salt pork and that I was Laura herself. She was short and small like me, and she savored every last touch of the salt on her tongue."[55] This parallelism in palates and stature is but a synecdoche of the larger connections that Nguyen identifies between her life and that of the Ingalls family: "In many ways, their pioneer life reminded me of immigrant life. As they search for new homesteads, they, too, experience isolation and the scramble for shelter, food, work, and a place to call home."[56] Again conflating immigrant and refugee positionalities, Nguyen's assertion of parallel searches for "a place to call home" elides the different *causes* of such a search for refugees displaced by war versus pioneers driven by settlement of Indigenous lands and waters.

Growing up in Michigan, Nguyen looked up to the Ingalls as "the epitome of American" and envied their "righteous belief in the idea of home, in the right to land, in the life of farming"—in other words, Thomas Jefferson's agrarian ideal, later legislated in 1862 via the Homestead Act and further promoted by Turner's frontier thesis.[57] As she grew older, Nguyen admits, she had "an increasingly uneasy time reading the books," though the central issue she critiques is not settler imperial violence but domestic "racism": "Ma Ingalls's hatred of Indians" as well as Pa's vaudeville performance of blackface in *Little Town on the Prairie*. Although Indigenous studies scholars have cautioned against reducing Indigeneity to racial difference, in this passage Nguyen attributes Ma's hatred of the Osage to inter-personal racism rather than the structure of settler colonialism, even though Indigenous peoples are not another minority group pursuing multicultural inclusion but rather independent nations fighting for sovereignty. Marking her family's similarities with the Osage and African Americans via shared experiences of racial exclusion rather than settler imperialism, Nguyen reflects, "I knew that people like me would also have been considered outcasts, heathens, and strangers; we didn't even count."[58] Such refugee settler desire to "count," however, is ultimately an example of what Lauren Berlant calls "cruel optimism": that which refugees cannot achieve but cannot help but desire.[59] Nguyen concludes the chapter: "Drawn to what I could not have, I kept seeking out landscapes in which I could not have existed. Deep down, I thought I could prove that I could be a more thorough and competent white girl than any of the white girls I knew."[60] In the continental United States, refugee settler desire for belonging is entangled with an aspiration for whiteness: a desire to exceed at whiteness, to write oneself into white spaces, and to inevitably, if unintentionally, reproduce the white settler logics of Indigenous displacement.

In sum, both Nguyen's novel *Pioneer Girl* and her memoir, *Stealing Buddha's Dinner*, explore parallels between refugee and pioneer narratives—and, by extension, structural antagonisms between refugee and Indigenous subjects. Although both the novel and the memoir critique the Manifest Destiny rhetoric and white entitlement depicted in the *Little House* books, this critique does not extend to the structural violence of settler imperialism. Indeed, both *Pioneer Girl* and *Stealing Buddha's Dinner* ultimately subordinate a critique of Indigenous dispossession to the seemingly more pressing goal of refugee inclusion in the US body politic: a pattern that is repeated in the secondary literature surrounding these texts.[61]

In *Pioneer Girl*, what motivates Lee's identification with Laura in the *Little House* series is not only a shared aspiration for (re)settlement but, counterintuitively, a feeling of perpetual *restlessness:* movement, displacement, exile, the perennial inability to ever feel settled or at home. Lee notes "a deep restlessness threading the *Little House* books together. Pa Ingalls is anxious to keep looking for a better homestead, to keep searching out the treasured West, and Laura too has that 'itchy wandering foot.' Perhaps her daughter Rose was able to translate and convey these feelings so well because she had grown up caged in her own desires, if not for westward exploration, then for worldliness, fame, glory, a life beyond the farm and small-town Missouri."[62]

Laura Ingalls's early childhood was one of constant movement: born in the Big Woods of Wisconsin, she traveled with her family through Missouri, Kansas ("Indian Country"), Minnesota, and Iowa before settling in De Smet, Dakota Territory, in 1879.[63] According to Lee, she and her brother "felt that restlessness too. The desire to be free of our family's choices, even though at the same time we knew how much we owed—our very existence—to them."[64] Laura's long list of midwestern homesteads is paralleled by Lee's own list of midwestern towns in which she grew up: Le Porte, Indiana; Battle Creek, Michigan; Naperville, Illinois; Joliet, Illinois; Waukesha, Wisconsin; Valparaiso, Indiana; Franklin, Illinois. Displaced from Vietnam as refugees, Lee's mother and grandfather elude traditional settlement, driving across the midwestern states with Lee and her brother in tow, in perpetual search of a better restaurant venture to replace the beloved Café 88 of Ong Hai's 1960s Sài Gòn. Throughout the novel, Lee feels haunted by this "old anxiety: my mother and grandfather, also searching, landing, restive in the Midwest."[65] In other words, Lee inherits her mother's intergenerational trauma of refugee restlessness: "Once in flight [my mother] was always in flight, glancing uneasily around before pushing on to another vista that promised better prospects. Maybe it kept her feeling safe. She couldn't have known that it would leave [my brother] and me feeling the opposite—permanently unsettled, unable to know what could be called home."[66] Like settler colonialism, refugee unsettlement is more akin to a structure than an event. It does not dissipate with the moment of arrival, but rather continues to haunt succeeding generations.

But does this sense of "deep restlessness" shared by Lee's family and the Ingalls— a modality of continual *un*settlement—undermine the violence of settler imperialism, or merely obfuscate and perpetuate it? Afterall, restlessness in the name of "westward exploration" or even "worldliness, fame, glory" is quite different from restlessness due to refugee displacement. The two rest on different logics of mobility and distinct planes of racial privilege. At the end of the novel, Lee identifies "restlessness" as a profoundly American experience—one that connects her family's refugee narrative to a longer genealogy of frontier expansion:

So far I have spent almost half of my life studying and thinking about American literature, and the landscape has seemed one of incredible, enduring, relentless longing.
Everyone is always leaving each other, chasing down the next seeming opportunity—
home or body. Where does it stop? Does it ever? I want to believe it all leads to something grander than the imagination, grander than the end-stop of the Pacific. Or is
that it: You get to the place where you land; you are tired now; you settle. You settle.
You build a home and raise a family. There are years of eating and arguing, working
and waking. There are years of dying. No one knows what the last image will be.[67]

Here, the frontier myth of the West—invoked by the "end-stop of the Pacific"—
seemingly concludes in settlement: "You get to the place where you land; you
are tired now; you settle." And yet the passage continues, suggesting an unfixed
future: "No one knows what the last image will be." On one hand, this invocation
of another image after "the end-stop of the Pacific" references the extension of US
settler imperialism beyond the West Coast, across Oceania, and into the "New
Frontier" of Vietnam. The last line of the novel, after all, invokes a "hoped-for
landscape that always lies just beyond the west."[68] On the other hand, the suggestion here of a not-yet-visible futurity marks an opening for alternative forms
of identification between Vietnamese refugees displaced by war and Indigenous
refugees displaced by frontier settlement. Neither settler imperialism nor refugee
settler desire are inevitable: "No one knows what the last image will be."

Instead of Laura Ingalls Wilder's "little house," I propose that the character
Lee Lien, and by extension Vietnamese American refugee settlers, consider a different abode: a birchbark house, built by the Anishinaabe of Moningwanaykaning, Island of the Golden-Breasted Woodpecker in Lake Superior, off the coast of
present-day Wisconsin. Anishinaabe author Louise Erdrich's *The Birchbark House*
(1999) has widely been regarded as an alternative to the *Little House* books: a mid-
nineteenth-century story of frontier encounters, as told from an Indigenous perspective. Born on 7 June 1954 in Little Falls, Minnesota, Erdrich, like Wilder, grew
up in the so-called Midwest. While her father's family hailed from Germany, her
mother's came from the Turtle Mountain Reservation in North Dakota, where
her grandfather was a tribal chair and traditional dancer.[69] According to Anishinaabe scholar Margaret Noodin, Erdrich "speaks in circles about Anishinaabe
language and identity the way a crow flies searching, the way a sunflower's seeds
spiral, the way seasons cycle—with subtle, undeniable purpose."[70]

Based on the life of Erdrich's great-grandmother, *The Birchbark House* tells the
coming-of-age story of seven-year-old Omakayas.[71] Seven is a significant number
in Anishinaabemowin in that it "represents the number of ways to specify who
is present as a speaker, audience, initiator, or object. . . . The seventh prophecy of
the Anishinaabe, made by the seven grandfathers, foretells a rebirth among the
people."[72] Set on and around Moningwanaykaning in 1847, *The Birchbark House*
takes place ten years after Michigan became a state, one year before Wisconsin statehood, and twenty years before Laura Ingalls Wilder was born. By this

time, the Three Fires Anishinaabe Confederacy—a long-standing alliance of the Ojibwe (Chippewa), Odawa (Ottawa), and Potawatomi—had been flourishing in the Great Lakes region for more than a thousand years.[73] Although the 1795 Treaty of Greenville had defined the boundary between the confederacy and the fifteen American states then in existence, *The Birchbark House* marks a moment of transition: a complex multicultural society of Anishinaabe and French traders soon to be disrupted by the encroaching *chimookoman* (white people), who bring smallpox and divide the land into private allotments. The following three books in Erdrich's series chronicle multiple displacements: the Sandy Lake Massacre of 1849, Omakayas's family's journey west to escape settler violence, and her later-in-life move farther west to live with the Métis of the Red River Valley.[74] Despite these displacements, the Anishinaabeg have persisted, and today, more than two hundred Anishinaabe nations are recognized across the United States and Canada.

Like many Anishinaabe stories, *The Birchbark House* is organized around the four seasons. Four is another important number in Anishinaabe epistemology, reflecting the four primary verb forms and the four cardinal directions.[75] The book's fourteen chapters are divided into four sections, entitled *Neebin, Dagwag-ing, Biboon*, and *Zeegwun*—four verbs, rather than nouns, that depict when the seasons *become* summer, fall, winter, and spring, respectively.[76] A standalone pro-logue, entitled "The Girl from Spirit Island," sets up the central mystery of the text. The first sentence reads: "The only person left alive on the island was a baby girl."[77] Ravaged by smallpox, "a sickness brought by the chimookoman," the Anishinaa-beg of Spirit Island had all passed away except for this unnamed baby girl.[78] Chapter One, "The Birchbark House," opens on a different island, Moningwanaykaning, and introduces the book's main character: "She was named Omakayas, or Little Frog, because her first step was a hop."[79] Throughout *The Birchbark House*, the reader is left to puzzle the relationship between the prologue's unnamed baby girl and the book's body chapters, which chronicle Omakayas's adventures and her growth as a healer. It is not until the last chapter, "Full Circle," that Erdrich reveals that Omakayas is indeed the "Girl from Spirit Island."

I share the story of *The Birchbark House* to propose an alternative source of identification for *Pioneer Girl's* Lee Lien, who feels haunted by her mother and grandfather's refugee displacement and inability "to know what could be called home" in the lands of the Three Fires Anishinaabe Confederacy, also known as the Midwest.[80] In some ways, Omakayas mirrors Laura Ingalls in *Little House on the Prairie*. *The Birchbark House* chronicles Omakayas's relationships with her siblings (including her pretty older sister, Angeline, reminiscent of Mary Ingalls) and her friendships with multiple animals. Like Laura, and by extension Lee, Omakayas is also shaped by a particular sense of restlessness: her family moves each season, constructing new houses and adapting to new threats posed by the encroaching *chimookoman*. But Omakayas's restlessness differs from that of the Ingalls. Omakayas's family's movement follows the patterns of the seasons, rather than the fantasy of frontier expansion: the building of a birchbark house in the summer, the canoe trek to a ricing camp in Kakagon in the fall, the construction of a cedar house in the winter, and the journey to a maple-sugaring camp on the other side of the island in the spring. Attuned to these seasonal patterns, Omakayas's family's archipelagic movement across multiple islands is shaped by a profound relationship to land and water, rather than an individualistic drive toward ownership and settlement. In sum, while "Wilder's stories depict the woods and the prairie as unsettled and unsettling," Erdrich's books "depict these places as home, harvest, and a web of comfort."[81]

In other ways, Omakayas is similar to Lee and thus bypasses Laura Ingalls as a mediating figure. Like Lee's family, who fled Vietnam in the wake US intervention and communist unification, Omakayas is also a refugee, driven from Spirit Island by the smallpox spread by the *chimookoman*. Indeed, Lee is not actually— or, rather, not only—a "pioneer girl" but also a daughter of displaced refugees whose own narrative intersects with that of Omakayas along this shared narrative of refugeehood. Refugeehood, however, does not preclude Omakayas's ability to establish a place-based sense of belonging in the Great Lakes region. And so, perhaps, Lee, and by extension Vietnamese American refugee settlers, can learn from Omakayas, substituting an identification with the white pioneer narrative of Laura Ingalls Wilder with an Anishinaabe epistemology of dwelling in place in order to quell her anxieties regarding perpetual restlessness. Erdrich writes:

> She couldn't help being just who she was. Omakayas, in this skin, in this place, in this time. Nobody else. No matter what, she wouldn't ever be another person or really know the thoughts of anyone but her own self. She closed her eyes. For a moment, she felt as though she were falling from a great height, plunging through air and blackness, tumbling down with nothing to catch at. With a start of fear, she opened her eyes and felt herself gently touch down right where she was, in her own body, here.[82]

Refugee flight can also feel like "falling from a great height, plunging through air and blackness, tumbling down with nothing to catch at." But refugee settler desire for a sense of belonging to counteract the fear associated with this fall need not necessarily take on the contours of frontier settlement—Manifest Destiny, white entitlement, and individualist ownership of the land. Instead, it can aspire toward bodily situatedness, as articulated by Omakayas via Erdrich. To be clear, I am not suggesting that Lee "play Indian"—a mode of parody interwoven with Native conquest and dispossession—but rather respectfully learn from the Anishinaabeg, on whose lands her family resettled.[83] Lee, daughter of Vietnam War refugees, might then be able to mitigate her family's sense of restlessness, the fear of the fall, by pausing to dwell "in her own body, here." Here, in the Midwest on Anishinaabe lands and waters, she can perhaps come to rest, cognizant of the interwoven nature of refugee and Indigenous displacement.

According to Anishinaabe writer Leanne Betasamosake Simpson, Anishinaabe understandings of Indigenous sovereignty are grounded in forms of relationality:

> I asked an Elder Gidigaa Migizi from Waashkigamaagki the word for "nation" or "sovereignty" or even "self-determination" in Anishinaabemowin (Ojibwe language). He thought for a long time, and then he told me that he remembered his old people saying "Kina Gchi Anishinaabe-ogaming," which was understood to mean, "the place where we all live and work together." On the surface, it seemed to me like such a simple answer, a description of sovereignty and nationhood that is at its core about relationships—relationships with each other and with plant and animal nations, with our lands and waters and with the spiritual world.[84]

Indigenous sovereignty can encompass refugee resettlement, insofar as refugees interrogate their refugee settler desire to identify with white settler narratives of nation-state belonging. The following section analyzes two films by Quyên Nguyen-Le in order to highlight the importance of "queer dis/inheritance" as a method of refusing the intergenerational perpetuation of settler colonial violence.[85]

## NƯỚC AND HOÀI: QUEER INTERROGATIONS OF REFUGEE SETTLER DESIRE

*Pioneer Girl*'s depiction of refugee settler desire is, I argue, emblematic of many Vietnamese Americans' response to the refugee settler condition: they embrace white settler narratives to mitigate the trauma of refugee uprooting, often failing to recognize connections between their forced displacement from the "New Frontier" of Vietnam and the dispossession of Indigenous peoples across Turtle Island. While calls for decolonial solidarity between Vietnamese Americans and Native Americans are growing, coalition still remains challenging for many to articulate.[86] I therefore turn to *Nước (Water/Homeland)* (2016) and *Hoài (Ongoing, Memory)* (2018), two experimental short films directed by queer Vietnamese American filmmaker Quyên Nguyen-Le, to think through more ethical forms of refugee home-making in the continental United States. Cultural production offers blueprints for unsettling the refugee settler condition and relating otherwise; whereas this section focuses on emergent solidarities across Turtle Island, part three of the book will develop this methodology in regard to Guam and Israel-Palestine.

*Hoài (Ongoing, Memory)*, cowritten with Ly Thúy Nguyễn, explicitly addresses Vietnamese refugee resettlement across Indigenous lands and waters. *Nước (Water/Homeland)*, on the other hand, grapples with the inherited images of war that produced refugee flight from Vietnam in the first place, providing a crucial context for querying refugee settler desire. Read together, archipelagically, these two films demonstrate how the afterlives of the Vietnam War shape contemporary refugee and Indigenous struggles. Via bilingual discourse and nonlinear dream sequences, the films interweave Vietnam and Turtle Island, past and present, refugeehood and resettlement.

Pairing stunning visuals with bilingual dialogue, simultaneously subtitled in English and Vietnamese, both *Nước (Water/Homeland)* and *Hoài (Ongoing, Memory)* feature genderqueer Vietnamese American protagonists and their relationships with their widowed refugee parents and progressive, mixed-race girlfriends. Whereas *Nước (Water/Homeland)* portrays a photographer grappling with the excess of Vietnam War imagery—images that threaten to drown out the quiet narrative of their own refugee mother—*Hoài (Ongoing, Memory)* depicts a broken-hearted activist arguing with their refugee father about the Vietnamese American community's role in protesting President Donald Trump's "America First" policies: the 2017 Muslim Ban and the imprisonment of undocumented Central American refugee children along the US-Mexico border. *Nước (Water/Homeland)* commences in a darkroom displaying signature black-and-white photos from the US War in Vietnam: Eddie Adams's 1968 photo of South Vietnamese major general Nguyễn Ngọc Loan shooting Việt Cộng prisoner Nguyễn Văn Lém; Nick Út's 1972 Putlitzer Prize–winning photo of Phan Thị Kim Phúc, also known as the "napalm girl"; Bernie Boston's 1967 Flower Power photo of American antiwar protesters placing carnations in soldiers' gun barrels; and an iconic photo of Vietnamese boat refugees. In the middle of these famous photographs is a closeup photo of the unnamed protagonist's mother's face. The other film, *Hoài (Ongoing, Memory)*, begins with a closeup shot of the eponymous main character Hoài's face against a geographically ambiguous blue sky. Hoài begins to slip and fall backward just as the camera cuts to black.

Both films grapple with the difficulty of translating across language, geography, generation, and political orientation. In *Nước (Water/Homeland)*, the protagonist speaks in English while their mother responds in Vietnamese. Although the two understand each other at the level of daily pleasantries, they do not have a shared language to discuss memories of war: "How do you ask about trauma when you don't even speak the same language anymore?"[87] In *Hoài (Ongoing, Memory)*, Hoài and their refugee father begin by speaking exclusively in their respective languages, and this leads to a generational clash: Hoài argues with their father, who warns that if Hoài joins their ex-girlfriend in punching white supremacists at political protests, Hoài will get arrested. In the final dialogue of the film, however, Hoài attempts faltering Vietnamese and their father responds in accented English. It is via this shared bilingual language that the two begin to articulate a cross-generational ethic of queer refugee home-making across Indigenous lands and waters.

The two films' genderqueer Vietnamese American protagonists also clash with their respective girlfriends about American left-wing interpretations of the Vietnam War and its aftermath. In *Nước (Water/Homeland)*, the girlfriend asserts, "Vietnam was such a mistake"—a comment that centers American perspectives and erases the South Vietnamese struggle for an independent democratic state.[88]

FIGURE 4. Film still from *Hoài (Ongoing, Memory)*, directed by Quyên Nguyen-Le. Poster art by Demian DinéYazhi'. Image courtesy of Quyên Nguyen-Le.

Hurt and offended, the protagonist responds, "Vietnam's a country, not a war. . . . You just ignored all Vietnamese people." Confused, having expected the protagonist to agree with her seemingly progressive statement, the girlfriend responds defensively: "All I'm saying is we shouldn't have been there." But the main character retorts: "We weren't there. It was a real thing that happened to real people like my mom. Don't idealize it."[89] Isolating the "we" to the two in dialogue, the protagonist questions the girlfriend's presumed "we" as inclusive of all Americans, across time and regardless of race. Instead, the protagonist recenters the specificity of the South Vietnamese refugee experience: those who lived through the war and experienced betrayal at the hands of retreating US allies.

*Hoài (Ongoing, Memory)* also depicts an argument between a progressive girlfriend, now an ex, and Hoài. This former girlfriend's intersectional leftist politics are established by her apartment's wall decorations: a "Yellow Peril Supports Black Power" poster, a "No Ban on Stolen Land!" protest sign, and black-and-white poster art by Diné artist Demian DinéYazhi' that declares: "This land: is not your land, was not your land, will never be your land."[90] While the first image references the cross-racial solidarity of the Vietnam War era, the latter two highlight an Indigenous critique of settler imperialism, foreshadowing the film's concluding dialogue, which interrogates refugee settler desire. This ex-girlfriend, in the interim, criticizes Hoài's father's concern about joining the protests: "You know, you'd think Vietnamese people would have more radical politics given the atrocity of the Vietnam War."[91] This comment again misrepresents the South Vietnamese experience of US allyship and refugee displacement, a past that intimately shapes multiple generations of Vietnamese Americans' relationships to the war.

Interestingly, while the arguments between the two protagonists and their respective girlfriends are never resolved on-screen, both *Nước (Water/Homeland)* and *Hoài (Ongoing, Memory)* conclude with dialogues of resolution between the protagonists and their respective parents. In both films, such resolutions are made possible by mediating dream sequences, or queer dis-orientations, that challenge the linear logics of settler colonial accumulation and interpolate the protagonists into their respective parents' experiences of war and resettlement, via what Marianne Hirsch calls "postmemory."[92] The dream sequence in *Nước (Water/Homeland)* is not a diegetic dream—the protagonist never falls asleep on screen—but rather a surrealist succession of moving images extrapolated from the signature black-and-white photographs hanging to dry in the opening scene's darkroom. Invoking the power of *nước* as an analytic, Ly Thúy Nguyễn notes, "the film's surreal style feels like a paper boat floating on water, and yet sternly anchors at the heavy questions of unspoken loss."[93] The dream sequence begins with a moving image of the protagonist's girlfriend as a Flower Power antiwar protester. This is followed by a series of quick shots of the protagonist as Major General Nguyễn Ngọc Loan shooting Nguyễn Văn Lém; as Nick Út shooting a photograph; and as a dark silhouette against a red curtain clinging precariously to an exposed umbilical cord, while the famous sex worker scene from Stanley Kubrick's *Full Metal Jacket* is projected across their body. This last image ends when the umbilical cord, symbolizing Vietnamese refugees' attachments to their lost motherland, snaps, causing the protagonist to fall backward into a black void. A quickly flashed image of the protagonist's mother working in a nail salon precedes the final shot of the protagonist as a drowning boat refugee, saved by the outstretched hand of their mother. In this dream sequence, generational positions are queered, the space of war bleeds into the space of escape by boat, and the shooting of a photograph is compared to the shooting of a gun: a warning against the violent potential for Vietnam War images to overdetermine the complex subjectivity of Vietnamese refugees.

The three diegetic dream sequences in *Hoài (Ongoing, Memory)*, in contrast, focus less on the war itself than on refugee escape and resettlement. In the first dream (which, following the film's nonlinear chronology, is actually connected to the third), Hoài is lying on the sand, their hair extending toward a tangle of seaweed, on the beach near the US-Mexico border wall that extends into the Pacific Ocean—recalling the image of the "end-stop of the Pacific" that concludes Nguyen's *Pioneer Girl*. In the second dream sequence, images of intimacy with the ex-girlfriend are followed by a photograph of Hoài's deceased mother, which is then interrupted by a close-up shot of Hoài's upper body suddenly being drenched in water, as if from a wave: a sensation that causes them to start awake, soaked in sweat. In the third dream sequence, the images of queer intimacy return, but are preceded first by the photograph of Hoài's mother, then by an image of Hoài's father hiding in a rice field in Vietnam while a US military helicopter flies across the sun. The helicopter in this last image sutures Vietnam to Turtle Island: the camera drops from the helicopter back down to the earth to capture an image of the father washed ashore on the same beach, near the US-Mexico border wall, that Hoài was lying on in the first dream, drawing parallels between Vietnamese and Central American refugees and reminding viewers that settler imperialism in Vietnam is interwoven with continental imperialism across the Américas. This final dream sequence ends with a scene of Hoài falling, out of the arms of the ex-girlfriend, through the wooden floor that provided the backdrop of the second dream's shock of water, and onto their bed—a scene that calls to mind the image, in *Nước (Water/ Homeland)*'s own dream sequence, of the Vietnamese American protagonist falling into a black void, as well as the image of Omakayas "falling from a great height, plunging through air and blackness, tumbling down with nothing to catch at" in *The Birchbark House*.[94] Falling, across these three forms of cultural production, is symbolic of displacement: by war, by lost love, by frontier expansion. Together, the three dream sequences in *Hoài (Ongoing, Memory)* beautifully layer multiple experiences of loss—Hoài's loss of love, the father's loss of a homeland, and the pair's loss of their mother/wife—as well as the multiple interconnected political issues at stake in the contemporary moment: Vietnamese refugee resettlement, Indigenous displacement, Central American refugee migration to the US-Mexico border, and Islamophobic backlashes against Muslim immigration to the United States. *Hoài (Ongoing, Memory)* ends with a single dream-like image of Hoài again on the beach, this time looking directly at the US-Mexico border wall: a survivor no longer falling, but rather standing in strength, buoyed by their father's refugee resilience and ready to fight for other displaced peoples. In the words of Lee Lien in *Pioneer Girl*: "No one knows what the last image will be."[95] Refugee survival can beget refugee struggle on behalf of future refugees.

The wordless dream sequences in *Nước (Water/Homeland)* and *Hoài (Ongoing, Memory)* facilitate the intergenerational resolutions articulated at the end of each film. In *Nước (Water/Homeland)*, the protagonist and their mother never explicitly talk about the war. However, their silence is bridged via a cross-generational sharing of sustenance. Sitting at the kitchen table together eating *cháo* (rice porridge), the mother recalls her own mother cooking *cháo* for her in Vietnam and offers to cook *cháo* for the protagonist's girlfriend, "a gesture that we can read as latent recognition and acceptance of a queer lineage."[96] In this way, the film affirms the main character's assertion that "Vietnam's a country, not a war." "Vietnam," in other words, need not be defined by iconic photographs of violence, but can instead encompass intergenerational acts of queer domesticity, that do not reproduce the heteronormative nuclear family structure. The concept of *nước*, meanwhile, is directly referenced by the rain falling outside the kitchen window: water that connects this domestic scene to the final image in the preceding dream sequence, of the mother pulling the drowning protagonist into a boat—only in this surrealist reinterpretation of Vietnamese boat refugee passage, the boat is stranded in a desert. The desert's dry land suggests a stuck-ness—an inability to move from the in-between space of refugeehood. Untethered from the homeland of Vietnam, yet still out of reach of a new home, the boat is temporarily immobile. Rain, however, promises newfound water, a rising sea, that can carry the refugee boat to new life. But new life need not be divorced from the homeland, understood as *nước*. According to Lan Duong, "Water is the liquid encasement that fuses together mother with motherland and life with feminist lineage; it is water that binds the diasporic subject to her mother/land."[97] Indeed, rain, as *nước*, connects Vietnam, the space of refugeehood, to the domestic space of the kitchen, suggesting a queer ethic of archipelagic home-making for displaced refugees.

But what if the domestic scene of resettlement takes place on Indigenous land? The final dialogue in *Hoài (Ongoing, Memory)* addresses this issue, which is foreshadowed by the Indigenous sovereignty posters hanging in Hoài's ex-girlfriend's apartment. Shot through the doorway, interspersed with close-ups of Hoài and their father's faces, this scene also takes place in a kitchen, emphasizing the significance of queer domestic spaces for facilitating intergenerational dialogue. Over steaming cups of tea, Hoài asks their father how he mitigates refugee settler desire for permanent settlement on Indigenous land. He responds in Vietnamese: "Đây đâu phải đất nước của mình. Mà không phải đất nước mình, thì mình phải chịu thôi. (This is not our homeland. If this is not our homeland, we just have to deal with it.)"[98] Initially, this seems like an explanation for why Hoài should not join the political protests: Vietnamese refugees have no place in refuting domestic US policies, and the father is worried that he might lose his child as he lost his wife. However, the father continues: "Nhưng mà tụi trắng nó cũng đâu phải dân gốc ở đây đâu. (But those white people, they're not native either.)" In this way, he notes structural differences between white settlers and natives, offering an opening for critiquing settler imperialism. Later in the dialogue, Hoài asks tentatively: "How do you make peace with living on land that doesn't belong to you?"[99] After a reflective pause, the father replies: "Mình làm người sống trong trời đất, nhưng mình không có sở hữ nó. (As humans living on earth, we only borrow the land and the sky.)"[100] Switching to English, he reiterates: "We do not own the land, or the sky. (Mình không sở hữ mặt đất, hay bả trời.)" On one hand, his words reflect a particular Vietnamese Buddhist sensibility of transitory belonging. The "we" here seems universalist, reflecting more a spiritual philosophy than a specific critique of refugee resettlement across Indigenous lands and waters. However, when juxtaposed with the father's above critique of white settlers' non-native status, these words can also be read as an Indigenous-centered critique of private property ownership, which is sustained by heteronormative forms of settler inheritance.[101] In other words, the father advocates for a queerer relationship to land/water, to *nước*, exemplifying what José Esteban Muñoz would call "disidentification" with refugee settler desire and Ly Thúy Nguyễn would term "queer dis/inheritance" of refugee trauma and the settler imperial violence that produced it.[102] Hesitantly, Hoài continues: "How do you make peace with not having a homeland?"[103] Here, Hoài invokes the sense of "deep restlessness" noted by Lee in *Pioneer Girl*: the difficulty for Vietnamese refugees and their descendants to ever feel truly at home on Turtle Island or in Vietnam. However, they also invite a specifically *refugee* answer to the question of displacement onto Indigenous lands and waters. Bypassing the question of restlessness, the father replies: "Sống trên đời đó—mình không như thế này thì mình như thế khác. Có ba đây. (Life happens—we adapt, we figure things out. I'm here.)"[104] Switching back to English, he concludes: "There will always be a place for you. (Ở đâu rồi cũng có chỗ cho con.)" Refugee settler desire for belonging, for a home to replace the lost homeland, is thus quenched not by an identification with white pioneer narratives of frontier expansion, but rather by an ethic of creating "a place" for one another: a queer familial refuge, in the face of forced displacement, that exceeds the nation-state's arbitration of asylum and citizenship. Such a queer ethic informs the film's refugee critique of the contemporary Muslim Ban and US-Mexico border wall.

But where do Turtle Island's Indigenous subjects fit in this queer refugee critique of the United States' xenophobic tightening of borders and erection of walls? Given its focus on interrogating refugee settler desire from a queer refugee perspective, *Hoài (Ongoing, Memory)* does not explicitly center Indigenous voices, though it features sovereignty posters to foreshadow the film's final dialogue. This raises the question: What would an Indigenous welcome of refugees look like? What are the political terms of such a welcome? Here I turn to Nathan Phillips, elder of the Omaha Nation, Vietnam-era veteran, and Indigenous rights activist. In a video that went viral in January 2019, Phillips stood defiantly as he was taunted by teenagers wearing "Make America Great Again" hats outside the White House. In an interview recorded by Chamorro rights activist Kaya Taitano, Phillips reports: "I heard them saying, 'Build that wall, build that wall.' This is Indigenous lands, you know. We're not supposed to have walls here. We never did. Before anyone else came here, we never had walls."[105] In this statement, Phillips articulates an Indigenous embrace of refugees. Native sovereignty encompasses the sovereign right to welcome displaced peoples, on Native terms. Refusing the genocidal logics of "Indian Country" and the American frontier, Phillips instead articulates a geography of multiplicitous belonging—one that critiques settler state borders designed to exclude and instead advocates mutual care between Indigenous peoples and refugees, two populations displaced by settler imperialism. Whereas Phillips speaks on behalf of Turtle Island, later chapters in this book elaborate the contours of Indigenous hospitality in Guam and Israel-Palestine.

Like *Nước (Water/Homeland)* and *Hoài (Ongoing, Memory)*, the cultural productions examined throughout this book are spectral and speculative: they gesture toward what is emergent and difficult to articulate, given the refugee settler condition. As noted above, there is not yet a sustained movement connecting Vietnamese American refugees and Native American sovereignty struggles. But *Hoài (Ongoing, Memory)* can spark important dialogue within the Vietnamese American community. Indeed, filmmaker Quyên Nguyen-Le wrote the final scene in *Hoài (Ongoing, Memory)* in hopes of one day being able to have a similar conversation with their own parents.[106] The film thus invites political action: the long-overdue project of building refugee-Indigenous solidarity across Turtle Island.

TURTLE ISLAND, GUAM, PALESTINE:
CHARTING AN ARCHIPELAGO OF
TRANS-INDIGENOUS RESISTANCE

This chapter has mapped the settler imperial dimensions of the US War in Vietnam, situating Vietnamese refugee resettlement across Turtle Island within a longer genealogy of frontier expansion. Together with chapter 1, it provides crucial context for understanding *why* Vietnamese refugees resettled in Guam and Israel-Palestine—the focus of the remaining chapters—as well as the settler imperial implications of refugee resettlement on Indigenous lands and waters. In short, these two opening chapters have mapped an archipelago of US settler imperialism, which in turn shaped the post-1975 archipelago of Vietnamese refugee resettlement.

But what about a corresponding archipelago of trans-Indigenous resistance, as discussed at the end of chapter 1? To return to the two poems that opened this chapter: the seventh and final stanza of Craig Santos Perez's "Interwoven" invites Indigenous subjects across Turtle Island *and* Oceania to "share our stories of hurt, / our stories of healing," "interweaving our struggles" for "seven generations" to come. Projecting an archipelago of decolonial futurity, the poem concludes: "I hope the stories we share today / and in the future will carry us / towards sovereign horizons."[107] Likewise, in stanza five of her untitled poem marking resonances between First Nation and Palestinian women, Erica Violet Lee emphasizes the importance of "telling / retelling / telling again / the stories they tried to take from us / and trying to remember the ones they did" as a mode of survivance.[108]

The following chapters unfurl as a series of stories: stories found in the archive, shared as oral histories, or fashioned into memoirs, blogs, poetry, and film. Such stories grapple with the refugee settler condition across Guam and Israel-Palestine. Part two details Vietnamese refugee migration to Guam and Israel-Palestine in the late 1970s, drawing from oral histories as well as archival research conducted at the Richard F. Taitano Micronesian Area Research Center, the Nieves M. Flores Memorial Library, and the Israel State Archives. Part three turns to cultural production to examine how this history of Vietnamese refugee resettlement has been re-storied, remembered, and retold. Solidarity between Indigenous peoples and Vietnamese refugees at these sites is still emergent; stories are therefore critical for imagining more ethical forms of refugee resettlement across Indigenous lands and waters.

Indeed, stories embody what Lisa Lowe has termed the "past conditional temporality" of "what could have been": a "space of reckoning that allows us to revisit times of historical contingency and possibility to consider alternatives that may have been *unthought* in those times, and might otherwise remain so now, in order to imagine different futures for what lies ahead."[109] Laura Ingalls Wilder's *Little House on the Prairie* is a white settler narrative of frontier expansion, of restless settler imperial domination across Osage lands. And yet the book's closing lines offer an unintentional opening for imagining otherwise. For *Little House on the Prairie* ends with a song about water, about *nước*, inadvertently calling to mind the voyage of Vietnamese boat refugees:

> Row away, row o'er the waters so blue,
> Like a feather we sail in our gum-tree canoe,
> Row the boat lightly, love, over the sea;
> Daily and nightly I'll wander with thee.[110]

Vietnamese American refugees often articulate refugee settler desire for national inclusion via interpolation in narratives of white pioneer settlement. But, conversely, read archipelagically, Vietnamese refugeehood may instead *unsettle* settlement, calling forth a politics of *nước*: of fluid attachments and liquid borders that drown out private property inheritances in favor of queerer and more relational forms of belonging. *Nước* may bring together currents of Indigenous resistance to challenge the settler imperial violence of the frontier.

# PART TWO

# Tracing Migrations

*Archipelagos of Settler Colonialism, US Empire,
and Refugee Refusal*

# 3

# Operation New Life

## *Vietnamese Refugees and US Settler Militarism in Guam*

On 5 April 1975, with the Fall of Saigon imminent, Chamorro governor Ricardo J. Bordallo sent a telex to President Gerald R. Ford, asserting Guam's willingness to participate in the "highly commendable humanitarian act" of Operation Babylift and "assist you in the nation's effort to provide relief for the refugees and orphan children from South Vietnam."[1] Two weeks later, Guam was transformed from a US military outpost for combating communism during the US War in Vietnam, to the first major US processing center for South Vietnamese refugees displaced by that war.[2] Although covering just 210 square miles and containing a 1975 population of roughly 93,000, from 23 April to 1 November 1975 Guam played a central role in US evacuation efforts, processing more than 112,000 refugees accepted for parole during what became known as Operation New Life: a name that starkly juxtaposes the co-constitutive forces of militarism and humanitarianism, or what historian Jana K. Lipman calls "military humanitarianism," at play.[3] While the term "Operation" recalled the very recent history of US military aggression in Vietnam—such as Operation Rolling Thunder and Operation Arc Light—"New Life" promised the rebirth of South Vietnamese refugees newly escaped from communist-unified Vietnam. Such a juxtaposition of terms also indexes the fact that the United States' humanitarian mission of refugee resettlement was underwritten—indeed, made possible—by US military occupation of Indigenous Chamorro land: a particular confluence of militarism and settler colonialism in Guam that is best described using Juliet Nebolon's term "settler militarism."[4]

Drawing from archival research conducted at the Richard F. Taitano Micronesian Area Research Center (MARC) at the University of Guam and the Nieves M. Flores Memorial Library in Hagåtña, as well as oral histories conducted between 2016 and 2021, this chapter details the development of the refugee settler condition in Guam. It argues that the humanitarian rhetoric that newspapers and politicians used to describe Operation New Life in 1975 retroactively justified settler militarism in Guam and, by extension, positioned Vietnamese refugees in a structurally antagonistic relationship to Chamorro decolonization struggles that opposed military settlement. Putting Neda Atanasoski's concept of "humanitarian violence" in conversation with Indigenous critiques of settler colonialism, I trace how Vietnamese refugees' narratives were appropriated to humanize the US military as a settler institution, irrespective of the refugees' intent.[5] Structural antagonisms are never totalizing, however. Attending to quotidian cross-racial encounters, this chapter highlights moments of contingency, echoing Catherine Lutz's assertion that empire and its discontents are "in the details"; in other words, identifying the "many fissures, contradictions, historical particularities, and shifts in imperial processes" can "make the human and material face and frailties of imperialism more visible" and, in so doing, "make challenges to it more likely."[6]

This chapter begins by historicizing settler militarism in Guam. It then outlines the structural antagonisms that were formed between Indigenous Chamorros and Vietnamese refugees—two populations differentially racialized by settler militarism—during Operation New Life. Vietnamese refugees were positioned as wards (albeit agential ones) of the very institution—the US military—that had dispossessed Chamorros of their land. However, as Bordallo's opening quote evidences, many Chamorros also empathized with the refugees' plight and welcomed them to Guam, suggesting alternative forms of relationality routed through Chamorro epistemologies of *inafa'maolek*. An expansive term, *inafa'maolek* means "to make good to each other" and "to promote goodwill, friendship, and cooperation," particularly after a conflict.[7] Whereas "conflict" traditionally refers to a dispute between two Chamorro families, it can also be understood in this context as the Vietnam War.[8] *Inafa'maolek* connotes generosity and hospitality, as well as reciprocity, interdependence, and mutual assistance. This chapter ends with moments of cross-racial encounter and refugee refusal, in which Chamorro subjects undermined the US military's efforts to divide them from the Vietnamese refugees, and Vietnamese refugees subverted American expectations to express unqualified gratitude for their rescue. Such quotidian acts of resistance challenge the seeming permanence of settler militarism and the refugee settler condition in Guam, suggesting decolonial traces of cross-racial solidarity.

## SETTLER MILITARISM: THE US MILITARY'S ROLE
## IN LAND EXPROPRIATION IN GUAM

Before analyzing the role that Vietnamese refugees played in justifying settler militarism in Guam during Operation New Life, it is important to first establish a longer genealogy of settler militarism on the island. Settler militarism, which I understand as a subset of settler colonialism, is distinguished by the US military's prominent role in dispossessing native Chamorros of their land. Land, according to Chamorro rights attorney Michael F. Phillips, is "literally the base" of Chamorro culture; it "incorporates special relationships: of clan, family, religion, and beliefs."[9] In the words of Governor Bordallo:

> Guam is not just a piece of real estate to be exploited for its money-making potential. Above all else, Guam is the homeland of the Chamorro people. This is a fundamental, undeniable truth. We are very profoundly 'taotao tano'—people of the land. This land, tiny as it is, belongs to us just as surely, just as inseparably, as we belong to it. No tragedy of history or declaration of conquest, no legalistic double-talk can change that fact. Guam is our legacy.[10]

Since Chamorro identity is intimately tied to the land, land dispossession produces a "genocidal effect."[11] Chamorro decolonization, conversely, is organized around the reclamation of land.

For the past two centuries, the US military in particular—rather than the US government writ large or individual settler citizens—has been the primary institution responsible for expropriating Chamorro lands and waters. Following the Spanish-American War and the 1898 Treaty of Paris, the US Navy colonized Guam. In 1899, Guam's first naval governor, Captain Richard P. Leary, issued General Order No. 15, mandating that Chamorro landowners register their lands with the US Navy. Such orders interpolated native Chamorros into a US system of private property relations that cleaved powerful extended family clans into separate nuclear family units.[12] General Order No. 15 resulted in mass land dispossession because it forced Chamorros to make an impossible choice: "either register their properties accurately and lose them because they could not pay the taxes, or not register their lands and lose them because they were not properly registered."[13] Naval governors wielded executive, legislative, and judicial authority, so resistant Chamorro landowners, as colonial subjects, had little legal recourse.

Nonetheless, some wealthy landowners were able to pay the required taxes and retain their lands, which they subsequently shared with other families in a demonstration of *inafa'maolek*.[14] Chamorros were thus largely able to uphold their traditional subsistence economy, organized around *låncho*, until Japanese occupation during World War II.[15] During World War II, American forces heavily bombed the island in order to force the occupying Japanese Army to surrender, destroying Guam's main population centers, Hagåtña and Sumay, as well as many other villages along Guam's western coast. About 80 percent of the island's homes and buildings were demolished.[16] Relocated from "the Japanese concentration camps into U.S. refugee camps," Chamorros lost their farmlands, coconut groves, and herds of cattle, the foundation of their economic and cultural livelihood, becoming internally displaced refugees—albeit Indigenous ones—on their own island.[17] After the "liberation" of Guam—alternatively remembered as the "reoccupation" of the island—the US Navy refused to rebuild the decimated villages and condemned more than 85,000 acres: two-thirds of Guam's surface area.[18] Although the US Navy promised to pay rent for the condemned lands and eventually return them to their original caretakers, the calculated rent was steeply below market value and almost none of the land was returned.[19] In 1946, Colonel Louis Hugh Wilson Jr., commander of the US Marine Corps, admitted the sometimes unlawful nature of land appropriation: "This is American territory and when we landed, the people were scattered and we took what we needed, occupied it, built up the roads, and so forth, *irrespective of the ownership*."[20] Judith Won Pat, Democratic speaker of the Guam legislature from March 2008 to January 2017, for example, remembers that her parents and relatives were permanently displaced from their ancestral villages in Sumay, where the 5th Naval Construction Brigade built Naval Base Guam.[21]

After World War II, Guam was transformed into a military fortress that served as a "launching point for strategic bombers carrying nuclear weapons," a "base for Polaris submarines," a "naval station with ship repair and tending capabilities," a "communications base allowing for world-wide military communications," and a "listening post for the tracking of Soviet submarines."[22] Within a year of US reoccupation, over twenty-one military bases were constructed in Guam.[23] Subsistence agriculture was replaced with race-based wage labor hierarchies that discriminated against Chamorro workers, reflecting the commander of US Naval Forces Marianas's judgment that the "economic development of relatively few native inhabitants should be subordinate to the real purpose for which these islands are held": "military value" and the "welfare of the United States."[24]

Even after the Organic Act of 1950 officially ended naval rule, the US military still wielded control over choice beaches and lands. In fact, a day before the Organic Act went into effect, Guam's first civilian governor, Carlton Skinner, signed a quitclaim deed transferring control of the condemned properties from Guam's government to the United States.[25] Three months later, on 31 October 1950, President Harry S. Truman issued Executive Order 10178, returning all property in the quitclaim deed to the navy, which divided the stolen land among the military branches without consulting the original Chamorro landowners. As a result, the US Navy and Air Force controlled roughly 49,600 acres, or over 36 percent of the island—a decrease from the initial 85,000 acres but still a substantial percentage.[26] In a statement dated 1951, a naval officer voiced the genocidal terra nullius fantasies of the occupying power: "Guam's value to the United States was entirely strategic, a communications point on the way to the Philippines and east Asia. From this point of view, it would probably have been *desirable if there had been no native population* to complicate matters."[27]

Today, the US military continues to control 39,287 acres in Guam, over onethird of the island's surface area. Moreover, no status of force agreement (SOFA) regulates US forces in Guam. It is this longer genealogy of settler militarism in Guam that provides crucial context for Operation New Life. The same military institution that has expropriated Chamorro land since 1898 facilitated the humanitarian transfer of Vietnamese refugees to Guam, implicating Vietnamese refugees in ongoing structures of settler militarism.

## GUAM: AN UNINCORPORATED PACIFIC PROCESSING
## CENTER FOR VIETNAMESE REFUGEES

To understand Guam's significance as the first major US processing center for Vietnamese refugees, it is illuminating to look at other counterfactual sites, such as Clark Air Force Base in the Philippines or a US military base in the continental United States. During spring 1975, a tent city adjacent to the Bamboo Bowl sports stadium at Clark Air Force Base had temporarily housed more than 30,000 refugees. Clark Air Force Base was thus initially the intended processing center for Vietnamese evacuees. However, on 23 April 1975, President Ferdinand Marcos announced that the Philippines would no longer accept political refugees.[28] Given the impending communist victory in Vietnam, Marcos worried that harboring South Vietnamese government and military officials would jeopardize the Philippines' diplomatic relations with the newly unified state of Vietnam.[29] That very same day, the United States pivoted plans to host its main refugee processing center in the Philippines to Guam, though State Department spokesman Robert Anderson "denied that the switch had anything to do with objections from the Philippine government."[30] According to First Lady Madeleine Bordallo, "Operation New Life began at 3:00am in the morning when Secretary Kissinger called the governor of Guam, my husband Ricky. We were both asleep and I heard the phone ring, and the security said it was a very important call."[31] In response to Kissinger's request that Guam host the Vietnamese evacuees, Governor Bordallo reportedly said, "Mr. Secretary, Guam was liberated by the US forces, particularly the Marines. Now, it's our time to give back to the US because of their generosity in liberating us from the occupation."[32] As a survivor of Japanese occupation during World War II, Governor Bordallo empathized with the Vietnamese refugees because he "knew firsthand about the misery of war."[33] He also believed that helping the Vietnamese refugees would honor the memory of the Chamorro soldiers who had sacrificed their lives in Vietnam. In a display of *inafa'maolek*, Bordallo therefore responded, "We got to open Guam up, and we got to show our hospitality, and try and take care of these people."[34]

Governor Bordallo's hospitality contrasted sharply with the general sentiment in the continental United States. Because of high rates of unemployment and the controversial status of the Vietnam War, many Americans strongly protested the resettlement of Vietnamese refugees, whom they deemed unassimilable aliens or potential communist infiltrators.[35] According to a May 1975 Gallup poll, 54 percent of all Americans were opposed to admitting Vietnamese refugees, with only 36 percent in favor.[36] A couple of weeks after the commencement of Operation New Life, four refugee reception centers were established on the continent for refugees who had already been vetted in Guam: Fort Chaffee Army Base in Arkansas, Camp Pendleton Marine Corps Base in California, Eglin Air Force Base in Florida, and later Fort Indiantown Gap in Pennsylvania. However, even these "militarized refuges" received virulent pushback: a placard in Arkansas read "Gooks, go home," and Representative Burt L. Talcott (R-CA) voiced the feeling in his district that "Damn it, we have too many Orientals."[37] Similarly, a journalist reporting from Fort Indiantown Gap observed that "Asians are about as welcome in some of the small towns surrounding the nation's newest refugee center as blacks might be at Ku Klux Klan gatherings."[38]

Operation New Life commenced in Guam when a planeload of Vietnamese refugees landed at Andersen Air Force Base at 4:01 p.m. on 23 April 1975.[39] By midnight, fifteen flights from Tân Sơn Nhứt Air Base near Sài Gòn had landed, bringing 2,487 Vietnamese refugees to Andersen Air Force Base and Naval Air Station Agana. Pacific Command representatives initially calculated that a "maximum of 13,000 people could be sheltered for a short period in Guam," but on 15 May 1975 the number of refugees in Guam awaiting transfer peaked at 50,430, representing an over 50 percent increase in the island's population at the time.[40] Roughly 15,000 Vietnamese refugees arrived by ship on 7 May alone, followed by another 15,000 on 12 May.[41] On 13 May the hundred thousandth refugee landed in Guam: an eleven-year-old girl named Phan Truc Chi "had a lei put around her neck," was photographed for the local newspaper, and then was rushed back "into the stream of refugees being processed."[42]

President Ford assigned Admiral George Steve Morrison, the commander-in-chief Pacific representative of Guam and the Trust Territory of the Pacific Islands and commander of US Naval Forces Marianas, to direct Operation New Life.[43] Under Morrison's command, the US military set up three main camps to host the refugees: "Tent City" at Orote Point (an overgrown World War II airstrip, which at its peak housed 39,331 refugees), Camp Asan at Asan Beach (former hospital barracks used during the Vietnam War and the site of Filipino insurrectionists' incarceration during the Philippine-American War), and "Tin City" at Andersen Air Force Base (a group of corrugated metal buildings).[44] Six smaller camps were established at the naval air station, the naval communications station in Barrigada, the Bachelors' Civilian Quarters in Apra Heights, the naval station gym, the Seabee Masdelco Sports Arena, and Camp Minron near Polaris Point. Private companies, including J & G Enterprises, Black Construction Co., Hawaiian Dredging Co., and the (recently closed) Tokyu Hotel also housed hundreds of refugees during the operation's height.[45] During the peak months of May and June, when more space was needed, more than 15,000 refugees were diverted to Wake Island, another unincorporated US territory in the Pacific.[46]

Although many Guamanians embraced the opportunity to contribute to Operation New Life—offering to adopt and sponsor refugees, as well as volunteer as babysitters and cooks—others expressed concerns about overcrowding.[47] Several of Guam's legislators noted potential food and housing shortages, public health risks, the probable inadequacy of federal funds to reimburse local transport and labor costs, and uncertainty as to whether tens of thousands of Vietnamese refugees would choose to stay in Guam, indefinitely straining the island's limited resources during an economic recession.[48] Although some of these complaints can be attributed to party politics—Republican senators criticizing the decisions of Democratic Governor Bordallo—they nonetheless leveled a distinct critique of settler militarism in Guam. Republican senator Ricky Salas, for example, said, "I felt it was always their plan to leave people on Guam. . . . Kissinger and the representatives from [the Department of D]efense will deceive the people of Guam again. That is the reason the U.S. cannot be believed all over the world. We can't believe the leaders of our nation."[49] He further accused the State Department of being "willing to sacrifice us on Guam to protect those citizens on the Mainland who don't want permanent resident aliens."[50] Highlighting the unequal weight of Guamanians' voices in US democracy, Republican senator Jerry Rivera observed: "Federal officials may be thinking that it is easier to handle the protests of Guam rather than the protests of the 50 states."[51] In these critiques, Vietnamese refugees figured as metonyms of federal overreach and exploitation: rather than merely reproduce the racist anti-refugee sentiments expressed on the continent, Guam's representatives invoked the Vietnamese refugee figure to condemn US settler militarism in Guam. Because Guam's residents were neither fully incorporated into the United States nor independently sovereign, however, they ultimately had little say in the matter, subject as they were to the federal government's plenary powers. Indeed, Guam's colonial status was a "precondition" for its role as the first major US processing center for Vietnamese refugees displaced by the US War in Vietnam.[52]

## OPERATION NEW LIFE: HUMANITARIANISM AS A JUSTIFICATION FOR SETTLER MILITARISM

According to media reports, Operation New Life prompted a marked shift in the US military's role in Guam from wartime aggression to humanitarian care. Newspapers praised the "tremendous compassion" of US military personnel who worked long shifts—sometimes up to twenty-four hours—to shelter and feed the Vietnamese refugees.[53] In an article chronicling the efforts of the US Construction Battalion (more commonly referred to as CBs or "Seabees") to hastily clear 500 acres of tangan-tangan trees and set up 3,200 tents, 191 wooden toilets, and 300 showers at Orote Point to house up to 50,000 incoming refugees, reporter Lyle Nelson notes the "Phoenix quality" of the operation, characterizing it as a "rebirth for [the Seabees'] efforts for the Vietnamese people and a symbolic windup to 13 years of sweat (and some blood)."[54] Likewise, Pacific Daily News (PDN) reporter Paul Miller wrote that "one of the many things in which Americans can take pride these days is the performance of our military in flying endangered thousands out of Vietnam and caring for them in hastily built staging areas such as the U.S. territory of Guam."[55] Staff Sergeant Clarence Randall, Company C, 1st Battalion, 5th Infantry Regiment, testified, "This is one of the few times in the Army that I've had a chance to be on a peace mission. Most of the time when the Army is called on, it's to destroy something. But here we have the opportunity to do something to help somebody. I am proud to be here."[56]

Building on the work of Jana K. Lipman, Ayako Saraha, Heather Marie Stur, and Yến Lê Espiritu, I argue that the media's characterization of Operation New Life as a Phoenix-like "rebirth" facilitated the discursive transformation of the United States "from a violent aggressor in Vietnam to a benevolent rescuer of its people," as well as the "material and ideological conversion of U.S. military bases into places of *refuge*—places that were meant to *resolve* the refugee crisis, promising peace and protection."[57] Such humanitarian rhetoric, however, entailed not the end of settler imperialism but rather what Simeon Man would call its "recalibration."[58] In other words, the rescue of Vietnamese refugees during Operation New Life was *co-constitutive* with the ongoing displacement of Indigenous Chamorro people; the "conversion" of US military bases in Guam into "places of refuge" for Vietnamese refugees did not preclude the settler imperialist role these bases continued to play in securing US interests across Asia and Oceania.

By centering US military actions, such humanitarian narratives also flattened the chaotic and often complex experiences of Operation New Life's Vietnamese refugees. Many Vietnamese subjects did not think they would become permanent refugees when they fled Vietnam. In "Of Luggage and Shoes," Thuy Dinh, who left Vietnam on 21 April 1975, writes, "While preparing for the trip, I never thought of the possibility that I may leave my birthplace forever, or at least for a very long time before I could return."[59] Lien Samiana has a similar story. In April 1975, Samiana had been living with her husband, Feliciano C. Samiana—a Filipino American employed by Pacific Architects and Engineers, Inc., and stationed with the US Army—and their five young children in Sài Gòn, when Feliciano received orders to leave Vietnam.[60] Hurriedly, they packed one suitcase with some clothes, important documents, and $1000, and rushed to Tân Sơn Nhứt Air Base, where they were loaded onto C-141 cargo planes. After a harrowing flight during which Samiana suffered motion sickness and witnessed a woman give birth, the family landed in Guam and were brought to Camp Asan.[61] There, the family slept on hard cement and endured long food lines. Samiana initially believed the indignities would be temporary; when she left Sài Gòn on 24 April in anticipation of the communist advance, she thought she would return to Vietnam. But as 30 April passed and she heard the sounds of Sài Gòn falling on the radio, she sobbed and resigned herself to her new life. Samiana's story attests to the contingent decisions Vietnamese evacuees were forced to make, qualifying the military's unilateral narrative of humanitarian rescue.

Overall, these narratives of humanitarian rescue provided moral justification for a US military outpost in Guam: without it, the settler militarist logic went, the anticommunist refugees would have perished at the hands of communist aggressors. Indeed, the temporal effects of these humanitarian narratives extend both backward and forward, retroactively vindicating the post–World War II construction of US military bases in Guam to combat communism during the Vietnam War, and proactively validating future military projects to further secure US-style democracy and racial capitalism across Asia and Oceania. Such settler militarist logic elides, however, the role that the US military played in displacing Vietnamese refugees from their homes in the first place, via aerial bombing campaigns, counterinsurgency plots, Agent Orange poisoning, and escalated tensions with North Vietnam.[62] It also interpolates the displaced Vietnamese as refugee settlers, structurally at odds with Chamorro efforts to liberate Guam from military rule.[63]

## CROSS-RACIAL ENCOUNTERS: CHAMORRO PARTICIPATION IN OPERATION NEW LIFE

According to Lanny Thompson, "Colonial discourses distinguish multiple 'others' with the intent to rule them differently."[64] However, as Patrick Wolfe reminds us, "the incompleteness of racial domination is the trace and the achievement of resistance, a space of hope."[65] The structural antagonisms that pitted Vietnamese refugees hosted by the US military against Chamorro self-determination efforts to challenge that same military's settler control were constantly being negotiated via quotidian cross-racial encounters. In truth, it is too simplistic to declare Operation New Life a unilateral settler militarist imposition. Many Guamanians, including native Chamorros, genuinely sympathized with the plight of the Vietnamese refugees and assisted the asylum efforts by volunteering in the refugee camps or donating toys and clothing to the new arrivals.[66]

Indeed, as the telex that opens this chapter reveals, Governor Bordallo actually *volunteered* Guam as a staging ground for refugee processing, weeks before President Ford demanded Guam's assistance. To note that Bordallo invited Operation New Life, which rhetorically worked to justify settler militarism in Guam, is *not* to suggest that Bordallo was a mere puppet of settler militarist control. On the contrary, in 1974 Bordallo ran his grassroots, patronage-based gubernatorial campaign for the Democratic ticket on a popular platform of Chamorro rights, articulated in both English and Chamorro.[67] Although his inaugural address seemingly embraced the US military—"You are a vital part of Guam. We welcome your valuable contributions to the growth of our island. You have our cooperation in all endeavors which are of mutual interest to our country and this territory"—Bordallo also emphasized that protecting Chamorro sovereignty over Guam's natural resources and affairs was a top priory of his administration.[68] *Los Angeles Times* reporter David Lamb described Bordallo's attitude toward the military as "cool but accommodating."[69] Bordallo's commitments to both Chamorro rights and Operation New Life are not contradictory; rather, they are an assertion of Chamorro self-determination. Chamorros fought—and continue to fight—for the right to

FIGURE 5. Guam school bus used in Operation New Life, 1975. From the collection of the Richard F. Taitano Micronesian Area Research Center.

determine when, how, and to whom they opened their island home. An embrace of displaced Vietnamese refugees need not entail an embrace of the military institution that hosted them.

During Operation New Life, barbed-wire fences and strict security protocols prevented substantial interactions between Vietnamese refugees and the island's residents. However, some Chamorros still found opportunities to interact with the Vietnamese refugees. Chamorro public school bus drivers transported refugees and supplies between the different camps; public health nurses gave refugees vaccines, checked for illnesses, and attended to pregnant Vietnamese women; Red Cross volunteers helped to locate and connect refugees; and others provided or prepared meals.[70] Norman Sweet, senior coordinator with the Agency for International Development (AID) refugee task force, observed that the "hospitable" people of Guam "show genuine interest in the welfare" of the refugees.[71] Even President Ford commended Guamanians' "warm and outgoing response" and upheld the island's residents as an "outstanding example to other Americans and the rest of the world in meeting an international emergency."[72]

Many Chamorros played key roles during Operation New Life. In April 1975, Raymond T. Baza (introduced in chapter 1) was invited by Admiral Morrison to help organize volunteers and translators to assist the Vietnamese refugees.[73] Baza tapped into his network of about ten Chamorro veterans who had married Vietnamese women. When the first plane of refugees landed at Andersen Air Force Base, Baza and the volunteers logged names, directed refugees to the food and clothing stations, and made sure they got on the right bus headed for Camp Asan, Orote Point, or Tumon Heights. His wife, Lee T. Baza, translated for the Vietnamese refugees, helped exchange money, assuaged fears about displacement, and explained the resettlement process.[74] During the height of Operation New Life, she worked twenty-four-hour days, attending to the people who arrived on planes at all hours.

Over the course of their interactions, the Baza couple developed close relationships with the Vietnamese refugees. When a refugee died, Raymond felt the loss personally and would accompany the family to Guam's naval cemetery for burial. He also loved engaging with the children: "That thing when a small child comes to you and says thank you, it really touches me because they needed help and we helped them."[75] During Operation New Life, the Bazas sponsored six Vietnamese refugee children and serve as godparents for several others. Their actions were not uncommon: "When we asked local people if they can sponsor, help us out, they were welcoming the children. Some of them adopted children. They offered shelter, families in their home."[76] Overall, Chamorros "really opened their arms and welcomed" the refugees during Operation New Life.[77]

Joaquin "Kin" Perez, meanwhile, was the youngest member of Governor Bordallo's cabinet and the commercial port director during Operation New Life. He remembers large US container vessels that had carried military cargo from Guam to Vietnam during the war being repurposed after the Fall of Saigon to transport 10,000–15,000 refugees at a time to Guam.[78] Other ships, which had transferred food supplies up and down the Mekong Delta, were Vietnamese owned. Most ships had no sanitary facilities, and refugees were given no food during the seventeen-day voyage from Vietnam to Guam. When the refugees reached the port, Perez ferried them by barge to the naval station, set up public health facilities to check for infectious diseases, and arranged for the refugees' transport to Orote Point. Afterward, the government commissioned Perez's team to clean the vessels that were still seaworthy: "We had to go in there with steam cleaners, and my people had to wear protective clothing because it was really bad."[79] Perez also arranged for the disposal of the unseaworthy ships in the Marianas Trench, the deepest natural trench in the world.

According to Perez, one time a Vietnamese captain refused to surrender her ship, which had been entrusted to her by her parents. "She tied herself to the mast and when the security tried to take her off, she opened up her dress, her jacket, and she had hand grenades tied around her!"[80] Fortunately, Perez was able to bring in translators who de-escalated the situation and explained to the captain that the vessel was no longer seaworthy and that the US government would compensate her for the ship's cost. Another Vietnamese captain refused naval orders to wait while the harbor was being cleared. Once he caught sight of Guam, he rushed through the harbor, with "all of these tugboats and these security vessels running after him," because he "just wanted to make sure that he got his people and the people that were on that ship to safety."[81]

One high-profile incident started with a rumor that one of the refugee ships, the 3,300-ton *Tan Nam Viet*, owned and mastered by Huynh Phy Qui, contained national treasures from Vietnam. On 23 May 1975, a refugee told port officials that the ship's fifty-four packing crates contained the South Vietnamese national archives and national art treasures worth as much as $150 million.[82] In response, the governor's office and the US military frantically debated over who had jurisdiction over the ship and its crates. Finally, they mobilized GovGuam customs officials and M16-toting Special Enforcement Detail policemen in an operation that began at 6:00 a.m. on 24 May 1975 and lasted for sixteen hours. As the commercial port director, Perez supervised the operation: "You would not believe the security that came down on that one. The State Department, they all gathered down at the port and told us to bring the ship up to the dock."[83] As it turned out, however, the rumor was false. Although the ship's cargo was worth between $70,000 and $80,000, it consisted not of national treasures but merely the household goods of a wealthy South Vietnamese civilian who had commissioned Huynh Phy Qui to transfer his belongings out of Vietnam.

According to Perez, Operation New Life did not hurt Guam's economy, as some senators had feared, and "actually helped a little bit" because the US government brought a lot of food, medicine, and housing supplies to Guam and purchased others from local vendors.[84] The Naval Regional Medical Center, for example, spent $35,857.27 in support of refugee medical aid.[85] Moreover, the Department of Defense reimbursed the government of Guam for expenditures related to Operation New Life.[86] Overall Perez described Operation New Life as "a good experience for Guam" and "a good experience for a lot of us that were personally involved in it." It was "a period in Guam history that showed us how man can be compassionate with other human beings."[87]

Monsignor David I. A. Quitugua, who grew up in Talofofo, lived through the Japanese occupation of Guam during World War II, and, on 11 February 1964, became the fifteenth Chamorro to be ordained, also played a key role during Operation New Life. In April 1975, Quitugua received orders from the archbishop and the United States Catholic Conference in Washington, DC, to set up a refugee resettlement office in Guam.[88] During Operation New Life, he managed social workers, processed refugee documents, and coordinated with military officials.[89] Vietnamese refugees who wished to stay in Guam were referred to Quitugua, who tapped into his church network to find sponsorship and employment for the refugees so they could be released from the camps. Often Quitugua would sponsor the refugees himself: "Sponsoring a family of refugees, I mean, it's a risk, because you are responsible for them, you know. But it's fine with me, as long as these people are out of the camp and can resettle in the place, then it's fine with me."[90] He remembered Operation New Life as "a great story" that he was "very happy to be a part of," and the Vietnamese refugees as "just so easy, they don't want trouble, all they want is peace, to have work, something to support their family, and that's it." In his view, Operation New Life brought "life to the people"—not only Vietnamese refugees but also Chamorros who participated in the process—and "culture to the island": a cross-racial encounter facilitated by settler militarism in Guam.[91]

Judith Won Pat, meanwhile, served as a teacher during Operation New Life. For a couple hours per day, she taught Vietnamese refugee children basic English through games and songs. Decades later, as a senator, she interacted further with the Vietnamese American community in Guam, whose members told her "how hard it was for them to just take whatever they could only physically carry, which is not a lot, you know, what they consider their valuables, and to start all over, and they just don't know how they are going to make it."[92] These stories of Vietnamese displacement reminded Won Pat of other forced displacements compelled by the US military, such as the dispossession of Chamorros from their villages after World War II to make room for US military base construction, and the removal of islanders from Diego Garcia in the Indian Ocean between 1968 and 1973 to make way for a joint US-UK military base. These archipelagic connections inform Won Pat's political critique of settler militarism in Guam today.

Rather than dismiss these Chamorro contributions to Operation New Life as examples of false consciousness—a settler militarist appropriation of Chamorro humanitarian labor made to further consolidate the US military's hold over

Guam—I take seriously these Indigenous acts of hospitality, or *inafa'maolek*, which undermine the structural antagonisms between refugees and natives that formed as part of the refugee settler condition in Guam. Even though Chamorro decolonization activists remain critical of colonial settlers, including refugee settlers, many Chamorros also recognized the plight of Vietnamese refugees in need of temporary asylum. Older Chamorros like Governor Bordallo drew comparisons between the experiences of the Vietnamese refugees and their own World War II experiences under Japanese occupation, associating the communist regime in Vietnam with the imperial Japanese occupiers. In a slightly different vein, Jesus Quitugua Charfauros, a retired Chamorro naval radioman chief who lived in Guam during Operation New Life, compared the US military to the Japanese occupiers, thereby critiquing the military's role in incarcerating the refugees in camps.[93]

Importantly, Chamorros' desire to aid Vietnamese refugees did not entail their acquiescence to the US military's continual destruction of and encroachment upon their native lands and waters. Although many Chamorros genuinely welcomed the opportunity to participate in Operation New Life, they did *not* sanction the presence of Agent Orange on Guam's military bases during the Vietnam War or the spraying of the pesticide malathion to kill mosquitoes in order to reduce the number of malaria and dengue fever outbreaks during the operation— toxins that seeped into the environment and likely tainted civilian water sources.[94] Won Pat recalls that when the military planes that dropped Agent Orange on Vietnam were hosed down at Andersen Air Force Base, the contaminated water ran off the tarmac and trickled down into civilian water wells located on the north side of the island, poisoning Chamorro residents living near the base.[95] Even in its destruction, Agent Orange posed a threat to Chamorros and other Micronesians. In 1977 the US Air Force incinerated the remaining herbicide left over from the Vietnam War off the coast of Johnston Island, contaminating the Pacific Ocean.[96] In his critique of Operation Pacer HO, Tony Hodges, Environmental Protection Board member of the Trust Territories, suggested that "the disposal be carried out in the courtyard of the inner ring of the Pentagon" because the "people who manufacture this material and use it should take the risk, not the people of Micronesia."[97] Micronesians had already borne the brunt of centuries of settler militarism; it was cruel to subject them yet again to the chemical afterlives of the US War in Vietnam.

In sum, Chamorro resistance to settler militarism in Guam did not manifest as a rejection of Vietnamese refugees during Operation New Life. It is true that Chamorros' acts of hospitality toward the Vietnamese refugees risked symbolic appropriation by settler militarist rhetoric, which conflated this hospitality with Chamorros' acquiescence to toxic contamination and land dispossession. Challenging this conflation, however, presents one way to undermine the structural antagonisms enacted by the refugee settler condition in Guam. Only then can we fully appreciate Chamorros' acts of critical empathy, grounded in the value of *inafa'maolek*, as expressions of sovereignty: a refusal to comply with settler militarist attempts to divide Indigenous subjects from refugees. *Inafa'maolek*, however, involves not one-sided hospitality but rather reciprocity, necessitating a response from Vietnamese refugees "to make good." The following section examines how Vietnamese refugees also subverted settler militarist attempts to fix them in the position of the "grateful refugee," thus challenging the humanitarian violence of settler militarism during Operation New Life in quotidian ways.

### REFUGEE SUBJECTIVITY, SOCIALITY, AND REFUSAL: NEGOTIATING FORTUNE, FAMILY, AND FOOD

Vietnamese refugees were agential subjects who made the most of their incarceration in the refugee camps. Via everyday acts of survival, they undermined the US military's dominant narrative of humanitarian rescue, which both retroactively and proactively sought to justify the US military's settler colonial presence in Guam. In contrast to previous refugee studies that have focused on the biopolitical and necropolitical dimensions of the camps as spaces of "bare life," in this section I attend to what Yến Lê Espiritu calls the "politics of living": "how Vietnamese refugees, as devalued people, scripted new life histories—and indeed new lives—on the margins of sovereign space."[98] I read these moments as acts of refugee refusal, in which Vietnamese refugees subverted American expectations to express unconditional gratitude for the "gift of freedom."[99]

Compared to the detention centers and closed camps for boat refugees established throughout Southeast Asia during the late 1970s, the Operation New Life camps in Guam were better resourced and structured for shorter stays.[100] The first wave of Vietnamese refugees processed in Guam, furthermore, consisted primarily of those who were well connected to the US military and government: ARVN military officials, political elites, those who worked for the US embassy or US businesses, and their families and loved ones. As a result, they were, on average, wealthier, more educated, and better connected than those in succeeding waves of forced migration from Southeast Asia. Moreover, sovereign power is never totalizing. Although the US military controlled refugees' mobility, sustenance, and political status in the camps, they still found ways to subvert military power via quotidian acts of survival.

Operation New Life refugees upended American stereotypes of the refugee as a poor, destitute, and malnourished figure, prone to recuperation as a passive object of humanitarian aid. *PDN* articles fixate on the "well-dressed" status of the refugees, noting their diamond rings and parasols and obsessing over their unexpected wealth: "Rumors about refugees carrying 'hundreds of thousands of dollars' are widespread."[101] Many refugees indeed brought large percentages of their life savings to Guam by sewing gold taels into their clothes or packing baht chains in their bags.[102] Once word got out, bank officials from Deak & Company, the American

FIGURE 6. Vietnamese refugees at Camp Asan, June 1975. From the collection of the Richard F. Taitano Micronesian Area Research Center.

Savings and Loan Association, and Bank of America flocked to the camps, setting up "little wooden building[s] amid the tents" to purchase the gold in exchange for opening savings accounts.[103] For several months in 1975, the refugee camps in Guam hosted "the most active gold exchange house in the world" and the "biggest gold rush in recent times," which amounted to "millions of dollars in gold wafers." In fact, "individual sales of up to $400,000" were "not uncommon."[104] Although selling their gold freed refugees from having to worry about theft inside the camps, some companies were accused of profiting off the refugees' plight, prompting Guam's government to step in to regulate gold prices.[105]

The Vietnamese refugees' deviation from the destitute-victim stereotype prompted some Guamanians to question whether they were even deserving of US aid. In a letter to the *PDN* editor dated 1 May 1975, for example, Betty L. Johnson, a self-identified US Navy dependent, wrote:

> Don't get me wrong, I don't begrudge the people help if they really need it, but just take a look at the pictures in the April 24 edition of the PDN. *They don't look like refugees to me.* Look at the clothes, the rings, watches etc. on these people. Look at the picture of all the baggage, people who can afford to buy suitcases like that certainly in my book cannot be classified as refugees. They say a picture is worth a thousand words so just take some good long looks at these pictures and tell me truthfully that these people are in need of food and clothing.[106]

What does it mean to "look like a refugee"? Previous studies have critiqued how displaced subjects from Vietnam were compelled to articulate a particular anticommunist narrative in order to be granted asylum in the United States.[107] Similarly, in the quoted passage, Johnson conflates class status with the condition of political asylum: despite (and often times because of) their material wealth, the refugees were unable to guarantee their safety in a communist-unified Vietnam.

Furthermore, Johnson's ahistorical focus on class elides the role that French colonization and US imperial aggression played in destabilizing the refugees' homeland in the first place. Johnson goes on to say that the United States should instead divert some of the resources spent on Operation New Life to "our own people," those "US citizens that are needy."[108] However, Johnson misidentifies the primary beneficiary of those resources: the bloated US military, which initiated the settler imperial wars in Asia in the first place, rather than the refugees displaced by that aggression, regardless of their former class status. Furthermore, despite her attempt to distinguish between worthy and unworthy refugees from Vietnam, Johnson betrays her nativist anxieties regarding *all* racialized refugees when she writes, "What will happen when all these 'refugees' get into the United States and try to take it over?"[109] Overall, this letter demonstrates the shortcomings of an oversimplified class analysis underwritten by yellow peril racism.

In spite of the financial concerns of Guamanians like Johnson, the US military spent millions of dollars funding Operation New Life. One of the main expenses was food. Over the course of the first month, refugees housed at Tent City alone ate "some $1.6 million worth of food"—roughly $63,870 per day, or about "$2 a day per refugee."[110] This amounted to "52,000 pounds of ham, pork chops, canned meat, rice, milk, eggs, and fruit."[111] Food studies scholars have argued that control over food distribution constitutes a form of biopolitics.[112] During Operation New Life, refugees were subject to the US military's control over their very bodily sustenance. However, refugees also pushed back, pressuring the US military to acquiesce to their culinary demands. Indeed, one of the biggest grievances that refugees had about the camps concerned the food. Although military personnel kept the kitchens running for twenty-four hours a day, food lines stretched for hours, especially during the first weeks of logistical confusion.[113] According to twenty-six-year-old Minh Luong Ngoc, a former security guard for the US consulate at Cần Thơ, life in Guam consisted of "getting up, standing in long lines for breakfast, eating fast, resting, standing in line for lunch, resting and standing in line for dinner."[114] Admiral Morrison, commander of Operation New Life, admitted that "our worst problem is too many people standing in line for food."[115]

Refugees also rejected American canned goods, demanding that the US military accommodate their palate preferences.[116] In response, the navy ordered "100,000 chopsticks" from Japan, diverted "500 tons of rice" to Guam from "a ship bound for other Far East destinations," and started placing "fish sauce, dried curry powder, coconut cream, bamboo shoots, greens and dried beef and pork" on "most tables"—what one journalist termed a "Vietnamizing" of the food, in ironic reference to Nixon's failed policy of Vietnamization.[117] Refugees were less successful in acquiring fresh leafy greens, though their lack of success should not be attributed to a lack of effort. Ronald Klimek, a white social scientist conducting research on "what the Vietnamese were like at the time of their immigration to America," recalls:

The refugees complained repeatedly that they were not being given vegetables and that the portions of meat and rice were more than they needed. They wanted vegetables, as they defined them [not the American-given legumes], substituted for meat. They argued that vegetables are cheaper than meat and that here was a chance for them to get what they wanted while the government saved money.

I had a number of evening parties for the Vietnamese who helped me conduct research. I always asked them what kind of festivities they wanted and the response always was the same—vegetable parties. I brought boxes of fresh vegetables—mostly lettuce, tomatoes and green peppers—and the Vietnamese quickly chopped and sliced the food for what turned out to be vegetable orgies.[118]

Although Klimek slips into Orientalist, sexualizing rhetoric, his article evidences how Vietnamese refugees negotiated with the US military to accommodate their culinary requests. The fact that they were unsuccessful in acquiring fresh vegetables speaks less to their efforts than to the general difficulty of shipping large quantities of perishable produce to an island whose own domestic agriculture had been all but obliterated by centuries of Spanish colonialism, Japanese occupation, US settler militarism, and unpredictable typhoons.[119]

Food was also one of the main commodities sold on the black market that developed in Tent City. Although an official navy spokesman attested that there "have been no reports of black marketeering" and only "two reports of prostitution," a PDN journalist's interview with Private First Class Timothy Brander and his anonymous friend "Jelly" suggests a different story.[120] According to the pair, both Vietnamese refugees and Guamanian civilians purchased food and cooking materials illegally from US military officials and mess attendants. In some cases, sex rather than money was the medium of exchange. Jelly said that "when an attractive Vietnamese girl asks for a can of meat or some other type of food she often 'pays' for it by sexual 'favors,'" and Brander recalled that "he and three other mess cooks were given five hours of extra duty for accidently interrupting a staff sergeant during intercourse with a refugee who wanted food."[121] These anecdotes remind readers that refugee agency was of course constrained by the racial and sexual power dynamics structuring the camps. They also demonstrate the extent of settler militarism: the fact that Guamanian civilians felt compelled to make black market deals with US soldiers in order to access federally funded food speaks volumes about Guam's status as an unincorporated territory rendered dependent on the US military.

Since food was such a large preoccupation for refugees during Operation New Life, it is unsurprising that the topic surfaces often in present-day oral histories. One refugee described an unforgettable day when her older children went out to stand in Tent City's multihour-long breakfast line while she stayed inside the tent to nurse her baby and young children.[122] When the children started to walk back with the food, rain began to pour. The paper plates disintegrated, the food melted to the ground, and the children were left with little except their tears to assuage them until they had to go and stand in line yet again for lunch. The refugee mother cried hard in despair.

For other refugees, the long lines were a marked improvement over their childhood of food insecurity in rural Vietnam. Wendy Trougher (born Le Nguyen Tuyet), who was eleven years old when she arrived in Guam, recalled: "Where I came from, it was the first time I felt safe because I could eat twice a day. You know, we stood in long lines in the sun [at Asan], but twice a day I could eat and that was a lot better than where I came from where every day it was thinking on how to outsmart someone, how to snatch and run. So, standing in line was no big deal at all."[123] After Operation New Life, Trougher was adopted by a strict American military family who forbade her to speak Vietnamese, but she reunited with her birth family when a senior in high school. She eventually married Mike Trougher, whom she met as a child growing up in Guam, and spent most of her life in Guam thereafter.

Another refugee, who joined her older sister in Guam in 1989, shared her sister's memory of Vietnamese refugees collecting snails (bắt ốc) and catching fish (câu cá) in the ocean bordering Camp Asan in order to supplement their military-supplied meals during Operation New Life.[124] According to Perez, the Vietnamese refugees "actually were permitted to go down to the beach and they would fish. They would catch crabs and they would bring them back up to the camp and they were permitted to have cooking facilities." They scoured the beach so thoroughly that Gab Gab Beach "actually turned white" and at one point "the EPA got scared that they would just wipe out the coral!"[125] The refugees also picked beans from local trees to eat as vegetables when green and to grind for coffee when roasted. Foraging food from the local environment, Vietnamese refugees subverted the US military's ability to exercise total control over their means of subsistence. In Perez's words: "They were able to take care of themselves."[126]

Refugees also exercised limited control over their forms of social organization. In negotiating US preferences for nuclear family formations, for example, refugees stretched the definition of "family" to ensure the safe passage of as many individuals as possible. One man claimed twenty-eight children as "his 'very own'" to immigration officials, even though he had to "check the[ir] name tags" before "he could fill out the entry forms."[127] Another couple "explained to immigration authorities that the baby they carried had been found in an abandoned field on their way to the airport and they 'just couldn't leave him there.'"[128] Sometimes refugees were accused of "fraud" for "adding names to family registers."[129] However, they also successfully changed the immigration laws restricting entrance into the United States. During Operation New Life, the category of "families" of US citizens and permanent-resident aliens who were allowed entry was expanded to include "aunts, uncles, cousins, etc., on both sides of family."[130] The Immigration and Naturalization Service even considered "admitting these persons' longtime domestic help," further qualifying what constituted a legitimate "blood relationship" in the eyes of the US government.[131]

Refugees also upended American expectations regarding romance and intimacy. In one "tear-jerking drama," chronicled breathtakingly across the front pages of multiple issues of the *PDN*, Thomas Heijl—a "brown-haired, wiry Farmingdale, N.Y., resident" who had been stationed at Nha Trang Air Base as an air force mechanic in 1971—reunited with his fiancée, Nguyen Thi Ut, at Camp Asan after three years of separation and the tragic loss of their daughter, Linda, who was "killed by Viet Cong bullets" as she and her mother "stood on the shore of Vietnam trying to evacuate the country on a fishing boat."[132] The couple promptly married, with Governor Bordallo presiding. However, Heijl found out later that the "cousin" Nguyen insisted that he sponsor and bring with them to New York was in fact Nguyen's Vietnamese lover, Tran Mong. Nguyen ended up leaving Heijl after a couple of months to live with Tran "in a motel in Florida."[133] Stories like this show how refugees worked creatively within bureaucratic constraints to safeguard passage for themselves and their loved ones.

Refugees also took leadership positions in the camps, at times taking "much work from their hosts, the U.S. Navy."[134] At the Naval Communications Station Barrigada barracks, the Vietnamese set up a plan to "work for themselves," "teaching English" and "performing most of the cooking, cleaning, medical duties as well as setting up lines of communications to help other refugees through the lengthy paperwork process needed by U.S. immigration officials."[135] The Vietnamese "camp commander," Tran Khanh Van, who held a "doctorate in civil engineering from University of California at Berkeley," formed "intracamp committees" for sanitation, health, cooking, and information. As a result, according to the *PDN* journalist, the refugees' "stay has been a comfortable one."[136]

Camp Asan also elected a "commanding officer," Tony Lam, an extroverted, bilingual, "5-foot-4 North Vietnamese native" and "former mahjong partner of Gen. Nguyen Cao Ky," who greeted flustered new arrivals, directed families to their tents, helped organize cleaning and sanitation committees, met with US military officials, comforted homesick refugees, arbitrated conflicts, and translated during immigration interviews, "scurrying from one scene to another, advising here and mediating there" over what often became a twenty-hour workday.[137] Lam's leadership in Guam prefigured his political career in the United States: Lam became the first Vietnamese American elected to political office when, in 1992, he won a seat on the Westminster, California, city council. For the Fourth of July celebrations organized at Camp Asan, Lam "eagerly directed" the games and contests, which included "sack races, slow-speed bicycle races, a tug-of-war, a beauty pageant, and a fishing contest," combined with other activities such as a volleyball tournament, special movie showings, and an evening dance.[138] Colonel General Jinx McCain, the marine officer in charge of the camp, interpreted the Vietnamese refugees' participation in the festivities as proof of their American patriotism, which, according to him, "was stronger than that in 75 percent of the cities back in the States."

Another onlooker observed, "The refugees brought out the red, white and blue of the American flag."[139] Although many refugees indeed felt a genuine desire to celebrate the patriotic holiday of the country that had fought alongside them during the Vietnam War, others likely just appreciated a break from the normal routine, which included long stretches of waiting and boredom.[140]

While Tony Lam was the star of the "national and international media," as evidenced by a relatively prominent *PDN* article lamenting his decision to finally leave for California after "90 days of volunteer management," other refugees at Camp Asan organized "Asan Refugee Camp Security," which consisted of a "commander, an assistant and 10 team leaders or supervisors" who then recruited "10 volunteers for security work."[141] Unwilling to trust the US Navy with something so important as their own security, the organization sought "to keep South Vietnamese from leaving the camp, to keep unauthorized outsiders from entering it, to protect and control the barracks compound, to prevent children from going to the beach and possibly drowning and to provide barrack sentries at night."[142] Using "five walkie-talkie radios" to communicate, the team patrolled the nineteen barracks of the camp on their own initiative.[143]

Lastly, rotating groups of refugees helped to run and write *Chân Trời Mới* (New Horizons), the Vietnamese-language newspaper that circulated throughout the refugee camps. *Chân Trời Mới* translated messages from the Red Cross and US military officials, demystified immigration procedures, cautioned refugees to save water, featured photographs and written coverage of camp events (such as dances, concerts, and art shows), kept refugees up-to-date on news from camps in the continental United States, and acted as a message board for family members and loved ones trying to find and send notes to one another. *Chân Trời Mới* was written by refugees, for refugees. Rather than describe refugee activities for a voyeuristic observer, the newspaper shared practical information to help refugees negotiate life in the camps.

In sum, camp residents carved out social spaces in which to continue living, refusing to let the war and the refugee crisis define them. They found moments of joy and entertainment within the camp's confines. Refugees attended mass in silk *aó dàis*, swam in the ocean, played volleyball and basketball, learned English, painted art that would be exhibited in Guam's Government House, traded comic books across a fence with children of naval families, and greeted Smokey the Bear.[144] At Camp Asan, "the G.I.s would show animated shorts in the open area in front of the barracks," where refugees would sit, "midway between Vietnam and the New World, with a full moon above us, and a huge white screen in front of us," watching Bugs Bunny, the Road Runner, *Popeye the Sailor Man*, *The Cat in the Hat*, and *Sinbad the Sailor*.[145] These anecdotes do not diminish the fact that the refugees were separated from the rest of Guam's residents by "barbed wire, chain-link fences, and armed guards" or that many felt depressed and homesick, to the point of considering suicide.[146] The US military's narrative of humanitarian rescue was underwritten by the refugees' carceral reality. Through everyday acts of survival, however, refugees could challenge the US military's totalizing control.

## ARCHIPELAGIC TRANSLATIONS: VIETNAM, GUAM, ISRAEL-PALESTINE

Vietnamese-Chamorro encounters during Operation New Life were facilitated by translation between English and Vietnamese, native and refugee. But who were these translators? Contrary to the dominant narrative, not all Vietnamese people in Guam during Operation New Life were refugees. Lee T. Baza, for example (cited above as well as in chapter 1) came to Guam several years before the Fall of Saigon. During Operation New Life, she worked around the clock to translate for the incoming refugees. Another key figure was Jennifer Ada, also known by her Vietnamese name, Mai Anh. Ada left Vietnam for California prior to 1975, when her mother remarried a US air force official. In 1974, when her stepfather deployed to Andersen Air Force Base, Ada and her mother moved to Guam, where they encountered the incoming refugees.

Ada was sixteen when Operation New Life commenced. One day, while swimming with a friend on base, she suddenly heard people speaking Vietnamese and thought, "Who are these Vietnamese? Am I dreaming?"[147] Ada walked into the barracks, where she met a military doctor, who was very grateful to see her once he realized that she could help translate for his refugee patients. From that day forward, Ada left her high school classes early every day to volunteer at Tin City and Orote Point, working "day and night" to help the refugees fill out paperwork, exchange their money, and come to terms with their displacement.[148] In response to their complaints about the food, she brought the refugees boxes of *nước mắm* (fish sauce), as well as Tabasco when she couldn't find hot peppers. Although not a refugee herself, Ada empathized with their loss of a country.

Ada's experiences during Operation New Life prefigured her lifelong ties to the island. After moving back to California in eleventh grade, Ada returned to Guam in 1988, became a successful businesswoman, and married into a well-known Chamorro family. Her husband, Peter "Sonny" Ada, is a prominent landowner and businessman; his first cousin, Joseph F. Ada, served as Speaker of the Guam legislature during Operation New Life and as the fifth governor of Guam from 1987 to 1995. These familial connections underwrite Ada's present-day commitment to the Chamorro community as a Vietnamese refugee settler.

Lee T. Baza's and Jennifer Ada's stories exemplify the lasting archipelagic connections between Vietnamese and Chamorros that persisted even after the conclusion of Operation New Life in 1975. They also serve as an important counterpoint to dominant representations of the operation, which have stressed the US military's humanitarianism in order to overwrite settler imperialism during the Vietnam War and morally justify settler militarism in Guam. Such narratives of humanitarian violence positioned Vietnamese refugee settlers in a structurally antagonistic relationship to Chamorro decolonial struggles against settler militarism. They also ignore the ways Chamorros welcomed the Vietnamese refugees in an expression of *inafa'maolek*, and the ways Vietnamese translators worked side by side with Chamorros to assist the refugees. According to Jennifer Ada, people today have forgotten Chamorros' role during Operation New Life. She seeks to counteract this forgetting, insisting that "the Chamorro people need to be recognized and remembered."[149]

Reflecting on Operation New Life, Monsignor David I. A. Quitugua enacts a different kind of archipelagic translation in comparing Vietnamese refugee displacement to the Jewish Exodus, Vietnamese escape from their war-torn homeland to the Jewish people's wandering through the desert for forty years, and the Vietnamese refugees' eventual resettlement in the United States to the Jews' arrival in the Promised Land.[150] In "Of Luggage and Shoes," Thuy Dinh also refers to the continental United States as the "Promised Land," marking archipelagic geographies.[151] These metaphors prefigure the narrative tactics that Israeli politicians used to represent Vietnamese refugees in Israel-Palestine, as discussed in the following chapter. Indeed, as the US military processed Vietnamese refugees in Guam during Operation New Life in order to morally justify settler militarism, so too did Israeli leaders resettle Vietnamese refugees in Israel-Palestine in order to direct international attention away from native Palestinians' ongoing dispossession. Like Vietnamese Americans in Guam, Vietnamese Israelis also became refugee settlers.

After chapter 4 details this analogous case study, chapter 5 returns to Guam to discuss cultural representations of Operation New Life and its afterlives. By November 1975, most Vietnamese refugees had left Guam, either to resettle in the continental United States or repatriate to Vietnam. However, an estimated 4,000 refugees decided to stay and make Guam their home. Chapter 5 explores how a critical refugee sensibility can be mobilized to undermine settler subjectivity in order to challenge the seeming permanence of settler militarism and the refugee settler condition in Guam.

# 4

## Refugees in a State of Refuge

*Vietnamese Israelis and the Question of Palestine*

On 5 June 1967, Israeli forces launched a series of airstrikes against Egyptian air-fields, initiating the Six Day War against the neighboring states of Egypt, Jordan, and Syria.[1] By the war's conclusion on 10 June 1967, Israel had radically expanded its territorial control over Palestine, commencing the ongoing occupation of Gaza and the West Bank and conquering the Sinai Peninsula, a territory it later rescinded, and the Golan Heights, the western portion of which remains occupied. Four hundred thousand Palestinian refugees were displaced in what became known as al-Naksa. Exactly one decade later, on 10 June 1977, Captain Meir Tadmor of the Israeli cargo ship *Yuvali* rescued a group of sixty-six Vietnamese refugees—thirty-four men, sixteen women, and sixteen children—who were floating adrift in the South China Sea, having escaped from the coastal town of Phan Thiết by fishing boat four days earlier.[2] One of the rescued people, Dr. Tran Quang Hoa, a former army surgeon, explained: "Conditions in Vietnam were unbearable. We feared for our lives. I couldn't support Communism—I suffered too long from them."[3]

Before Captain Tadmor picked up the refugees, five ships had passed by without offering assistance, thereby violating international maritime law. The *Yuvali* had initially rushed by as well, but when Tadmor caught sight of the boat and heard the refugees' cries for help, he turned the ship around.[4] Tadmor initially tried to drop the displaced Vietnamese off at a refugee camp, but they were denied asylum in Taiwan, Japan, and Hong Kong. Finally, after weeks of debate, on 21 June 1977, newly elected prime minister Menachem Begin announced that the State of Israel would resettle the sixty-six Vietnamese refugees as his first official act in office—the first time that a non-Jewish population would be offered asylum and eventual citizenship in the self-proclaimed Jewish nation.[5] Two more waves would follow in 1979, bringing the total number of Vietnamese refugees resettled in Israel-Palestine to 366.[6]

I begin with this temporal juxtaposition—10 June 1967 and 10 June 1977—in order to emphasize that Israel's resettlement of Vietnamese refugees was inherently structured by its settler occupation of Palestine—an occupation that Zionists argue is necessary to ensure refuge for displaced Jews. Indeed, Prime Minister Begin empathized with the Vietnamese refugees because "their plight evoked memories of Jews fleeing Nazi Germany and being denied entry to Palestine."[7] In a speech with President Jimmy Carter on the White House lawn on 19 July 1977, he elaborated: "We remember, we have never forgotten that boat with 900 Jews, having left Germany in the last weeks before the Second World War for Cuba. . . . We have never forgotten the lot of our people, persecuted, humiliated, ultimately physically destroyed. And therefore, it was natural that my first act as Prime Minister was to give those people a haven in the land of Israel."[8] Explaining his executive decision to offer asylum, Begin translated the post-1975 Vietnamese refugee crisis into a Jewish context, drawing visual parallels between "that boat with 900 Jews"—the SS *St. Louis*, which left Germany on 13 May 1939 but was turned away by the United States at Havana and forced to return to Europe, where many died at the hands of Nazis—and the iconic images of Vietnamese boat people that were then circulating in the postwar international media. Focusing on the figure of the boat refugee, Begin suggested that the Jewish experience of Holocaust refugeehood uniquely positioned the self-identified Jewish nation of Israel to empathize with the displaced Vietnamese refugees, the majority of whom had fled Vietnam, also by boat, following the withdrawal of US troops from Vietnam, the Fall of Saigon, and the anticolonial reunification of the country under communist rule.

In his welcome speech to Prime Minister Begin, President Carter also projected parallel histories of Jewish and Vietnamese refugeehood:

> I was particularly impressed that the first official action of [Begin's] government was to admit into Israel sixty-six homeless refugees from Vietnam who had been floating around in the oceans of the world, excluded by many nations who are their neighbors, who had been picked up by an Israeli ship and to whom he gave a home. It was an act of compassion, an act of sensitivity, and a recognition of him and his government about the importance of a home for people who are destitute and who would like to express their own individuality and freedom in a common way, again typifying the historic struggle of the people of Israel.[9]

In his praise of Begin's humanitarian gesture, Carter noted the "historical struggle of the people of Israel" brought on by Holocaust displacement. By referencing the anticommunist Vietnamese refugees' own pursuit of "individuality and freedom" in Israel, he also drew implicit parallels between Israel and the United States as Western nations similarly positioned to safeguard such democratic values.

Carter and Begin's characterization of Israel as a democratic nation of Jewish refugees capable of extending empathy to Vietnamese refugees did not account for the contemporaneous context of Palestinian refugeehood. Indeed, any discussion of Vietnamese and Jewish refugeehood must also triangulate Palestinian refugee-hood—the settler colonial removal of Palestinians from their native homeland. In the speech quoted above, Carter elided the archipelagic history of both US inter-vention in Vietnam, which exacerbated Southeast Asian displacement, as well as US financial and military support of Israel, which has facilitated Palestinian dis-placement. By doing so, he helped Begin to direct international attention *away* from Israel's settler occupation of Palestine and instead depict Israel as a humani-tarian state of refuge.

Based on an analysis of newspaper articles, Israel State Archives (ISA) docu-ments, and interviews conducted with Vietnamese Israelis between 2015 and 2016, this chapter posits that Israel's resettlement of 366 Vietnamese refugees during the late 1970s should be read as a performance of humanitarianism intended to recuperate Israel's image in the international sphere. Whereas the US military used humanitarian rhetoric during Operation New Life to justify settler militarism in Guam, as discussed in the previous chapter, the Israeli government mobilized humanitarian discourse to elide international critiques of Palestinian dispos-session, instead emphasizing Israel's own history of Holocaust displacement to project a shared sense of refugeehood with the most visible refugee crisis at the time, the Southeast Asian boat refugee exodus.[10] Publicizing Israel's humanitarian act of Vietnamese refugee resettlement, furthermore, helped to depict Israel as a benevolent Western democracy rather than a settler colonial aggressor—a rhetori-cal move that Candace Fujikane has identified as "yellowwashing" and Rebecca L. Stein has characterized as a "humanitarian alibi."[11] Vietnamese refugees were thus positioned in a structurally antagonistic relationship to the Palestinian liberation struggle, regardless of individual intent.

This chapter details the three waves of Vietnamese refugee resettlement to Israel-Palestine that facilitated Vietnamese Israelis' refugee settler condition: the vexed positionality of refugees made citizens in a settler colonial state. It asks: How and why were these Vietnamese refugees resettled by the Zionist state, despite their non-Jewish status? How did they fit into Israel's existing racial landscape? How has the exemplary case of Vietnamese refugee resettlement been discussed in regard to Israel's more recent refugee crises? My objective in this chapter is not to debate the sincerity of Israel's actions but rather to critique how the humanitarian resettlement of Vietnamese refugees went hand in hand with the settler colonial displacement of Palestinian refugees. Refugee acts of refusal of such Zionist rheto-ric present openings for relating otherwise.

## THREE WAVES: VIETNAMESE REFUGEE RESETTLEMENT ON NATIVE PALESTINIAN LAND

To unpack the refugee settler condition in Israel-Palestine, it is important to first map out Jewish, Palestinian, and Vietnamese subjects' overlapping claims to refu-geehood. In the State of Israel, Ashkenazi Jews maintain a monopoly over refugee discourse. Despite the fact that Israeli citizens who trace their family histories to the Holocaust constitute a demographic minority in Israel-Palestine, the historical catastrophe of Holocaust refugeehood figures prominently in the Israeli state's overarching story of Jewish refugeehood: a national narrative that traces its origins to Jewish exile following the fall of the Second Temple in 70 CE, and that depicts Zionism as the rightful return of the Jewish people to the Holy Land from which they were displaced. Indeed, this privileging of the figure of the Holocaust refugee in Israel's national narrative elides other waves of Jewish immigration and racial formation in Israel: Ashkenazi Jewish elites, inspired by European forms of nationalism and socialism, who settled Palestine prior to World War II; Yemeni Jewish laborers recruited by these Ashkenazi pioneers to build the Zionist state; Mizrahi and Sephardic Jews from North Africa, Spain, and the former Ottoman Empire who fled their Muslim-dominated Arab nations after 1948 and who remain underrepresented in positions of power despite their demographic majority in Israel; Indian and Ethiopian Jews who suffer discrimination via simultaneous forms of invisibility and hypervisibility; and post-Soviet "Jews"—many of whom are actually Christian—who were allegedly brought to Israel-Palestine to "whiten" the Arab-majority population in the late 1980s and 1990s.[12] Today, white-presenting Ashkenazi Jews are disproportionately represented in Israel's government, businesses, and higher education, despite their demographic minority status. This elitist control over key positions of power further consolidates their influence in shaping Israel's self-image as a nation of Holocaust refugees.

Israel's national narrative of Jewish refugeehood can, in turn, either be activated to enact empathy with other refugee populations—such as the Vietnamese boat people—or deny refugee status to them—as is the case with Palestinians. In 1977, Prime Minister Begin asserted that "the Israeli people, who have known persecution, and know, perhaps better than any other nation, what it means to be a refugee, couldn't watch the suffering of these wretched people. It's only natural to grant them a refuge in our country."[13] In this quote, "wretched people" refers exclusively to the Vietnamese refugees; such a designation did not extend to displaced Palestinians, who were excluded from "our country."

Palestinians, meanwhile, have had a vexed relationship to "refugee" status ever since the term's inception as an internationally recognized legal category. The 1951 United Nations Refugee Convention, which Israel signed yet never adopted into its own national legislation, purposely excludes displaced Palestinians. Initially written in response to the mass uprooting of European peoples following World War II, the 1951 Convention, and the later 1967 Protocol Relating to the Status of Refugees, declared that Palestinians were already protected by the United Nations Relief and Works Agency for Palestine Refugees (UNRWA), established in 1949 following the State of Israel's declaration of sovereignty on Palestinian land. To complicate matters, some early General Assembly resolutions refer to Palestinians as "refugees," but following Resolution 3236's passage in 1974, Palestinians were referred to as a "people," reflecting arguments that their displacement was not a problem of refugeehood per se but rather a denial of their national right to self-determination.[14] Adding another layer of complexity, the UNWRA's own registry of Palestinian refugees is incomplete because it defines Palestinian refugees "in relation to relief, not rights."[15] According to Ilana Feldman, "Because the definition was developed to implement the UNRWA relief mandate, rather than to account for Palestinian loss and displacement (as relevant to UN resolutions and Palestinian political claims), it did not ever include the whole of the population that had claims to property, to return, and to national self-determination."[16] Since refugee status is a precondition for the Palestinian Right of Return, should UN General Assembly Resolution 194, which resolved that "refugees wishing to return to their homes and live at peace with their neighbors should be permitted to do so at the earliest practicable date," ever come to fruition, lacking an official body to register Palestinian refugee status—especially for later generations born outside of their national homeland—is particularly problematic. Such ambiguities highlight the fraught relationship that displaced Palestinians have to the legal category of "refugee" under international law.

Arab nationalists initially supported the decision of the United Nations High Commissioner for Refugees (UNHCR) to leave jurisdiction over Palestinian refugees to the UNRWA, since they worried that the 1951 Convention, which advocated the resettlement of refugees in other nation-states of asylum, would preclude Palestinians' Right of Return to their ancestral lands in occupied Palestine.[17] Such preclusion would effectively surrender the newly established State of Israel to the Zionist settlers. In practice, however, this distinction between the jurisdiction of the UNHCR and the UNRWA has often benefited Israel. This effect is evidenced, for example, in meeting notes from the twenty-ninth and thirtieth sessions of the UNHCR during the late 1970s, which largely focused on the Southeast Asian refugee crisis. At the twenty-ninth session, held at the Palace of Nations in Geneva 9–17 October 1978, High Commissioner Poul Hartling stressed the "universality of refugee problems," even as the issue of Palestinian refugeehood remained woefully underdiscussed.[18] In one instance, Lebanon's delegate asked for assistance regarding "the vast problems confronting the displaced persons in his country as a result of recent events," but the UN press release detailing this exchange refrained from explicitly naming the Palestinian refugees as such or identifying the cause of their displacement: the Israel Defense Forces (IDF) invasion of Lebanon in March 1978.[19] Such rhetorical elision effectively erased Palestinian refugeehood from the UNHCR archive.

A year later, an unpublished report sent by Israeli ambassador Eviatar Manor to the International Organizations Department in Israel detailing the thirtieth session of the UNHCR, held at the Palace of Nations in Geneva 8–16 October 1979, drew special attention to a speech by Iran's delegate, who invoked Palestinian refugeehood in relation to the contemporaneous Southeast Asian refugee crisis and expressed his support for the Palestine Liberation Organization's (PLO) struggle.

To Manor's relief, however, the "conflict in the Middle East" was not otherwise mentioned, and the session's delegates agreed that the UNHCR's jurisdiction did not extend to Palestinian refugees.[20] As a whole, this session, which invoked the 1951 United Nations Refugee Convention to emphasize the UNHCR's commitment to "saving refugees at sea," privileged the rescue of Southeast Asian refugees at the same time that it rejected the plight of Palestinian refugees as beyond its purview—a decision that implicitly worked to Israel's benefit.[21]

Such complicated and competing definitions of refugeehood lead to conflicting politics of national belonging and "return." Israel's Law of Return—which grants automatic citizenship to diasporic Jews who "return" to Israel—precludes not only Palestinians' Right of Return but also any codified legal procedure for non-Jewish refugees to gain asylum, let alone citizenship, in the State of Israel. Furthermore, Jewish immigration to Israel is conceived of in biblical terms as *aliyah*, an accession to Mount Zion in Jerusalem; the Hebrew word for (presumed Jewish) immigrants to Israel, *olim*, is derived from this term. To this day, Israel has no standardized legal process for naturalizing non-Jewish persons.

Prime Minister Begin's resettlement of sixty-six Vietnamese refugees (*plitim mi-Vietnam*) in 1977 was therefore quite an exception to Israel's own immigration and asylum policy. According to Yehudit Hueber, a Ministry of Interior official, this was "the first time Israel had received a party of non-Jewish refugees." Furthermore, he said, although "Israel normally gives no aid to non-Jewish immigrants," the "Vietnamese would receive the same aid offered to Jewish newcomers."[22] Upon arrival at Ben Gurion Airport on 26 June 1977, each refugee was given $70 in shekels, canned food, and a packet of tea. They were transferred to Ofakim, a Zionist development town consisting of Yemenite and North African immigrants located seventy-five miles south of Tel Aviv, where they were greeted with welcome signs and a youth band playing "Jerusalem the Gold." At the welcome ceremony, Israeli minister of immigrant absorption David Levi chastised the other ships that had ignored the leaking boat full of refugees, urging them and others to instead follow Israel's humanitarian example: "Let them do as we have. May they lend a hand to save women and children who are in the heart of the sea without a homeland, and lead them to safe shores."[23] Contrasting the response of those ships' respective nations with the magnanimity displayed by Israel, this statement was directed toward an international audience of nation-state leaders.

During the first six months of resettlement, the Vietnamese refugees stayed at an absorption center in Ofakim, learned Hebrew, and received subsistence subsidies and free medical insurance from the government.[24] In December 1977, they moved to more permanent housing around Tel Aviv where they were given loans and grants to purchase new furniture and appliances. Eventually the refugees found employment in tourism, industry, fishing, and medicine; one family opened a Vietnamese restaurant. All the refugees were of ethnic Vietnamese origin, and several spoke English and French in addition to Vietnamese.

Because the 1952 Entry into Israel Law does not offer any standardized natu-ralization policy for non-Jewish immigrants to Israel-Palestine, the Vietnamese refugees' legal status was largely improvised. They first received special tourist visas that granted them permission to find permanent work.[25] Then they were given identity cards and temporary residency permits that included limited civil rights to employment, fair housing, social security, pensions, and medical insur-ance. Finally, those who chose to stay in Israel-Palestine were granted permanent residency status and the promise of citizenship after five years.

From a purely demographic perspective, Prime Minister Begin's resettlement of a mere sixty-six Vietnamese refugees may appear insignificant, especially when compared to the hundreds of thousands of Southeast Asian refugees reset-tled by the United States, Canada, France, and Australia. The event's rhetorical significance, however, outweighs its demographic impact, as evidenced by the pro-fusion of press articles documenting it. Israel made sure to publicize its human-itarian act of Vietnamese refugee resettlement in order to promote a favorable image in the international sphere, particularly given ongoing critiques of Israel's treatment of Palestinians within its 1948 borders and in the occupied territories of Gaza and the West Bank. In December 1978, for example, Kastel Films wrote to the Israel Film Service with a proposal to create a film about the resettlement of the first wave of refugees, which would have great "propaganda value": "We are talking specifically about a positive 'publicity film' whose aim is to show the attrac-tive side of Israel, without disguises and reservations, as a nation of refugees ready to give shelter to other refugees from a distant country, without having any cultural, religious or ethnic connection with them."[26] In this proposed film, Vietnamese refugees would be racialized as passive victims upon which to write a narrative of Israeli humanitarian aid. The words of one Israeli reporter succinctly pinpoint the problem of Israel's seeming obsession over international representation: "There's something suspicious about the self-gratitude of the heads of the establishment, the wish to prove with the media to the whole world how moral and pretty we are, how we look after the Holocaust refugees of other countries, as if we can't follow our own conscience without the whole world knowing about it."[27] In sum, Israel's resettlement of Vietnamese refugees was a self-conscious performance of humani-tarianism for an international audience.

Part of Israel's publicity campaign was in response to the specificity of Begin's positionality within Israeli politics. Earlier in his career, Begin had served as the leader of the Zionist paramilitary organization Irgun, which operated in Man-date Palestine between 1931 and 1948, and then as the head of the early right-wing political party Herut, meaning "Freedom." Given their militant tactics, both orga-nizations have been accused of terrorist activities, making Begin a controversial figure. In 1977, Begin's candidacy for prime minister as the head of the Likud party was supported by a coalition of working-class Mizrahi Jews and Orthodox Jewish conservatives, both of whom felt alienated by the Ashkenazi socialist elite. His electoral victory marked the first time in Israeli history that a right-wing party had won control of the theretofore left-wing-dominated government. Begin's resettlement of the sixty-six Vietnamese refugees as his first act in office was therefore partly intended to quell Western concerns that his newly formed right-wing government would jeopardize Israel's established legacy of Ashkenazi liberalism.

We can also read Begin's act as a strategic response to United Nations General Assembly Resolution 3379 (1975), which denounced Zionism as a "form of racism and racial discrimination." This resolution severely harmed Israel's reputation internationally and would not be revoked until the 1991 passage of Resolution 46/86, which was put before the UN General Assembly at the United States' behest. With the resettlement of the Vietnamese refugees, Begin sought to counter Resolution 3379's characterization of Israel as a racist nation of Zionist aggressors by reframing the country as a multicultural haven for displaced refugees. Such multicultural inclusion, however, did not extend to Palestinian refugees, let alone most non-Jewish asylum seekers who followed the Vietnamese.

Media representations of Vietnamese refugees in Israel-Palestine tend to narrate the second and third waves of resettlement as natural progressions following the first. However, Israel did not initially plan to accept more refugees following Begin's original humanitarian gesture. In 1978, when Yigael Yadin, serving temporarily as deputy prime minister while Begin traveled overseas, proposed that Israel absorb another group of Vietnamese refugees, the majority of the Cabinet, Israel's executive branch, rejected the proposal.[28] Then, on 11 November 1978, Dov Shilansky (Likud) and Akiva Nof (Democratic Movement), two members of the Knesset, Israel's legislative body, made separate procedural motions to either fully absorb or offer temporary shelter to 2,500 Vietnamese refugees stranded on the *Hai Hong*, a ship that had anchored off the coast of Port Klang in October but was refused permission to land in Malaysia. The motion was sent first to the Knesset Committee and then to the Committee of Interior Ecology. By the time Israeli leaders addressed the issue, Canada had already offered to resettle the ship's refugees.[29] In a similar vein, at a UN meeting that took place 11–12 December 1978 in Geneva on the question of Southeast Asian refugees, Israeli leaders agreed that Ambassador Joel Barromi should offer medicaments but that Israel should not commit to absorbing more refugees at that time.[30] In his initial protest of the decision, Barromi highlighted the public relations advantages of Vietnamese refugee resettlement: "Our participation is of value for propaganda purposes since a refugee tragedy is involved."[31] Furthermore, he argued, "it is not good for us now to show indifference to a problem which many compare to the story of the Exodus."[32] Barromi was ultimately overruled, however, and Israel refrained at the UN meeting from offering to resettle more refugees.

Israel's stance would change less than a month later, however. In late December 1978, the rusty freighter *Tung An* marooned in Manila Bay, leaving more than 2,300 Vietnamese refugees stranded.[33] About 240 of these refugees were granted asylum in countries such as France, West Germany, New Zealand, Switzerland, Britain, and Hong Kong. On 8 January 1979, Begin and the Cabinet ministers offered to resettle 100 refugees from the *Tung An*.[34] The Cabinet vote on the question of Vietnamese refugee absorption was 11–2 with four abstentions. According to a press report,

> Religious Affairs Minister Aharon Abu Hatzeira of the National Religious Party and Housing Minister Gideon Patt of Likud voted against the airlift on grounds that Israel should not become involved in a refugee problem that was beyond its ability to solve. Three of the four abstaining were Foreign Minister Moshe Dayan, Interior Minister Yosef Burg and Agriculture Minister Ariel Sharon. The fourth minister abstaining was not identified. The majority of the Cabinet, however, felt Israel should set a moral example in this instance.[35]

Although it is unclear what precipitated the majority of the Cabinet to change its stance regarding the resettlement of more Vietnamese refugees in less than a month's time, they were likely swayed in part by the deluge of earnest letters from Israeli citizens and the Jewish diaspora that echoed Begin's 1977 assertion that as a nation of Jewish refugees, Israel should empathize with the Vietnamese refugees and absorb a greater number of them.[36]

When announcing the Cabinet's decision, Cabinet secretary Arye Naor echoed Begin in citing the Jewish experience of the Holocaust as influencing the Cabinet's vote: "We remember the experience of our brethren during World War II who were seeking in vain for shelter."[37] He also stressed that this decision to absorb a second wave of Vietnamese refugees was largely symbolic, meant to encourage "other nations to follow."[38] Likewise, the Committee of Interior Ecology noted, "Israel should serve as an example to richer, bigger, and more developed countries which did not display generosity and did not agree to allow displaced people to enter their countries."[39] Israel sought to frame itself as a moral nation, rather than a settler colonial one. Indeed, following Naor's announcement, Avi Pazner, chancellor of the Israeli Embassy in Washington, DC, and head of the Foreign Ministry's Press Division, promptly wrote to Israel's Department of Journalism and Publicity and the Government Press Office, "It would be of much use for our image if the arrival of the refugees to Israel will receive wide coverage on the media, particularly the television networks. I suggest we think how to bring about maximum coverage, including interviews with refugees who will express their thanks to the State of Israel for the humanitarian gesture."[40] Pazner sought to solicit expressions of gratitude from the Vietnamese refugees in order to augment Israel's performance of humanitarianism in the international sphere.

In January 1979, Israeli leaders dispatched Jewish Agency representative Yehuda Weissberger to Manila from Bombay to help select the refugees to be offered asylum in Israel. Via private correspondence, they instructed Weissberger to favor multilingual and professional refugees who had traveled with their families.[41] He was to avoid unmarried adults or orphans: individuals who compromised not only the heteronormative ideal but also the fiction of racial purity. Such deviations from the nuclear family norm increased the likelihood of miscegenation, which could disrupt the ever-fragile Jewish national identity.[42] Unmarried adults, it was speculated, would marry Jewish partners; Jewish parents would have to adopt refugee orphans. Nuclear families of refugees, in contrast, would presumably remain self-sufficient. Thus, the Israeli state's humanitarian gesture of refugee resettlement was underwritten with concerns about intermarriage, inadvertently echoing the yellow peril racialization of Asian immigrants in North America.

By the time Weissberger arrived in Manila Bay, the refugees had been stranded on the *Tung An* for several weeks, having been refused entry into the Philippines. They had run out of provisions and were dehydrated and starving. According to Tran Tai Dong, who was eighteen at the time, Weissberger approached the *Tung An* in a small boat, called out to the captain, and explained that Israel would offer asylum and resettlement to large, "complete" families of seven to ten people.[43] The families who met this criteria were then invited onto the small boat for an interview. Weissberger ended up offering asylum to Tran and his family: an ethnic Chinese father, a Vietnamese mother, and nine children. Although they did not know anything about Israel-Palestine at the time, the family accepted Weissberger's offer since they had "no other choice."[44] As a whole, the group Weissberger selected were of ethnic Chinese background and middle-class status—part of the large exodus of Chinese Vietnamese merchants from South Vietnam who were targeted by the country's communist leaders after the Fall of Saigon.

In public interviews, Weissberger was careful to hide Israel's selection preferences and to focus instead on parallels between the boat refugees escaping Vietnam and Jewish refugees fleeing the Holocaust, as other Israeli leaders had done. On 14 January 1979, for example, Weissberger told a Reuters reporter that the sight of the *Tung An* was "tragically reminiscent" of the more than sixty refugee boats he remembered coming to the Mandate of Palestine after World War II.[45] However, the *Tung An* was "far worse than almost any boat which brought refugees to Israel in the 1940s except perhaps for the famous refugee ship *Exodus*," which was turned away by the British Mandate authorities. Drawing parallels between Vietnamese refugees seeking asylum in the present and Holocaust refugees seeking refuge in Historic Palestine, Weissberger thus not only represented Israel as a nation of Jewish refugees well positioned to empathize with the Vietnamese refugees, but also moralized the history of Zionist settlement in Palestine as one of refugee displacement.

Eliding Israeli leaders' initial hesitancy to resettle more Vietnamese refugees after the first wave of sixty-six, Weissberger asserted that "everyone in Israel was unanimous in welcoming those refugees." He also claimed that, even if the refugees were not Vietnamese, "we would still take some, because we have suffered so greatly as refugees ourselves and cannot remain indifferent and watch the

FIGURE 7. The second wave of Vietnamese refugees, from the freighter *Tung An,* marooned in Manila Bay, are greeted at Ben Gurion Airport by the first wave of resettled Vietnamese, January 1979. Photo by Milner Moshe, courtesy of the Government Press Office (GPO) of Israel.

sufferings of our fellow beings crowded on a refugee ship."[46] Israel, however, had and continues to have a strict asylum policy, and Weissberger's statement has been disproven time and again. For example, around the same time the Cabinet was debating whether to admit the second wave of Vietnamese refugees from the *Tung An,* it also discussed whether to send assistance to Ethiopian Jews who had been the principal victims of civil warfare ever since Ethiopian emperor Haile Selassie had been deposed in 1974 and replaced by a military regime.[47] Although the Israeli rabbinate had decided in 1975 that the Ethiopian Jews were indeed "legitimate" Jews, the government had been slow to act, prompting Ethiopian Israeli protesters to hold a demonstration in Jerusalem on 8 January 1979. Shouting in Amharic, "Begin, hear our voice and save our brothers," they waved signs that read "S-O-S" and "Begin Let My People Come."[48] The case of the Ethiopian Jews was complicated by not only the Israeli government's support of the Ethiopian government in its war with the Arab-backed Somalis, and by extension Emperor Selassie's policy of rejecting Ethiopian Jewish immigration to Israel, but also by Israel's latent politics of anti-Blackness.[49] This juxtaposition emphasizes the exceptionalism of the Vietnamese refugee case: not only were Vietnamese refugees absorbed (while Palestinian refugees were expelled) and given resettlement benefits similar to those of Jewish immigrants, but they were also offered asylum quicker than this group of Ethiopian Jews, who shared a religious background with the Israeli Jews

FIGURE 8. Vietnamese refugee child, wearing a *kova tembel* and holding an Israeli flag, at Ben Gurion Airport, January 1979. Photo by Sa'ar Ya'acov, courtesy of the Government Press Office (GPO) of Israel.

but lacked the preferred whiteness implicit in the Zionist project. It would not be until the 1980s that Israel would engage in large-scale operations to bring Ethiopian Jews to Israel, such as Operation Solomon in 1991. Vietnamese Israelis therefore exist in an uneasy "third space" created by a "racial triangulation" of Israeli Jews and Arab Palestinians, as well as white Ashkenazi Jews and Black Ethiopian Jews—two binaries that admittedly erase those caught in between, such as Arab Jews, the Mizrahim.[50]

On 24 January 1979, the second wave of Vietnamese refugees—fifteen families consisting of 103 people total—landed in Tel Aviv, having left the *Tung An*, boarded a KLM plane in Manila, and transferred to an El-Al plane in Athens.[51] After being welcomed at Ben Gurion Airport by the first wave of Vietnamese refugees, they were promptly driven to an absorption center in Afula, a Zionist settlement town in

Marj ibn ʿAmir (Jezreel Valley) in northern Israel-Palestine that had displaced the Arab village of Al-ʿAffūla. Founded in 1925 on lands purchased by the American Zion Commonwealth, Afula was the first planned urban settlement in Historic Palestine, indexing the United States' early archipelagic entanglement with Palestinian dispossession. As with the first wave of Vietnamese refugees, the Israeli government provided subsidized, furnished apartments and free Hebrew lessons to the new arrivals. Tran remembers arriving in his family's assigned apartment in the middle of the night and finding bread on the table for breakfast the next morning.[52] After several months, the refugees found jobs at the Afula Hospital, the Ford factory in Nazareth, and the dairy factory at Kibbutz Tel Yosef and moved into more permanent government-subsidized housing in upper Afula. Even so, they faced discrimination for their non-Jewish status. For example, although the refugees were promised tax exemptions for the first six months by a representative of the Ministry of Immigrant Absorption in Haifa, the local tax evaluation clerk insisted that the tax exemption was only given to Jewish immigrants, or *olim*, with an *oleh* certificate.[53] Furthermore, whereas the refugees were promised three months of Hebrew language instruction, their *ulpan* classes were cut short after just a month and a half, forcing the refugees to take on working-class jobs inferior to the ones they had held in Vietnam as middle-class professionals.

Despite these setbacks, the second wave of Vietnamese refugee resettlement was largely seen as successful—a point that Israel made sure to stress to the international community and the UNHCR. In a telegram dated 1 February 1979, Minister of Foreign Affairs Moshe Dayan—who, as noted above, had originally abstained from the Cabinet vote on whether or not to resettle the second wave of Vietnamese refugees—thanked High Commissioner Poul Hartling for the UN's assistance in transferring the Vietnamese refugees, "whose ordeal reminds of the ships carrying Jews around the world, during the darkest hours of our history."[54] Like previous Israeli leaders, Dayan translated the Vietnamese refugee crisis into a particular Holocaust refugee context, emphasizing Israel's position as a historic victim—a nation of Jewish refugees—over its concurrent role as an oppressor—a settler colonial state.

After the first two waves of Vietnamese refugee resettlement, Israel again hesitated to accept additional refugees. Around this time, the Association of Southeast Asian Nations (ASEAN)—including Thailand, Singapore, the Philippines, Malaysia, and Indonesia—expressed concern over the unexpectedly large influx of boat refugees from Vietnam, Cambodia, and Laos and the slow rate of refugee resettlement in Western countries.[55] On 25 May 1979, UN secretary general Kurt Waldheim sent an urgent telegram to world leaders requesting more financial contributions and increased commitments to refugee resettlement.[56] In a response to Waldheim dated 5 June 1979, Begin wrote that Israel would send an additional financial contribution to the UNHCR but that it was unable to accept more Southeast Asian refugees at the time, given the "heavy burden laid on Israel in providing a home and shelter for *Jewish* immigrants and refugees" via the Law of Return.[57] Begin reminded Waldheim of Israel's resettlement of the first two waves of Vietnamese refugees, and again reiterated Israel's special connection to the Southeast Asian refugee crisis: "The grave and compelling humanitarian problem arouses profound sympathy and understanding amongst our people, with its own history and experience of persecution and homelessness. The Jewish People [are] uniquely familiar with the tragedy of the unwanted refugee and his plight."[58]

An escalation in the boat refugee crisis stirred Begin to action just two weeks later, however. On 18 June 1979, Prime Minister Hussein Onn told Waldheim that due to overcrowding in Malaysia's refugee camps, "Any boat carrying Vietnamese illegal immigrants that tries to enter Malaysian waters and attempts to land will be towed away and given assistance to proceed on its journey."[59] Furthermore, refugees currently residing in Malaysia who were not accepted by resettlement countries or their country of origin would be expelled, "the only alternative to their being left to rot in the camps."[60] Rumors spread that Malaysian officials would start shooting boat refugees to deter their arrival.[61] Alarmed, Hartling called for an emergency UNHCR conference in Geneva.

In a letter sent to world leaders on 19 June 1979, Begin expressed concern that an international conference would be an "exercise in futility," given the past inefficiency of such meetings in safeguarding Holocaust refugees during World War II: "As a Jew I cannot forget the useless conferences at Evian [in 1938] and Bermuda [in 1943], whose end results were the non-saving of even one Jewish child out of the one-and-a-half million Jewish children who were dragged to wanton death. Among the Vietnamese refugees there are many children and they, too, may lose their lives until such a time as an international conference convenes, until its deliberations get under way and until its resolutions are adopted."[62] Establishing a special connection between Jewish refugees and Vietnamese refugees, Begin again interpolated the Southeast Asian refugee crisis in a longer history of Jewish refugeehood, going so far as to characterize the contemporary moment as another "Holocaust." He urged state leaders to, rather than convene an international conference, tell Hartling directly that they would commit to resettling a portion of Malaysia's refugee population proportionate to their country's "size of territory and population," thus ensuring a quicker humanitarian outcome.[63] Begin thus positioned himself as an international leader on refugee issues, even as he limited the demographic burden imposed on his small country. In response, the PLO criticized Begin's letter as "a cynical and blatant propaganda gesture on the part of the state, which deliberately caused the exodus of hundreds and thousands of [Palestinians] out of their homeland."[64] Begin's humanitarian gesture toward the Southeast Asian refugees again elided Israel's role in displacing Palestinian refugees.

Begin sent his proposal to President Jimmy Carter, the UNHCR in Geneva, and forty-nine prime ministers. He received replies from countries as diverse as Samoa, Italy, the Dominican Republic, Singapore, Papua New Guinea, Japan,

Australia, Luxemburg, Colombia, Uruguay, Costa Rica, Greece, Lesotho, Finland, Jamaica, Germany, Canada, the United Kingdom, South Africa, and Chile.[65] At Begin's urging, the Knesset unanimously approved a similarly worded resolution on 20 June 1979: "In the name of a nation that in this generation has experienced the most terrible of all holocausts, the Knesset calls upon all parliaments to take action towards the acceptance and absorption of the Vietnamese refugees."[66] Waldheim responded that he thought an international conference would still be prudent and asked Begin whether his government would comply.[67] Begin telegrammed his agreement to participate in the conference, which would take place 20–21 July 1979 in Geneva, though he again expressed concerns that the conference would be a tragic repeat of Evian and Bermuda.[68]

On 1 July 1979, in response to the UNHCR's request, Begin's administration committed to resettling an additional 200 refugees.[69] At the UN Conference on Indochinese Refugees in Geneva three weeks later—the largest international conference to date on Southeast Asian refugees—US vice-president Walter F. Mondale echoed Begin's political rhetoric when he cited the Evian conference and drew parallels between the Southeast Asian refugee crisis and the Jewish Holocaust three decades prior: "If each nation at Evian had agreed on that day to take in 17,000 Jews at once, every Jew in the Reich could have been saved."[70] Evidencing the political entanglements between the United States and Israel, Mondale urged international leaders, "Let us not re-enact [the Evian conference's] error. Let us not be the heirs to their shame."[71] Other US politicians invoked similar parallels. For example, in a November 1978 letter to Israeli ambassador to the United States Zvi Rafiah, New York congressman Stephen J. Solarz explained that he was driven to help the "15,000 homeless and helpless Cambodian refugees in Thailand" by the "haunting reminder of the European refugees who tried without success to find a refuge in our own country from the horrors of Hitlerism almost forty years ago."[72] He concluded that "our own government, mindful of its failure to do anything for those who were fleeing the previous European Holocaust, is determined not to turn its back on the victims of the present Asian Holocaust."[73] In a July 1979 letter to the UNHCR, Vietnamese refugees recently resettled in California also invoked the Holocaust to critique the Vietnamese communist government's human rights abuses and stress the urgency of Vietnamese refugee resettlement: "As long as the present mad rulers in Hanoi stay in power the Indochinese exodus will continue just like the Jewish holocaust ended only after the fall of Hitler. We need help in ridding our homeland of the criminals who are as vicious and coldblooded as any Nazi storm-trooper."[74] In comparing Vietnamese refugee flight to the "Jewish holocaust," these Vietnamese Americans invoked a sense of moral imperative. That moral imperative, however, privileged a history of Jewish refugeehood over the contemporaneous reality of Palestinian refugeehood.

In August 1979, A. Ben-Yohanan, director of the Asia and Oceania Division of the Ministry of Foreign Affairs, instructed Weissberger to return to Southeast

Asia to select 200 more candidates for refugee resettlement. This time, the Israeli committee in charge of Vietnamese refugee resettlement expressed a preference for refugees of ethnic Chinese descent and warned Weissberger to avoid refugees from Cambodia or Laos.[75] Such preferences, however, reproduced global hierarchies as to which refugees were considered worthy of care: refugees from Laos and Cambodia were often overlooked in favor of refugees from Vietnam, given the widespread knowledge of the United States' controversial war in Vietnam and the relative ignorance of President Nixon's "Secret War" in the neighboring nations. Furthermore, ethnic Chinese entrepreneurs in Vietnam—who had made up the second wave of refugees resettled in Israel-Palestine—were often wealthier and more educated than ethnic Vietnamese refugees from the countryside and, therefore, would presumably have an easier time readjusting to their new home. In sum, Israel's explicit ethnic preferences betrayed the pragmatic calculations underwriting the Zionist state's humanitarian gesture.

Guided by the committee's specifications, Weissberger's initial plan was to offer asylum to 63 relatives of Vietnamese refugees already resettled in Israel-Palestine—most of whom were stationed in the Malaysian refugee camps—and to select an additional 120 refugees from the Philippines.[76] The 200-person refugee quota would be filled soon after, once the number of family reunification cases had been confirmed. However, when Weissberger arrived in Malaysia, 36 out of the 45 refugee relatives *refused* to go to Israel-Palestine—a country that they either did not recognize or did not think could offer them many opportunities—and Weissberger could not track down the other nine.[77] Such refusals evidence the ways refugees enacted agency over their own futures, however limited and constrained. In the end, Weissberger did not select any refugees from Malaysia—the country that had precipitated Begin's call to resettle an additional 200 refugees in the first place.

Weissberger also encountered problems at Camp Palawan in the Philippines, where he judged that most of the "good" refugees had already departed, having been offered asylum in the United States or Australia, and only what he called "problematic families" (*mishpakhot ba'ayatiyot*) remained.[78] For Weissberger, the category of "problematic families" included single parents, orphans, and widows—those who, as with the second wave of refugees, were presumably more likely to invite miscegenation with the Jewish population. Although he spent a month interviewing hundreds of refugees in Manila, Weissberger ended up selecting only fifty-five individuals (thirteen families) from Camp Palawan. Included in this group were Hoài Mỹ Nguyễn and his wife, who when they fled Vietnam by boat, never expected that they would end up in *nước Do Thái*, the "land of the Jewish people."[79] By the time Weissberger offered them asylum, they had been waiting in the refugee camp for almost two years and were eager to secure permanent resettlement. Once in Israel-Palestine, they would give birth to Vaan Nguyen, a prominent Vietnamese Israeli poet (discussed in chapter 6).

Under pressure to complete the 200-refugee quota, Weissberger sent a flurry of telegrams to various ministries in Israel to secure permission to visit the refugee camps in Thailand and Hong Kong.[80] They obliged. At the Songkhla refugee camp in Thailand, however, Weissberger encountered a similar situation: "90% of the residents were selected by the U.S. (that began to absorb at a rate of 6,000 a month) and what was left were fractures of families" that had been waiting in the camps for months, passed over by other resettlement nations.[81] Furthermore, no refugees expressed interest in traveling to Israel-Palestine, since only a few had even heard of the country before, so Weissberger advertised Israel's asylum offer over the local radio station.[82] Tellingly, these radio announcements were made in Chinese rather than Vietnamese, betraying Israel's preference for ethnic Chinese refugees from Vietnam. Of the group of refugees who finally expressed interest in immigrating to Israel-Palestine, 35 percent were infected with tuberculosis and twelve had leprosy, so, in the end, Weissberger accepted only 63 refugees (nineteen families) from Thailand.

Weissberger then proceeded to Kai Tak camp in Hong Kong, where he found "exemplary order, discipline and control of the residents, which were clearly missing in the previous three countries."[83] Here, too, however, he faced difficulties. First, the heads of refugee families were required to go out and work for their sustenance, so Weissberger encountered only women and children in the camp. Second, as in Thailand, very few refugees desired to go to Israel-Palestine, which they viewed as a war-stricken country, so Weissberger distributed publicity pamphlets, which included positive testimonies from the second wave of refugees in Afula, to encourage interest. Of those who eventually expressed the intent to resettle in Israel-Palestine, 41 passed the required medical tests and were accepted by Weissberger. However, on the day of departure, a woman went into labor, so her family was left behind and told to petition for immigration to Israel-Palestine at a later date. In the end, Weissberger accepted 38 people (nine families) from Kai Tak camp.

Meanwhile, in mid-September 1979, the Israeli ship ZIM *Sydney*, steered by Captain Ilo Eidelstein, was directed by a US scout plane to a nearby boat containing 41 refugees.[84] The Israeli ship dropped the Vietnamese refugees off in Singapore, with the promise to resettle them if no other state would take them. Although Israeli officials had initially decided that the 41 refugees would not count toward the country's 200-refugee quota, they soon changed their minds once they encountered so many difficulties in locating refugees willing to immigrate.[85] These 41 also initially refused to go to Israel-Palestine, unanimously demanding resettlement in the United States. However, after a "vigorous publicity action," the refugees finally agreed, and Israel was, in Weissberger's words, "saved . . . from disgrace."[86]

On 22 October 1979, the 197 refugees from the Philippines, Thailand, Hong Kong, and Singapore were flown from Bangkok via Athens to Israel-Palestine, where they were housed in a new absorption center in Sderot, a city in southern

Israel-Palestine near Gaza that at the time was mostly populated by Moroccan Jews.[87] Sderot was founded as a development town in 1954 on the remains of the Palestinian village of Najd, whose residents had fled Zionist violence during al-Nakba. Although Weissberger had initially sought out ethnic Chinese refugees with entrepreneurial experience, the group he ended up recruiting consisted mostly of ethnic Vietnamese families who had worked as fishermen and farmers.[88]

This third wave of refugees was met with mixed reactions in Israel-Palestine. The minister of immigrant absorption, Azriel Veldman, and the head of the Sderot town council, Amos Hanania, accompanied Vietnamese refugees from the first two waves to the airport to welcome the third group.[89] The local schoolchildren of Sderot gave the newcomers red roses and Israeli flags. But some Jewish residents expressed resentment at the Vietnamese refugees' special treatment. One commented, "It hurts me to see that they are bringing here non-Jews that will get better apartments than ours."[90] Like the first two waves of Vietnamese refugees, this third wave did not qualify for all the rights granted *olim* under the Law of Return; however, the fact that they were given special assistance at all still generated resentment from those who believed that the Israeli state should privilege the needs of its Jewish citizens.[91] These negative feelings would continue to haunt the Vietnamese refugees in the following decades, even as they gained Israeli citizenship and birthed a generation born in Israel-Palestine yet largely still considered perpetual foreigners.

So far, this chapter has argued that both Israeli and American politicians drew symbolic parallels between Jewish refugees and Vietnamese refugees, between the Holocaust and the Vietnam War, in order to assert Israel's special role in alleviating the Southeast Asian refugee crisis and to retroactively underscore the morality of Zionist settlement of Historic Palestine during World War II. Such rhetorical overtures, however, were made at the expense of Palestinian refugees, as a short article in the *Jerusalem Post* dated 18 June 1979 makes explicit. This article begins by comparing the expulsion of ethnic Chinese minorities from Vietnam with the genocide of Jews in Europe, and ends by calling on the United Nations to turn its attention *away* from Palestinians, who allegedly do not constitute a "real" refugee problem: "The UN's refugee effort has for long been bogged down in the political entanglements of the Palestinian refugees, whose problem it is committed, under pressure from the Arab world, not to solve. It would be refreshing, for a change, if it devoted its energies to a *real refugee problem* that urgently requires the saving of tens if not hundreds of thousands of lives."[92] Blaming Arab nations for exacerbating Palestinian refugeehood by insisting upon the Right of Return, this article pits Palestinian refugees against Southeast Asian refugees in a seeming competition for the UN's limited resources. In a parallel critique, Israeli leaders publicly derided Israel's neighboring Arab gulf states for *not* assisting with the Southeast Asian refugee crisis, distinguishing Israel as the sole Western democracy in the so-called Middle East.[93] Such rhetoric, by extension, positioned Vietnamese Israelis as refugee settlers whose asylum and eventual citizenship in the settler colonial state of Israel was predicated on the ongoing displacement, dispossession, and disenfranchisement of native Palestinians. Thus did the refugee settler condition in Israel-Palestine develop, marking structural antagonisms between Vietnamese refugees and Palestinian refugees, Vietnamese Israelis and Palestinian liberation fighters—two groups differentially positioned in relation to Israel's own national narrative of Jewish refugeehood.

## GIVING VOICE: REFUGEE GRATITUDE, REFUGEE REFUSAL

As part of its attempt to frame Israel as a nation of Jewish refugees uniquely positioned to empathize with the Southeast Asian refugee crisis, the Zionist state has often called upon Vietnamese refugees to express gratitude for their humanitarian rescue. The series *Features from Jerusalem*, for example, features Tran Thuan, an English-speaking spokesman for the second wave of ethnic Chinese refugees from Vietnam, who had told "Israelis how grateful I am" shortly before landing at Ben Gurion Airport in January 1979.[94] Five months later, Tran followed up: "People have been very helpful and kind and we're already beginning to feel very much at home."[95] More extensively, a July 1979 promotional booklet entitled "The Absorption of Vietnamese Refugees: The Israel Experience / L'Integration des Refugies Vietnamiens: L'expérience d'Israël," published by the Israeli Department of Information for Immigrants (*Olim*) and stamped by the Ministry of Immigrant Absorption, includes three letters from resettled refugees expressing gratitude to the Zionist state. Invoking fraternal language, Minister of Immigrant Absorption David Levi opens the booklet by emphasizing that Israel was "among the first to accept brother refugees from Indo-China" because "we the People of Israel know the taste of being pursued and to wander—homeless—amongst the peoples of the world."[96] Presenting the booklet as the "story of the successful integration of two groups of Vietnamese refugees to my country," Levi addresses an international audience when he calls on "other countries to follow suit and accept similar groups of refugees."[97]

The first letter in this booklet was written by Dr. Tran Quang Hoa (quoted at the beginning of this chapter). On behalf of the first wave of refugees, he expresses "deep thanks and deep gratitude coming from our heart[s] and our mind[s]."[98] Tran reports that after two years, all members of the first group have resettled in the Tel Aviv region in "houses provided by the Ministry of Immigrant Absorption and by the administration of the places where people are working." Furthermore, he writes, "we all feel happy and satisfied with our social and professional life in the places where we are living." He concludes, "We always remember that we owe all our success to the generosity of the people and the Government of Israel."[99] Tran depicts Israel as a humanitarian nation and the refugees' resettlement as a success—a testimony that the Ministry of Immigrant Absorption intentionally packaged and distributed in this booklet to showcase Israel's magnanimity.

Similarly, in the second letter, translated into English and French from Hebrew, Long Li Tin Lau, a youth who traveled to Israel-Palestine with the first wave of refugees ahead of his parents and siblings, recounts his harrowing flight from Vietnam, his rescue by the Israeli ship *Yuvali*, and his first days in the country: "The people of Ofakim were very kind to us. After a year, we 10 children who had no parents, were told that we will be moved to a youth village where we will live and study together with other Israel kids. They brought us to a beautiful place called *Meier Shfeyah* Youth Village. They received us with open arms and provided us with everything. We learned Hebrew and other subjects and felt like everyone else."[100] Although Lau says he was made to feel "like everyone else," his experience may have been an exception. Indeed, his testimony is at odds with the experiences of many Vietnamese Israelis I interviewed in 2015–16, suggesting that his positive testimony might have been hand-selected for this promotional booklet. Meanwhile, in the third letter, Tran Thuan (quoted above from *Features from Jerusalem*), details the second wave of refugees' experiences: a generous welcome in Afula, receipt of free health care for six months plus meal subsidies, ease in finding jobs, and resettlement in more permanent housing thanks to grants from the Jewish Agency. He ends his letter by thanking the "kind-hearted and helping friends as we have here in Israel!"[101]

The expressions of heartfelt gratitude depicted in this promotional booklet are countered, however, by instances of refugee refusal to ventriloquize the Zionist narrative of state benevolence and refugee indebtedness. These are moments of slippage when the Israeli state could not orchestrate the intended refugee response. As discussed in the previous section, Yehuda Weissberger encountered many examples of refugee refusal to move to Israel-Palestine while on his mission to select the third wave of refugees. Refugees refused to evidence Israel's self-representation as an attractive refuge, instead holding out for the chance to resettle elsewhere.

A 1986 Associated Press story by Jonathan Immanuel likewise depicts refugee refusal alongside refugee gratitude. He reports that the "young Vietnamese tend to see themselves as Israelis. Huynh Minh, for example, says his favorite subject in school is the Torah, the five Books of Moses which speak of God's promise to give the land of Israel to the Jews."[102] However, when he interviews Dr. Tran Quang Hoa, who by 1986 had found a job as a heart surgeon at Tel Hashomer military hospital near Tel Aviv, the doctor expresses concern whether Vietnamese refugees would ever be truly welcomed into Israeli society: "This society looks Western, but in its depths it is basically religious. Can we really be Israeli without being Jewish?"[103] This tone is markedly different from the unreserved gratitude Tran expresses in the letter featured in "The Absorption of Vietnamese Refugees: The Israel Experience," discussed above. Israeli leaders meanwhile attempted to dismiss Tran's concerns. In the article, Ministry of Religious Affairs official Daniel

Rossing insists that Judaism does not encourage conversions and, therefore, "there is no reason at all why they should feel they have to change their religion in order to be Israelis."[104] Immigration official Arieh Korat, in contrast, acknowledges the material disadvantages of not converting to Judaism: because the Israeli-born children of Vietnamese refugees are not automatically drafted into the Israel Defense Forces (IDF), they could "miss out on job opportunities and government benefits restricted to veterans."[105] These structural disadvantages exacerbated many Vietnamese refugees' feelings of alienation and discrimination in Israel-Palestine. Refusing Israel's narrative of successful resettlement, by 1986 "scores" of refugees had "left to join relatives in Western Europe and the Americas because they were unable to fully integrate, and only 200 remain." Furthermore, "most of those who stayed are scattered throughout the country, and the community is not closely knit."[106] Driven apart by economic precarity, Vietnamese Israelis struggled to maintain a sense of ethnic community in Israel-Palestine.

Today, Vietnamese Israelis continue to practice refugee refusal by countering Israel's exclusive claims to their identity. Disrupting a narrative of unidirectional resettlement, some individuals embody archipelagic orientations, living and working in Vietnam or the United States for several weeks or years at a time before returning to Israel-Palestine.[107] Others acquire multiple passports and nationalities. Hoài Mỹ Nguyễn, for example, recently petitioned the Vietnamese embassy in Tel Aviv for Vietnamese passports for himself and his family.[108] In 2015, he served as a translator for Vietnamese foreign laborers recruited to work in Israel's agriculture and irrigation sectors, thereby bridging the gap between the Vietnamese embassy in Israel, the overseas laborers, and Israeli society. Putting aside the communist-anticommunist divisions of Vietnam's civil war, Nguyễn and others work to develop a more archipelagic vision of Vietnamese community—one that recognizes kinship across nation-state borders.

## VIETNAMESE ISRAELIS TODAY: TWENTY-FIRST CENTURY REPRESENTATIONS OF "MODEL REFUGEES"

After the third wave of Vietnamese refugees resettled in Sderot in October 1979, Israel did not absorb any more refugees from Southeast Asia, refusing even family reunification requests.[109] Between 1979 and 2009, Israel offered asylum to only four other non-Jewish groups: 84 Bosnian Muslim refugees in 1993, who were granted temporary residence in Israel-Palestine until the end of the Bosnian War (a humanitarian act that was critiqued for directing attention away from the contemporaneous deportation of 400 Palestinian Muslims); 112 Albanian Muslim refugees from the Balkan War in 1999, who were granted six-month tourist visas but not absorbed like the Vietnamese; 5,895 Lebanese Christians (Southern Lebanon Army members and their families) in 2000, following Israel's withdrawal from southern Lebanon; and 500 Sudanese asylum seekers from Darfur, who were granted temporary residency permits in 2007.[110] None of these groups were considered "convention refugees," meaning that their asylum in Israel-Palestine was not structured by the 1951 United Nations Refugee Convention but was left, rather, to the discretion of the Ministry of Interior, precluding any legal precedent.[111] In 2009, in an attempt to standardize asylum policy in response to a large influx of asylum seekers, Israel established a Refugee Status Determination Unit (RSD) under the Ministry of Interior, which works closely with the UN to process asylum claims.[112]

Today, asylum seekers come to Israel-Palestine from three main regions: the majority from African countries (mostly Eritrea and Sudan but also Congo, Liberia, Ghana, and Somalia); a few from Europe (including Yugoslavia, Russia, and Ukraine); and a more recent surge from Syria.[113] In 2018, there were about 36,000 stateless African asylum seekers living in Israel.[114] More often than not, these asylum seekers are imprisoned, granted temporary residence but forbidden to work or apply for citizenship, or deported to seemingly neutral third countries such as Rwanda or Uganda (sometimes under the smokescreen of "voluntary repatriation").[115] The Vietnamese refugee case, therefore, is exceptional: not only was it the first instance of non-Jewish resettlement in the self-proclaimed Jewish nation, but it has since proven to be a key exception to Israel's otherwise strict asylum policy. Indeed, Hebrew distinguishes between "refugees" and "asylum seekers"—*plitim* versus *mevakshei miklat*—and while the former is used to refer to the Vietnamese, the latter is reserved for contemporary stateless peoples in Israel-Palestine. At the very level of language, then, Israel draws parallels between Vietnamese "refugees" and Jewish refugees, even as it denies such parallelism to Black and Arab "asylum seekers," let alone displaced Palestinians.

Why were the Vietnamese refugees granted asylum and eventual citizenship in Israel-Palestine in the late 1970s, while the vast majority of asylum seekers since then have been turned away? The answer to this question is complex, indexing both domestic and international concerns. First, Israeli leaders could control the number of Vietnamese refugees they resettled. The Southeast Asian boat refugee crisis was both geographically and politically distant from the State of Israel. Sans escort by transcontinental flight, unwanted refugees from Southeast Asia had no means to claim asylum within Israel's borders. Furthermore, the international community did not hold Israel politically responsible for the Southeast Asian refugee exodus and, therefore, praised rather than critiqued the token number of refugees it did absorb. In other words, 366 was seen as humanitarian excess, rather than a woefully inadequate response. In contrast, current refugee crises are geographically and politically much more proximate to Israel. Many of today's asylum seekers cross into Israel-Palestine by foot, given its shared border with Syria and its geographically intermediary location between Africa and Europe. As a result, the number of asylum seekers from such places as Syria, Eritrea, and Sudan is much larger in scale, and Israeli leaders worry that resettling a handful of these asylum seekers would set a dangerous precedent that could threaten the Zionist state's precarious Jewish demographic majority. Then there is the case of Palestinian refugees, to whom the State of Israel continues to deny the Right of Return. The 366 Vietnamese refugees, in contrast, never presented a demographic threat to the Zionist nation.

Second, as argued above, Israel's resettlement of the Vietnamese refugees was a performance of humanitarianism for an international audience. The hypervisibility of the Southeast Asian refugee crisis presented an already set stage upon which Israeli leaders could rehabilitate their national image after the Six Day War. In contrast, more recent refugee displacement from Eritrea and Sudan has not generated as much international concern, in part because the United States has not pledged as much support; and although the Syrian refugee crisis *has* generated international sympathy in recent years, the potential benefits to Israel's self-image that would come from granting asylum to Syrian refugees are far outweighed by Israel's demographic concerns regarding a mass influx of non-Jewish Syrian refugees, some presumed to be Palestinian "terrorists."

In sum, the Zionist framing of the Vietnamese refugee case as exceptional reproduces anti-Black and anti-Arab stereotypes of Asian docility. Within Israel's racial landscape, Vietnamese refugees have become "model refugees" who do not threaten to disrupt the existing social order: a stereotype that then codes non-Vietnamese subjects—primarily Black and Arab asylum seekers, as well as displaced Palestinians—as always already suspect. Such a conception of "model refugees" resonates with the racialization of Asian subjects in the North American context as "model minorities." When drawing such comparisons, it is important to note, however, the distinct racial politics in Israel-Palestine versus the United States. In Israel-Palestine, white-presenting Ashkenazi Jews constitute a demographic minority even as they dominate key positions of power, and nonwhite Mizrahi and Sephardic Jews have often aligned themselves politically with right-wing populist leaders, given their exclusion from elite Ashkenazi socialist circles. In the United States, in contrast, white Americans who have dominated key positions of power constitute a demographic majority, while people of color have largely turned to left-of-center political parties and organizations to form effective coalitions. As such, although Vietnamese Israelis cannot be considered "model minorities" in the North American sense, many of the characteristics attributed to this stereotype—such as incorporation into what Quynh Nhu Le calls "settler racial hegemonies" at the expense of Indigenous, non-Vietnamese, and nonwhite subjects—apply, solidifying their structural position as "model refugees" within Israel-Palestine's racial landscape.[116]

Given Israel's strict asylum policy and its ongoing settlement and occupation of Palestine, the exceptional case of Vietnamese Israeli refugee resettlement continues to be re-cited in the contemporary context in order to either critique or rehabilitate Israel's image in the international sphere. A 2015 article in the *Los Angeles*

*Times* entitled "One Country That Won't Be Taking Syrian Refugees: Israel" and a 2017 feature essay in *Foreign Policy* entitled "Inside Israel's Secret Program to Get Rid of African Refugees," for example, reference Prime Minister Menachem Begin's 1977 resettlement of sixty-six Vietnamese refugees in their critique of Israel's contemporary asylum decisions.[117] These two articles notably fail to acknowledge the subsequent two waves of Vietnamese refugee resettlement, which generated less international attention than the first, spectacularized act. They also do not account for the ways Vietnamese refugee resettlement continues to direct international attention away from ongoing Palestinian displacement.

Zionist writers cite the case of Vietnamese refugee resettlement as well, though with the opposite intent of promoting a more positive image of Israel to a global readership. In 2012, for example, both Shoshana Bryen's article "Israel and the Boat People" in the *Times of Israel* and Menucha Chana Levin's "Vietnamese Boat People in the Promised Land: Memories of Holocaust Refugees, but with a Different Ending" on *aish.com*, a Jerusalem-based Jewish-content website launched in 2000, commemorated the thirty-fifth anniversary of the arrival of the first wave of Vietnamese refugees to Israel in 1977.[118] Both articles portray Israel sympathetically, and both echo earlier rhetoric that interpolates the Vietnamese case in a longer national narrative of Jewish refugeehood. For example, Bryen writes:

> The experience of Jewish refugees and the hopelessness of statelessness made Israel sensitive to the hopelessness of people from another place, another culture, another war, giving the Vietnamese a place to start over.
>
> (For those rolling their eyes on behalf of stateless Palestinian refugees: It is precisely the Jewish experience with statelessness that impels Israel to continue to seek a mechanism by which Palestinians can achieve the state the Arab states declined on their behalf in 1948—without losing the State of Israel.)[119]

According to Bryen, Israel's resettlement of the Vietnamese refugees was not hypocritical in regard to Israel's policy toward Palestinian refugees, since Israel officially supports a two-state solution. This invocation of a two-state solution, however, fails to acknowledge the settler colonial foundation of the State of Israel, the continual disenfranchisement of Palestinians living within Israel's 1948 borders, and the ongoing settlement of the occupied West Bank and Gaza. Blaming Arab nationalism rather than Zionist aggression for the current lack of an independent Palestinian state, Bryen invokes Vietnamese Israelis as a form of "yellowwashing" in her attempt to defend Israel from criticism.[120]

Sarit Catz's 2012 article "On Refugees and Racism, a Double Standard against Israel," published by the Committee for Accuracy in Middle East Reporting in America (CAMERA), is even more defensive of Israel. In response to major news outlets that had critiqued Israel for the recent repatriation of undocumented African migrants, Catz offers examples of Israel's benevolence toward racialized refugees, such as the "*black* Ethiopian Jews" in the 1980s and 1990s and the

Vietnamese in the 1970s.[121] Catz's use of italics here is pointed, as well as her vehement assertion that "never before had black Africans been taken from Africa, not from freedom to slavery but from slavery to freedom. No other nation has ever done that. Only Israel." In a move that can be called "blackwashing"—akin to Fujikane's theorization of "yellowwashing"—Catz paints Israel as a haven for African diasporics, denying a longer history of structural anti-Blackness in Israel.[122] As the United States promotes a narrative of American exceptionalism in order to elide the archipelagic nature of its military empire, so too does Israel promote a story of Israeli exceptionalism: one of unparalleled morality and supposed racial liberalism.

Some Zionist writers cite the Vietnamese case to argue that the Israeli state's recent asylum decisions tarnish Israel's reputation. In her 2012 article "I Remember When Israel Rescued Non-Jewish Refugees," Lisa Goldman juxtaposes a portrait of Eritrean refugees "who were left to bake in the desert sun for a week without food or medical help, while the army prevented activists from bringing food or a physician to examine them," with an image of Israeli magnanimity toward the Vietnamese refugees.[123] Israeli writer Hillel Halkin offers a pragmatic solution to the question of Sudanese asylum seekers in his 2007 article "A Shame on Israel." Chastising Prime Minister Ehud Olmert's unsympathetic response to the Sudanese refugees who crossed the border from Egypt into Israel-Palestine, Halkin argues that Olmert should have accepted a small number of Sudanese refugees as a symbolic gesture, akin to Begin's move of "pure theater" in the 1970s.[124] Halkin agrees with Olmert's assertion that Israel cannot solve the Sudanese refugee problem—indeed, he believes that Israel already suffers from too many "illegal foreign laborers." Nonetheless, he posits that absorbing a token number of Sudanese refugees would help to counter some of Israel's negative "propaganda."[125]

Extending Halkin's argument, Hirsch Goodman, in a 2014 *New York Times* op-ed entitled "Losing the Propaganda War," bemoans the fact that "Israel is letting itself be branded an apartheid state—and even encouraging it."[126] In addition to citing the military buildup in the occupied territories as contributing to this negative propaganda, Goodman writes: "Instead of welcoming Eritrean and Sudanese refugees seeking asylum—the way that a former Likud Party prime minister, Menachem Begin, did in 1977 with the Vietnamese boat people, saying they reminded him of Jewish refugees during the Holocaust—Israel is confining today's asylum-seekers to a camp in the desert, providing reams of footage to those who want to prove Israel is a racist society."[127] Conversely, to accept a token number of Eritrean and Sudanese refugees in the present would vastly improve Israel's vexed image in the international sphere. Such open displays of political calculation in the contemporary moment shed light on some of the rhetorical considerations at play during the original period of Vietnamese refugee resettlement in the 1970s. The image of Begin welcoming the Vietnamese refugees to Israel helped to recuperate Israel's reputation by directing attention away from the Zionist state's apartheid policies.

Other Zionist organizations appropriate the case of Vietnamese refugee resettlement to assert Israel's moral superiority in the Middle East.[128] For example, as part of their "Israel: The Oldest Democracy in the Middle East" campaign, BlueStar, a nonprofit 501(c)(3) organization "dedicated to empowering the next generation of Israel advocates and leaders," distributed a poster asking, "Which Middle Eastern Country Provided Refuge and Citizenship to 350 Homeless Vietnamese Desperately Seeking Political Asylum? Only Israel." On the poster, the question and answer appear in stark white text against a ruby-red backdrop.[129] Designed to criticize the surrounding Arab nations as a region of "tyranny and unrest" and align Israel with a Western political order of liberal democratic rule, this poster again translates Vietnamese refugee displacement into a longer history of Jewish Israeli refugeehood. Two black-and-white photos of seemingly destitute Southeast Asian refugees are followed by the statement, "Many Israelis know first-hand what it is like to be shut out from freedom. Despite its small size, Israel has managed to reach out and provide humanitarian relief and aid to others in times of need."[130] Such assertions of course neglect to account for Israel's tendency to deny asylum to the vast majority of its asylum seekers and to continually dispossess native Palestinians.

And what about Israel's special relationship with the United States? An archipelagic framework prompts recognition that Israel's reticence to offer asylum to contemporary asylum seekers was paralleled by the Trump administration's own policy of severely reducing refugee resettlement to the United States. Like Israeli leaders, President Donald Trump justified his position by painting refugees from Muslim countries as potential terrorist infiltrators. Interestingly, the "model refugee" rhetoric used to depict Vietnamese Israelis has also been used in reference to resettled Vietnamese American refugees, as made apparent by headlines such as "As Trump Bans Syrian Refugees, a Look Back at When California welcomed 50,000 Displaced People" and subtitles such as "The US was once a leader on refugee policy—then Trump came to power."[131] Indeed, like the pro-Israel articles cited above, these newspaper articles point to the United States' humanitarian resettlement of the Vietnamese refugees in the 1970s to establish a point of contrast to the nation's recent asylum policy. They also argue that such humanitarianism ultimately benefited the United States' geopolitical influence abroad. According to political scientist Idean Salehyan, "When the United States is seen as a good actor on the international stage, that's incredibly important as a tool of some would say soft power in generating goodwill and fostering cooperation with other things that we care about as well."[132] In both the Israeli and US contexts, then—and here we must include the unincorporated territory of Guam—Vietnamese refugees have been depicted as "model refugees": those whose resettlement generated a positive image for their respective nations while directing international attention away from ongoing settler colonial violence.

## "REFUGEETUDE": FIRST- AND SECOND-GENERATION MEDIA FATIGUE

According to Vinh Nguyen, "refugeetude" is a "form of subjectivity—an experience, consciousness, and knowledge that lingers even when the legal designation is lifted."[133] Even after gaining citizenship in the State of Israel, many Vietnamese Israelis continued to feel like refugees: unsettled, unwelcome, not fully at home in the Zionist state. Furthermore, many passed this condition of refugeetude down to their children, via what Marianne Hirsch calls "postmemory."[134] In response to media narratives that depict Vietnamese Israelis as "model refugees," first- and second-generation Vietnamese Israelis have sometimes expressed media fatigue: that is, a frustration that the media constantly turn to them to evidence Israel's humanitarianism in order to rehabilitate the Zionist state's image in the international sphere.

Media fatigue is exemplified in Simona Weinglass's 2015 article "35 Years On, Where Are Israel's Vietnamese Refugees?", which responds to Prime Minister Benjamin Netanyahu's recent refusal to offer asylum to Syrian refugees.[135] What is striking about this article, however, is that it veers in style from previous articles of this genre. Weinglass openly describes her *difficulty* in finding Vietnamese Israeli informants. She scouts out a restaurant owned by ethnic Chinese refugees from Vietnam in Bat Yam, for example, but the husband and wife refuse to talk to her:

> Asked if he could be interviewed, a 50-ish Vietnamese man smoking outside said, "No, I am just a cook, go inside and talk to the management."
>
> Inside, a woman who appeared to be his wife, said in fluent Hebrew, "No, my Hebrew is not good enough."
>
> Why do you think people in the Vietnamese community are so reluctant to be interviewed?
>
> The woman smiles and shrugs.
>
> Is it because you want to be left in peace?
>
> The woman nods, a glint of assent in her eye, then looks away. The conversation is over.[136]

Weinglass messages twenty Vietnamese Israelis over Facebook, but only one responds with "Hi! I'm not interested, thanks." She also contacts Vietnamese Israeli poet Vaan Nguyen, but Nguyen "declines an interview on the subject of Vietnamese refugees," saying she would rather be interviewed regarding her book of poetry.[137]

Nguyen explains, "Whenever there is a humanitarian crisis somewhere, I get calls from various media outlets asking to interview me about the refugee experience. I don't feel like a refugee. I'm the daughter of refugees."[138] Nguyen bears witness to the media's frequent attempts to recuperate Israel's reputation by recalling the narrative of Vietnamese refugee resettlement whenever Israel is critiqued for its contemporary asylum policies. Such narratives flatten Vietnamese Israelis into one-dimensional "model refugees," eliding their complicated subjectivities. Nguyen resists Weinglass's questions, refusing to participate in Israel's performance of multicultural humanitarianism for an international readership.

Nguyen also critiques Netanyahu's exclusion of Syrian refugees, asserting that "compassion has no race."[139] Yet she is also careful to qualify her argument, distinguishing it from those who hope to restore Israel's international image in order to perpetuate the state's discrimination against and dispossession of native Palestinians: "Bibi will only enhance his resume if he absorbs a few hundred refugees who will not change Israel's demographic balance one iota. My family is not thriving here, but they have hope and a future. It's all relative: at least we're alive."[140] Nguyen refuses to play the role of the grateful refugee—she insists that her family is "not thriving"—yet she also pragmatically advocates the resettlement of Syrian refugees, acknowledging the material precarity of statelessness. In the contemporary political moment, it is the Vietnamese Israeli, then, rather than the Jewish refugee, who calls for Israel's compassion.

Such refugee compassion, it must be noted, does not always translate into Vietnamese Israeli solidarity with displaced Palestinians. In other words, Vietnamese Israelis' media fatigue with the "model refugee" stereotype does not necessarily entail wholesale rejection of the Zionist monopoly on refugee discourse—a discourse that embraces Vietnamese refugees and their descendants as legitimate refugees, akin to Jewish refugees, even as it rejects the asylum claims of Syrians, Eritreans, and Sudanese and refuses the Right of Return to displaced Palestinians. According to Tran Tai Dong (quoted above in regard to the second wave of resettled Vietnamese refugees), "The government doesn't complain about us, and we don't complain about the government."[141] By not complaining, however, Vietnamese Israelis register their tacit acceptance of the Zionist state's ongoing settler colonial violence, evidencing the refugee settler condition.

I end this chapter with the story of Cuc Huynh Sears, whom I met in 2016 in Petah Tikvah, a Jewish suburb 6.59 miles east of Tel Aviv. Petah Tikvah was founded in 1878, following the sale of Palestinian lands in the village of Mulabbis to Orthodox Jewish settlers from Europe, and became a permanent settlement in 1883 with the financial help of early Zionist Baron Edmond de Rothschild. Sears's refugee journey evidences archipelagic connections between Vietnam, Guam, and Israel-Palestine. After fleeing Vietnam in April 1975, Sears and her daughter My Linh were processed in Guam during Operation New Life.[142] One week later, Sears's husband, a US serviceman who had stayed behind in Vietnam, arrived in Guam, called Sears's name on the intercom loudspeaker, and escorted her and her daughter to first Hawai'i and then California. Haunted by the war, this husband unfortunately passed away. When she was thirty, Sears met her current husband, an American Jew, in Oxnard, California, where he was serving in the US Navy. This husband had always dreamt of retiring in Israel-Palestine, and in the mid-2000s Sears acquiesced, becoming the first Vietnamese in the country to convert to Judaism. Tracing the *nước* that connects Sears's multiple movements across Guam, the continental United States, and Israel-Palestine—seemingly disparate "islands" of settler colonialism, US militarism, and Indigenous struggle—renders visible an interconnected archipelago of Vietnamese refugee resettlement.

Part three turns to cultural production in order to theorize potentials for solidarity between Vietnamese refugees and Indigenous Chamorros and Palestinians across the structural antagonisms produced by the refugee settler condition. Attending to what Quynh Nhu Le calls "settler racial tense," chapters 5 and 6 engage the temporal dimensions of settler colonialism in Guam and Israel-Palestine, respectively.[143] Because solidarity does not yet exist in the social sphere, these chapters are speculative and aspirational, offering a political vocabulary for relating otherwise. Chapter 6 returns to the Israel-Palestine context via a close reading of Vaan Nguyen's poetry in relation to Palestinian poet Mourid Barghouti's *I Saw Ramallah*, as well as the film *The Journey of Vaan Nguyen*. Read together, these chapters enact an archipelagic methodology—one that maps the refugee settler condition and challenges to it across Vietnam, Guam, and Israel-Palestine.

# PART THREE

# Unsettling Resettlements

*Archipelagos of Decolonization across Guam,
Israel-Palestine, and Vietnam*

# 5

# The Politics of Staying

## The Permanent/Transient Temporality of Settler Militarism in Guam

By 22 May 1975, the Vietnamese refugee camp called Tent City at Orote Point, Guam, boasted many of the amenities and characteristics of an urban metropolis: "two newspapers, an orphanage, two hospitals and 19 doctors," "hotdog vendors, beggars, thieves and daily church services," "eight dining halls, five movies, 300 showers, 303 bathrooms and a bank that's open seven days a week," plus "a beach, a civic stationery, and a squad of Xerox machines spitting out copies of forms, copies of sheets and copies of copies."[1] This "city"—a square mile block consisting of 3,200 tents to house more than 39,000 Vietnamese refugees—even had its own fire department, police force, and zip code: F. P. O. San Francisco 96630. Despite its approximation of normative urban life, however, Tent City remained an "unincorporated community," mirroring Guam's own status as an unincorporated territory with limited rights under the US Constitution.[2] Moreover, despite its illusion of permanence, Tent City was ultimately transient: "Thirty years ago," the *Honolulu Star Bulletin* reported in 1975, "this rocky plot of red coral dust was an airfield for Japanese Zeros. Thirty months ago it was a drag-strip for off-duty sailors in T-shirts. Thirty days ago the area was an overgrown clump of stubby trees, scrubby brush and snails."[3] And roughly thirty days later, on 25 June 1975, Tent City would be closed in anticipation of the upcoming typhoon season, the majority of refugees having already left for permanent resettlement elsewhere.

Tent City's permanent/transient dynamic is indicative of a larger permanent/transient temporality of settler militarism in Guam—a temporality, I argue, that makes Guam distinct from other spaces of settler colonialism.[4] In the continental United States and Israel-Palestine, settlers project a permanent attachment to territory: a long-term investment in private property that disregards preexisting and ongoing Indigenous relationships to native lands and waters. In Guam, in contrast, the as-of-yet *permanence* of militarized occupation is undercut by military *transience*—the turnover of individual servicemen who transfer between different military bases, caught up in an archipelagic circuit of deployment. Stationed in Guam for short periods at a time, these military settlers are unable to invest in long-term property ownership at the individual and nuclear family level. Their relative *transience* as individuals does not preclude, however, the concurrent *permanence* of the US military's occupation of Guam as an ongoing and iterative structure.

Nonmilitary settlers who immigrate to Guam also play a role in upholding settler militarism. Leland R. Bettis, who served as executive director of the Guam Commission on Self-Determination from 1988 to 2003, offers insight into how "colonial powers have often used immigration to distract, confuse, and subvert the issues of decolonization." According to Bettis, "Immigrants serve to dilute the strength of the native people in a colonized area. Since most immigrants are either citizens of the colonizing country or attempting to become citizens, their loyalties and support will lean toward the colonizing country. This makes them useful colonial tools. In essence, immigrants are part of the colonizing process. They are colonizers not colonized."[5] Lured by the promise of US citizenship, many immigrants come to Guam to pursue the American Dream. In the process, they disrupt Chamorros' genealogical relationships to the lands and waters and undermine decolonial efforts to counter US colonization. Moreover, like military settlers, many of these immigrant settlers embody the peculiar permanent/transient dynamic of settler militarism in Guam. Between the US reoccupation of Guam in 1944 and the lifting of the US Navy's mandatory security clearance in 1962, for example, Guam was overrun by "transient migrants," to quote Bettis, recruited by the US military to build new infrastructure after the devastation of World War II: "U.S. military personnel were only assigned temporarily, and non-U.S. citizen laborers were usually transient hires."[6] The transience of individual military and immigrant settlers, however, coincided with a more permanent increase in the percentage of non-Chamorro settlers in Guam, as "'turn-over' rates were offset by newly-arriving military personnel or contract hires."[7]

After 1962, the demographic makeup of Guam's non-native population changed but did not abate. While the percentage of white Americans from the continent dropped, the number of immigrants from the Philippines, Korea, and the surrounding Pacific Islands increased sharply, attracted by the promise of US wages through participation in Guam's tourism and military industries. Like many of the pre-1962 immigrants, these new arrivals, in Bettis's analysis, "tend to be transient," using Guam "merely as a stepping stone to secure U.S. citizenship before moving on to the U.S."[8] As these immigrant settlers leave for the continent, they are replaced by new waves of immigrants, ever decreasing the demographic percentage of native Chamorros in Guam.[9]

In contrast to immigrant settlers who migrate to Guam in search of better economic opportunities, Vietnamese refugees were products of war, displaced by both communist repression and US military intervention in Vietnam. As such, they had less agency over their routes of resettlement. Nonetheless, when refugees seek refuge in settler colonial states, they too become structurally implicated in settler colonial policies of Indigenous dispossession, evidencing the refugee settler condition. During Operation New Life, Vietnamese refugee settlers embodied the permanent/transient temporality of settler militarism in Guam. Their processing in the unincorporated territory of Guam marked both their permanent incorporation into the settler colonial United States as well as their transient stay in Guam in particular, which served as a temporary layover for the vast majority of refugees. Likewise, the refugee camps that housed Vietnamese refugees during Operation New Life were but transitory infrastructural iterations of the ongoing settler militarist project of occupation, which has shifted forms as Guam's role in US settler imperial policy has changed over time.

Today, Chamorros in Guam must contend with the US military's decision to host an additional 2,500 marines transferred from Okinawa (a decrease from the original proposal of 8,000 thanks to activist pressure) and to destroy sacred sites such as Pågat and Litekyan to build a live-fire range.[10] According to political geographers Jenna M. Loyd, Emily Mitchell-Eaton, and Alison Mountz, support for such military buildup projects in the present are "at times premised upon the memory of the Vietnamese refugee operations" during Operation New Life.[11] Indeed, "many of Guam's public officials have pointed to historical refugee operations in Guam as evidence of the island's capacity for expanded populations (i.e. refugees, asylum-seekers, *or military troops) and military operations.*"[12] A former immigration officer in Guam cited the island's capacity to house the Vietnamese refugees in 1975, albeit temporarily, as evidence that it could accommodate the influx of 2,500 marines and their dependents—whose stay would be indefinite.[13] Conflating the *impermanent* temporality of Operation New Life with the *transitory* circulation of individual marines in a more *permanent* structure of military buildup, this officer collapsed the multiple temporalities and contradictions of settler militarism, arguing that Guam's humanitarian response to the Vietnamese refugees in 1975 necessitated an equivalent hospitable welcome of the incoming marines in the present. The settler militarist rhetoric surrounding Operation New Life, therefore, continues to haunt the present, justifying further militarization of the island and necessitating a decolonial analysis of the distinct temporality of settler militarism in Guam.

To unpack the dynamics of this permanent/transient temporality, this chapter examines three narrative representations of Operation New Life and its afterlives: a Chamorro high school student's article from 1975, a Vietnamese refugee repatriate's memoir translated into English and published in 2017, and a Chamorro-Vietnamese college student's blog from 2008–9. Countering settler militarism's material and rhetorical force in Guam necessitates a turn to these more quotidian sources: forms of self-expression available to subjects with little cultural or political capital.

Cutting across hierarchies of value, these texts are not only intimate and personal but also indicative of how settler militarism attempts to cement structural antagonisms between Indigenous decolonization activists and refugee settlers. As textual objects, they embody settler militarism's permanent/transient temporality in both form and content: they are simultaneously cultural ephemera—transient snapshots of lived experiences of settler militarism that have not yet risen to the status of the literary or historical canon—that have nonetheless persisted, finding their ways into more permanent archives and online platforms. Together, these texts evidence how Operation New Life and its legacies have been understood by native Chamorros, Vietnamese refugees, and Chamorro-Vietnamese subjects—the last of whom embody both Indigeneity and refugeehood. A decolonial analysis of these texts reveals potentials for unsettling the refugee settler condition in Guam.

Overall, this chapter grapples with the politics of staying: refugee settler homemaking in the unincorporated territory of Guam. The vast majority of Vietnamese refugees who were processed during Operation New Life left Guam after a few months, resettling more permanently in the continental United States. One might argue that this departure absolves them from ongoing processes of settler militarism in Guam—that they have complied with Chamorro decolonization activists' calls for self-determination by vacating Chamorro land. This argument, after all, has been made in many other settler colonial states such as Israel, where decolonization entails the removal of illegal settlements and repatriation of native Palestinian land.

Given the distinct permanent/transient temporality of settler militarism in Guam, however, transient populations that pass through Guam, avoiding permanent resettlement, do not necessarily disrupt settler militarism but rather occlude and even facilitate its endurance. By vacating the space of contested sovereignty, these transient populations evade calls for decolonization, leaving the US military's control over the island unchallenged. In the words of one refugee processed during Operation New Life, "Yeah, I forgot about the Guam thing."[14] Therefore, this chapter makes the counterintuitive proposition that it is actually Vietnamese refugee settlers who stayed in Guam, rather than those who left for resettlement elsewhere, who more intimately bear witness to the ongoing violence of settler militarism and Chamorros' calls for decolonization. Such intimacy informs emergent potentials for cross-racial coalition building. Even though a mass solidarity movement between Chamorro decolonization activists and Vietnamese refugee settlers has yet to be realized in the present, the cultural texts discussed in this chapter present examples of what Quynh Nhu Le identifies as "inchoate refusals" of the refugee settler condition: "workings that move and are moved by the dynamic processes and assemblages that compose the thickness of their settler colonial worlds."[15] Such solidarities are as of yet speculative. Nonetheless, they present a political blueprint for relating otherwise in Guam.

## RACIAL MISATTRIBUTIONS: CHAMORRO AND
## VIETNAMESE IDENTIFICATIONS IN
## THE CARCERAL CAMP

Buried under layers of official newspaper clippings, military documents, and government speeches that make up the "Operation New Life" documents archived at the Richard F. Taitano Micronesian Area Research Center is an issue of George Washington Senior High's school newspaper, *The Banana Leaf*, dated 16 May 1975. Named after one of the founding fathers of the US settler state, George Washington Senior High was the first public high school in Guam to serve native Chamorros. In this particular issue of the *Banana Leaf*, a two-page article by Edith Iriate entitled "Concert for Orote Point Refugees" chronicles Iriate's experience visiting Tent City with a group of classmates a few days prior.[16] Such encounters between Chamorro students and Vietnamese refugees were not uncommon: in another article in the *Banana Leaf*, a classmate reports that three busloads of students—chorus members and the Girls' Glee Club—went to sing at Camp Asan to entertain the refugees.[17] What makes Iriate's story notable, however, is its narrative arc of shifting racial identification: though she begins the article by marking her racial difference from the foreign Vietnamese refugees, she is then misidentified as a refugee by American soldiers at Tent City. By the end of her story, this misattribution is replaced with a more genuine sense of identification with the Vietnamese refugees along an axis of parallel yet distinct experiences of US military violence.

One day in mid-May 1975, Iriate and about twenty students from George Washington Senior High rode to Tent City in three pickup trucks and a Volkswagen to attend a concert. This was the first time Iriate had encountered the Vietnamese refugees in person. Initially, she marks her distance from the refugees, voicing shock at their poor living conditions: "'Wow!' The johns were just boxes . . . and the air was full of their scent."[18] Staring openmouthed at the sheer mass of refugee bodies, she observes, "It looked as though this camp went to the tip of the island, you couldn't see the end of the rows of tents." Packed so closely together, the refugees, she comments, "were like ants." This insectoid simile betrays her apprehension at the thought of being overwhelmed by the crowd of "25,000 foreign people"—a potential Indigenous critique of colonial immigration that nonetheless echoes nativist fears of yellow peril invasion.[19] But Iriate also expresses sympathy for the plight of the refugees: displaced by war and temporarily resettled by the US military in Guam, they were suffering crowded conditions in the carceral space of the camp.[20]

Iriate's fear of getting lost amid all the foreign refugees became accentuated when she and several other girls got separated from the other students. Starting to feel "panicky" as the sky began to darken, Iriate and her friends approached three pairs of military personnel to ask for directions.[21] The first pair of GIs laughed at the girls and assumed they were joking about a concert. The second pair of GIs also cracked jokes at the girls' expense, misidentifying them as Vietnamese refugees. The third pair, "two navy dudes," repeated the mistake, asking Iriate and the girls again if they were refugees. In the *Banana Leaf* article, Iriate complains, "We couldn't understand why everyone asked us that. To us it seemed obvious that we weren't Vietnamese."[22]

This point of the story marks the first shift in Iriate's racial identification. At the beginning of the article, Iriate expresses distance from and even slight repulsion by the nameless mass of "foreign" refugees. However, in the eyes of these American soldiers at Tent City, Iriate, a native Chamorro high school student, was racialized as a Vietnamese refugee. In other words, she was racialized as a homogeneous brown Other; although Indigenous to Guam and a US citizen, she was misread as a foreigner. The race of these individual navy sailors remains unmarked in Iriate's account; regardless, their comments reproduce the structural white gaze of the US military as an institution, which racialized both native Chamorros and Vietnamese refugees alike as nonwhite wards of US military jurisdiction.[23]

Although it is the GIs and navy men in this story who are actually more "foreign" to Guam than Iriate and the other native Chamorro students, it is *the students* who were racialized as not belonging in Guam—or rather, as belonging too much, to the carceral space of the camp in particular. On one hand, Iriate and her friends' misidentification as Vietnamese refugees stripped them of their US citizenship and marked them as foreign to Guam. On the other hand, the students' misattribution as refugees suggested that they belonged *in excess*—not to Guam as a Chamorro homeland but to the refugee camp in particular as a space of military control. Although it seems "obvious" to Iriate and her friends that they are not Vietnamese, in the eyes of these military men, the differences between the two nonwhite populations, placed in positions of military dependence, were blurred. In this encounter, native Chamorros—whose homeland had been militarized—and Vietnamese refugees—processed in Guam by the US military—became interchangeable. Both were depicted as passive subjects of military care: Chamorros as natives not yet ready for self-government and the Vietnamese as victims of a bloody civil war. Rhetorically, these racializing practices worked to justify the continued settler militarist presence in Guam: the US military, it was rationalized, must stay to look after of its dependents.

This racialization—this blurring of the native and the refugee as a composite brown Other—was violently imposed from without. But, by the end of the story, Iriate starts to identify with the Vietnamese refugees *on her own terms* as a Chamorro student. Fortunately, the last pair of navy men take pity on Iriate and her friends and offer to drive them around the camp to find the concert. Eventually, "we got close to Gab Gab beach and we heard the band." To shake off their unsettling experience of militarized racialization, Iriate and her friends "went to a coke machine" and put "quarters in like crazy, because we all needed a drink."[24]

The girls end the adventure-filled night by dancing and socializing with the Vietnamese refugees. Iriate is especially taken by a French-Vietnamese refugee named Nick Tran, who had just arrived in Guam from Vietnam that morning: "He is 16 years old, in eleventh grade, he speaks Vietnamese and French, and a little German and Spanish, he loves to play tennis, and his father owns a coffee and tea plantation." Communication prompts connection and identification: "I really got to know him and I was amazed at how much his life was similar to ours."[25]

In her article, Iriate focuses on common high school experiences as the impetus for her identification with Tran: "He knows how to play tennis, and I don't, he goes to a French school and learns to speak English, he said that once his professor was asking him something and he answered him with a 'yeah' rather than a 'yes' and his professor told him don't try to get the American accent. Weird huh."[26] But what connects Iriate and Tran are not only their mutual experiences as students and consumers of American language and culture, but also their shared racial difference in the eyes of the US military. Both are marked by US military intervention in their communities—settler militarism in Guam and settler imperialism in Vietnam. This shared racialization may have sparked a politics of recognition in Iriate. While she began her story by voicing apprehension at the faceless mass of "foreign" refugees, by the end of her account in the *Banana Leaf* she acknowledges the refugees' individuality and expresses a desire to get to know them better: "[Tran] was so nice, now it's got me thinking how many more of him are there around of the 25,000, maybe more!"[27] Distinct yet entangled histories of US militarism ultimately shaped Iriate's sense of connection with the Vietnamese refugees.

Iriate's penultimate sentence best encapsulates the permanent/transient dynamic of this racial encounter between the two youths: "When we were leaving [Tran] asked me to stay, I told him I couldn't but if he ever gets out of there to check-it-out at GW!!"[28] This sentence marks the residual structural difference between native Chamorros and Vietnamese refugees: the latter are confined to the camp, while the former are free to leave after the concert ends. This suggests Iriate's relative mobility and Tran's lack thereof. However, at the level of syntax, this sentence actually indexes Iriate's lack of mobility, not Tran's: "he asked me to stay, I told him *I couldn't*."[29] Tran may suffer from *temporary* immobility: as a refugee, he must be processed by the US military before he can leave the carceral space of the camp. But in the long run, Tran's class privilege as the mixed-race son of plantation landowners, plus his status as a parolee absorbed by the US government, affords him greater transnational mobility than Iriate has. As a transient refugee, Tran will have the option to leave Guam and remake his life abroad; in contrast, it is actually Iriate, as a native Chamorro, who will continue to be misread and underestimated by US military personnel stationed in Guam. Iriate may not want to leave Guam: indeed, as an Indigenous subject, she could likely be invested in a politics of staying, to decolonize her native homeland. However, to stay is also to continue to bear the brunt of US military power on the island. Tran, in contrast, can forget his temporary participation in the settler militarist project in Guam, vacating his body from the space of ongoing occupation. If he resettles in the continental United States, he will have to confront the refugee settler condition there—but he would be seemingly absolved from grappling with his vexed positionality on Indigenous Chamorro land. In sum, Iriate's story makes apparent the complex dynamics structuring the permanent/transient temporality of settler militarism in Guam: without decolonial intervention, transient refugees facilitate rather than challenge the more permanent structure of US military occupation of Chamorro land.

## *SHIP OF FATE*: VIETNAMESE REPATRIATES AND THE POLITICS OF RETURN

In contrast to native Chamorros like Edith Iriate who have stayed in Guam to contend with the US military's ongoing occupation, the vast majority of Vietnamese refugees who were processed during Operation New Life went on to resettle in the continental United States. This steady flow of refugees to the US continent was interrupted, however, by a vocal group of roughly two thousand Vietnamese protesters who over the course of six months demanded repatriation to their homeland of Vietnam. Their reasons were manifold: some wanted to return to families left behind in Vietnam, some pledged loyalty to their homeland irrespective of communist control, and a few even identified with the new communist government.[30] Vicky Ritter, a local Chamorro who volunteered with the Red Cross during Operation New Life, recalls: "People got separated in the chaos of leaving, in the panic. Families got separated. Kids came without parents. Some were pretty young. . . . So, a lot of them wanted to go back."[31] Her husband, Gordon Ritter, who was also working for the Red Cross when the two met, remembers one blue-eyed Vietnamese refugee in particular who helped to sew "black-and-blue, typical pajama-colored dark clothes" for the repatriates to wear "so at least when they got back [to Vietnam] they weren't wearing US T-shirts."[32] According to historian Jana K. Lipman, the Vietnamese repatriates "inverted Americans' understanding of 'rescue' and positioned themselves as the captives and the U.S. military as the captor," drawing strategic comparisons between their situation and that of American POWs in Vietnam, given parallel conditions of "barbed wire, military security, and indefinite waiting."[33] In this way they challenged the US military's narrative of humanitarian rescue—a narrative that in turn has been used to scaffold settler militarism and Indigenous land dispossession in Guam, as detailed in chapter 3.

By emphasizing the carceral dimensions of Operation New Life, these refugee protesters argued that they were being held in the military camps against their will. They demanded that Governor Ricardo J. Bordallo, the US government, and the UNHCR allow them to return home to Vietnam. The federal government pushed back, citing a lack of diplomatic relations between the United States and

FIGURE 9. Governor Ricardo J. Bordallo and First Lady Madeleine Bordallo wave to the
Vietnamese repatriates aboard the *Việt Nam Thương Tín*, October 1975. From the collection of
the Richard F. Taitano Micronesian Area Research Center.

the Democratic Republic of Vietnam. Resorting to public protests, hunger strikes,
and riots to pressure the federal government to give in to their demands, these
repatriates asserted that they had never intended to leave Vietnam permanently.
Some had been stationed on a military plane or ship that had been diverted to
the Philippines or Guam after the Fall of Saigon; some had been under the false
impression that their stay in US custody would be temporary; and some had simply changed their minds regarding their desire to resettle abroad. In one of the
more extreme accounts, thirteen Vietnamese men alleged that the US military had
drugged and kidnapped them to bring them to Guam.[34]

After months of protests, the US government finally gave in to the repatriates'
demands. Phone conversations between Governor Bordallo and Secretary of State
Henry Kissinger resulted in the United States granting the repatriates a ship—the
largest South Vietnamese ship that had evacuated to Guam, the *Việt Nam Thương
Tín*—to facilitate their return.[35] On 17 October 1975, 1,652 repatriates sailed back
to their communist-unified homeland under the leadership of Trần Đình Trụ, a
former naval captain of the fallen Republic of Vietnam (RVN).[36] Stressing a "politics of contingency," Lipman cautions against reading this reversal of the dominant
flow of refugees out of Vietnam to the United States as a "triumphant rejection
of U.S. imperialism or a romanticized revolutionary victory."[37] Despite the *Việt
Nam Thương Tín*'s efforts to fly the Vietnamese communist flag and display a huge

portrait of Hồ Chí Minh, the southern Provisional Revolutionary Government (PRG) and the northern Democratic Republic of Vietnam (DRV) interpreted the repatriation initiative as an American scheme to sabotage Vietnam. As a result, the repatriates were imprisoned in reeducation camps upon their return.[38]

After thirteen years in a reeducation camp, Trần, the naval captain who piloted the *Việt Nam Thương Tín* from Guam back to Vietnam, immigrated to the United States with his family in 1991 under the Humanitarian Operation, a program that, like Operation New Life, sought to rehabilitate US imperialism as an act of humanitarianism by stressing the comparative *in*humanity of the communist government that had imprisoned the repatriates as political prisoners.[39] Soon after his arrival in the United States, Trần began to document his life story "in stolen hours between working the night shift in a convenience store and helping his children adjust to life in the United States."[40] He initially published two thousand copies of his four hundred–page memoir under the title *Việt Nam Thương Tín: Con tàu định mệnh*, one copy of which he donated to the Library of Congress and the rest he distributed to Vietnamese American bookstores. Almost twenty years later, Lipman found the memoir while conducting research at the Library of Congress. With Trần's permission, she edited and translated it into English with the help of Vietnamese American language instructor Bac Hoai Tran.

Published in 2017, *Ship of Fate* is notable for providing a first-person account of the refugee camps in Guam, as well as a full snapshot of Trần's life beyond the high-profile repatriate experience. In matter-of-fact prose, Trần details his *multiple* experiences of forced displacement structured by Western intervention in the decolonizing country of Vietnam. Born in 1935 in Ninh Bình Province in northern Vietnam, Trần joined other Catholic families in moving south in 1954, following the French colonists' defeat at Điện Biên Phủ and the political division of Vietnam at the 17th parallel. This was his first refugee displacement. He then volunteered for the RVN Navy and, after two years of training, became a naval officer. Displaced from the land to the sea, Trần sailed far from home for months at a time. Right before the Fall of Saigon, Trần and his crew evacuated Vietnam on a ship bound for Subic Bay in the Philippines, initiating a months-long separation from his family left behind in Năm Căn. On 13 May 1975 Trần landed in Guam, where he was interned first at Tent City and then, following Tent City's closure in June 1975, Camp Black Construction Co. and Camp Asan. Unable to imagine life without his family, Trần joined the repatriate movement to reunite with his loved ones. After five months in Guam, Trần sailed back to Vietnam, only to be incarcerated in a reeducation camp until 1988. In 1991, Trần moved a final time: bypassing Guam, he flew to the continental United States under the tutelage of the US government, this time accompanied by his wife and children.

Unlike other Vietnamese American writing that focuses almost exclusively on life in the United States, Trần's memoir details multiple journeys out of Vietnam that preceded the post-1975 refugee exodus, evidencing pre-1975 settler militarist

connections between Asia, Guam, and the continental United States. Following the 1961 escalation of US involvement in Vietnam, for example, US officials
began inviting RVN sailors to train at US military bases in Japan, the Philippines,
California, and Guam.[41] Trần's five-month internment in Guam as a refugee was
actually prefigured by two prior visits to the island as an RVN sailor, including a
five-month stay to service a broken RVN ship in 1972—an experience that he
describes in his memoir as a "beautiful" memory.[42] Standing in Tent City in May
1975, he recalls that, just three years before, he had "gone for many picnics on rest
days on this hill, which was covered with trees and located near Gab Gab Beach,"
the site of Iriate's concert.[43] Now that hill had been leveled, and the military uni-
form of his fallen country shed. Trần's "beautiful" experience of Guam as an RVN
sailor belonged to the past.

In her introduction to the memoir, Lipman observes that although Trần does
not explicitly use the "language of empire" to describe Guam, his diction
does index Guam's "nebulous, almost limbo status" as an unincorporated territory.[44] At times Trần refers to Guam as "American soil," "free land," and a "part of
the United States," but at other points he notes Guam's isolated and colonial status,
describing it as a "lonely small island in the middle of the Pacific Ocean, so distant from every continent," that remains "under the control" of the United States.[45]
In a passage lamenting his loneliness in the camps, Trần compares the status of
the refugee repatraites with that of Guam itself: "In some ways, Guam's isolation
reminded me of my own separation from my loved ones. For these six months, I
had lived like a parasite, day in and day out, stretching out my hand to receive food
like a beggar. My life had no meaning whatsoever."[46] Extending the analogy in the
first sentence to the following two lines, this quote evidences, in this moment of
slippage, a radical critique of Guam's territorial status: as long as Guam remains a
"parasite" dependent on the US government for recognition, "life"—that is, political life, what the ancient Greeks distinguished as *bios*—would be meaningless.

Although Trần depended on the US military for food and shelter during Operation New Life and, during the war, had collaborated with the United States as
an RVN naval officer, his memoir does not unilaterally praise the Americans. In
fact, at one point he even characterizes them as "imperialists."[47] What makes *Ship
of Fate* unique, however, is its articulation of an *anticommunist* critique of US
imperialism, distinct from both the communist critique of imperialism outlined
in chapter 1 and anticommunist displays of gratitude more commonly associated
with resettled refugees. "Americans always placed the interests of their country
above all else," Trần observes, "and so small and weak countries were only pawns
in a larger game. America had taken part in the war in Vietnam for years, but not
only did it *not* win the war in that country, it had also abandoned it. To the United
States, the war had been a game."[48] Identifying foremost as a South Vietnamese
nationalist, Trần faulted the United States for putting its own imperialist interests
above its political commitment to defend democracy in South Vietnam.

In his memoir, Trần also repudiates the carceral logics of the military-controlled refugee camps. He notes that although the camp had "plenty of activities, and all our basic needs were met," it was was still "surrounded by barbed wire and had a gate. On the one hand, the base could be seen as an apartment complex, but on the other hand, it could also be seen as a detention camp. It was all the same."[49] This last insight—"It was all the same"—highlights the confluence of humanitarianism and carcerality that characterized Operation New Life, exemplifying the paradoxical rhetoric of imperial benevolence.[50]

Trần's critique of US militarism does not, however, necessarily entail a critique of *settler* militarism—that is, the *settler colonial* aspects of US military occupation in Guam that work to dispossess native Chamorros. Indeed, in *Ship of Fate*, Trần does not distinguish Chamorros from the larger population of Guamanians. When Trần notes "Guam's ongoing hospitality" during Operation New Life, he conflates native and settler positions, homogenizing the two groups.[51] Likewise, when he quotes Governor Bordallo's compassionate response to the repatriates' riots—"We have been trying our best to create a comfortable life for you on the island of Guam. Even though you have organized many protests and created instability on the island, we have tried to help"—he elides Bordallo's concurrent advocacy of Chamorro rights as well as contemporaneous discussions of Indigenous self-determination.[52] Lastly, Trần reproduces stereotypes of Guam as a tranquil island paradise and thus occludes a longer history of transpacific militarized violence. For example, he writes that Guamanians were likely shocked by the repatriates' sometimes violent protests because "the people here lived in peace and had never experienced anything that upset their lives."[53] Such commentary erases Guam's recent history of Japanese occupation during World War II, as well as the role that Guam's military bases played in facilitating US intervention during the Vietnam War. In sum, although Trần's story of Vietnamese repatriation critiques the carceral logics of US militarism, it does not account for the concurrent structure of *settler* militarism on Chamorro lands and waters.

Like Nick Tran in Edith Iriate's story recounted above, Trần and the other Vietnamese repatriates embodied the permanent/transient temporality of settler militarism in Guam: as transient refugee settlers, their stay in Guam was temporary, even as the US military that incarcerated them has so far remained permanent. Although the repatriates' act of returning to Vietnam challenged the dominant US narrative of humanitarian rescue and unidirectional resettlement in the continental United States, it did little to undermine the US military's ongoing settler militarist occupation of Guam. Indeed, even though the repatriates physically vacated Chamorro land, by leaving Guam, they also avoided any responsibility for addressing the military's role in expropriating the land in the first place. If anything, the repatriates' return to Vietnam contributed to the postcolonial Vietnamese state's own nation-building project, which discriminated against Indigenous ethnic minorities within its own borders in an attempt to organize what Nguyễn-võ Thư-hương has called a "national singular": a cohesive Viet-namese body politic predicated on the elimination of "the nation's racial other to make imaginable redemptive universal citizenship."[54] Effective challenges to the permanent/transient temporality of settler militarism in Guam necessitate a politics of staying, then, rather than a politics of repatriation. To theorize pos-sibilities for decolonial solidarity, the following section examines moments of mutual recognition between native Chamorros and Vietnamese refugee settlers who stayed in Guam.

## VIETNAMESE REFUGEE SETTLERS: A
## "DECOLONIZATION CONVERSATION" IN GUAM

Although most of the 112,000 Vietnamese refugees processed in Guam during Operation New Life continued on to the continental United States or repatriated to Vietnam, an estimated 4,000, or roughly 3.6%, decided to stay and work on the island, contributing to the fishing, cooking, agriculture, banking, cosmetics, engi-neering, and airline industries, among other skilled professions.[55] On one hand, the refugees who resettled in Guam became permanent rather than transient set-tlers in the sense that their US citizenship is predicated on, and indeed upholds, US military occupation of the island. On the other hand, their decision to stay in Guam positions them to be more accountable to Chamorro decolonization struggles than those who left. To these refugee settlers, Guam became a perma-nent home rather than a temporary stepping-stone on the way to the continental United States and the full privileges of US citizenship that such a move afforded. Bearing everyday witness to Guam's ongoing colonial status may spark moments of recognition that the US military that occupies Guam is the same institution that intervened in Vietnam and incarcerated refugees during Operation New Life. Such recognition, in turn, would be the first step in forging decolonial solidarity.

Some of the Vietnamese refugees who chose to stay in Guam after Operation New Life were married to US servicemen stationed on the island or sponsored by other Guamanian relatives; dozens of Vietnamese orphans were adopted by island families. Other refugees cite an interest in Guam's tropical climate, prox-imity to Vietnam, and welcoming culture as reasons for staying. One resettled refugee, Kien, praised the "community of good feeling" in Guam.[56] Another, Gia, explained: "I love Guam. Here the people are very open. They're friendly. The cli-mate is like Saigon. It is just like home."[57] To these displaced refugees, Guam felt warm and familiar: an island connected to their homeland by nước, where they could rebuild their lives.

Many of this initial group of Operation New Life refugee settlers eventually left Guam in search of other opportunities; other Vietnamese have since settled on the island, either migrating from the continental United States or coming directly from Vietnam. Today, an estimated three hundred to four hundred Vietnamese

Americans reside in Guam. Those who have stayed since the 1970s are passionately committed to their compatriots, drawing distinctions between the close-knit sense of community in Guam and the competitive individualism of Vietnamese Americans on the continent. According to one refugee, "The Vietnamese community here really loves each other . . . they help each other out a lot."[58] Whereas Vietnamese American friends on the continent tell stories of closed doors and avoided eye contact, this refugee knows she can count on her community in Guam for assistance. When she recently had to go to the hospital, for example, her Vietnamese American friends visited, brought food, and called her children who were studying in the States. Another refugee who came to Guam in the 1980s from the continental United States agrees with this assessment, citing instances of Vietnamese Americans in Guam helping each other with doctor's appointments, immigration difficulties, and car troubles.[59] According to Kim Bottcher, the Vietnamese community in Guam "has taken on many characteristics of Chamorro culture," including the hospitality and reciprocity embodied in *inafa'maolek*.[60]

Today, Vietnamese Americans in Guam work in a wide range of professions: many own popular Vietnamese restaurants, run bars or nightclubs that cater to military personnel, or work in the local agriculture industry, farming and selling vegetables and fruit. Vietnamese-owned restaurants include Pho Basil, Pho Viet, and Lieng's Restaurant in Tamuning; Queen Bee Lounge in Tumon; and Hoa Mai in Harmon. One former refugee is an optometrist at the 2020 Vision Center in Tamuning; another recently retired from working in the IT department at the University of Guam; one opened up Thiem's Upholstery & Supply in Dededo; another runs Mai Market in Dededo; and more recent waves of Vietnamese immigrants have opened nail salons in Tamuning Shopping Center and surrounding strip malls. Overall, Vietnamese American businesses in Guam reflect settler militarism's permanent/transient temporality: although they have been a persistent presence on the island since the 1970s, many individual restaurants and storefronts are short-lived, lasting only a few years before their owners fold them in pursuit of other business ventures.

Other businesses have found more lasting success. Dr. Hoa Van Nguyen, a retired lieutenant colonel with the US Air Force, retired state air surgeon with the Guam Air National Guard, and founding member of the American Medical Center, owns several clinics on the island.[61] In April 1975, when Nguyen was a child, he and his family left Vietnam. During Operation New Life, they stayed at Camp Asan in Guam for two weeks, transferred to Camp Pendleton, California, and finally resettled in Fort Walton Beach, Florida with their sponsor, US Air Force colonel Thornton Peck.[62] Nguyen first returned to Guam when the US Air Force, which sponsored his college tuition, gave him a choice of serving in either Guam, Hawai'i, or Korea. He fell in love with the island again, and once he had earned his medical degree, he returned to Guam in 1995 to work in a medical clinic. In 2005, he opened the American Medical Center, which serves tens of thousands of patients. Overall Nguyen is grateful for the opportunities Operation New Life gave his family and is happy to give back to the community in Guam. Every Sunday he goes fishing on his boat, enjoying the Pacific waters.

For the most part, Vietnamese Americans in Guam are not active in politics. Jennifer Berry left Vietnam as a child in 1975 and was recruited by the Guam Department of Education in 1993 from her teaching position in Washington State to replace the English-speaking but heavily accented Filipino teachers who had previously been instructing the children of US military personnel on base. She attests that Guam is like a "small boat and everyone needs to get along."[63] Here, the vehicle of many refugees' escape—the boat—becomes a metaphor for Guam itself: a precariously balanced vessel hosting a diverse community. Continuing the metaphor, Berry explains that Vietnamese Americans are "not activists, so they don't rock the boat. You don't have demonstrations or anything like that. . . . I just think the Vietnamese living here, they're more interested in making money, making a living, and most of them are in survivor mode, and so [they're] just trying to survive."[64] Another longtime refugee resident and community leader agrees with Berry's assessment: "In general speaking, the Vietnamese on Guam [are] rarely involve[d] in the local politics. . . . They are afraid to take side[s], Republican or Democrat, because they want to maintain neutral to keep everybody happy. They don't pay much attention to local politics."[65] As for native Chamorros, in contrast, "politics is in their blood."[66] While not explicitly advocating decolonization, the last-quoted refugee noted that Vietnamese Americans should follow Chamorro activists' example, "first to exercise their rights, and second, to help with the community. With me, having a voice is better than there's no voice."[67]

In 1985, Vietnamese American leaders founded the Vietnamese Community of Guam. Much of their political activism has centered on helping other Vietnamese refugees establish a haven in Guam. One of the organization's first actions was to apply for federal funding to sponsor one or two Vietnamese families from the refugee camps in the Philippines. Then, in 2008, community leaders heard about two undocumented Vietnamese refugees working on a farm in Cetti Bay who had been stateless for almost twenty years. After leaving communist Vietnam two decades before, the two refugees had hidden in the jungles of Indonesia and then traveled by small boat to Borneo, Palau, Chuuk, and Yap, charting archipelagic connections along the way. Unable to qualify for citizenship on the other Pacific islands, they sailed to the US territory of Guam to apply for political asylum. There, they met a Vietnamese businessman who ultimately extorted them by promising refuge in exchange for agricultural labor and exorbitant fees.[68] The Vietnamese Community of Guam contacted Dr. Nguyen Dinh Thang, director of SOS Boat People, who made a couple of trips to Guam's immigration court to argue on behalf of the refugees. Eventually, they were granted asylum.

Around the same time, five young Vietnamese men who had escaped abusive labor conditions on Korean and Taiwanese fishing ships, and who were also secretly living and working on Vietnamese-owned farms in Guam, approached the Vietnamese Community of Guam for help. Although the men were denied political asylum, Guam attorney general Anne Alicia Garrido Limtiaco prosecuted the case as one of human trafficking, with help from officials on Saipan. After a year of legal battles, the men were granted T-visas and were able to safely resettle in both Guam and the continental United States. More recently, Vietnamese Americans in Guam and the continental United States raised money to sponsor a Lone Sailor statue at the Ricardo J. Bordallo Governor's Complex to symbolize "the significant relationship between the Navy, the sea services, Guam, and the thousands of Vietnamese citizens who found refuge on the island during Operation New Life in the ending days of the Vietnam War."[69] For Nga Pham, attending the dedication ceremony on 30 April 2019 "brought back my memory that, the first time I came here with a thousand refugees, we didn't know the future of our lives, but American people, especially in Guam, opened their arms [and] welcomed us to give us hope."[70] By characterizing Guamanians as "American people," however, she elides the specificity of Chamorro hospitality grounded in inafa'maolek, as discussed in chapter 3.

According to one Vietnamese American in Guam, "Involvement in politics is beneficial for our own Vietnamese community as well as the larger community of Guam."[71] By invoking the "larger community of Guam," this refugee promotes multicultural inclusion in the US body politic: a right that she believes all displaced refugees and victims of human trafficking, not just those from Vietnam, should have access to. However, this liberal politics does not take into account the refugee settler condition. Political activism regarding refugee resettlement is important and necessary, particularly in the wake of war and displacement; however, in appealing to the US government for asylum and citizenship, Vietnamese Americans naturalize US sovereignty over Guam, in effect upholding the US military's settler occupation of Chamorro land.

As of yet, most Vietnamese Americans in Guam do not actively advocate decolonization. As refugee settlers, they are invested in maintaining Guam's territorial status because their US citizenship rights are predicated upon US jurisdiction over Guam. Given the opportunity, some Vietnamese Americans would perhaps vote for statehood, though others cite the lower tax rates and decreased regulation that come with Guam's unincorporated status as beneficial to their small businesses. In sum, because Vietnamese Americans have few incentives to give up the privileges of US citizenship in exchange for an uncertain political and economic status under Chamorro self-rule, they become structurally invested in upholding settler militarism in Guam. Overall, Guam, like Hawaiʻi, manifests "a more liberal multicultural form of settler colonialism" whereby Guam's hospitable culture and ethnic diversity are celebrated at the expense of Chamorro decolonization efforts aimed at curtailing US military jurisdiction.[72]

Such "colliding histories," to quote Asian settler colonialism scholar Dean Itsuji Saranillio, point to the challenges to forging solidarity between

Chamorro decolonization activists and Vietnamese refugee settlers in Guam.[73] I therefore turn to *The Decolonization Conversation*, a blog created in 2008 by Vietnamese-Chamorro student-turned-teacher Bianca Nguyen, to offer hints of what a yet-to-be-realized solidarity between Vietnamese refugee settlers and Chamorro decolonization activists in Guam could look like. Nguyen's blog encompasses many of the formal qualities of what Marxist cultural critic Raymond Williams termed "structures of feeling," conditions that are emergent but have yet to be fully articulated in the social realm.[74] According to Henry Jenkins, blogs are "grassroots intermediaries" that can challenge governmental, military, and corporate media control over news cycles and knowledge production. They document the gestural and evolving thoughts of a blogger working through complex ideas in front of a virtual audience.[75] Anna Poletti notes that blogs facilitate a "kind of co-presence"—a "transformational environment" and "means of creating scenes" for the blogger to "encounter others in."[76] Blogs therefore can call into being an activist public; they embody an inherent *potentiality* for engagement and eventual translation into political praxis.[77] For South Vietnamese refugees and their descendants in particular, blogs constitute a "diasporic refugee archive."[78] Furthermore, as with the temporality of settler militarism in Guam, blogs are both transitory and permanent: they are simultaneously short-lived and performative, outside the economy of traditional publication and yet archived online to achieve a certain permanence, as long as the website remains active.

Bianca Nguyen grew up in Yigo, Guam, in a Vietnamese-Chamorro household: "Christmas time and any type of holiday, it's always a mix of both cultures on the table. You definitely will have Vietnamese lumpia, fried lumpia, fresh lumpia. But you'll also have red rice and chicken kelaguen on the same table. . . . Some mornings you wake up and you hear my dad playing his Vietnamese music, some days you hear my mom playing some Johnny Sablan or Chamorro music."[79] Sponsored by Nguyen's aunt who had married a US soldier, Nguyen's father and his family left Vietnam as refugees in April 1975, landed at Andersen Air Force Base after a brief stop in Manila, and arrived at Orote Point just a couple hours before the tents of Tent City were pitched. Nguyen's Chamorro mother, meanwhile, was the first in her family to earn a college degree, from the University of Guam, and currently works as a Chamorro language teacher. For Nguyen, "having two different sides, one that is Indigenous Chamorro and one that is fleeing from a country during a time of war," deeply influences her thoughts about decolonization, which to her is fundamentally about "correct[ing] a historical injustice."[80] In other words, Nguyen has inherited the historical legacies of not only US settler imperialism in Southeast Asia but also settler militarism in Guam. After graduating from the University of Guam with a degree in business administration, Nguyen worked as a ghostwriter for a campaigning politician before earning a master of science in early childhood education from Capella University. She currently works as an elementary school teacher for the Guam Department of Education.[81] By invoking asymmetrical histories linked via US military intervention, Nguyen's blog invites readers to consider how archipelagic histories of US military violence present one analytic by which to theorize cross-racial solidarity between Chamorro decolonization activists and Vietnamese refugee settlers and thereby unsettle the refugee settler condition and address the structural antagonisms formed by settler militarism.

Nguyen started *The Decolonization Conversation* blog in 2008 while she was a student at the University of Guam. In fall 2008, Bianca and her mother attended the Second Chamorro Summit at the university, a convention that sought to educate the Chamorro populace about their different political options regarding decolonization.[82] Eleven years earlier, the Guam legislature had established the Commission of Decolonization for the Implementation and Exercise of Chamorro Self-Determination. The commission originally scheduled a plebiscite for 2000, endorsed by the United Nations, for Chamorros to vote on whether to change Guam's unincorporated territorial status to either independence, free association, or statehood. Notably, this 1997 law restricted the "self" of "self-determination" to Indigenous Chamorros, and instituted a companion Chamorro Registry to register eligible voters as well as record "the progress and identity of the Chamorro people" for "historical, ethnological, and genealogical purposes" more broadly.[83] The Chamorro Registry legislation defined Chamorro people as

> all inhabitants of the Island of Guam on April 11, 1899, including those temporarily absent from the island on that date and who were Spanish subjects who after that date continued to reside in Guam or another territory over which the United States exercises sovereignty and have taken no affirmative steps to preserve or acquire foreign nationality; all persons born in the island of Guam, who resided in Guam on April 11, 1899, including those temporarily absent from the island on that date who after that date continued to reside in Guam or other territory over which the United States exercises sovereignty and have taken no affirmative steps to preserve or acquire foreign nationality; and their descendants.[84]

Although this legislation refrained from articulating a race-based definition, the plebiscite was still critiqued by detractors as a "Chamorro-only vote" that violated the Fifteenth Amendment of the US Constitution and the Voting Rights Act of 1965. Accordingly, the 2000 plebiscite was postponed.

To address these criticisms, Guam's legislature passed Public Law 25-106 in March 2000, creating a Guam Decolonization Registry (GDR) to replace the Chamorro Registry for recording eligible plebiscite voters. Unlike the Chamorro Registry—a "registry of names of those CHamoru individuals and their descendants who have survived over three hundred years of colonial occupation and continue to develop as one"—the GDR was, more narrowly, "an index of names established by the Guam Election Commission for the purposes of registering and recording the names of the native inhabitants of Guam eligible to vote in an election or plebiscite for self-determination."[85] The law defined "native inhabitants" as "those persons who became US citizens by virtue of the authority and enactment of the 1950 Organic Act of Guam and descendants of those persons," thus changing the date of legal nativity from 1899 to 1950.[86] In response to criticism of the Chamorro Registry, Public Law 25-106 insisted that the "political status plebiscite shall not be race-based, but based on a clearly defined political class of people resulting from historical acts of political entities in relation to the people of Guam." In other words, what united eligible plebiscite voters was not a shared racial category but the political condition of being forcefully interpellated as US citizens of an unincorporated territory following the Organic Act of 1950. To ensure a representative mandate, the law also specified that 70 percent of the island's eligible voters must be registered on the GDR before a political status plebiscite could be held.[87]

By 2008, the year of Nguyen's first blog post, Guam still had not held a decolonization plebiscite. Because of underfunding, lackluster support from Guam's leaders, and confusion regarding the overlap between the Chamorro Registry and the Guam Decolonization Registry, the GDR had yet to accumulate the requisite 70 percent of eligible voters. As a result, in 2007 the United Nations included Guam in its "Report of the Special Committee on the Situation with regard to the Implementation of the Declaration on the Granting of Independence to Colonial Countries and Peoples."[88] Citing General Assembly Resolution 1514, the report reaffirmed that "in the process of decolonization, there is no alternative to the principle of self-determination, which is also a fundamental human right"; and that "it is ultimately for the peoples of the Territories themselves to determine freely their future political status" after educating the populace about their "legitimate political status options," namely, immersion in the administrating power (in this case US statehood), free association, or independence.[89] Regarding Guam specifically, the report noted Chamorros' concerns about the "impacts of the impending transfer of additional military personnel" from Okinawa to Guam and requested that the United States continue to "transfer land to the original landowners of the Territory" and "recognize and respect the political rights and the cultural and ethnic identity of the Chamorro people of Guam."[90] In short, the UN recognized Chamorros as Indigenous people who had been unjustly dispossessed by settler militarism in Guam.

At the Second Chamorro Summit at the University of Guam, Nguyen and her mother listened to a debate between Trini Torres and Joe Garrido, spokespeople for the Independence and Free Association options, respectively, and spoke to different decolonization activists. They left the summit feeling shocked that they had not heard about the decolonization plebiscite before, as well as uncertain as to which option presented a "realistic plan of action for the protection and preservation of the Chamorro culture and the people residing on the island."[91] This experience motivated Nguyen to start her blog, *The Decolonization Conversation: A Journey through the Events, the Opinions, and the Decisions in Regards to a Burning Question Left Unanswered*. Despite its permanent archiving on the host blogspot. com, the blog is transitory in nature: as of the time of writing, it consists of four posts spanning 25 October 2008 and 24 May 2009, plus a follow-up post dated

19 December 2020, written after my initial interviews with Nguyen. The blog is thus akin to what Walter Benjamin characterized as an image that flares up at a historical juncture, rather than a sustained political movement that has fully erupted into the social sphere.[92] However, *The Decolonization Conversation* is significant for representing a mixed-heritage perspective on the question of decolonization: one that grapples with transpacific relationalities between Indigenous and refugee subjects.

A one-dimensional racial analysis might attribute Nguyen's urgent interest in decolonization events—such as a rally at Skinner's Plaza entitled "Reclaim Guahan: Chule Tatte Guahan" and an event hosted by the Guam Humanities Council entitled "8000: How Will it Change Our Lives? Community Conversations on the US Military Buildup on Guam"—solely to the Chamorro part of her identity. However, I want to emphasize the significance of her Vietnamese refugee inheritances as well. In other words, what if Nguyen is invested in questions of self-determination in the face of military buildup not *despite* her Vietnamese refugee heritage but *because* of it? Given her inherited history of US settler militarism in Guam *as well as* US military imperialism in Vietnam, Nguyen is *doubly-positioned* to critique the proposed military buildup of an additional 8,000 marines to Guam, announced by the US military in 2005, which, in her words, "calls into mind our colonial status; did anyone ask the People of Guam first 'would you like a couple of Marines in a couple of years?' Was there a poll to see whether we wanted it or not? No one asked, but gave an order, and they are coming whether we like it or not."[93] Identifying as one of the "People of Guam," Nguyen critiques the island's lack of self-determination. Indexing Chamorros' complex entanglement with the US military—a large percentage of Chamorros serve in the armed forces and the economy has come to rely on US defense dollars—Nguyen quickly qualifies her statement, however, pointing out that she is "not anti-military or what have you" but that she's "just been kicking back and observing this for awhile"— "this" being Guam's "colonial status" as an unincorporated territory, which doesn't afford residents the same rights or privileges as those residing in the continental United States.[94]

In another blog post, Nguyen recounts an experience of trying to sign up for more information on an American online school's website, facing restricted access because she resides outside the fifty states, and then emailing the webmaster to kindly explain that "Guam was a U.S. Territory." The webmaster responded, "'We don't cater to international institutions.'" Nguyen ends the post—the last from 2009—with this insight:

> Ahh. International. So, we're a part of this thing, but not really.
>     So I guess Guam's kind of like the new kid in school; he's sort of part of the school (transcript-wise), but socially he isn't. So what do we do about it?[95]

Nguyen's words characterize not only Guam's seemingly paradoxical status as an unincorporated territory of the United States—"a part of this thing, but not really"—but also Vietnamese refugees' status as recent US citizens living in Guam—"sort of part" of the group but "socially" not. "Group" here can refer to the United States: although US citizens, Vietnamese Americans in Guam face the same political restrictions as other Guamanians, such as the inability to vote for US president. "Group" can also refer more specifically, however, to Guam: although Guamanian, Vietnamese Americans are not Indigenous and thus not typically included in decolonization conversations.

What role can Vietnamese refugee settlers, shaped by a history of US war-turned–rescue operation, play in native Chamorro decolonization efforts? Given their inadvertent role in humanizing and justifying the US military's occupation of Guam during Operation New Life, as elaborated in chapter 3, Vietnamese refugees embody "the power to represent or enact" settler militarism on native Chamorro lands and waters.[96] As settlers who stayed in Guam, they contribute to the ongoing dispossession of native Chamorros. However, Vietnamese refugees' experiences of US military imperialism also present potential points of solidarity with Chamorro decolonization activists who resist US settler militarism. US intervention in Vietnam was predicated upon the colonization of Guam, after all, as outlined in chapter 2. The decolonization of Guam could therefore inhibit future US military interventions in Asia and Oceania, preventing further displacement of refugees by war. In other words, settler militarism in Guam harms not only native Chamorros but also refugees displaced by US military ventures; as such, effective organizing around archipelagic histories of US empire could activate a coalitional critique of US military violence in its myriad forms.

Moreover, on a small island with high rates of interracial marriage, subject positions and personal histories have become increasingly entangled, making it difficult to discuss "distinct" experiences of settler militarism. For individuals like Bianca Nguyen, caught between divergent histories of Indigeneity and refugee-hood, subjectivity is hybrid and liminal—a reflection of Guam's own unincorporated status—as well as "archipelagic," manifesting what Yu-ting Huang calls a "congregation of various geopolitical relations" informed by "interlacing stories" of militarized displacement and settlement.[97] "So," to repeat Nguyen's question, "what do we do about it?" Vietnamese refugees, Chamorro natives, and those caught in the mix must engage in a "decolonization conversation" in order to become "multilingual in each other's histories"—the only way to resist the structural antagonisms enacted by settler militarism in Guam.[98]

## "HORIZON OF CARE": DECOLONIZATION IN GUÅHAN TODAY

Since Bianca Nguyen first started *The Decolonization Conversation* blog in 2008, the decolonization movement in Guam has grown dramatically: activist groups such as Independent Guåhan, the Fanohge Coalition, and Prutehi Litekyan: Save Ritidian regularly host events, protests, and educational sessions. Decolonization is discussed openly on podcasts and the radio, and more people have expressed interest in learning the Chamorro language as well as traditional arts.[99] Yet Guam remains an unincorporated territory, neither fully independent nor fully integrated in the settler imperial United States. In March 2012, Arnold "Dave" Davis, a white American settler and longtime resident of Guam, filed a lawsuit against Guam's government asserting that the Guam Decolonization Registry discriminates against non-Chamorro US citizens. A retired officer of the US Air Force, Davis embodies settler militarism's ongoing attempts to undermine Chamorro self-determination. Davis argued that the GDR violates his Fifteenth Amendment rights against voter discrimination based on race: as a US citizen, he too should have the right to vote in a decolonization plebiscite held in a US territory where (most) constitutional rights apply. In March 2017, US district court chief judge Frances Tydingco-Gatewood ruled in favor of Davis, striking down Guam's plebiscite law as unconstitutional and prohibiting the decolonization plebiscite to proceed. According to Judge Tydingco-Gatewood, the plebiscite law violated the Fifteenth Amendment by discriminating against settler voters for not having the "correct ancestry or bloodline."[100]

Judge Tydingco-Gatewood's reference to the Fifteenth Amendment in her ruling naturalized US military occupation of Guam as a permanent ontology, denying the existence of a historical moment *before* the temporality of settler militarism. In other words, the decolonization plebiscite was meant to address not only the structure but also the *event* of US military occupation: to acknowledge that there was a time *prior to* US jurisdiction over Guam and, by extension, prior to the application of the Fifteenth Amendment.[101] Participating in a decolonization plebiscite is *not* the right of all US citizens in Guam, but rather only those who experienced the life-shattering event of colonization, plus their descendants.

Guam's governor at the time, Eddie Calvo, vowed to fight Judge Tydingco-Gatewood's decision in an appeals court. Attorney Julian Aguon argued that the GDR's designation of "native inhabitants" was a political classification, not a racial one. In July 2019, however, the Ninth US Circuit Court of Appeals ruled against Guam. Contradicting the United Nations Declaration on the Rights of Indigenous Peoples to "freely determine their political status," Circuit Judge Marsha Berzon affirmed the district court's ruling that "Guam's limitation on the right to vote in its political status plebiscite to 'Native Inhabitants of Guam' violates the Fifteenth Amendment," again mistakenly categorizing Indigeneity as a race rather than a political subjectivity.[102] On 4 May 2020, the US Supreme Court denied Guam's appeal of the Ninth Circuit Court decision. The fact that the US courts have the power to arbitrate Chamorros' struggle for decolonization at all further highlights Guam's continued colonial status.

Refusing defeat, Chamorro activists and their allies persist in strategizing different methods for decolonization. Bianca Nguyen expresses hope that "within my daughter's lifetime, we actually do have a plebiscite."[103] Effective decolonization, however, must take into account the distinct temporality of settler militarism in Guam: the ways the structural permanence of the US military as an institution is often occluded, and even upheld, by the transience of individual settlers, including refugee settlers. Indigenous decolonization does not preclude what Glen Coulthard (Yellowknives Dene First Nation) terms "radical hospitality" toward refugees.[104] Indeed, as Michelle Daigle and Margaret Marietta Ramírez argue, native displacement by settler militarism "compels Indigenous peoples to welcome other dispossessed peoples into their/our homelands, according to their/our own laws, as they become displaced through the violence of racial capitalism" and military imperialism.[105]

In "Care," the first poem featured in his 2018 triptych "Crosscurrents (Three Poems)," Chamorro poet Craig Santos Perez models such "radical hospitality," alternatively understood as *inafa'maolek*, while also critiquing the role Western nations play in displacing refugees. Across nineteen stanzas of two lines each, "Care" refracts Perez's admiration for Syrian refugee resilience through his own efforts to soothe and protect his then sixteen-month-old daughter. Imagining what would happen if the space between Syria and his current home on the island of O'ahu were to suddenly collapse, he writes of the "Pacific trade winds suddenly / [becoming] helicopters" and the shadows cast by "plumeria / tree branches" morphing into "soldiers and terrorists marching / in heat." Perez asks himself if he would be able to display the same strength and fortitude as those Syrian refugees fleeing war: "Would we reach the desperate boats of / the Mediterranean in time? If we did, could I straighten / my legs into a mast, balanced against the pull and drift / of the current?"[106] Here, Syrian refugee passage is marked by water, by *hånom*, by *nước*, calling to mind the passage of Vietnamese boat people four decades earlier. Perez thus enacts not only a spatial suturing—Syria to O'ahu—but a temporal one—the refugee crises of the 1970s and 1980s to today.

"Care" ends by calling on Western countries to open their homes to those in need of refuge, compelled not by paternalistic benevolence but by the instructive teaching of refugees, whose resilient love defies borders and walls. Expressing hope that refugees' love "will teach the nations that emit / the most carbon and violence / that they should, instead, remit the most / compassion," Perez represents refugees not as helpless victims, but as teachers of compassion; resettlement nations, in turn, are depicted not as humanitarian saviors but as perpetrators responsible for violence and global warming, who should learn from refugees.[107] The poem's closing lines query distinctions between "legal refugee[s]"—those who adhere to narrow UN definitions of political asylum—and "illegal migrant[s]"—a term used to describe Syrian as well as Central American asylum seekers to the United States, and which disavows the role Western intervention has played in destabilizing these Global South economies in the first place. In place of these distinctions, Perez envisions a "horizon of care," indexing an opening of homes, an offering of refuge, that does *not* reify the exclusionary power of settler nation-states but rather suggests a multiplicity of belonging—one that can account for Indigenous sovereignty and refugee home-making alike.[108] In this poem, an archipelagic critique of settler colonialism encompasses both Indigenous "radical hospitality" *and* refugee pedagogies of compassion. Here, distinct yet entangled histories of displacement, via settler militarism and settler imperialism, beget a shared vision of decolonization across Guåhan and the Global South.

# 6

## The Politics of Translation

*Competing Rhetorics of Return in Israel-Palestine and Vietnam*

In the second stanza of "Packing Poem," Vietnamese Israeli poet Vaan Nguyen translates between images of stillness and movement, rest and migration, to capture the complex contradictions of being both an Israeli-born citizen in Historic Palestine and the daughter of Vietnamese boat refugees displaced by war:

> The chopsticks rest diagonally
> matching the movement of birds along a waterfall.
> How can they stall their transmission and keep eating rice
> before their night migration?[1]

Invoking images of Vietnamese culture—chopsticks, birds, rice—Nguyen paints a scene of reluctant "night migration": a desire to "rest" and "stall" before leaving one's homeland for the unknown. When offered resettlement in Israel, Vietnamese refugees often hesitated, uncertain about their prospects in a seemingly embattled Zionist state. For Vietnamese Israelis, resettlement, or "rest," is therefore always undercut by the "movement of birds": an unsettled and migratory form of belonging in the settler colonial state.

This incessant translation between stillness and movement informs the narrator's invocation of Armageddon in the latter part of the poem's second stanza, in what can be read as a nod to more recent waves of refugee migration to Israel-Palestine:

> Under the cover of delusions,
> all I wanted was to point and warn everyone "that's Armageddon"
> to ask whether foreigners have
> inflatable boats.[2]

Dismissing as "delusions" the Israeli media's alarmist representations of recent asylum seekers from Eritrea, Sudan, and Syria as a foreign invasion, the narrator instead warns of impending "Armageddon," referring to the biblical battle between good and evil before the Day of Judgement. Anticipating a conflict over the nation's soul, the narrator wonders: Will Israel embrace the new refugees or succumb to exclusionary rhetoric? And, if turned away, will the refugees have "inflatable boats" to carry them along their "night migration," or will they sink into the sea, the *nước*, as so many Vietnamese boat refugees did during the exodus of the 1970s and 1980s?

This chapter analyzes cultural representations of Vietnamese Israelis and their descendants—the first non-Jewish, non-Palestinian group of refugees to be granted asylum and eventual citizenship in Israel-Palestine—through the trope of translation. Translation indicates both physical movement, the removal from one place to another, from the Old French *translater*, derived from the Latin *translates* (*trans* "across, beyond" + *latus* "borne, carried"), as well as linguistic movement, from one language to another, a meaning that developed in the early fourteenth century. The spatial translation of Vietnamese refugees from Vietnam to Israel-Palestine and back necessitates a series of symbolic translations across language, nation, culture, and memory: translations that are ongoing and multilayered, shaped by both Vietnam's anticolonial civil war and Israel-Palestine's settler colonial context. In "The Task of the Translator," Walter Benjamin argues that seamless translation is impossible, given inherent differences in syntax, symbols, and worldview. Likewise, postcolonial theorist Gayatri Chakravorty Spivak emphasizes translation's inevitably "catachrestic" nature.[3] Both argue, however, that translation is a necessary and ethical project, as every translation extends closer to the horizon of "pure language," which Benjamin defines not as an expression or approximation of thought but rather as something greater: the Word itself.[4] Whereas Benjamin probes the spiritual dimensions of pure language, in this chapter I explore its decolonial possibilities. Like Spivak, I argue that the goal of translation is not to collapse difference, but to recognize and communicate across it: to understand translation as an "incessant shuttle" that can destabilize structural antagonisms between Vietnamese Israelis and native Palestinians in order to render legible emergent solidarities between seemingly incommensurable subject positions.[5]

Translation intimately shapes Vietnamese Israelis' modes of subject formation. Linguistically, Vietnamese Israeli families must translate between Vietnamese, the language of first-generation refugees, and Hebrew, the language of subsequent generations born in Israel-Palestine, in their everyday interactions. Conceptually, Vietnamese Israelis translate their understandings of home-making, belonging, and refugeehood from Vietnam to Israel-Palestine and back. Analytically, researchers who study Vietnamese Israelis must translate between existing scholarship on Vietnamese refugees, the majority of which derives from North America, and the racial politics of Israel-Palestine. Translation, in sum, operates across multiple vectors—language, culture, space, time—and multiple scales—local, global, diasporic, archipelagic.

This chapter analyzes the politics of translation in Israel-Palestine and Vietnam via the work of the prominent Vietnamese Israeli poet and actress Vaan Nguyen. Born in 1982 in the coastal city of al-Majdal Asqalan (renamed Ashkelon by Israeli settlers), Nguyen is one of five daughters of Vietnamese refugees who came to Israel-Palestine in 1979 as part of the third wave of refugee resettlement. After moving around, her family settled in Jaffa Dalet, a working-class neighborhood in the southern part of Yafa (renamed Tel Aviv–Jaffa) heavily populated by both Mizrahi immigrants from abroad and Palestinians displaced from the older part of Yafa, near the sea.[6] In 2005, Nguyen starred in Duki Dror's documentary film *The Journey of Vaan Nguyen*; in 2008, she published her first chapbook of poetry, *The Truffle Eye* (*Ein Ha-kemehin*); and in 2018, she published her second collection of poems, *Vanity Intersection* (*Hituch Hehavalim*). Nguyen participated in "Guerrilla Culture" (*Gerila Tarbut*), an activist collective founded by Mati Shemoelof in 2007 that staged social justice demonstrations through poetry and music.[7] Issues addressed include the occupation of Palestine, labor unionization, and antiracist critique.

Originally written in Hebrew, Vaan Nguyen's poems are marked by their translation into English. Indeed, Vaan Nguyen's name itself is inflected by its passage from Vietnamese, to Hebrew, to English, reflecting Trinh T. Minh-ha's insight that "translation seeks faithfulness and accuracy and always ends up betraying either the letter of the text, its spirit, or its aesthetics."[8] "Vân," meaning "cloud" in Vietnamese, becomes the homophonic "ואן" in Hebrew, which is transliterated into "Vaan" in English—the doubling of the vowel *a* a characteristic absent from both the Hebrew and Vietnamese. "Vaan" is thus an inherently archipelagic name, bearing the residue of its translation across multiple languages, continents, and cultures.

Translation, furthermore, invites comparison across seemingly incommensurable rhetorics of return: the Law of Return for Jewish immigrants to Israel, the Right of Return for Palestinian refugees and exiles to Palestine, and the journey of return for Vietnamese refugees to postwar Vietnam. Whereas Jewish return has been facilitated by militarized violence and settler colonialism, Palestinian return, rooted in humanitarianism and international law, remains a yet-to-be-realized aspiration. Vietnamese return, in turn, does not necessarily resolve the refugee settler condition. Translation, however, can facilitate decolonial solidarities between Vietnamese Israelis, displaced by war, and Palestinians, displaced by settler colonialism: two groups otherwise divided by structural antagonisms in Israel-Palestine.

As Israeli citizens, resettled Vietnamese refugees and their descendants are politically implicated in the Israeli state's ongoing settler colonial violence against Indigenous Palestinians. It is important to note that Vietnamese Israelis such as Vaan Nguyen serve in the Israel Defense Forces, which terrorize Palestinians within

Israel as well as the Occupied Territories. Although both Vietnamese Israelis and Palestinians are marginalized by the Zionist state, wherein cultural citizenship is equated with Jewish identity, their marginalization operates unequally: while the former suffer cultural exclusion despite their de jure citizenship, the latter are systematically dispossessed and displaced from their lands. While the Israeli state racializes Palestinians as terrorist threats to national security, Vietnamese Israelis are upheld as proof of a multicultural democracy. De jure inclusion of Vietnamese Israelis directs attention away from Israel's settler colonial exclusion of Palestinians, a strategy that Candace Fujikane has critiqued as "yellowwashing."[9] Indeed, the very inclusion of Vietnamese Israelis in the so-called Jewish democratic state promulgates the racialization of Palestinians as the ultimate Other, against which Vietnamese Israelis as "model refugees" can be comparatively absorbed.[10]

Palestinians, in turn, are not a homogeneous group. Rather, their different political statuses derive from their distinct geographical relationships to Israeli settler colonialism: third-class citizens within Israel's 1948 borders, surveilled subjects in the Occupied Territories of the West Bank and Gaza, displaced refugees in a neighboring camp, or resettled exiles residing abroad. Politically, however, Palestinians embody a unified nation; as displaced native people, they are united in their Indigenous claim to Palestine. The refugee settler condition, therefore, implicates Vietnamese Israelis in the dispossession of *all* Palestinians, regardless of political status, inhibiting any meaningful coalition between the two communities from yet being realized in the present. Indeed, Vietnamese Israelis often come to identify with the Israeli security state, seeing their fate as tied to that of Jewish Israelis (*người Do Thái*). Despite the fact that "the overwhelming majority of Palestinians have not demanded Jewish-Israelis removal" in their calls for decolonization, but rather "only a relinquishment of their desire to rule," Vietnamese Israelis worry that if Palestinians were to regain sovereignty, they too would be expelled from Palestine, becoming refugees yet again.[11] Therefore, Vietnamese Israelis' affective and material investment in resettlement—what this book calls refugee settler desire—translates into an implicit investment in settler colonialism.

Given this refugee settler condition, how can we begin to theorize solidarity between Vietnamese Israelis and Palestinians? As in the previous chapter about settler militarism in Guam, countering such structural antagonisms between refugee settlers and displaced natives necessitates a turn to the literary and visual arts. We do not yet have the political vocabulary to articulate solidarity between Vietnamese Israelis and Palestinians across the impasses of settler colonialism, but a close reading of poetry and film from these respective communities renders legible resonant "structures of feeling" that have yet to be fully articulated in the present.[12] Such resonances, in turn, invite emergent translations between Vietnamese Israelis and Palestinians along the axis of displacement from ancestral lands: a key theme in Palestinian cultural production.[13] In this analysis, cultural production is not prescriptive but rather suggestive: slippages and gaps opened up by translation's catachresis present opportunities for imagining otherwise.

This chapter proceeds in two parts. Identifying affective and thematic connections between Mourid Barghouti's *I Saw Ramallah* and Vaan Nguyen's *The Truffle Eye*, the first section attends to incessant translations between the unstable signifiers of native, settler, refugee, and exile. Destabilizing the very categories that divide Palestinians and Vietnamese Israelis under the refugee settler condition, I posit an exilic poetics that critiques the settler colonial state's forms of exclusion in favor of more pluralized modalities of belonging. Such poetics not only "disrupt the incommensurability of Jewish and Palestinian belonging" but challenge the seeming incommensurability of native Palestinian and Vietnamese refugee settler belonging as well.[14] Key here is an engagement with temporality: a critique of linear narratives of autochthony in favor of recognizing what Barghouti calls overlapping "shape[s] of time" (*shakl awqātinā fīhi*).[15]

The chapter's second section focuses on Duki Dror's 2005 film, *The Journey of Vaan Nguyen*, to examine the translation—or rather, inevitable mistranslation—of the refugee setter condition from Israel-Palestine back to Vietnam. What happens when Vietnamese Israelis travel to Vietnam to reclaim their own ancestral lands, which were redistributed by the communist government when they fled Vietnam as refugees, and translate the political vocabulary of competing land claims from Israel-Palestine to their own postwar homeland? In a key scene in the film, Vaan Nguyen's father, Hoài Mỹ Nguyễn, identifies the Vietnamese family that settled on his ancestral lands in Vietnam as *olim khadashim*, or "new immigrants," which in the Israeli context refers exclusively to Jewish immigrants who migrate to Israel under the Law of Return. Derived from the Hebrew term *aliyah*, *olim* infuses Jewish immigration to the Holy Land with the religious connotation of an ascension to Mount Zion. In another layer of translation, the film's English subtitles translate *olim khadashim* not as "new immigrants" but as "settlers," with all of the latter word's political connotations in the Zionist state. This startling translational collision of multiple political contexts invites archipelagic comparisons between the distinct yet parallel processes of settlement and land appropriation that have structured both Israel-Palestine and postwar Vietnam. In sum, an archipelagic framework probes how questions of land, water, Indigeneity, refugeehood, settlement, and exile resonate across multiple narratives of belonging and return, shaping political possibilities for Jewish settlers, Palestinian natives, and Vietnamese refugee settlers in a reimagined Israel-Palestine.

## EXILIC POETICS: TRANSLATING BETWEEN NATIVE, SETTLER, REFUGEE, AND EXILE

Born in the West Bank in 1944, Mourid Barghouti (Murīd Barghūthī) was "struck by displacement" on 10 June 1967.[16] Because he was taking his final exams at Cairo University when Israeli forces conquered Ramallah, Barghouti graduated a stateless man. Published in 1997 under the Arabic title *Ra'aytu Rām Allāh*, *I Saw Ramallah* charts Barghouti's reflections upon returning to Ramallah after thirty years of forced exile. Blending memoir, essay, and prose poetry, *I Saw Ramallah* contrasts Barghouti's memories of Ramallah and the neighboring village of Deir Ghassanah, his hometown, with the reality of his present moment, marking continuities and disjunctures between his experience as a displaced exile returning to Palestine and the experiences of Palestinians who stayed in the occupied West Bank after the Six Day War of 1967, which Palestinians commemorate as al-Naksa. Originally published in the wake of the 1993 Oslo Accords, the book negotiates the politics of fledgling statehood, embodied by the Palestinian Authority's newfound, though limited, jurisdiction over the Occupied Territories and the subsequent "legal and geographic fragmentations separating Palestinians from one another."[17] According to Anna Bernard, *I Saw Ramallah* addresses this national fragmentation by employing "a materialist aesthetic which emphasizes both the circumstantial diversity of Palestinian lives and Barghouti's sense of his own responsibility, as a poet, to resist the temptation to reify the dynamic materiality of that diversity."[18]

Awarded the Naguib Mahfouz Medal for Literature in 1997 and the Palestine Prize for Poetry in 2000, *I Saw Ramallah* was promptly translated into English by Egyptian novelist Ahdaf Soueif in 2000. In his foreword to the English edition, Edward Said praises *I Saw Ramallah* as "one of the finest existential accounts of Palestinian displacement."[19] Translation thus mediates the book's international circulation as a representative Palestinian text.[20] Although *I Saw Ramallah* does not claim to represent the Palestinian experience writ large, especially given the varying political subjectivities of those living under occupation, as third-class citizens in Israel, and as refugees and exiles outside Palestine, it does "envision a Palestinian unity that does not rely on a narrative of shared identity" and is therefore a productive text for examining the diversity of Palestinian positionalities vis-à-vis Vietnamese Israeli refugee settlers.[21] While this section attends to the specificity of Barghouti's positionality as a Palestinian exile, it also forwards Norbert Bugeja's reading of *I Saw Ramallah* as an "exilic-realist" narrative that forges "specific affinities between different forms of exilic conditions both within and beyond the homeland itself."[22] Barghouti's exilic poetics, in turn, resonate with the exilic affects of Vietnamese Israelis resettled in a Zionist state that too often excludes them.

As the daughter of Vietnamese refugees, Vaan Nguyen was granted citizenship at birth into the very state that displaced Barghouti. In 2005, her first published poems appeared in *Ma'ayan*, an Israeli anti-establishment journal committed to social justice.[23] Three years later, *Ma'ayan* released both digital and print copies of Nguyen's chapbook, *The Truffle Eye* (*Ein Ha-kemehin*), the first collection of Hebrew poetry published by a Vietnamese Israeli. In 2013, Nguyen's chapbook was revised and expanded into a book with the same title, and in 2021, Adriana X. Jacobs published an English translation. Rich, sensual, and fleeting, *The Truffle Eye*'s free-verse poems interweave images of sexuality, illness (both physical and mental), beauty, and decay, citing cosmopolitan cities in Israel-Palestine, Vietnam, France, the Netherlands, and the United States. According to Jacobs, the title of the collection "invokes the image of the truffle in opposition to domestication, settlement, adaptation, and absorption"—themes that resonate across the poems.[24] Eschewing the affective investment in permanent settlement upon which settler colonialism hinges, Nguyen's poems instead imbue a second-generation restlessness: a refusal to exemplify the "model refugee."

Whereas some Israeli critics have deployed Nguyen's biography to exotify her work, other scholars have emphasized *The Truffle Eye*'s resonance with Jewish literary themes of diaspora and exile.[25] Jacobs, for example, argues that Nguyen's work instantiates "cosmopolitan and transnational movements" characteristic of "twenty-first century Israeli mode[s] of travel and translation."[26] What has yet to be examined, however, is how Nguyen's poetry may instead be translated into a *Palestinian* literary tradition of displacement and dispossession, as exemplified by Barghouti's *I Saw Ramallah*. Although Nguyen's and Barghouti's poetry differ in style, parallel themes of dislocation and alienation across the two texts work to unsettle the settler colonial state. More specifically, *I Saw Ramallah* and *The Truffle Eye* translate across and, in the process, destabilize the seemingly fixed categories of native, settler, refugee, and exile.

Barghouti's text does not explicitly refer to Vietnamese Israelis, who, confined by Israel's borders, do not reside in the West Bank. Similarly, when I asked Palestinians in the West Bank about the Vietnamese, they fondly recalled Palestine's solidarity with Vietnam during the Third World Liberation movement (discussed in chapter 1) but had little knowledge of the Vietnamese refugees resettled in Israel-Palestine less than a decade later.[27] Nguyen's poetry, in turn, does reference Palestinian subjectivity across different geographies of settler colonialism. In "Nomad Poem," Nguyen bears witness to the Zionist erasure of native Palestinian villages: "At the entrance of every city / there's an address written by the victors."[28] Calling to mind Mahmoud Darwish's *Memory for Forgetfulness*, "Chaos" depicts collapsing "buildings in Beirut," the site of four major Palestinian refugee camps, and characterizes the contemporary moment of settler colonial violence as "an ongoing epidemic, poetry's slaughter."[29] In "For the Sake of Innocence," Nguyen depicts the militarization of Israel-Palestine's landscape—"Tanks / are standing quietly in the desert"—and indexes the Zionist logic of elimination with a haunting image of an old poet "on the bus / from Abu Dis," an occupied Palestinian village bordering Jerusalem, who "wonders / if his dead wife is / his last one."[30] "Status," meanwhile, juxtaposes the defeatist sense that "nothing will change" with a call to "liberate Gaza and shake up our parents."[31]

In *I Saw Ramallah* and *The Truffle Eye*, Barghouti and Nguyen "shake up" the Zionist state's monopoly on refugee discourse. As elaborated in chapter 4, Israel enshrines the figure of the Holocaust refugee while denying Palestinian claims to refugeehood and, by extension, the Right of Return. Indeed, Palestinians have had a vexed relationship with the term "refugee" ever since its codification as a legal category. Following the establishment of the United Nations Relief and Works

Agency for Palestine Refugees in the Near East (UNRWA) in 1949, Palestinians were excluded from the purview of the international 1951 Refugee Convention and the United Nations High Commissioner of Refugees (UNHCR). Moreover, after 1967, many Palestinians shed a "self-perception as mere refugees" and adopted a concurrent "new identity as revolutionaries," a moniker that noted refugeehood's "connotations of defeat, passivity, and reliance" and instead emphasized "self-reliance, agency, and pro-activeness in reclaiming their homeland."[32] In *I Saw Ramallah*, Barghouti further problematizes the use of the term "refugees" to describe Palestinians who fled their villages in 1948 to resettle in the West Bank, in the hope of one day returning home:

> How can we explain today, now that we have grown older and wiser, that we on the West Bank treated our people as refugees? Yes, our own people, banished by Israel from their coastal cities and villages in 1948, our people who had to move from one part of the homeland to another and came to live in our cities and towns, we called them refugees! We called them immigrants! Who can apologize to them? Who can apologize to us? Who can explain this great confusion to whom?[33]

In a series of provocative questions and exclamations, Barghouti cautions against identifying the part of Palestine that lies within the State of Israel's 1948 borders as ontologically distinct from the Occupied Territories of the West Bank and Gaza—a political division that the Palestinian Authority, since the Oslo Accords, has indeed accepted. The legal-political category of the refugee marks geographic displacement from one's native land—Palestinians displaced to refugee camps in Beirut, for example—rather than the renaming of one's land by a colonizing power. To call '48 Palestinians "refugees" (*lāji 'īn*) and "immigrants" (*muhājirīn*), therefore, is in effect to naturalize and dehistoricize the State of Israel's control over '48 Palestine, relinquishing Indigenous claims of belonging. Put another way, Barghouti's searching questions—"Who can apologize to them? Who can apologize to us? Who can explain this great confusion to whom?"—criticize not only the Zionist state's policies of forced displacement but also the Palestinian Authority's acquiescence in abandoning a politics of resistance.[34]

Barghouti's own Indigenous claim to Palestine does not reproduce Zionist logics of exclusion: a mere transposition of "Israel for Jewish Israelis" to "Palestine for Arab Palestinians," which would in effect erase the subjectivity of Arab Jews, the Mizrahim, who make up the majority of Israel's population.[35] According to Palestinian American legal scholar Noura Erakat, although Zionist sovereignty "engenders fragmentation, partition, separation, and population transfer," the "inverse is not true: Palestinian sovereignty is not to control; it is to belong."[36] Belonging, furthermore, is marked in Barghouti's text by exilic poetics. According to Bryan Cheyette, the term "exile" is "disruptive and intransigent and not redeemed by a sense of nationalist return."[37] Likewise, in "Reflections on Exile," Said eschews the term "refugee"—"a creation of the twentieth-century state"—in favor of "exile,"

positing the latter's "contrapuntal" "plurality of vision."[38] This plurality is characterized by a recognition of the multiple cultures, narratives, and homelands existing
within a single landscape, necessitating what Zahi Zalloua identifies as a "double
consciousness, a parallax perspective" that can "bear witness to the interdependence of viewpoints or voices."[39] Exilic poetics, in turn, "unsettle the cultural script
of rootedness and national belonging" and, by extension, unsettle the exclusionary
logics of the settler colonial state.[40]

Barghouti's exilic poetics are apparent in a passage near the beginning of *I Saw
Ramallah* that identifies overlapping narratives of belonging. Crossing the Amman
Bridge separating Jordan from Palestine for the first time in thirty years, he
reflects: "And now I pass from my exile to their . . . homeland? My homeland? The
West Bank and Gaza? The Occupied Territories? The Areas? Judea and Samaria?
The Autonomous Government? Israel? Palestine? Is there any other country in the
world that so perplexes you with its names?"[41] Barghouti acknowledges multiple
mappings of the land: what was once Palestine is now claimed by Israel; what the
international community, since the Six Day War, has called the Occupied Territory
of the West Bank, is to the Israeli government the Judea and Samaria Area and to
the Palestinian Authority the jurisdiction of its Autonomous Government. But
these mappings are also claims to belonging, at once political, historical, imagina-
tive, and affective: "their . . . homeland?" (*waṭanihim*); "my homeland?" (*waṭanī*).
Barghouti's use of punctuation here undercuts any false equivalence between
these two claims to Palestine. While "their . . . homeland?" seems to acknowledge Zionists' claim to autochthony—the assertion that the Jewish people, prior
to exile, lived in Eretz Israel long before the arrival of Palestinians—Barghouti's
ellipses and question mark simultaneously query and challenge such a claim. This
is followed not by a declarative claim of his own but rather by another, albeit less
hesitant, question: "My homeland?" By posing his Indigenous claim to Palestine
as a question, Barghouti destabilizes divisions between the native and exile positions, embodying both: as a native Palestinian, Barghouti insists upon Indigenous
claims to the land while simultaneously acknowledging overlaid temporalities of
belonging, thus demonstrating an exilic contrapuntal sensibility that, in Said's
words, "diminish[es] orthodox judgment and elevate[s] appreciative sympathy."[42]
To be clear, such sympathy does not condone Zionist dispossession of native Palestinians but rather opens up a space for recognizing Palestinians' Right of Return
alongside Jewish claims for refuge. More probing than declarative, Barghouti's
string of questions points us toward an emergent binationalist politics that would
encompass native Palestinians and Jewish (refugee) settlers alike under a unified,
democratic Palestine, as has historically been imagined by leftist groups such as
the Popular Front for the Liberation of Palestine (PFLP).

In *Parting Ways: Jewishness and the Critique of Zionism*, Judith Butler also
invokes the promise of binationalism to bring justice to displaced Palestinians.
Arguing that the "Palestinian diaspora" remain crucial to "any understanding of

the Palestinian nation," she proposes a deterritorialized conception of nationhood wherein "the nation is partially scattered," the "rights of those who have been forcibly expelled from their own homes and lands" are honored, and "Palestine is not bound by any existing or negotiated borders."[43] Butler explores how a radical sense of binationalism—that is, a nationalism articulated through the differences and connections between Palestinian and Jewish exilic longings for home, rather than the cementation of ethno-nationalist difference propagated by a two-state solution—could reimagine the very configuration of the nation-state.[44] Connecting Butler's theory of binationalism to Indigenous critiques of settler colonialism, Erakat questions how "a state-centric legal order that sanctifies the sovereignty of settler states [can even] rectify and stem ongoing dispossession and native erasure."[45] She concludes that "statehood, as a remedy, does not correspond to the reality and scope of Palestinian grievances today."[46] Likewise, in "We Refugees," Giorgio Agamben highlights the contested territory of the Golan Heights as a model of archipelagic belonging organized around refugee subjectivity:

> The no-man's-land [between Lebanon and Israel] where [Palestinians] have found refuge has retroacted on the territory of the state of Israel, making holes in it and altering it in such a way that the image of that snow-covered hill has become more an internal part of that territory than any other region of Heretz Israel. It is only in a land where the spaces of states will have been perforated and topologically deformed, and the citizen will have learned to acknowledge the refugee that he himself is, that man's political survival today is imaginable.[47]

While it is important not to romanticize forced displacement or colonial occupation, what Butler, Erakat, and Agamben identify is the potentiality of Palestinian refugeehood, as a political "vanguard," not only to unsettle the settler colonial state of Israel but also to trouble the exclusionary logics of nation-statehood more broadly.[48] Such refugee politics is refracted through exilic poetics and Indigenous resistance, as exemplified in Barghouti's writing. Pushed further, this archipelagic reconfiguration, which challenges the exclusionary Westphalian logic of "one people, one land" and destabilizes the divisions between the native, settler, refugee, and exile positions, opens up a "third space" for those who are neither Palestinian nor Jewish in a reimagined Israel-Palestine.[49] That is, a radical *multi*nationalism may engender a form of Vietnamese Israeli belonging predicated not on Palestinian dispossession but instead more ethical forms of relationality.

Like displaced Palestinians, Vietnamese Israelis such as Vaan Nguyen have a vexed relationship to the term "refugee." In interviews, Nguyen often protests being labeled a refugee: "Whenever a humanitarian crisis pops up, various communication outlets approach me to request an interview on the refugee experience, but the only thing I can do is read poetry at one of *Ma'ayan*'s flash readings, because I am a poet who does not feel like a refugee."[50] Because she was born in Israel-Palestine, Nguyen does not fit the legal-political category of a refugee who crosses borders in order to secure asylum outside their homeland. However, her citizenship in the Zionist state *is* predicated on her *parents'* status as Vietnamese refugees, since Israel does not grant automatic birthright citizenship to non-Jewish subjects. In other words, Nguyen's status as an Israeli citizen derives not from the Law of Return, which governs Jewish immigrants, nor the Citizen Act of 1952, which restricted Israeli citizenship to Palestinians who did not leave their villages during al-Nakba, but from her parents' exceptional absorption into the State of Israel under Prime Minister Menachem Begin.

In 1977, Nguyen's parents escaped Vietnam by boat and ended up in Camp Palawan in the Philippines. After years of waiting, they were granted asylum in Israel-Palestine in 1979 as part of the third wave of Vietnamese refugees. Once they were resettled in the Negev town of Sderot, however, they were "forgotten forever":

> My parents were transparent: No one took any interest in them. They left the *ulpan* [intensive Hebrew course] after three months without having learned Hebrew, in order to work in factories in the Sderot area. Very quickly they decided to move to the big city in the expectation of finding a better livelihood. They moved around between Holon, Rishon Letzion and Bat Yam, and in the end settled in Jaffa—not the pastoral tourist part, but the section that is far from the sea. My parents worked mostly in kitchens, doing jobs that did not require language.[51]

Unable to smoothly assimilate into the Hebrew-speaking country, Nguyen's parents struggled to accomplish the upward mobility they had hoped for.

Nguyen's family's narrative reflects many Vietnamese Israelis' experiences. Today, Vietnamese Israelis number between 150 and 200. Since the 1970s, many Vietnamese refugees have left for resettlement elsewhere, a number of Vietnamese women were brought over from Vietnam to marry Vietnamese Israeli and Jewish Israeli men, and a handful of children were adopted from Vietnam during the 1990s.[52] Most Vietnamese Israelis live in urban, immigrant neighborhoods and are concentrated in low-income jobs such as restaurant cook, hotel chambermaid, or factory worker. A couple of families own Chinese restaurants, but there is a distinct lack of the sort of Vietnamese-language storefront signage that characterizes other Vietnamese diasporic communities.[53] First-generation refugees struggle to learn Hebrew, and second-generation citizens face racial and religious discrimination in an already saturated job market.[54] Moreover, Vietnamese Israelis are often mistaken for Asian guest workers from Thailand, China, or the Philippines, who have no legal pathway to citizenship in the Zionist state.[55]

Such experiences of alienation and cultural exclusion inform the exilic aspects of Nguyen's poetry in *The Truffle Eye*. But do exilic poetics preclude refugee aesthetics? Timothy K. August contrasts the aesthetics of Southeast Asian refugees to that of exiles, arguing that while the latter—often marked by the figure of the elite intellectual—occupy multiple worlds and thus critique the very idea of a singular mode of belonging, the former defiantly claim space within the nation-state in order to critique exclusionary nationalism from within.[56] But what are the ethical and political implications of claiming space in a *settler colonial* state, which inevitably implicates refugee settlers in Indigenous dispossession? Exilic poetics, as exemplified by the contrapuntal layers of Nguyen's poetry, present one potential way for Vietnamese Israelis to move beyond the structural antagonisms imposed by the refugee settler condition. Read next to Barghouti's *I Saw Ramallah*, Nguyen's *The Truffle Eye* troubles the refugee/exile distinction by questioning the presumed teleology of the refugee as a "problem" to be solved via absorption into the "national order of things."[57] Instead, refugeehood is inherited by the second generation in the form of exilic affects. In other words, exilic affects are not in opposition to refugee subjectivity but rather to just the narrow legal definition of refugee status. Indeed, Nguyen's exilic poetics align with the cross-generational temporality and mode of relationality captured by the term "refugeetude."[58]

Like *I Saw Ramallah*, which opens with Barghouti's crossing of the Jordan River into Palestine, *The Truffle Eye* begins with a scene of *nước*. In the opening poem, "Mekong River," Nguyen invokes exilic affects to describe her second-generation condition of refugeetude. Over twenty-six lines divided into two odd-numbered stanzas, the poem shifts between the rivers and seas of Southeast Asia and West Asia, marking fleeting but intense bodily encounters. Charting restless movement and multiple entanglements, the first stanza begins by tracing the multiple geographies that shape Nguyen's Vietnamese Israeli identity—a bricolage of places that are simultaneously grounded in spatial referents and metaphorically brought together in the archipelagic space of Nguyen's poem:

> Tonight I moved between three beds
> like I was sailing on the Mekong
> and whispered the beauty of the Tigris and Euphrates.[59]

"Mekong" refers to the Mekong River, which runs through Vietnam and enters the sea at its southeastern border. Although the narrator references the Mekong, suggesting placement in Southeast Asia, she also whispers "the beauty of the Tigris and Euphrates" (*yephi ha-Perat ve-hakhideqel*), rivers that run through Syria, Iraq, Iran, Turkey, and Kuwait—Arab countries that surround Israel and challenge the Zionist state's settlement and occupation of Palestine. Moreover, the narrator's boat voyage serves as a simile for her movement "between three beds," suggesting the inability to find any one bed, or one space, to call home. Here, Nguyen characterizes exile not as loss but as multiplicity. It is this multiplicity, or this refusal to claim Israel as one's sole bed or space of belonging, that renders possible another plurality—the inability to claim Israel solely for oneself.

As Said reminds us, multiplicity is not to be romanticized; rather it is always already conditioned by the exile's forced displacement and "discontinuous state of being."[60] Marking this violence, the first stanza of "Mekong River" continues:

> Under an endless moment
> looking
> below the left tit

I have a hole
and you fill it
with other men.[61]

Problematizing the refugee settler condition, the refugee/exile narrator calls attention to modalities of alienation: how Vietnamese Israelis remain unsettled, futilely
looking "under an endless moment" for the sense of belonging promised by the
Zionist state. The state, in turn, violently penetrates the narrator, violating her
body with its own multicultural narrative: "I have a hole / and you fill it / with
other men." Staged as a sexual encounter, these lines call attention to Vietnamese
Israelis' intimate entanglement with the settler colonial state that "saved" them
from statelessness, yet continues to overwrite their narratives. In a similar vein,
other poems in *The Truffle Eye* also employ gendered second-person address to
index Vietnamese Israelis' complicated feelings of indebtedness to a state that
militarizes their everyday lives: "I'll drool just for you, / solider, master of beret,
rank, and whip"; "Once, you were a pilot with seven strikes on enemy territory."[62]
Via spatial and affective proximity, Vietnamese Israelis become implicated in the
Zionist state's military violence as "model refugees."

To return to the beginning of the first stanza of "Mekong River": If we read
Vietnam (Mekong) as one bed/home of belonging, and Arab nations (the Tigris
and Euphrates) as another, then what space does the third bed connote? Interpreted as metonymy, the concluding two lines of the first stanza—"Notes of Tiger
beer / on your body."—offer one suggestion: the United States.[63] Tiger Beer, an
American Adjunct Lager–style beer brewed by Asia Pacific Breweries Ltd., indexes
the obfuscated role of the United States in connecting the previous two beds/
homes in an archipelagic manner, thus producing the conditions of emergence
for the Vietnamese Israeli figure. US military intervention in Vietnam contributed to
the post-1975 refugee exodus, and US defense aid to Israel supports Israeli settlement and occupation of Palestine.[64] In order to project itself as a Western democracy sympathetic to international concerns, Israel followed the United States'
humanitarian example of resettling Vietnamese refugees.

A turn to another poem in *The Truffle Eye*, "Highway 1," supports this reading of
the United States as the third bed/home in "Mekong River." The title of the poem,
"Highway 1," references not only Highway 1 in Israel, which connects Tel Aviv
and Jerusalem, but also National Route 1A (Quốc lộ 1A) in Vietnam, which runs
the length of the country, and US Highway 1, which runs along the East Coast.[65] The
poem's first stanza—"On Highway 1, America's fixed on a gun / The hilltop green-
ing / *a place and a name*."—invokes the name of the Holocaust museum in Jerusalem, Yad Va-shem (Isaiah 56:5), entangling US militarism with Holocaust exceptionalism, which in turn denies refugeehood to displaced Palestinians.[66] The poem
goes on to suggest that such Zionist narratives, which "stitch an ancestry for you /
and a tradition" on Palestinian soil, are ultimately untenable, built as they are on a
decaying foundation of "worms."[67]

The second stanza of "Mekong River" continues the first stanza's images of restless movement and fraught sexual encounters, referencing the "crickets [that] drone south of Laos," the "showers of cold air from Hanoi," and an "ink stain on the belly."[68] The poem concludes with six lines that further question the political implications of Vietnamese refugee resettlement in Israel-Palestine:

I'll release roots at your feet,
I want to come to puke
specks of dust
in my crotch. Rest your hand
in my pants. Make it personal
Who dares abandon a disease mid-sea?[69]

Comparing the releasing of roots to the puking of specks of dust, the narrator problematizes the romanticized narrative of the refugee planting new roots in the adoptive country of rescue. Roots instead signify a settler colonial attachment, that—like an invasive species—threatens the Indigenous landscape. Furthermore, the act of releasing roots originates not from personal desire but from external imperative: "I'll release roots at your feet" suggests an imposed genuflection, an enforced capitulation, to the settler colonial narrative touted by the Zionist state—one that upholds Vietnamese refugees as proof of Israel's multicultural democracy while directing attention away from displaced Palestinian refugees and exiles.

The poem's last line—"Who dares abandon a disease mid-sea?" (*Mi me'ez la-azov ma-halah be-emtsah yam?*)—exemplifies a politics of refugeetude refracted through exilic poetics. Israel, like many nation-states, represented the Vietnamese boat refugees as a "disease"—an aberration to the nation-state order—that needed to be cured via resettlement and citizenship. As political philosophers such as Arendt and Agamben have shown, however, the normative body of the nation-state inevitably *produces* displaced populations, by the very nature of its exclusive borders.[70] Parodying Israel's self-righteous accusation that its neighboring Arab nations are *not* humanitarian since they did not absorb Vietnamese refugees—"Who dares abandon a disease mid-sea?"—the poem reminds the reader that Israel itself is responsible for millions of Palestinians' forced displacement. Lastly, the poem leaves the temporality of "disease" ambiguous: once resettled, do Vietnamese Israelis continue to be marked as diseased subjects, suggesting a latent threat to the Jewish body politic? If so, then perhaps this association with illness is one vector by which Vietnamese Israeli refugee settlers can infect the settler colonial state from within via a radical politics of refugeetude: "I *want* to come to puke / specks of dust / in my crotch."[71]

"Mekong River" marks geography via *nước*, blurring divisions between Southeast Asia and West Asia, refugee and settler, exile and citizen. At first glance, the poem's last line—"Who dares abandon a disease mid-sea?"—seems to characterize the "sea" as a transitory space from which to be saved. The sea, however, teems with possibility. To embrace the sea is to open oneself up to more archipelagic forms of belonging. In Vietnamese diasporic literature, the sea (*biển*) marks boat refugee passage as well as rebirth and renewal. In post-1948 Palestinian literature, the sea (*al-baḥr*) represents the promise of reunification: a return to the Mediterranean for Palestinians confined to the West Bank and exiled abroad. In Hebrew literature, from the Book of Jonah to contemporary Israeli poetry, the sea (*yam*) is "a space for voyage and discovery, loss and transformation, not to mention a radical alternative to settlement and territory."[72] In sum, the sea, with its fluid borders and shifting perimeters of belonging, has the potential to erode the exclusionary logics of the settler colonial state.

"Culture Stain," the twelfth poem in *The Truffle Eye*, builds upon the themes introduced in "Mekong River." In this three-stanza poem, "culture" operates as a "stain," a disease, that marks Vietnamese Israelis' ethnic and political difference and inhibits easy assimilation into the Zionist state. In the first stanza of "Culture Stain," the Mekong, Tigris, and Euphrates rivers, introduced in "Mekong River," converge on a "riverbank," near which a second-person character digs to extract "seeds of nothing."[73] Such seeds, like the roots in "Mekong River," are infertile. If the second-person "you" is understood as the figure of the Vietnamese Israeli, these lines suggest the ultimate failure of refugee resettlement—a failure that can be characterized not as a loss but as an opening for relating otherwise to the land of Palestine. If "you" references the figure of the Jewish Israeli, however, as other poems in *The Truffle Eye* seem to suggest, these lines also indicate the inevitable collapse of what Lila Sharif has termed the Zionist project of "eco-occupation"— that is, "the planting of nonnative trees to resemble European landscapes and the appropriation of the natural habitat to expand colonial settlement."[74] In "Culture Stain," Zionists' attempts at settler eco-occupation are ultimately "seeds of nothing" that will fail to take permanent root in the land of Palestine.

In the third stanza of "Culture Stain," Nguyen depicts a vexed romantic encounter between the Vietnamese Israeli narrator and a Jewish Israeli addressee:

A rosy sun sets
on a musical Monetbach lake in your eyes—
When we hold each other
you'll ask where I came from. I'll say
I came from this rot.
Where did I come from, you're asking,
I mean, parents?[75]

The couple's intimate embrace—indicative of the way Israel embraced the Vietnamese refugees in the 1970s by offering asylum—is interrupted by the Jewish Israeli lover's query as to the narrator's origins, a question that calls to mind the perpetual foreigner stereotype often imposed on Asian immigrants who do not fit the phenotypical markers associated with the presumed national body politic. The narrator, however, disrupts expectations by answering "I came from this rot," simultaneously insisting on her belonging to Israel-Palestine as an Israeli-born citizen while also eschewing any pride in that nativity. "Rot" indicates the dust and decay of the underresourced neighborhoods Vietnamese Israelis like Nguyen grew up in, as well as the rotten seeds of Zionist settler colonialism—and by extension, Vietnamese Israelis' refugee settler condition—in Palestine more broadly.

While the lover attempts to clarify the question as one about the narrator's parents' origins—indexing how parental refugeetude is inherited by the second generation—the poem undermines this very line of questioning. According to Jacobs, the syntax of the last two lines actually "dislocates the subject," so that "Where did I come from" is "both a question posed to the speaker and the one that the lover appears to ask himself."[76] Turning the question of origins and "seeds of nothing" back on the questioner, the poem prompts Jewish Israelis to interrogate their own claims to settlement and occupation and instead consider Palestinian calls for decolonization. This interrogation of origins is marked by water, by *nước*, framed as it is "on a musical Monetbach lake" in the lover's eyes. *Nước*, then, marks geographies of decolonization that trouble settler colonial claims to Indigenous land.

In *The Truffle Eye*, Nguyen's poems translate not only across different spaces but also across different verb tenses, bringing together an archipelago of temporalities in a collage-like manner. Translating between multiple temporalities is key to articulating contrapuntal forms of belonging that destabilize exclusionary divisions between natives, settlers, refugees, and exiles. Such temporal translations can be characterized by Barghouti's concept of a "shape of time" (*shakl awqātinā fīhi*).[77] Toward the middle of *I Saw Ramallah*, Barghouti asks what David Farrier has identified as the "central question" of the text: "Does a poet live in space or in time?"[78] Answering his own query, Barghouti replies: "Our homeland is the shape of the time we spent in it."[79] For exiles, "homeland" is not only a space but also a time, a memory of a place prior to forced displacement. This temporality of memory, however, need not be characterized by nostalgia or autochthony, a teleological logic of property rights based on the question of origins: Who was here first? Who owns the original title to the land? Rather, this temporality of memory invites new forms of political organization, a "project of building something new" and "going back to an unknown future."[80] In other words, this forthcoming "shape of time" can encompass Palestinian claims to Indigenous belonging while also acknowledging Jewish Israeli attachments to the Holy Land and Vietnamese Israelis' longing for a state of refuge.

Indexing overlapping modalities of belonging, Barghouti writes of Israel-Palestine: "the place is for the enemy and the place is for us, the story is their story and the story is our story. I mean, *at the same time*."[81] Such parallelism and coevality do not equate to "two equal rights to the land," however, given that the Zionists "took our entire space and exiled us from it." Barghouti clarifies that "when we were in Palestine, we were not afraid of the Jews," and only *after* they "took the space with the power of the sacred and with the sacredness of power, with the imagination, and with geography" did they "bec[o]me an enemy."[82] Barghouti orients readers toward a time and place before Zionist settlement and occupation—a shape of time *before* Jewish settlers and native Palestinians were considered enemies, *before* Vietnamese Israelis would have been positioned as refugee settlers—in sum, a shape of time toward which to orient decolonial futures. Although Zionists used "imagination" (*al-khayāl*) and "geography" (*al-jughrāfiyyā*) as tools for Palestinian dispossession, such tools can be repurposed to build a radically multinational, contrapuntal Palestine.

In the middle of the second stanza of "Mekong River," Nguyen also questions the teleology of origins, suggesting more archipelagic understandings of time:

> Sketch me a monochrome
> flow chart
> on fresh
> potted flowers.[83]

While a "monochrome / flow chart" (*tarshim zerimah / be-tsevah akhid*) connotes linear temporality and unambiguous causality, "fresh / potted flowers" promise verdant growth, marking the potential for this flow chart to blossom and elongate in unexpected directions. These fertile shoots—which disrupt linear causality by extending forward, backward, and horizontally—resonate with Barghouti's vision of a shape of time oriented simultaneously toward the memory of pre-1948 Palestine and the future of decolonization. Indeed, when Barghouti writes that he "want[s] borders that I later will come to hate"—the modicum of security promised by the Palestinian Authority's autonomous government—he articulates a desire for a "flow chart" that can flower and change, blooming into a more expansive vision of Palestinian self-determination.[84]

Translating Vaan Nguyen's *The Truffle Eye* into a Palestinian literary tradition, as exemplified by Mourid Barghouti's *I Saw Ramallah*, presents one way to work through the structural antagonisms produced by the refugee settler condition. In these two texts, exilic poetics, refracted through refugeetude and Indigenous politics, query not only the exclusionary logics of the settler colonial state but also the "sovereignty trap" of the Palestinian Authority's politics of statehood, in order to imagine more contrapuntal visions of a decolonized Palestine.[85] In *The Truffle Eye*, poems traverse space and time, marking tendrils of belonging in both West Asia and Vietnam. The following section hones in on the space-time of postwar Vietnam and interrogates what happens when Vietnamese Israelis translate the vocabulary of land settlement and occupation from the Israel-Palestine context back to their communist-unified homeland.

## "OLIM KHADASHIM": TRANSLATING "NEW IMMIGRANTS" FROM ISRAEL-PALESTINE TO VIETNAM

Prior to the release of *The Truffle Eye*, Vaan Nguyen starred in the 2005 documentary film *The Journey of Vaan Nguyen* (*Hamasa shel Vaan*). Directed by Duki Dror, an Israeli filmmaker of Iraqi heritage, *The Journey of Vaan Nguyen* premiered at the Jerusalem Film Festival on 29 September 2005 and proceeded to achieve global acclaim: it won a Remi Award at the WorldFest-Houston International Film Festival and was an Official Selection of the International Documentary Film Festival Amsterdam.[86] The documentary is one of the first cultural texts to prominently circulate the story of Vietnamese Israelis to a global audience, as well as debut Nguyen as a poet: shots of Nguyen journaling, speaking into a voice recorder, and writing in her online blog, "A Jaffran in Saigon," are interspersed with archival footage of Vietnamese refugees arriving in Israel-Palestine in the late 1970s and receiving Hebrew language instruction at an *ulpan*.

Whereas *The Truffle Eye* destabilizes the categories of native, settler, refugee, and exile via exilic poetics, *The Journey of Vaan Nguyen* more explicitly grapples with the politics of Vietnamese Israeli return to Vietnam in order to reclaim the lands they left behind as refugees. This emphasis on return may at first seem to reify an ethno-nationalist politics of nativity: an anti-immigrant belief that Vietnamese Israelis suffer alienation in Israel-Palestine because they rightly "belong" in Vietnam. However, read archipelagically, the film actually invites surprising translations between, on one hand, Vietnamese Israelis' journey of return to Vietnam and, on the other, the Law of Return for Jews and the Right of Return for Palestinians in the Israel-Palestine context. In fact, the film suggests the *inadequacy* of a nation-state framework for unsettling the refugee settler condition in Israel-Palestine. Theorizing potentials for Vietnamese Israeli and Palestinian solidarity becomes possible only when one considers questions of land dispossession and competing rhetorics of return in Israel-Palestine *in relation to Vietnam*. This relational politics is captured by Palestinian American scholar Loubna Qutami's concept of the "Palestine analytic," which "elucidates how Palestine/Palestinian resistance can present new global anti/de-colonial opportunities and new solidarities between causes and communities that are not bound by the nation-state."[87] Indeed, the Palestinian struggle for liberation presents one vector by which Vietnamese Israelis can come to understand their own experiences of land dispossession in Vietnam; such archipelagic analogies may in turn engender solidarity with Palestinian liberation in Israel-Palestine, rather than identification with the Zionist state.

The politics and problematics of translation feature prominently in *The Journey of Vaan Nguyen*, which shows first-generation Vietnamese refugees speaking most comfortably in Vietnamese while their Israeli-born children speak primarily Hebrew. When reading their own poetry, the two main characters of the film, Vaan Nguyen and her father, Hoài Mỹ Nguyễn (identified in the film as "Hoimai Nguyen"), speak in their respective native languages, Hebrew and Vietnamese. But when they speak to each other, they switch, sometimes mid-sentence, between (native) Hebrew, (Vietnamese-accented) Hebrew, (native) Vietnamese, and (Hebrew-accented) Vietnamese, cobbling together a shared language across linguistic difference. Translation also operates at the level of the film's subtitles.

FIGURE 10. Film still from *The Journey of Vaan Nguyen* © Zygote Films.

Because very few viewers are fluent in both Hebrew and Vietnamese—even the Vietnamese Israelis in the documentary sometimes experience difficulty communicating across generation and language—subtitles are indispensable for understanding the film. For Hebrew-language audiences, the film needs to translate only the Vietnamese dialogue. For Anglophone audiences, in contrast, the film offers English subtitles for both the Hebrew and Vietnamese dialogue and, regrettably, does not distinguish between the two. Unless they can identify the auditory differences between Vietnamese, Hebrew, and their respective accented variations, Anglophone viewers may therefore miss the characters' constant linguistic negotiations. In sum, English subtitles mediate Anglophone viewers' understanding of the film: not only are they often inaccurate, but they also smooth out the grammatical inconsistencies and hesitant vocabularies of the Vietnamese Israelis, who communicate with one another without formal training in each other's native tongue. In essence, the film's English subtitles mask Vietnamese Israelis' everyday labor of translation in their quotidian interactions.

At the level of narrative, the film also translates—incessantly shuttles—between two main narratives: that of Hoài Mỹ Nguyễn and his daughter, Vaan Nguyen. In 1972, Hoài Mỹ Nguyễn fled his village in Hội An district, Bình Định province, in central Vietnam, his life threatened by the communist-sympathetic mayor who poisoned his father, Nguyễn Khắc Minh. After his escape and eventual resettlement in Israel-Palestine, Hoài Mỹ's family lands were confiscated by the Vietnamese communist government and redistributed as part of the post-1975 land reform program.[88] In the film, Hoài Mỹ returns to Vietnam to reclaim his ancestral lands. Nguyen's narrative, in turn, emphasizes the exilic affects that characterize her life in Israel-Palestine as a Vietnamese Israeli. Halfway through the film, Nguyen follows her father to Vietnam to help him reclaim the family's lands. The film frames her journey as one of hopeful return: a desire to assuage feelings of alienation and cultural dissonance in Israel-Palestine with a final sense of belonging in the land of her ethnic heritage. The documentary ends, however, with a scene of irresolution. Nguyen tearfully divulges to the camera that she "feels Vietnamese in Israel and Israeli in Vietnam," bypassing any form of identification with Palestinians.[89]

In *The Truffle Eye*, Nguyen is able to reframe her exilic affects as exilic poetics, with all the contrapuntal possibilities à la Said that such engender. In contrast, in *The Journey of Vaan Nguyen*, shot and edited by Duki Dror, second-generation exile is represented as a failure to assimilate rather than an opening for radical multiplicity: Nguyen is depicted as unable to fully belong in either Vietnam or Israel-Palestine. In Vietnam, Nguyen's Hebrew-accented Vietnamese, assertive manner, and Western clothes mark her as *Việt Kiều*, an overseas Vietnamese. According to Võ Hồng Chương-Đài, "Despite its seemingly neutral translation, *Việt Kiều* often is used derogatorily and carries with it the baggage of civil war and imperial history—local Vietnamese's resentment toward those who were able to flee the devastated country and who are now citizens and residents of more prosperous, usually Western, nations."[90] For Nguyen and her family, however, this resentment is somewhat misplaced: Vietnamese Israelis typically did not prosper in Israel-Palestine, and they remain alienated in Israeli society. In fact, in the beginning scenes of *The Journey of Vaan Nguyen*, the majority of Vietnamese Israelis who have gathered in the Nguyens' living room in Jaffa Dalet to watch archival footage of themselves arriving in Israel-Palestine express desire to return to Vietnam and belief that their livelihoods would now be better in their postwar homeland than in the Zionist state.

In an oft-quoted monologue halfway through the film, Nguyen elaborates on the cultural estrangement Vietnamese Israelis feel in Israel-Palestine. Shots of Nguyen packing, waiting in the Tel Aviv airport for her flight to Vietnam to join her father, and then riding in a taxi in Sài Gòn are sutured together by a bitter voiceover in which Nguyen addresses the Zionist state directly:

> Goodbye wonderful country, your humble servant offers you this song on the way to Vietnam. This journey is made out of bitterness and anger—may I never return. I'm not accepted . . . because of my appearance, my religion, my nationality, my immigrant soul. Enough. I'm tired, fed up, traumatized by life's experiences. I want to write. I want to go to the store without having people pry into my private life, asking so many questions because I look suspicious or so very interesting. I want them to quit the UFO investigations and the demand that I politely clap my hands and sing: "I was born in Israel, my parents are Vietnamese refugees, who came in 1979, when Prime Minister Menachem Begin, who had just been elected, decided that his first official act would be to let in some Boat People as a humanitarian identification with the exile so familiar to the Jewish people." No, I'm not Jewish. I don't know if I'll convert and whether or not my child will be circumcised. I don't know in what section

of the cemetery I prefer to be buried or according to which religious affiliation. Yeah, I feel sorry for everyone who died or was jailed regardless of whatever religion or nationality was reported in most recent statistics of the last Intifada. I observe Holocaust Day . . . and anyhow I'm not fucking any Arabs at the moment. I have no idea how you tell the difference between Chinese, Japanese, Thai, [Filipino], and Korean. I don't think that my eyes are slanted because I grew up eating rice every day. Yes, I bet my skin is smoother. Yes, I do have cellulite. No, I don't comb my hair a hundred times a day. No, I'm not related to Bruce Lee or Jackie Chan. Hello in Vietnamese is *chào*, I love you is *Anh yêu em*. And [Vân (Vaan)] is a synonym for cloud. Now can I have some peace and quiet?[91]

In this frustrated soliloquy, Nguyen indexes the endless questions about her appearance and her place in Israeli society that she is compelled to answer in her everyday interactions. Despite her birth in Ashkelon and fluency in Hebrew, Nguyen's Vietnamese features mark her as a perpetual foreigner and Orientalist oddity in Israel-Palestine.

As this monologue reveals, Vietnamese Israelis are also considered "suspicious" because they do not easily fit into the presumed binary opposition between Jewish Israelis and Arab Palestinians. Vietnamese Israelis' loyalties thus remain suspect: Do they plan to convert to Judaism? Whose "side" did they sympathize with during the last Intifada? Do they observe Holocaust Day? Do they sleep with Palestinians, implying both illicit sexual relations and a reproductive threat to the Zionist state's precarious Jewish demographic majority? In this scene, Nguyen refuses to choose a "side," expressing sympathy "for everyone who died or was jailed regardless of whatever religion or nationality was reported in most recent statistics of the last Intifada." At first glance, this refusal to take a "side" may seem an aspiration to binationalism, as discussed in the previous section. However, under the oppressive conditions of the settler colonial state, failing to take a stance effectively translates into upholding the status quo of Palestinian dispossession. Radical binationalism, and by extension multinationalism, is possible only in and through Palestinian liberation.

In *The Journey of Vaan Nguyen*, solidarity between Vietnamese Israelis and Palestinians is depicted as not yet a reality but rather as potentiality—shared experiences of structural as well as interpersonal discrimination that, if not acknowledged, may, like Walter Benjamin's image of the past that "flashes up at the instant when it can be recognized," dissolve into missed opportunities.[92] Two scenes in particular depict how Vietnamese Israelis are often grouped with Palestinians, rather than Jewish Israelis, in the bifurcated political geography of Israel-Palestine. About ten minutes into the film, Nguyen's parents visit a Muslim cemetery in Yafa to light incense at the foot of two parallel gravestones featuring Vietnamese as well as Arabic script. In a Vietnamese voiceover, Nguyen's mother explains that in 1983, her twin daughters were born stillborn.[93] Speaking directly to the camera in Vietnamese-accented Hebrew, Hoài Mỹ divulges that the family struggled to find a cemetery where they could bury the children. They were turned away from first a Jewish synagogue in Yafa and then a Christian cemetery; finally, this Muslim cemetery accepted them. In the film, Hoài Mỹ shares this information matter-of-factly; instead of dwelling on the political implications of this encounter, he concludes simply, "That's all."[94] But this scene presents an opening for cross-racial connections, raising the specter of possible solidarities. The vast majority of Muslim subjects in Israel-Palestine are Palestinian; therefore, this Muslim cemetery can be read as a space of Palestinian sovereignty, in death if not yet in life. By extension, this scene suggests that Vietnamese Israelis may find a final resting place of resettlement not in the Zionist *state* of Israel but in the *land* of Palestine. Indeed, Palestine, liberated from the restrictive logics of nation-statehood, can encompass radical multiplicity, whereas the settler state inevitably reproduces exclusions. Ironically, in Hebrew the word most commonly used for cemetery is also the word for home: *bayit*.[95] Excluded from the possibility of refugee home-making in the Zionist state, Vietnamese Israelis instead have the potential in this scene to align with Palestinian land-based struggles.

In a following scene, Nguyen's younger sister, Hong Wa, visits a neighborhood playground with her friend Jamillah. Like "Vaan," "Hong Wa" is a name marked by multiple translations: the original Vietnamese name Hoa Hồng, meaning rose, gets transliterated through Hebrew back into English as Hong Wa. In the film, Hong Wa also goes by her Hebrew name, Vered, which similarly means rose.[96] In this scene, the two girls discuss their bilingual experiences while balancing on a swing set. Hong Wa talks about speaking Vietnamese at home with her parents, and Jamillah shares that her family primarily speaks Arabic, though, unlike Hong Wa's parents, Jamillah's parents are also fluent in Hebrew. Their conversation is interrupted by the offscreen taunts of Jewish Israeli children who call Hong Wa "Japanese" and tell Jamillah to "go home."[97] Like the cemetery scene described above, this scene of cross-racial friendship between Hong Wa and Jamillah suggests potentials for solidarity: shared vulnerability to Zionist exclusions that mark the two girls' ethnic difference as well as strengthen their young friendship. If we read copper-skinned and dark-eyed Jamillah as Palestinian rather than Mizrahi, then the children's provocation to "go home" is particularly ironic given that Jamillah is already at home in Palestine; in fact, the right to "go home" is exactly what displaced Palestinians are fighting for via the Right of Return. The film, however, does not explicitly frame this encounter between the two girls as one of political solidarity, and in that way, it risks fading into a missed opportunity.

This scene on the playground is sutured to the previous scene at the Muslim cemetery by a shot of Nguyen's mother brushing her daughter Hong Wa's hair while in a voiceover Nguyen reads, in Hebrew, one of her journal entries chronicling the racial discrimination she has experienced growing up in Israel-Palestine. Nguyen concludes: "At some age I started to blame my parents and to be ashamed of them. Later I started hating the elitist Jewish society. I became angry and rude.

Finally, I remained hating myself, trying to come to terms with those whom I was ungrateful to: family, state, community of any kind. Loneliness of a foreigner who grew up in a desert out of sand storms."[98] In this confession, Nguyen tries to pinpoint who should be held accountable for her experiences of cultural exclusion as a second-generation Vietnamese Israeli. Frustration with her refugee parents evolves as she grows older into a more structural critique of the Zionist state and "elitist Jewish society"; however, in this particular narration of her political development, structural critique ultimately disintegrates back into stultifying exilic affects of self-hatred and loneliness. In sum, Nguyen's narrative, as depicted by Dror in *The Journey of Vaan Nguyen*, seems to foreclose political agency and, by extension, the potential for solidarity between Vietnamese Israeli refugee settlers and native Palestinians in Israel-Palestine.

But is Nguyen's story the main narrative of the film? The film's title, *The Journey of Vaan Nguyen*, definitely seems to suggest so. Further analysis of the film's trailer reveals, however, that the title is actually a product of an English subtitle's *mistranslation*—or, more generously, creative interpretation—of the film's Vietnamese dialogue, suggesting that viewers' assumptions about the prominence of Nguyen's narrative over that of her father's may actually be misplaced. In the trailer's penultimate scene, a Vietnamese villager who currently owns a house on Hoài Mỹ's ancestral lands tells Hoài Mỹ as Nguyen looks on, "Người ta nói, cuối cùng, không có đâu giống như quê hương." The English subtitles translate this as "At the end of the journey, there is no place like home," after which the trailer cuts to a closeup of Nguyen walking by herself at night along the streets of Sài Gòn, framed to the left by the text of the film's English title in yellow letters: *The Journey of Vaan Nguyen*. The on-screen visual repetition of the word "journey," juxtaposed against the truism "There's no place like home"—a *Wizard of Oz* reference—calls into question the inanity of this supposed truism.[99] For Nguyen, a Vietnamese Israeli who feels alienated both in Israel-Palestine and Vietnam, the platitude "there is no place like home" might speak less to a sense of the cherished uniqueness of an abstract home than to the fact that for those marked by refugee displacement and exilic affects, there is indeed "no place [that can feel] like home." Alternatively, one can read this platitude through the lens of exilic poetics discussed in the previous section, in which case home becomes contrapuntal and archipelagic, exceeding the borders of the settler state. In other words, for those caught in translation between multiple cultures, continents, and languages, there is no *one* place that can feel like home and, by extension, no *one* population that can monopolize Israel-Palestine or Vietnam as their national homeland, to the exclusion of others. Furthermore, it is at the end of the film, "at the end of the journey," to quote the film's Vietnamese character—that is, "the journey of Vaan Nguyen" (from Israel-Palestine to Vietnam)—that Nguyen, and the viewer, may come to this conclusion.

This reading of the trailer's play on words, however, is premised on the film's English subtitles, flashed—not spoken—on the bottom of the screen in white text, moments before the yellow text of the film's English title appears in the next shot. In fact, a more accurate translation of the Vietnamese man's statement does not even include the word "journey" (*cuộc hành trình*). "Người ta nói, cuối cùng, không có đâu giống như quê hương" translates more precisely to "People say, *in the end*, there is no place like home." Furthermore, the word for "home" used here, *quê hương*, means not only one's hometown or village but also one's homeland or country. In other words, there is no place that can surpass the significance of one's homeland, one's *nước*. Without the repetition of the English word "journey" to connect this Vietnamese man's quote to the title of the film, *The Journey of Vaan Nguyen*, the above reading of the title's significance, and the centrality of Nguyen's narrative that it purports, unravels.

If the film's title is based on a mistranslation ("in the end" versus "at the end of the journey") and therefore misrepresents the relative prominence of Nguyen's second-generation narrative, then perhaps the film does not completely foreclose the potential for solidarity between Vietnamese Israelis and Palestinians. Indeed, a turn to the other main narrative thread of the film, that of Nguyen's father, Hoài Mỹ, opens up the question of Palestinian liberation to a relational analysis of land contestations in postwar Vietnam. If we understand *quê hương* in the previous quote to refer not only to "home" in the abstract but more precisely to one's ancestral village lands—the lands a family has cultivated for generations—then Hoài Mỹ's narrative invites archipelagic connections between distinct yet parallel experiences of land dispossession in Israel-Palestine and Vietnam.

For Palestinians, the Right of Return to ancestral lands is an Indigenous issue—a political refutation of the Zionist state's ongoing policies of settler colonialism. But how do Vietnamese Israelis conceive of their own politics of return to their ancestral lands in postwar Vietnam? A scene a quarter of the way through the film provides some answers. As the camera cuts between shots of Hoài Mỹ reading a letter addressed to his diasporic siblings, Nguyen and her sisters listening, and Nguyen's mother cooking in the family's small apartment in Jaffa Dalet, Hoài Mỹ's voiceover details how he and his siblings left their homeland decades ago, escaping through the rainfall of bombs. In the letter, written during Lunar New Year (Tết), Hoài Mỹ prays to his ancestors for the ability to return to the family's ancestral lands, bemoaning poetically, "Xa hang đưa vòng trái đất." The English subtitles translate this phrase as "I was torn from roots and lands."[100] The word for land used here, "*trái đất*," takes on the planetary dimensions of Earth, extending beyond the provincial connotations of "*quê hương*" to invite archipelagic connections between spaces on opposite sides of the globe: Israel-Palestine and Vietnam.

In another key scene regarding land rights in the postwar Vietnam context, Hoài Mỹ visits Chú Kỳ, the landlord in Vietnam who currently owns and rents out his ancestral lands. Distinguished as an "Honorable War Hero" by the communist government, Chú Kỳ received the Nguyễn family's lands as part of the Vietnamese state's postwar land redistribution program, which transferred land deeds from anticommunist traitors to communist patriots. As the camera looks on, Hoài Mỹ explains his family's attachment to the land and asks Chú Kỳ to "transfer it back to my family, to give it back so that my children may know their roots."[101] But Chú Kỳ responds that the "government has the right to grant [the land] to someone else," and it is he who is the legitimate owner of the house; he has "all of the (Communist) committee's paperwork" to back up his claims.[102] According to Võ, "Hoimai and Chú Kỳ's claims to ownership of the land rest on different systems of legitimacy—the former insists on family lineage whereas the latter asserts the authority of the state."[103] While Hoài Mỹ appeals to the force of tradition—his family's long-term cultivation of the land—Chú Kỳ insists on the newfound government's system of law and bureaucracy.

In this scene, to what degree does Hoài Mỹ's ancestral claim to his family's lands parallel Palestinians' insistence on the Right of Return, in the face of the Israeli government's imposed Law of Return, which legitimizes Jewish immigration to Israel-Palestine at the same time that it denies Palestinians access to the homes that they have lived in for generations prior to forced displacement? When comparing these two cases of contested land claims—Vietnamese refugees in postwar Vietnam and Palestinians in Israel-Palestine—it is important to attend to historical specificity and acknowledge structural differences. Not all ancestral claims to land are Indigenous claims. The Vietnam War was both a war against imperialism and a civil war, in which Vietnamese communists, anticommunists, and those caught in between all claimed national belonging to *nước Việt Nam*. Although the Vietnamese state has enacted settler colonial policies that displace Indigenous minorities, Hoài Mỹ here is not an Indigenous minority but rather an anticommunist former landowner who left Vietnam as a refugee.[104] In contrast, the Zionist foundation of Israel was characterized by a mass influx of Jewish settlers whose rhetorical claim to the land of Palestine was articulated as a "return" to the Holy Land after millennia of exile—an affective attachment that the State of Israel then codified as the Law of Return via the rhetoric of *aliyah*, which infuses Jewish immigration with the religious connotation of an ascension. Both the Vietnamese government and the Israeli government deny the land claims of the families that fled their lands at the time of the government's foundation: 1975 and 1948, respectively. In the Israeli case, the politics of difference is bolstered by the rhetoric of racial and religious difference: the Islamophobic Othering of the Arab Muslim Palestinian figure, regardless of demographic accuracy. Furthermore, the Israeli government continues to wield settler colonial control over Palestinians living within its 1948 borders and in the Occupied Territories of Gaza and the West Bank—power that the Vietnamese government does not retain over its postwar refugee diaspora.

In Israel-Palestine, Vietnamese Israelis occupy a vexed political positionality in between Jewish Israelis and displaced Palestinians, between the Law of Return and the Right of Return. But what happens when they travel from Israel-Palestine to Vietnam, necessitating an archipelagic analysis of their refugee settler condition?

Are Vietnamese Israelis' journeys of return to Vietnam more akin to the Law of Return or the Right of Return in Israel-Palestine? In other words, when Vietnamese refugees return to reclaim their ancestral lands in postwar Vietnam, are they asserting a birthright, akin to Jewish Israelis, or are they challenging the legality of the newfound state's land acquisition and redistribution, akin to displaced Palestinians? Or both?

To answer this question, one can turn to another moment of cultural and linguistic translation, or mistranslation, in the film. In a scene toward the end of *The Journey of Vaan Nguyen*, Hoài Mỹ guides Nguyen and the documentary film crew through tropical trees and rice fields in search of his father's plot of land. As they walk, Hoài Mỹ asks on-looking villagers for directions, invoking the name of his father, Nguyễn Khác Minh. They wave him forward down the road. After orienting himself, Hoài Mỹ raises his arms and calls out excitedly to the surrounding trees, "Ô, ba má, con đây!" ("Oh father, mother, I'm here!").[105] Nguyen follows, asking her father (in Hebrew) where his house would be. He responds (in Vietnamese) that the house is most likely gone by now. Nguyen spots another house nearby and suggests (again in Hebrew) that they approach and inquire about Hoài Mỹ's familial home. Switching to Hebrew, Hoài Mỹ replies that the neighbors probably wouldn't know, since they are "olim khadashim," or "new immigrants."[106] Surprised by the use of this term, which in the Israeli context refers specifically to Jewish immigrants who immigrate to Israel-Palestine under the Law of Return, Nguyen parrots incredulously, "Olim khadashim? Me-epho?" ("New immigrants? From where?").[107] But before the viewer gets a response, the scene cuts to a different shot of Hoài Mỹ pointing out the vast reach of his ancestral lands while Nguyen looks on admiringly.

Hoài Mỹ's usage of the term *olim khadashim* translates this scene of Vietnamese refugee land reclamation into the vexed vocabulary of Israel-Palestine's own land contestations. *Olim khadashim*, derived from the word *aliyah*, refers specifically to Jewish immigrants who "return" to Israel-Palestine. In identifying the postwar, communist-sympathetic Vietnamese newcomers as "olim khadashim," or "new immigrants" who have the backing of state authority, Hoài Mỹ implicitly positions himself as a dispossessed native Palestinian in this metaphor's binary. To be clear, such a metaphor risks ahistorical erasure of the particular settler colonial dynamics structuring Israel-Palestine. However, by translating the vocabulary of land rights so charged in the Israel-Palestine context into the postwar Vietnamese context, Hoài Mỹ also introduces a possible vector of distinct yet parallel experiences of land dispossession, along which solidarity between Vietnamese Israelis and Palestinians in Israel-Palestine can be further developed. A turn to the English subtitles for this scene further facilitates this possibility. Although the term *olim khadashim* is politically neutral, perhaps even celebratory of Jewish "return" to Israel-Palestine, the film's English subtitles translate "olim khadashim" not as "new immigrants" but as "settlers," adding another complex layer of politicized rhetoric.

They are new settlers.
-Settlers?

FIGURE 11. Film still from *The Journey of Vaan Nguyen* © Zygote Films.

The word "settlers" in white text flashes across the screen twice—once for Hoài Mỹ's assertion, and then again for Nguyen's surprised follow-up question—more explicitly framing Jewish immigration to Israel-Palestine as part of the Zionist state's structure of settler colonialism.

According to Qutami, "The Palestine analytic moves beyond thinking of Palestine as an isolated issue, or an ethnic- or geographic-based cause, and instead allows for thinking through the particularities of Zionist settler-colonialism as informed by and informing structures of oppression globally."[108] Hoài Mỹ's usage of the term *olim khadashim* invites archipelagic comparisons between land dispossession in the settler colonial state of Israel and the postwar communist state of Vietnam, between Palestinians' Indigenous politics of return and Vietnamese Israelis' refugee politics of return. As the previous section on *I Saw Ramallah* and *The Truffle Eye* elaborated, both Palestinians and Vietnamese Israelis suffer exilic affects, though such affects can be rearticulated into contrapuntal exilic poetics, inviting a decolonial future of radical multinationalism. Exilic poetics, in turn, can destabilize divisions between natives, settlers, refugees, and exiles, thereby calling attention to a subject's concurrent location across multiple positionalities. *The Journey of Vaan Nguyen*, meanwhile, reminds viewers that exilic poetics are entangled with land politics—the politics of return to the very soil, plants, and waters that sustained one's family for generations. Although the structural antagonisms dividing Vietnamese Israelis and Palestinians remain material, the film proposes potential grounds for solidarity between Vietnamese Israelis and displaced Palestinians around distinct yet parallel experiences of land dispossession, and subsequent struggles for land reclamation, in Israel-Palestine and Vietnam.

Recognizing their own attachments to their ancestral lands, Vietnamese Israelis can perhaps come to empathize with Palestinian refugees' and exiles' own desires to return to their ancestral villages in Palestine, and work to make those aspirations a reality.

## HOME AS AN ARCHIPELAGO

In "Exiled at Home: Writing Return and the Palestinian Home," Palestinian feminist scholars Nadera Shalhoub-Kevorkian and Sarah Ihmoud testify, "Our geographies of home transcend territorial borders and nation states and a symbolics of national struggle, even as we insist on our belonging to the homeland we call Palestine, on justice for our people, on survival and life. Home is a space where we remember who we are and where we have been, from our multiple locations across the homeland and the shatat [diaspora]."[109] Here, Shalhoub-Kevorkian and Ihmoud articulate an archipelagic understanding of home—one that insists upon Palestinian liberation at the same time that it deterritorializes nation-state claims to sovereignty and instead recognizes multiple geographies of home-making for Palestinian natives, refugees, and exiles. In "Winter City Poem" ("Shir 'arim chorpi"), Vaan Nguyen, too, theorizes home as an archipelago. Israel-Palestine, France, and Vietnam—the land of her birth, the former colonizer of Vietnam, and the homeland of her parents—are connected across four stanzas by the image of rain, which provides the backdrop to the narrator's series of missed romantic encounters in Herzliya, Paris, and Đà Lạt. In the poem, rain, another form of *nước*, brings together these different abodes, calling to mind the epigraph by Chamorro poet Craig Santos Perez that opened this book: "home / is an archipelago of belonging."[110]

Shalhoub-Kevorkian and Ihmoud, moreover, conceptualize home as a "psychological and epistemological space" of "radical thinking and becoming."[111] As this book has endeavored to show, archipelagic understandings of home can unsettle the settler colonial state, calling forth decolonial futures of radical multiplicity that facilitate more ethical forms of relationality between refugee settlers and Indigenous subjects. The following afterword elaborates on visions of Vietnamese refugee futurity through the analytics of islands and archipelagos, articulating home-making in and through *nước*.

# Afterword

## Floating Islands: Refugee Futurities
### and Decolonial Horizons

In their book-length manifesto on "seasteading," Joe Quirk (a "seavangelist") and Patri Freidman (grandson of economist Milton Friedman and founder of the Seasteading Institute) extoll the virtues of "floating nations on the sea," arguing that ocean-based living configurations will restore the environment, enrich the poor, cure the sick, and liberate humanity from oppressive government structures.[1] Characterized as a "globally emerging Blue Revolution" and a "Silicon Valley of the Sea," this seasteading initiative replaces land-based despotism with "fluidity of movement," such that "political power would be radically decentralized and shared."[2] Certain components of Quirk and Friedman's seasteading manifesto resonate with *Archipelago of Resettlement*'s critiques of nation-state borders and its proposal for more archipelagic forms of belonging. Indeed, this book's concerns are not isolated to the specific case studies of Vietnamese refugee settlers across Guam and Israel-Palestine but rather engage broader conversations about refugeehood, displacement, and settler colonialism. Whereas Quirk and Friedman propose a limitless future of libertarian freedom, however, this book takes seriously histories of war, displacement, and colonial occupation. Its imagination of a futurity routed through *nước* is shaped by refugee migration and Indigenous sovereignty.

Quirk and Friedman's color-blind vision of a world of floating nations, in contrast, reproduces settler colonial fantasies of uncharted lands—or, in this case, seas—ripe for conquest. Seasteaders are positioned as pioneers charged with settling the "Blue Frontier"—a twenty-first-century manifestation of President Kennedy's "New Frontier," as discussed in chapter 2.[3] Whereas Kennedy's "New Frontier" elided the United States' history of continental imperialism and charted a future of transpacific militarism, Quirk and Friedman's "Blue Frontier" furthers what Kanaka Maoli scholar Maile Arvin calls a "logic of possession through whiteness": white settler attempts to appropriate Pacific Islanders' lands, seas, bodies, and ideas as their own.[4] The Seasteading Institute's proposal of modular units that can detach, travel, and reattach, offering seasteaders radical freedom to experiment with different modes of living and governance, elides preexisting Indigenous lifeworlds and long histories of expert seafaring. Furthermore, the group's emphasis on untethered mobility raises questions: Who can choose to move, and who is forced to move? Who must fight for the right *not* to be moved?

The preceding chapters have queried the "national order of things" and unsettled the settler colonial state, proposing more fluid understandings of belonging through the Vietnamese concept of *nước:* water, country, homeland.[5] They have challenged land-based understandings of collective organization in favor of more archipelagic imaginaries, rendering visible relations of US empire, militarism, and settler colonialism as well as resettlement, resistance, and decolonization. By way of conclusion, this afterword asks: What would a seasteading project that takes into account Indigenous and refugee histories, epistemologies, and futurities look like? How can a politics of refugeetude inform our decolonial horizons?[6]

According to Quirk and Friedman, humanity as we know it "is poised to plunge in 2050. We can drown or we can float."[7] It is in the year 2049, on the brink of such a civilizational collapse, that Vietnamese American author Linh Dinh sets his one-page futuristic story, "A Floating Community" (2004). In contrast to Quirk and Friedman's utopic vision of seasteading, Dinh's floating community, "discovered eighty miles off the coast of Guam," is marked by forced displacement and precarious resettlement: "ninety-nine individuals" drift aimlessly on "eleven rotting boats, lashed together by ropes," surviving on "flying fish and rain water."[8] The sea is described as both "holy and toxic," the "final resting place of their ancestors" who drowned during the refugee exodus.[9] According to Vinh Nguyen, Dinh's sea is "reconfigured as home rather than transit; or, water becomes a home *in* transit, a drifting home moored in motion."[10] In other words, *nước* and transit are not in opposition to Vietnamese refugee resettlement but rather inherent in it, disrupting the "primacy of linear, property-centric, landlocked liberal individualism and settler-colonial governmentality."[11]

This floating community also retains a certain fungibility, suggesting archipelagic resonances across multiple histories of displacement. While the reference to Guam in the story's first line calls to mind Vietnamese refugees processed during Operation New Life in 1975, the story's invocation of "boat people" refers to later waves of Vietnamese refugees who braved uncertain waters to escape the aftermath of war. Dinh's floating community, therefore, encompasses both the Vietnamese refugees processed in Guam (discussed in chapter 3) and the Vietnamese boat refugees that resettled in Israel-Palestine (discussed in chapter 4). Furthermore, although the narrator speculates that the ninety-nine subjects *might* be "the last of the Vietnamese boat people," they are ultimately described as "individuals of indeterminate nationality."[12] This indeterminacy of nationality—versus ethnicity or race—suggests a critique of nation-state borders: nationhood becomes irrelevant in an apocalyptic future of mass displacement.

Indeed, if the current rate of war, militarism, imperialism, and settler colonialism continues, refugee futurity—understood as a future of mass refugeehood—would not be circumscribed to today's refugees but would come to encompass humanity writ large. This is the future explored in *The Island* (2017), Tuan Andrew Nguyen's forty-two-minute single-channel video installation featured at the 2017 Whitney Biennial. Set in the wake of global nuclear destruction, around the same time as Dinh's "A Floating Community," *The Island* features Pulau Bidong, an island off the coast of Malaysia that served as the largest and longest-operating Southeast Asian refugee camp following the Vietnam War. Between 1978 and 1991, when the United Nations High Commissioner for Refugees closed the camp and repatriated the remaining inhabitants, roughly 250,000 Southeast Asian refugees, including Nguyen and his family, had inhabited the island.[13] According to refugee Han Hai Van, "Many people had an unfounded fear that the island would sink into the sea, and disappear completely with the weight of all the people. I felt as if the planet had stopped, and had forgotten about us."[14] *The Island* takes up these themes of arrested temporality and the politics of memory, cutting between archival footage of the Vietnamese refugee camp during the 1970s and '80s, home videos of refugees returning to Pulau Bidong decades later, and scenes shot by Nguyen in the present to represent Pulau Bidong in the future.

Van's comment about the planet stopping presages the future depicted in *The Island*. In the video installation, only two characters survive the world's nuclear annihilation: a male Vietnamese refugee and a female United Nations scientist. Like *Nước (Water/Homeland)* and *Hoài (Ongoing, Memory)* (discussed in chapter 2) and *The Journey of Vaan Nguyen* (discussed in chapter 6), *The Island* engages refugee politics of translation: the refugee, played by Phạm Anh Khoa, speaks exclusively in Vietnamese accompanied by English subtitles, while the UN scientist, played by Donika Do Tinh, responds in English accompanied by Vietnamese subtitles. Their dialogue is interrupted twice by Khánh Ly's famous song "Biển Nhớ" (The sea remembers), which would play regularly over the camp intercom during the 1970s through the 1990s whenever someone arrived or departed from the island. Having evaded forced repatriation, the unnamed refugee tends to Pulau Bidong alone, rebuilding a memorial commemorating the Vietnamese boat people and serving as a living archive for the human race: "The last wars made refugees out of the entire world. I am now the last on Earth. The one that carries the voices."[15] Vietnamese refugeehood prefigured humanity's refugeehood; humanity's memory is subsequently refracted through an ageless Vietnamese refugee's memory. About a quarter of the way into the video installation, the UN scientist washes upon the shore of Pulau Bidong, having been set adrift when her home, "one of the last ships on the ocean" that had been working toward nuclear disarmament, was destroyed.

Echoing Dinh's "A Floating Community," she recalls: "I must have floated for over a month. No map. No record of how long."[16]

Although the refugee and the UN scientist communicate fluidly across languages, they disagree on how to move forward in the wake of global disaster. The latter becomes frustrated with the refugee's seeming refusal to care about life beyond the island's confines. She stresses that since they are the only two people left on earth, it is up to them to rebuild human civilization. The refugee responds, "So this is the last refugee camp?"[17] This line recalls the specificity of Vietnamese refugeehood on Pulau Bidong, as well as suggests a finality to the condition of refugeehood writ large: no future camp will be necessary in the wake of humanity's destruction. But the scientist, more practical and global in her concerns, insists, "It is the only refuge now. But it won't be for long. We have to think about the future. We have to think of leaving the island."[18] For the scientist, futurity exists beyond the island, which she interprets via the trope of insularity. The refugee reminds viewers, however, that specificity is not in opposition to universality; indeed, one can address global history, memory, and displacement only through specific case studies and situated contexts. Furthermore, no island is in isolation, but rather exists as a part of an archipelagic "sea of islands."[19] *The Island* recalls another island of importance in Vietnamese refugee history, Guam, which served as the first major US processing center for Vietnamese refugees in 1975. Israel-Palestine, in turn, is also caught up in this story. Recall that Prime Minister Hussein Onn's 1979 declaration that he would tow away refugee boats seeking landfall in Malaysia was what spurred Prime Minister Menachem Begin to resettle the third wave of Vietnamese refugees in Israel-Palestine, including the parents of Vietnamese Israeli poet Vaan Nguyen. Indeed, *The Island* asserts that Vietnamese refugee history impresses not only upon the Vietnam War diaspora but also upon the world writ large.

Pulau Bidong is at once a cautionary tale against global refugeehood and the cradle of a new world order following global destruction. The refugee and the scientist argue about the organization of this new world:

Scientist: . . . We have to rebuild. We have to repopulate.

Refugee: You think we live in a fairy tale like the Mountain Fairy and the Dragon King?

Scientist: What I am talking about is not the origin story of the nation. It's the opposite. I am talking about the end of the world, and our responsibility to think of the future.

Refugee: A future for whom?

Scientist: For us. For humans.

Refugee: You've seen the brutality humans have caused.

Scientist: What do you know about anything? You've been on an island your entire life. Have you ever imagined an elsewhere?

Refugee: In that case, we are going to end the brutality right here. In the most
gentle way possible.[20]

According to the scientist, global nuclear destruction serves as an opening for
reorganizing the world anew, not around nations or settler colonial states but
around more ethical and contrapuntal forms of belonging as theorized in the
preceding chapters. The refugee reminds viewers, however, that such visions for
the future are not untethered from history, as Quirk and Friedman seem to suggest
in their seasteading manifesto, but are rather rooted in place-based mythologies.
Recall the story of the Mountain Fairy and the Dragon King that opened this
book's introduction: the pair bore one hundred children who then split, half following their mother to the mountains and the other half following their father
to the sea. The refugee observes that this is a "story of how the past predicted
the future. Seems we've been caught between separation and exodus ever since."[21]
"Future" here refers both to the Vietnamese refugee exodus of the 1970s and '80s
and to the postnuclear future of Dinh's and Nguyen's 2049. In other words, Vietnamese refugeehood is not incidental to global history but profoundly premoni-
tory, warning of a postapocalyptic future if the current world order of forced displacement continues unabated. If humanity does get annihilated, according to
the scientist, the solution is to rebuild and repopulate. In contrast, the refugee,
acknowledging humanity's role in the world's environmental and nuclear destruction, proposes a more Indigenous cosmological approach in which humans give
way to a different world order that acknowledges human entanglements with non-
human collectives.

Such refugee futurity is characterized not by defeat but by a different articulation of refugee resilience. Although the video installation's final scene consists
of a gender-ambiguous figure's back—either the refugee's or the scientist's—suddenly disappearing under the ocean's surface, this image of drowning is undercut
by the refugee's voiceover, which insists, "We must keep afloat."[22] This imperative
is preceded by a provocation: "We exist only in the traces we leave behind. And
those traces are echoed only in our memories of them. The relics, the mementos,
the mythologies, the mysteries, the memorials, the monuments. All in an ocean of
sinking memories. Which ones do we cling to in order to keep adrift?"[23]

This book insists on the importance of mapping archipelagic histories of refugee resettlement in order to envision decolonial futures. Yet history must not be
uncritically memorialized. We must sift through the traces of the past, to figure out
which ones "we cling to in order to keep adrift." I suggest we let go of attachments
to settler colonialism, refugee displacement, and nation-state exclusion and work
instead toward an archipelago of decolonization. *Nước*, or what Vinh Nguyen calls
"*oceanic spatiality*—the waterscape of the boat and of the sea"—can help to wash
away the debris.[24]

In *The Island*, Pulau Bidong is described as "an island that became a refuge. The
second country. An in-between existence."[25] This in-betweenness marks a space of

transition, between one home and another, one world and another. But it is also, according to the refugee, "a space between life and death, land and sea, past and future." Like *nước*, an island bridges land and water. Like the present, it connects past and future. Only by engaging refugee pasts, and working through the refugee settler condition in the present, can we begin to theorize refugee futurities and decolonial horizons.

Only then can we keep afloat.

## INTRODUCTION

1. lê thi diem thúy, *The Gangster We Are All Looking For* © 2003 by lê thi diem thúy. Used by permission of Alfred A. Knopf, an imprint of the Knopf Doubleday Publishing Group, a division of Penguin Random House LLC. Reprinted by permission of the author and Aragi Inc. All rights reserved.

2. Mahmoud Darwish, *Memory for Forgetfulness: August, Beirut, 1982* © 1995 by the Regents of the University of California. Used by permission of University of California Press.

3. Craig Santos Perez, "Off-Island Chamorros," *Craig Santos Perez*, 25 July 2017, https://craigsantosperez.wordpress.com/2017/07/25/off-island-chamorros/. Used by permission of Craig Santos Perez.

4. Epeli Hau'ofa, "Our Sea of Islands," *Contemporary Pacific* 6, no. 1 (Spring 1994): 152.

5. Huỳnh Sanh Thông, "Live by Water, Die for Water: Metaphors of Vietnamese Culture and History," *Vietnam Review* 1 (Autumn–Winter 1996): 143.

6. Vinh Nguyen, "*Nước*/Water: Oceanic Spatiality and the Vietnamese Diaspora," in *Migration by Boat: Discourses of Trauma, Exclusion, and Survival*, ed. Lynda Mannik (New York: Berghahn Books, 2016), 67.

7. Patrick Wolfe, "Settler Colonialism and the Elimination of the Native," *Journal of Genocide Research* 8, no. 4 (Dec. 2006): 388.

8. Wolfe, 387; Lila Sharif, "Vanishing Palestine," *Critical Ethnic Studies* 2, no. 1 (Spring 2016): 18.

9. Leanne Betasamosake Simpson, "Indigenous Resurgence and Co-resistance," *Critical Ethnic Studies* 2, no. 2 (Fall 2016): 19–34.

10. Yến Lê Espiritu, *Body Counts: The Vietnam War and Militarized Refuge(es)* (Berkeley: University of California Press, 2014), 10–11.

11. Giorgio Agamben, "We Refugees," trans. Michael Rocke, *Symposium* 49, no. 2 (Summer 1995): 117; Hannah Arendt, "We Refugees," in *Altogether Elsewhere: Writers on Exile*, ed. Marc Robinson (Boston: Faber and Faber, 1994), 110–19.

12. Hannah Arendt, *The Origins of Totalitarianism* (New York: Harcourt, 1973), 267–302; Liisa H. Malkki, "Refugees and Exile: From 'Refugee Studies' to the National Order of Things," *Annual Review of Anthropology* 24 (1995): 495–523.

13. Agamben, "We Refugees," 117.

14. Espiritu, *Body Counts*, 11.

15. Eman Ghanayem, "Colonial Loops of Displacement in the United States and Israel: The Case of Rasmea Odeh," *WSQ: Women's Studies Quarterly* 47, nos. 3–4 (2019): 87.

16. Espiritu, *Body Counts*, 2 (emphasis in original).

17. Yến Lê Espiritu, "The 'We-Win-Even-When-We-Lose' Syndrome: U.S. Press Coverage of the Twenty-Fifth Anniversary of the 'Fall of Saigon,'" *American Quarterly* 58, no. 2 (2006): 330.

18. Lorenzo Veracini, *The Settler Colonial Present* (New York: Palgrave Macmillan, 2015), 35.

19. Jodi A. Byrd, *The Transit of Empire: Indigenous Critiques of Colonialism* (Minneapolis: University of Minnesota Press, 2011), xxxv.

20. Haunani-Kay Trask, "Settlers of Color and 'Immigrant' Hegemony," in *Asian Settler Colonialism: From Local Governance to the Habits of Everyday Life in Hawai'i*, ed. Candace Fujikane and Jonathan Y. Okamura (Honolulu: University of Hawai'i Press, 2008), 45–65; Haunani-Kay Trask, "Settlers, Not Immigrants," in *Asian Settler Colonialism*, vii.

21. Candace Fujikane and Jonathan Y. Okamura, eds., *Asian Settler Colonialism: From Local Governance to the Habits of Everyday Life in Hawai'i* (Honolulu: University of Hawai'i Press, 2008); Dean Itsuji Saranillio, "Why Asian Settler Colonialism Matters: A Thought Piece on Critiques, Debates, and Indigenous Difference," *Settler Colonial Studies* 3, no. 3–4 (2013): 280–94; Dean Itsuji Saranillio, *Unsustainable Empire: Alternative Histories of Hawai'i Statehood* (Durham, NC: Duke University Press, 2018); Manu Karuka, *Empire's Tracks: Indigenous Nations, Chinese Workers, and the Transcontinental Railroad* (Berkeley: University of California Press, 2019); Karen J. Leong and Myla Vicenti Carpio, eds., "Carceral States," special issue, *Amerasia Journal* 42, no. 1 (2016): vi–152; Quynh Nhu Le, *Unsettled Solidarities: Asian and Indigenous Cross-Representations in the Américas* (Philadelphia: Temple University Press, 2019); Juliana Hu Pegues, *Space-Time Colonialism: Alaska's Indigenous and Asian Entanglements* (Chapel Hill: University of North Carolina Press, 2021); Erin Suzuki, *Ocean Passages: Navigating Pacific Islander and Asian American Literatures* (Philadelphia: Temple University Press, 2021); Candace Fujikane, *Mapping Abundance for a Planetary Future: Kanaka Maoli and Critical Settler Cartographies in Hawai'i* (Durham, NC: Duke University Press, 2021).

22. Iyko Day, *Alien Capital: Asian Racialization and the Logic of Settler Colonial Capitalism* (Durham, NC: Duke University Press, 2016), 19; Yu-ting Huang, "Between Sovereignties: Chinese Minor Settler Literature across the Pacific" (PhD diss., Department of Comparative Literature, University of California, Los Angeles, 2015), UCLA Electronic Theses and Dissertations, ii.

23. For recent work that has grappled with Vietnamese refugee-Indigenous relations in settler colonial states, see Evyn Lê Espiritu, "Vexed Solidarities: Vietnamese Israelis and the Question of Palestine," *LIT: Literature, Interpretation, Theory* 29, no. 1 (2018): 8–28; Quynh

Nhu Le, "The Colonial Choreographies of Refugee Resettlement in Lan Cao's *Monkey Bridge*," *Journal of Asian American Studies* 21, no. 3 (Oct. 2018): 395–420; Vinh Nguyen, "Refugeetude: When Does a Refugee Stop Being a Refugee?" *Social Text* 139, no. 2 (June 2019): 109–31; Christina Juhasz-Wood, "Contesting Historical Enchantment: Militarized Settler Colonialism and Refugee Resettlement in New Mexico" (PhD diss., University of New Mexico, 2020), UNM Electronic Theses and Dissertations; Evyn Lê Espiritu Gandhi, "Historicizing the Transpacific Settler Colonial Condition: Asian–Indigenous Relations in Shawn Wong's *Homebase* and Viet Thanh Nguyen's *The Sympathizer*," *MELUS* 45, no. 4 (Winter 2020): 49–71; and Yến Lê Espiritu and J. A. Ruanto-Ramirez, "The Philippine Refugee Processing Center: The Relational Displacements of Vietnamese Refugees and the Indigenous Aetas," *Verge* 6, no. 1 (Spring 2020): 118–41. This is the first book-length study, however, to address the refugee settler condition.

24. "The Blue Mountain Forts," *Wilkes-Barre (PA) Record*, 10 June 1869, 7; "The Indian Troubles," *Osage County Chronicle*, Burlingame, KS, 13 June 1878, 1; "The Indian War," *Wilkes-Barre (PA) Record*, Wilkes-Barre, PA, 13 June 1878, 1; "The Indian Troubles," *News Journal*, Wilmington, DE, 13 June 1878, 3; "Idaho Indian Trouble," *Public Ledger*, Memphis, TN, 13 June 1878, 2; "News of the Day," *Alexandria (VA) Gazette*, 13 June 1878, 2; "Indian Troubles," *Indianapolis News*, Indianapolis, 13 June 1878, 1; "Six Hundred Warriors Terrifying Idaho," *Evening Star*, Washington, DC, 13 June 1878, 1; "Indians on the War Path," *Raleigh News*, Raleigh, NC, 14 June 1878, 1; "The Indian Trouble," *Daily Democratic Statesman*, Austin, 14 June 1878, 1; "The Indians," *Wilmington (NC) Morning Star*, 14 June 1878, 4; "The Idaho Indians," *Daily American*, Nashville, TN, 14 June 1878, 4; "The Hostile Indians," *Poughkeepsie Eagle-News*, 14 June 1878, 2; "Hostile Indians," *The Times*, Philadelphia, 14 June 1878, 1; "Evening Telegrams," *Montgomery Advertiser*, 14 June 1878, 3; "San Francisco," *Times-Picayune*, New Orleans, LA, 14 June 1878, 8; "The Nation's Red Wards in the West," *Observer*, Raleigh, NC, 14 June 1878, 1; "The Indians," *Philadelphia Inquirer*, 14 June 1878, 1; "The Warlike Indians," *New York Times*, 14 June 1878, 1; "The Red Rascals," *Cincinnati Enquirer*, 14 June 1878, 5; "The Indian War," *Daily Constitution*, Atlanta, 14 June 1878, 1; "The Noble Red Men," *Charlotte Observer*, 14 June 1878, 2; "Serious Trouble with Indians Anticipated," *Tri-Weekly Herald*, Marshall, TX, 15 June 1878, 3; "The Nation's Red Wards in the West," *Weekly Observer*, Raleigh, NC, 18 June 1878, 4; "By Telegraph," *Deseret News*, Salt Lake City, 19 June 1878, 308; "A General Indian Uprising," *Summit County Beacon*, Akron, OH, 19 June 1878, 2; "Indian Outrages," *Valley Spirit*, Chambersburg, PA, 19 June 1878, 2; "Indian War," *Helena (MT) Weekly Herald*, 20 June 1878, 2; "Petaluma Creek," *Petaluma (CA) Weekly Argus*, 26 June 1878, 2; "The Freedman's Aid Association of Dunlap, Kansas," *Greenley (KS) News*, 3 Nov. 1881, 3; "City and Neighborhood," *Salt Lake Tribune*, 23 Jan. 1891, 8; "The Indian Forts of the Blue Mountains," *Reading (PA) Times*, 10 Mar. 1896, 2; "Old Indian Forts," *Allentown (PA) Daily Leader*, 12 Mar. 1896, 1; "Blue Mountain Forts," *Wilkes-Barre (PA) Semi-Weekly Record*, 12 June 1896, 5; "Frontier Forts," *Pike Country Press*, Milford, PA, 28 Jan. 1898, 2; "Settlers Are Returning to Their Homes," *Dayton (OH) Herald*, 13 Oct. 1898, 1; "Redskin Trouble Is Ended," *Marion (OH) Star*, 13 Oct. 1898, 1; "Indian War Council," *Pittsburgh Press*, 13 Oct. 1898, 3; "Indian Council Held Last Night," *Elmira (NY) Gazette*, 13 Oct. 1898, 1; "Indians Have Backed Down," *Buffalo (NY) Enquirer*, 13 Oct. 1898, 6.

25. Evan Taparata, "'Refugees As You Call Them': The Politics of Refugee Recognition in the Nineteenth-Century United States," *Journal of American Ethnic History* 38, no. 2 (Winter

2019): 10; Nick Estes, *Our History Is the Future: Standing Rock versus the Dakota Access Pipeline, and the Long Tradition of Indigenous Resistance* (London: Verso, 2019), 247.

26.  Mary Carnahan, "The Ideal American," *Randall (KS) Enterprise*, 15 May 1924, 6.

27.  For examples referring to displaced Indigenous subjects as "refugees," see Roxanne Dunbar-Ortiz, *An Indigenous Peoples' History of the United States* (Boston: Beacon Press, 2014), 74, 77, 84, 87, 157; James Spady, "As if in a Great Darkness: Native American Refugees of the Middle Connecticut River Valley in the Aftermath of King Philip's War," *Historical Journal of Massachusetts* 23, no. 2 (Summer 1995): 183; Christopher Vecsey and Robert W. Venables, eds., *American Indian Environments: Ecological Issues in Native American History* (Syracuse: Syracuse University Press, 1980), ix; Laurence M. Hauptman, "Refugee Havens: The Iroquois Villages of the Eighteenth Century," in *American Indian Environments*, 128–39; Taparata, "'Refugees as You Call Them,'" 9–11, 24–29.

28.  Ikuko Asaka, *Tropical Freedom: Climate, Settler Colonialism, and Black Exclusion in the Age of Emancipation* (Durham, NC: Duke University Press, 2017), 120.

29.  Richard G. Massock (AP), "Parley Hunts Refuge for Persecuted," *Detroit Free Press*, 18 Apr. 1943, 10; AP, "Refugee Problem Is Under Study," *Big Spring (TX) Daily Herald*, 18 Apr. 1943, 6; AP, "Refugee Aid Soon Is Goal," *Baltimore Sun*, 18 Apr. 1943, 7; AP, "Refugee Parley to Be Practical," *Indianapolis Star*, 18 Apr. 1943, 5; AP, "Haven Sought for Refugees of Nazism," *Leader-Telegram*, Eau Claire, WI, 18. Apr. 1943, 1, 12; AP, "Places South for Persecuted," *Poughkeepsie Sunday New Yorker*, 18 Apr. 1943, 8; AP, "Refuge for Persecuted Under Study," *Shreveport Times*, 18 Apr. 1943, 5; AP, "U.S. Delegates Seeking Haven for Refugees," *Pantagraph*, Bloomington, IL, 18 Apr. 1943, 1; AP, "War Victims Cannot Be Fed While under Control of Nazis, Bloom Says," *Cincinnati Enquirer*, 18 Apr. 1943, 13; AP, "Pressure Put on Parleys to Aid Refugees," *Courier*, Waterloo, IA, 18 Apr. 1943, 1; AP, "Bermuda Parley to Seek Place for Refuge," *Decatur (IL) Sunday Herald and Review*, 18 Apr. 1943, 25; Richard G. Massock (AP), "Pressure Felt by Refugee Conferees," *Monitor*, McAllen, TX, 18 Apr. 1943, 3; AP, "Haven Sought for Refugees," *Des Moines Register*, 18 Apr. 1943, 8; AP, "U.S. to Seek Refugee Homes on Strictly Practical Basis," *Ashbury Park (NJ) Press*, 18 Apr. 1943, 9; AP, "To Seek Havens for Refugees from Nazi-Ridden Territories," *Daily Press*, Newport News, VA, 18 Apr. 1943, 8B; "Homes Sought for Refugees from Europe," *Sunday Times*, New Brunswick, NJ, 18 Apr. 1943, 7; Richard G. Massock (AP), "Refugee Conference Hopes to Find Homes for Persecuted Groups," *Tennessean*, Nashville, 18 Apr. 1943, 17; Richard G. Massock (AP), "Parley Begins to Find Homes for Refugees," *Arizona Republic*, Phoenix, 19 Apr. 1943, 3.

30.  Referring to Jewish refugees who settled Palestine, Patrick Wolfe asserts that "there is no necessary tension between being a refugee and being a settler." See Patrick Wolfe, "Purchase by Other Means: Dispossessing the Natives in Palestine," in *Traces of History: Elementary Structures of Race* (London: Verso, 2016), 203.

31.  Michael Rothberg, *The Implicated Subject: Beyond Victims and Perpetrators* (Stanford, CA: Stanford University Press, 2019).

32.  Espiritu, *Body Counts*, 21.

33.  Nhi T. Lieu, *The American Dream in Vietnamese* (Minneapolis: University of Minnesota Press, 2011); Isabelle Thuy Pelaud, *This Is All I Choose to Tell: History and Hybridity in Vietnamese American Literature* (Philadelphia: Temple University Press, 2011); Mimi Thi Nguyen, *The Gift of Freedom: War, Debt, and Other Refugee Passages* (Durham, NC: Duke University Press, 2012); Espiritu, *Body Counts*; Viet Thanh Nguyen, *Nothing Ever Dies: Vietnam and the Memory of War* (Cambridge: Harvard University Press, 2016); Phuong Tran

Nguyen, *Becoming Refugee American: The Politics of Rescue in Little Saigon* (Urbana: University of Illinois Press, 2017); Marguerite Nguyen, *America's Vietnam: The Longue Durée of U.S. Literature and Empire* (Philadelphia: Temple University Press, 2018); Long T. Bui, *Returns of War: South Vietnam and the Price of Refugee Memory* (New York: New York University Press, 2018); Timothy K. August, *The Refugee Aesthetic: Reimagining Southeast Asian America* (Philadelphia: Temple University Press, 2021).

34. Byrd, *The Transit of Empire*, xx.

35. Eve Tuck and K. Wayne Yang, "Decolonization Is Not a Metaphor," *Decolonization: Indigeneity, Education & Society* 1, no. 1 (2012): 31.

36. Chadwick Allen, *Trans-Indigenous: Methodologies for Global Native Literary Studies* (Minneapolis: University of Minnesota Press, 2012), xxxii.

37. Allen, xix.

38. Jana K. Lipman, *In Camps: Vietnamese Refugees, Asylum Seekers, and Repatriates* (Oakland: University of California Press, 2020).

39. Daniel Wolf and Shep Lowman, "Toward a New Consensus of the Vietnamese Boat People," *SAIS Review* 10, no. 2 (1990): 103.

40. Michael F. Phillips, "Land," in *Kinalamten Pulitikåt: Siñenten I Chamorro / Issues in Guam's Political Development: The Chamorro Perspective* (Agaña, Guam: Political Status and Education Coordinating Commission, 1996), 4.

41. In his dissenting opinion in one of the cases, Supreme Court justice John Marshall Harlan wrote: "The idea that this country may acquire territories anywhere upon the earth, by conquest or treaty, and hold them as mere colonies or provinces—the people inhabiting them to enjoy only such rights as Congress chooses to accord to them—is wholly inconsistent with the spirit and genius, as well as with the words, of the Constitution." See *Downes v. Bidwell*, 182 U.S. 244, 372–73 (1901).

42. Robert F. Rogers, *Destiny's Landfall: A History of Guam* (Honolulu: University of Hawai'i Press, 1995), 206–33; Doloris Coulter Cogan, *We Fought the Navy and Won* (Honolulu: University of Hawai'i Press, 2008); R. D. K. Herman, "Inscribing Empire: Guam and the War in the Pacific National Historical Park," *Political Geography* 27 (2008): 630–51.

43. Timothy P. Maga, "The Citizenship Movement in Guam, 1946–1950," *Pacific Historical Review* 53, no. 1 (1984): 71.

44. Rogers, *Destiny's Landfall*, 207.

45. Bart Stinson, "Civilian Government Was Born from the Organic Act in 1950," *Pacific Daily News* (hereafter *PDN*), 9 Oct. 1986, 4.

46. Catherine Lutz, "US Military Bases on Guam in a Global Perspective," *Asia-Pacific Journal* 30, no. 3 (26 July 2010), http://apjjf.org/-Catherine-Lutz/3389/article.html.

47. Juliet Nebolon, "'Life Given Straight from the Heart': Settler Militarism, Biopolitics, and Public Health in Hawai'i during World War II," *American Quarterly* 69, no. 1 (Mar. 2017): 25.

48. Setsu Shigematsu and Keith L. Camacho, eds., *Militarized Currents: Toward a Decolonized Future in Asia and the Pacific* (Minneapolis: University of Minnesota Press, 2010).

49. Wolfe, "Purchase by Other Means."

50. Theodor Herzl, *The Jewish State*, trans. Harry Zohn (New York: Herzl Press, 1970).

51. Judith Apter Klinghoffer, *Vietnam, Jews, and the Middle East: Unintended Consequences* (New York: St. Martin's Press, 1999), 70.

52. Alan George, "'Making the Desert Bloom': A Myth Examined," *Journal of Palestine Studies* 8, no. 2 (Winter 1979): 88.

53. Michael Brenner, *Zionism: A Brief History*, trans. Shelley L. Frisch (Princeton, NJ: Markus Wiener, 2006).

54. Walid Khalidi, ed., *All That Remains: The Palestinian Villages Occupied and Depopu-lated by Israel in 1948* (Washington, DC: Institute for Palestine Studies, 2006); Rochelle Davis, *Palestinian Village Histories: Geographies of the Displaced* (Stanford, CA: Stanford University Press, 2011); Ahmad H. Sa'di and Lila Abu-Lughod, eds., *Nakba: Palestine, 1948, and the Claims of Memory* (New York: Columbia University Press, 2007).

55. George, "'Making the Desert Bloom'"; Edward W. Said, "Reflections on Exile," in *Reflections on Exile and Other Essays* (Cambridge, MA: Harvard University Press, 2000), 141.

56. During the war, Israel also conquered the Sinai Peninsula, which it later rescinded, and the Golan Heights, the western portion of which remains occupied.

57. Joseph R. Farag, *Politics and Palestinian Literature in Exile: Gender, Aesthetics and Resistance in the Short Story* (London: I. B. Tauris, 2017), 75; Ilan Pappé, *A History of Modern Palestine: One Land, Two Peoples* (Cambridge: Cambridge University Press, 2004), 139.

58. Byrd, *The Transit of Empire*, xv.

59. Karuka, *Empire's Tracks*, xii.

60. Tiara R. Na'puti and Michael Lujan Bevacqua, "Militarization and Resistance from Guåhan: Protecting and Defending Pågat," *American Quarterly* 67, no. 3 (Sept. 2015): 837.

61. Amy Kaplan, *Our American Israel: The Story of an Entangled Alliance* (Cambridge, MA: Harvard University Press, 2018).

62. Steven Salaita, *The Holy Land in Transit: Colonialism and the Quest for Canaan* (Syracuse, NY: Syracuse University Press, 2006); David Lloyd and Laura Pulido, "In the Long Shadow of the Settler: On Israeli and U.S. Colonialisms," *American Quarterly* 62, no. 4 (Dec. 2010): 795–809; Steven Salaita, *Inter/Nationalism: Decolonizing Native America and Palestine* (Minneapolis: University of Minnesota Press, 2016); Juliana Hu Pegues, "Empire, Race, and Settler Colonialism: BDS and Contingent Solidarities," *Theory & Event* 19, no. 4 (2016): http://muse.jhu.edu/article/633272; Ghanayem, "Colonial Loops of Displacement."

63. Craig Santos Perez, *from Unincorporated Territory [lukao]* (Oakland, California: Omnidawn Publishing, 2017), 55. Used by permission of Omnidawn.

64. Ibrahim Muhawi, "Introduction," in *Memory for Forgetfulness: August, Beirut, 1982* (Berkeley: University of California Press, 1995), xxv.

65. Mishuana Goeman, "Land as Life: Unsettling the Logics of Containment," in *Native Studies Keywords*, ed. Stephanie Nohelani Teves, Andrea Smith, and Michelle H. Raheja (Tucson: University of Arizona Press, 2015), 72–73.

66. Irene Watson, "Settled and Unsettled Spaces: Are We Free to Roam?" in *Sovereign Subjects: Indigenous Sovereignty Matters*, ed. Aileen Moreton-Robinson (Crows Nest, New South Wales: Allen & Unwin, 2007), 20. See also Leanne Betasamosake Simpson, "The Place Where We All Live and Work Together: A Gendered Analysis of 'Sovereignty,'" in *Native Studies Keywords*, ed. Stephanie Nohelani Teves, Andrea Smith, and Michelle H. Raheja (Tucson: University of Arizona Press, 2015), 18.

67. Glen Coulthard and Leanne Betasamosake Simpson, "Grounded Normativity/ Place-Based Solidarity," *American Quarterly* 68, no. 2 (2016): 254.

68. Simpson, "Indigenous Resurgence and Co-resistance," 22.

69. Wolfe, "Settler Colonialism and the Elimination of the Native," 388; Goeman, "Land as Life," 71.

70. Tiffany Lethabo King proposes another land/water formation—the shoals—as a medium and metaphor for comparative ethnic studies. However, while King risks reifying Blackness as water and Indigeneity as land, this book insists upon the nonopposition of land and water, of Indigenous and refugee. See Tiffany Lethabo King, *The Black Shoals: Offshore Formations of Black and Native Studies* (Durham, NC: Duke University Press, 2019).

71. Jodi A. Byrd, "American Indian Transnationalisms," in *The Cambridge Companion to Transnational American Literature*, ed. Yogita Goyal (Cambridge: Cambridge University Press, 2017), 177.

72. Albert Wendt, "Towards a New Oceania," *Mana Review* 1, no. 1 (1976): 49–60; Vicente M. Diaz and J. Kehaulani Kauanui, "Native Pacific Cultural Studies on the Edge," *Contemporary Pacific* 13, no. 2 (2001): 315–42; Tiara R. Na'puti, "Oceanic Possibilities for Communication Studies," *Communication and Critical/Cultural Studies* 17, no. 1 (2020): 95–103.

73. Lanny Thompson, "Heuristic Geographies: Territories and Area, Islands and Archipelagoes," in *Archipelagic American Studies*, ed. Brian Russell Roberts and Michelle Ann Stephens (Durham, NC: Duke University Press, 2017), 70.

74. Édouard Glissant, *Poetics of Relation* (Ann Arbor: University of Michigan Press, 1997), 11.

75. Vicente M. Diaz, "No Island Is an Island," in *Native Studies Keywords*, 90–91, 97.

76. Michel Foucault, *Discipline and Punish: The Birth of the Prison*, trans. Alan Sheridan (New York: Vintage Books, 1995), 297; Paul Amar, *The Security Archipelago: Human-Security States, Sexuality Politics, and the End of Neoliberalism* (Durham, NC: Duke University Press, 2013); Sylvia Wynter, "Unsettling the Coloniality of Being/Power/Truth/Freedom: Towards the Human, After Man, Its Overrepresentation—An Argument," *CR: New Centennial Review* 3, no. 3 (Fall 2003): 257–337; Gleb Raygorodetsky, *The Archipelago of Hope: Wisdom and Resilience from the Edge of Climate Change* (New York: Pegasus Books, 2017); Alison Mountz, "Political Geography II: Islands and Archipelagos," *Progress in Human Geography* 39, no. 5 (2015): 636–46; Harrod J. Suarez, "Archipelagoes and Oceania in Asian American and Pacific Islander Literary Studies," *Oxford Research Encyclopedia of Literature*, July 2018, https://doi.org/10.1093/acrefore/9780190201098.013.874.

77. Brian Russell Roberts and Michelle Ann Stephens, eds., *Archipelagic American Studies* (Durham, NC: Duke University Press, 2017). See also Hester Blum et al., eds., "Archipelagoes/Oceans/American Visuality," special issue, *Journal of Transnational American Studies* 10, no. 1 (2019): 1–222.

78. Lanny Thompson, *Imperial Archipelago: Representation and Rule in the Insular Territories under U.S. Dominion after 1898* (Honolulu: University of Hawai'i Press, 2010); Bruce Cumings, *Dominion from Sea to Sea: Pacific Ascendancy and American Power* (New Haven, CT: Yale University Press, 2009), 393.

79. Brian Russell Roberts, *Borderwaters: Amid the Archipelagic States of America* (Durham, NC: Duke University Press, 2021).

80. For more on how the history of Japanese and American colonial administration across the Mariana Archipelago has shaped Chamorro cultural memory, see Keith

L. Camacho, *Cultures of Commemoration: The Politics of War, Memory, and History in the Mariana Islands* (Honolulu: University of Hawai'i Press, 2011); Keith L. Camacho, *Sacred Men: Law, Torture, and Retribution in Guam* (Durham, NC: Duke University Press, 2019).

81. After World War II, the Northern Marianas voted in favor of reintegration with Guam in a series of four referendums. Decades of colonial divisions, however, prompted Guam's residents to reject the proposed integration in 1969. In the 1970s, the Northern Mariana Islands (NMI) decided to push for commonwealth status instead of independence, and in 1978 it officially established the Commonwealth of the Northern Mariana Islands (CNMI) as an insular area and commonwealth of the United States.

82. Tiara R. Na'puti, "Archipelagic Rhetoric: Remapping the Marianas and Challenging Militarization from 'A Stirring Place,'" *Communication and Critical/Cultural Studies* 16, no. 1 (2019): 6.

83. Jennifer Lynn Kelly, "Asymmetrical Itineraries: Militarism, Tourism, and Solidarity in Occupied Palestine," *American Quarterly* 68, no. 3 (Sept. 2016): 725.

84. Bousac's map unwittingly feeds into Zionist accusations that Palestinian revolutionaries seek to annihilate Jewish settlers by pushing them into the sea. It is not my intent to condone such genocidal rhetoric. See Moshe Shemesh, "Did Shuqayri Call for 'Throwing the Jews into the Sea'?" *Israel Studies* 8, no. 2 (Summer 2003): 70–81.

85. Loubna Qutami and Omar Zahzah, "The War of Words: Language as an Instrument of Palestinian National Struggle," *Arab Studies Quarterly* 42, nos. 1–2 (Winter/Spring 2020): 76.

86. Qutami and Zahzah, 82.

87. Qutami and Zahzah, 81–82.

88. lê thi diem thúy, *The Gangster We Are All Looking For* © 2003 by lê thi diem thúy. Used by permission of Alfred A. Knopf, an imprint of the Knopf Doubleday Publishing Group, a division of Penguin Random House LLC. Reprinted by permission of the author and Aragi Inc. All rights reserved.

89. Stephanie Nohelani Teves, Andrea Smith, and Michelle H. Raheja, "Indigeneity," in *Native Studies Keywords*, 109.

90. Linda Tuhiwai Smith, *Decolonizing Methodologies: Research and Indigenous Peoples*, 2nd edition (London: Zed Books, 2012), 7.

91. Smith, 7.

92. Teves, Smith, and Raheja, "Indigeneity," 116.

93. "Chamorro vs. Chamoru," *Guampedia*, accessed 12 May 2017, http://www.guampedia.com/chamorro-vs-chamoru/.

94. "Guamanian" originated in the late 1940s, following World War II, when Chamorros in Guam asked the US naval government to refer to them as such in order to differentiate themselves from Chamorros in the Northern Marianas Islands, who were not US nationals and who had sided with the Japanese during World War II. "Guamanian" was also a way to identify with the land, as the Hawaiians, Rotanese, and Saipanese had done. "Chamorro" and "Guamanian" were used interchangeably in Guam up until the 1970s when the Chamorro decolonization movement realigned the term "Chamorro" with Indigenous rights.

95. Susan Guffey, "Evacuee Flood Flows On," *PDN*, 25 Apr. 1975, 3.

96. Jana K. Lipman, "'Give Us a Ship': The Vietnamese Repatriate Movement on Guam, 1975," *American Quarterly* 64, no. 1 (2012): 7.

97. Lipman, 7.

98. Nguyen, "Refugeetude," 110; Khatharya Um, *From the Land of Shadows: War, Revolution, and the Making of the Cambodian Diaspora* (New York: New York University Press, 2015), 213.

99. Marianne Hirsch, "Past Lives: Postmemories in Exile," *Poetics Today* 17, no. 4 (Winter 1996): 659.

100. Nguyen, "Refugeetude," 112.

101. Trinh T. Minh-ha, "An Acoustic Journey," in *Rethinking Borders*, ed. J. Welchman (London: Macmillan Press; Minneapolis: University of Minnesota Press, 1996), 6. Reproduced with permission of SNCSC and University of Minnesota Press.

102. Raymond Williams, *Marxism and Literature* (Oxford: Oxford University Press, 1978), 132.

103. Mourid Barghouti, *I Saw Ramallah*, trans. Ahdaf Soueif (New York: Anchor Books, 2003), 41.

## 1. ARCHIPELAGIC HISTORY

1. "Egypt, Israel Agree on Terms: Kissinger," *PDN*, 2 Sept. 1975, 1; Arafat, quoted in "Palestine Guerrillas on Offensive," *PDN*, 2 Sept. 1975, 1.

2. James A. Hebert, "U.S. Marshal Injured in Violence at Asan," *PDN*, 2 Sept. 1975, 1.

3. Lipman, "'Give Us a Ship.'" The Vietnamese repatriates are discussed in chapter 5.

4. See, for example, Akira Iriye, *Global and Transnational History: The Past, Present, and Future* (London: Palgrave Macmillan, 2013).

5. Lisa Lowe, *The Intimacies of Four Continents* (Durham, NC: Duke University Press, 2015), 6.

6. Sunaina Maira and Magid Shihade, "Meeting Asian/Arab Studies: Thinking Race, Empire, and Zionism in the U.S.," *Journal of Asian American Studies* 9, no. 2 (2006): 117–40; Junaid Rana and Diane C. Fujino, "Taking Risks, or The Question of Palestine Solidarity and Asian American Studies," *American Quarterly* 67, no. 4 (2015): 1027–37; Lisa Kahaleole Hall, "Which of These Things Is Not Like the Other: Hawaiians and Other Pacific Islanders Are Not Asian Americans, and All Pacific Islanders Are Not Hawaiian," *American Quarterly* 67, no. 3 (2015): 727–47; Vicente M. Diaz, "'To "P" or Not to "P"?': Marking the Territory between Pacific Islander and Asian American Studies," *Journal of Asian American Studies* 7, no. 3 (Oct. 2004): 183–208.

7. Amy Kaplan, "Violent Belongings and the Question of Empire Today: Presidential Address to the American Studies Association, Hartford, Connecticut, October 17, 2003," *American Quarterly* 56, no. 1 (2004): 12.

8. Françoise Lionnet and Shu-mei Shih, eds., *Minor Transnationalism* (Durham, NC: Duke University Press, 2005); Lowe, *The Intimacies of Four Continents*, 19.

9. Kris Manjapra, *Age of Entanglement: German and Indian Intellectuals across Empire* (Cambridge, MA: Harvard University Press, 2014), 13.

10. "A Heartfelt Welcome to Guam," *Guam Daily News* (hereafter *GDN*), 20 Mar. 1967, 4.

11. George Mariscal, ed., *Aztlán and Viet Nam: Chicano and Chicana Experiences of the War* (Berkeley: University of California Press, 1999), 37–46. During the Vietnam War, Chicano soldiers expressed "uneasy recognition of shared experiences with the Vietnamese"—an analytic that also pertains to Chamorro soldiers (38).

12. For more on how all archives are political projects of a given state, see Jacques Derrida, *Archive Fever: A Freudian Impression*, trans. Eric Prenowitz (Chicago: University of Chicago Press, 1998).

13. A note regarding citations: many of the documents archived and anthologized by the Institute of Palestine Studies (hereafter IPS) in the annual *International Documents on Palestine* (hereafter *IDP*) anthologies have been previously published. In order to credit the work of the IPS, to which I am indebted, I have cited both the original publication and its placement in these anthologies.

14. This section builds on existing scholarship on Chamorro soldiers. See Michael Lujan Bevacqua, "The Exceptional Life and Death of a Chamorro Soldier: Tracing the Militarization of Desire in Guam, USA," in *Militarized Currents: Toward a Decolonized Future in Asia and the Pacific*, ed. Setsu Shigematsu and Keith L. Camacho (Minneapolis: University of Minnesota Press, 2010), 33–61; and Keith L. Camacho and Laurel A. Monnig, "Uncomfortable Fatigues: Chamorro Soldiers, Gendered Identities, and the Question of Decolonization in Guam," in *Militarized Currents*, 147–79.

15. Klinghoffer, *Vietnam, Jews, and the Middle East*, 2.

16. Klinghoffer, 2.

17. Klinghoffer, 2.

18. Jodi Kim, *Ends of Empire: Asian American Critique and the Cold War* (Minneapolis: University of Minnesota Press, 2010), 9.

19. Kaplan, *Our American Israel*, 94.

20. George W. Ball, "We Should De-escalate the Importance of Vietnam," *New York Times* (hereafter *NYT*), 21 Dec. 1969, 35.

21. George W. Ball, "Suez Is the Front to Watch," *NYT*, 28 June 1970, 62.

22. Klinghoffer, *Vietnam, Jews, and the Middle East*, 155.

23. Ball, "Suez Is the Front to Watch," 63.

24. Richard Nixon, "Television Interview Statements on American Middle East Policy," National Broadcasting Company, Columbia Broadcasting System, and American Broadcasting Company, transcript printed in *Department of State Bulletin LXII*, 27 July 1970, 112–13, repr. *IDP 1970*, ed. Walid Khadduri, Anne R. Zahlan, Hussein Sirriyyah, and George K. Nasrallah (Beirut: IPS, 1973), 198.

25. Nixon, "Television Interview Statements," 197.

26. Klinghoffer, *Vietnam, Jews, and the Middle East*, 70.

27. Avery, cited in Klinghoffer, 70.

28. Klinghoffer, 70.

29. Ben-Gurion, quoted in Klinghoffer, 70.

30. Paul Thomas Chamberlin, *The Global Offensive: The United States, the Palestine Liberation Organization, and the Making of the Post–Cold War Order* (Oxford: Oxford University Press, 2012), 33; Klinghoffer, *Vietnam, Jews, and the Middle East*, 71; Melani McAlister, *Epic Encounters: Culture, Media, and U.S. Interests in the Middle East since 1945* (Berkeley: University of California Press, 2005), 157; Pamela E. Pennock, *The Rise of the Arab American Left: Activists, Allies, and Their Fight against Imperialism and Racism, 1960s–1980s* (Chapel Hill: University of North Carolina Press, 2017), 96.

31. Mitchell G. Bard, "U.S. Israel Strategic Cooperation: The 1968 Sale of Phantom Jets to Israel," *Jewish Virtual Library*, accessed 8 July 2017, http://www.jewishvirtuallibrary.org/jsource/U.S.-Israel/phantom.html.

32. Yasser Arafat, "Statement by the Chairman of the Executive Committee of the PLO," *United Nations General Assembly 2282nd meeting*, 13 Nov. 1974, excerpted from the provisional verbatim record, UN doc. A/PV 2282, pp. 2–51, repr. *IDP 1974*, ed. Jorgen S. Nielsen and George K. Nasrallah (Beirut: IPS, 1977), 134.

33. Ball, "Suez Front," 62; Nixon, "Television Interview Statements," 197; Kaplan, *Our American Israel*, 119.

34. Farag, *Politics and Palestinian Literature in Exile*, 80.

35. Ba'ath Party of Syria and the Communist Party of the Soviet Union, "Joint Communiqué on the Visit of a Soviet Communist Party Delegation to Syria," Damascus, 6 Aug. 1968, printed in *Al-Thawra*, Damascus, 7 Aug. 1968, repr. *IDP 1968*, ed. Zuhair Diab (Beirut: IPS, 1971), 115.

36. Soviet Union Government, "Statement following the Israeli Attack on Karameh, Jordan," 22 Mar. 1968, Moscow, printed in *Soviet News*, London, 26 Mar. 1968, 158–67, repr. *IDP 1968*, ed. Zuhair Diab (Beirut: IPS 1971), 41.

37. Executive Secretariat of the Afro-Asian–Latin American Peoples' Solidarity Organization, "Appeal to All Revolutionary Forces and Socialist Countries to Support the Arab and Palestinian Peoples' Struggle against Israel's Aggression," 29 May 1969, Havana, printed in *Al-Ba'ath*, Damascus, 5 June 1969, repr. *IDP 1969*, ed. Walid Khadduri, Walid Qaziha, George Dib, George K. Nasrallah, and Husain Sirriyyah (Beirut: IPS, 1972), 92.

38. See also the "Statement of Policy Released by the First International Convention for the Support of the Palestinian People," originally published in *Al-Sha'b*, Algiers, 30 Dec. 1969, repr. *IDP 1969*, ed. Walid Khadduri, Walid Qaziha, George Dib, George K. Nasrallah, and Husain Sirriyyah (Beirut: IPS, 1972), 853: "Zionism is a racialist, expansionist and colonialist system that is inseparable from world imperialism, headed by the United States. It is a tool in the hands of world imperialism, directed not only against the Palestinian people but all Arab peoples and other national liberation movements in the world as well."

39. Yugoslav president Josip Broz Tito, "New Conference Remarks during Visit to the United Arab Republic," 7 Feb. 1968, Cairo, printed in *Al-Ahram*, Cairo, 8 Feb. 1968, repr. *IDP 1968*, ed. Zuhair Diab (Beirut: IPS, 1971), 23–25.

40. Houari Boumediene, "Press interview statements commenting on Arab measures to secure the rights of the Palestinians granted to the Japanese daily Asahi Shimbun," Jan. 1974, Algiers, printed in *al-Shaab*, Algiers, 15 Jan. 1974, trans. from Arabic and repr. *IDP 1974*, ed. Jorgen S. Nielsen and George K. Nasrallah (Beirut: IPS, 1977), 390.

41. For a more thorough critique of this binary Cold War framework, see Heonik Kwon, *The Other Cold War* (New York: Columbia University Press, 2010).

42. "U.S.-Soviet Conspiracy to Strangle Arab People's Anti-imperialist Struggle," *Peking Review*, 14 June 1968, 25, 29, repr. *IDP 1968*, ed. Zuhair Diab (Beirut: IPS, 1971), 89. The *Peking Review* was known for its Maoist propaganda in support of the "Great Proletarian Cultural Revolution." The People's Republic of China's position would shift in 1972, following the resumption of diplomatic relations with the United States.

43. "U.S.-Soviet Conspiracy," 89.

44. "U.S.-Soviet Conspiracy," 90.

45. See, for example, interview granted by Dr. George Habash, Secretary General of the Central Committee for the PFLP, to a United Press Correspondent, 4 Mar. 1969, Amman, printed in *Al-Nahar*, Beirut, 5 Mar. 1969, repr. *IDP 1969*, ed. Walid Khadduri, Walid Qaziha, George Dib, George K. Nasrallah, and Husain Sirriyyah (Beirut: IPS, 1972), 630–31.

46. Keith P. Feldman, *A Shadow over Palestine: The Imperial Life of Race in America* (Minneapolis: University of Minnesota Press, 2015), 59–101; Keith P. Feldman, "Representing Permanent War: Black Power's Palestine and the End(s) of Civil Rights," *CR: New Centennial Review* 8, no. 2 (Fall 2008): 193–231; Alex Lubin, *Geographies of Liberation: The Making of an Afro-Arab Political Imaginary* (Chapel Hill: University of North Carolina Press, 2014), 111–41.

47. "Mao Condemns U.S.-Israel Link," *Black Panther* 2, no. 12 (Nov. 1968).

48. "An Appeal by a Group of Black Americans against U.S. Support for Israel," *NYT*, 1 Nov. 1970, printed in *Action*, New York, 2 Nov. 1970, 6–7, repr. *IDP 1970*, ed. Walid Khadduri, Anne R. Zahlan, Hussein Sirriyyah, and George K. Nasrallah (Beirut: IPS, 1973), 364.

49. "An Appeal by a Group of Black Americans," 364.

50. "An Appeal by a Group of Black Americans," 365.

51. Quoted in Pennock, *The Rise of the Arab American Left*, 56.

52. Quoted in Pennock, 35.

53. Quoted in Pennock, 35.

54. Naseer H. Aruri, "AAUG: A Memoir," *Arab Studies Quarterly* 29 (Summer–Fall 2007): 38.

55. Pennock, *The Rise of the Arab American Left*, 59–60, 97.

56. Bernadine Dohrn, "Communiqué #4 from the Weatherman Underground," *San Francisco Good Times*, 18 Sept. 1970.

57. Robert J. C. Young, *Postcolonialism: An Historical Introduction* (Oxford: Blackwell, 2001), 2.

58. Maha Nassar, "'My Struggle Embraces Every Struggle': Palestinians in Israel and Solidarity with Afro-Asian Liberation Movements," *Arab Studies Journal* 22, no. 1 (Spring 2014): 88.

59. Samih al-Qasim, "Min al-Tha'ir fi al-Sharq," *al-Ittihad*, 18 Dec. 1964, trans. into English by Maha Nassar, 90. Reprinted with permission by Nassar.

60. See, for example, "1970 Resolutions of the Seventh Session of the Palestinian National Assembly," 4 June 1970, Cairo, trans. from Arabic and repr. *IDP 1970*, ed. Walid Khadduri, Anne R. Zahlan, Hussein Sirriyyah, and George K. Nasrallah (Beirut: IPS, 1973), 820–26; "Joint Communiqué issued on the occasion of the PLO Executive Committee Chairman Arafat's visit to Yugoslavia," 30 Mar. 1972, Belgrade, printed in *Review of International Affairs*, Belgrade, no. 529, 20 Apr. 1972, 17–18, and repr. *IDP 1972*, ed. Jorgen S. Nielsen and George K. Nasrallah (Beirut: IPS, 1975), 165; "Statement by the Palestine People's Conference affirming the unity of the Arab and Palestine liberation movements and urging the Arab states to sever relations with Jordan," 10 Apr. 1972, Cairo, printed in *Fateh*, Damascus, no. 333, 12 Apr. 1972, 20, trans. from Arabic and repr. *IDP 1972*, ed. Jorgen S. Nielsen and George K. Nasrallah (Beirut: IPS, 1975), 314–17; "Communiqué issued by the Second Conference of the General Union of Palestinian Women," 10 Aug. 1974, Beirut, repr. *IDP 1974*, ed. Jorgen S. Nielsen and George K. Nasrallah (Beirut: IPS, 1977), 479–80.

61. Daoud Talhami, former official of Democratic Front for the Liberation of Palestine (DFLP), interview with author, Ramallah, Palestine, 7 July 2016.

62. Baruch Kimmerling and Joel S. Migdal, *The Palestinian People: A History* (Cambridge, MA: Harvard University Press, 2003), 250; Kaplan, *Our American Israel*, 120.

63. "Statement of Basic Policy of the Popular Front for the Liberation of Palestine," Aug. 1968, printed in *IDP 1968*, ed. Zuhair Diab (Beirut: IPS, 1971), 424.

64. "The Political Strategy of the Popular Front for the Liberation of Palestine [PFLP]," Feb. 1969, excerpts from PFLP Pamphlet repr. *IDP 1969*, ed. Walid Khadduri, Walid Qaziha, George Dib, George K. Nasrallah, and Husain Sirriyyah (Beirut: IPS, 1972), 610.

65. Yasser Arafat, "Press Interview Statements on Relations with Socialist States and the Proposed Democratic State in Palestine to the Correspondent of the Algerian News Agency in Cairo," June 1970, Cairo, printed in *al-Sha'b*, Algiers, 6 June 1970, trans. from Arabic and repr. *IDP 1970*, ed. Walid Khadduri, Anne R. Zahlan, Hussein Sirriyyah, and George K. Nasrallah (Beirut: IPS, 1973), 829.

66. Talhami, interview with author.

67. Saadi Salama, interview with author, Hanoi, Vietnam, 22 July 2015.

68. This would be the first of more than ten visits Arafat made to Vietnam over his lifetime. Salama, interview with author.

69. Quoted in Chamberlin, *The Global Offensive*, 1.

70. Quoted in Chamberlin, *The Global Offensive*, 26. For other references to a "second Vietnam," see "Press Conference Statements by Executive Committee Chairman Arafat of the P.L.O. on the Situation in Jordan," Amman, 14 June 14 1970, printed in *al-Muharrir*, Beirut, 15 June 1970, excerpts trans. from Arabic and repr. *IDP 1970*, ed. Walid Khadduri, Anne R. Zahlan, Hussein Sirriyyah, and George K. Nasrallah (Beirut: IPS, 1973), 840; and "Press Conference Statements by Secretary-General Habash of the PFLP on the Front's Attitude towards the Rogers Plan and Its Acceptance by Certain Arab Governments," 25 July 1970, Tripoli (Lebanon), printed in *al-Hadaf*, Beirut, 1 Aug. 1970, excerpts trans. from Arabic and repr. *IDP 1970*, ed. Walid Khadduri, Anne R. Zahlan, Hussein Sirriyyah, and George K. Nasrallah (Beirut: IPS, 1973), 880.

71. "Statement of Palestinian Commando Organizations on Current Moves Aimed at 'Liquidating' the Palestinian Cause," 9 Aug. 1970, Amman, printed in *Fateh*, 10 Aug. 1970, trans. from Arabic and repr. *IDP 1970*, ed. Walid Khadduri, Anne R. Zahlan, Hussein Sirriyyah, and George K. Nasrallah (Beirut: IPS, 1973), 888.

72. Quoted in Chamberlin, *The Global Offensive*, 175.

73. For more on how the Palestinian struggle has resonated globally, see John Collins, "Global Palestine: A Collision for Our Time," *Critique: Critical Middle Eastern Studies* 16, no. 1 (Spring 2007): 3–18.

74. Mahmoud Darwish, quoted in "Yasser Arafat in Berlin," *Journal of Palestine Studies* 3, no. 1 (Autumn 1973): 166–68.

75. Hồ Chí Minh, "Message of Greeting to the International Conference for the Support of Arab Peoples," 24 Jan. 1969, Cairo, printed in *IDP 1969*, ed. Walid Khadduri, Walid Qaziha, George Dib, George K. Nasrallah, and Husain Sirriyyah (Beirut: IPS 1972), 12.

76. Hồ Chí Minh, 12.

77. See also "Declaration by the Democratic Republic of Vietnam on the Middle East Cease-Fire," 12 Aug. 1970, broadcast on Hanoi Radio, issued as an article in the official daily *Nhan Dan* and printed in *Free Palestine* (Washington, DC), II, 5 Sept. 1970, 6, repr. *IDP 1970*, ed. Walid Khadduri, Anne R. Zahlan, Hussein Sirriyyah, and George K. Nasrallah (Beirut: IPS, 1973), 250–51; and "Message from President Nguyen Huu Tho of the Provisional Revolutionary Government of South Vietnam to PLO Executive Committee Chairman Arafat expressing support for the Palestine Revolution," June 1974, printed in *Wafa*, 27 June 1974, Beirut, 1, trans. from Arabic and repr. *IDP 1974*, ed. Jorgen S. Nielsen and George K. Nasrallah (Beirut: IPS, 1977), 309–10.

78. Yasser Arafat, "Speech at the First International Conference of the Committees for Solidarity with the Palestinian People," 27 Dec. 1969, Algiers, printed in *Al-Sha'b*, Algiers, 29 Dec. 1969, repr. *IDP 1969*, ed. Walid Khadduri (Beirut: IPS, 1972), 834.

79. Stuart Symington, "Television Interview on U.S.-U.S.S.R. Relations and Middle East Policy," Face of the Nation: Columbia Broadcasting System, 12 July 1970, St. Louis, MO, excerpts printed in *IDP 1970*, ed. Walid Khadduri, Anne R. Zahlan, Hussein Sirriyyah, and George K. Nasrallah (Beirut: IPS, 1973), 215.

80. McAlister, *Epic Encounters*, 159.

81. McAlister, 158.

82. Edward W. Said, "Chomsky and the Question of Palestine," *Journal of Palestine Studies* 4, no. 3 (Spring 1975): 93.

83. "Speech by Ambassador Saadi Salama on the Occasion of the International Day for Solidarity with the Palestinian People," *Embassy of the State of Palestine in Hanoi, Vietnam*, 1 Dec. 2014, http://www.palestineembassy.vn/index.php?option=com_content&view=arti cle&id=251%3Aspeech-by-ambassador-saadi-salama-&lang=en. In 1976, the PLO opened a resident representative office in Hà Nội. This office was upgraded to an embassy in 1988, when Vietnam became one of the first nations to recognize Palestine as an independent state.

84. Saadi Salama, quoted in "VN Push for Independence Inspires Palestine," *Viet Nam News*, 30 Dec. 2014, http://vietnamnews.vn/life-style/264668/vn-push-for-independence -inspires-palestine.html.

85. For more on Saadi Salama, see Evyn Lê Espiritu, "Cold War Entanglements, Third World Solidarities: Vietnam and Palestine, 1967–75," *Canadian Review of American Studies* 48, no. 3 (Nov. 2018): 352–86.

86. Salama, interview with author.

87. Salama, interview with author.

88. Joseph F. Ada, "The Quest for Commonwealth, the Quest for Change," in *Kinalamten Pulitikåt*, 130.

89. Mark Forbes, "Military," in *Kinalamten Pulitikåt*, 43.

90. Max V. Soliven, "Where the Political 'War' Is Ending, and They're Getting Set for Another 'War,'" *PhilStar Global*, 5 Nov. 2002, http://beta.philstar.com/opinion/2002 /11/05/182667/where-political-145war146-ending-and-they146re-getting-set-another -145war146.

91. Lutz, "US Military Bases on Guam in a Global Perspective."

92. Joe Murphy, "Pipe Dreams," *PDN*, 30 Apr. 1975, 16; Bob Klitzkie, "Guam Played Major Role during War," *PDN*, 23 Apr. 2000, 20; Anonymous 1, interview with author, Mangilao, Guam, 3 June 2016.

93. Pedro C. Sanchez, *Guahan/Guam: The History of Our Island* (Agana, Guam: Sanchez Publishing House, 1991), 352; Lipman, "'Give Us a Ship,'" 6.

94. George McArthur, "What's Vietnam Outlook As Guam Conference Begins?" *GDN*, 20 Mar. 1967, 3.

95. "Plans for LBJ Visit Laid; 12 Coordinators at Work," *GDN*, 15 Mar. 1967, 1.

96. "Gov. Guerrero Issues Welcome," *GDN*, 15 Mar. 1967, 1.

97. Joe Murphy, "What, You Ask, Is a Guam?" *GDN*, 20 Mar. 1967, 7. Joe Murphy also reported on Operation New Life in 1975. In thanks, some refugees gave Murphy paintings that

they had made in the camps. Shannon Murphy, interview with author, Mangilao, Guam, 27 May 2016.

98. Murphy, "What, You Ask, Is a Guam?" 8.

99. "Guam Goes All Out to Greet President Johnson," *GDN*, 21 Mar. 1967, 1. See also Juan P. Cruz, "Voice of the People," *GDN*, 18 Mar. 1967, 9; "Welcome Him Well," *GDN*, 19 Mar. 1967, 4.

100. "Guam Goes All Out," 15. The proliferation of signs that read "Bomb Hanoi" was also stressed by Anonymous 1, in interview with author.

101. "A Job Really Well Done," *GDN*, 23 Mar. 1967, 4.

102. Anonymous 1, interview with author; Rose Franquez Brown, interview with author, Zoom, 3 May 2021.

103. Joe Murphy, "Pipe Dreams," *GDN*, 21 Mar. 1967, 4.

104. "Statement by Johnson," *GDN*, 21 Mar. 1967, 7.

105. "Statement by Johnson," 7.

106. "Statement by Johnson," 7.

107. "Statement by Johnson," 7.

108. Carol McMurrough, "Johnson Says No Decisions of Military Nature Made," *GDN*, 21 Mar. 1967, 1; George A. Carver Jr., "115. Memorandum for the Record, Working Notes on First Day's Session of Guam Conference, Agana, Guam, March 20, 1967, 3–5:30 p.m.," in *Foreign Relations of the United States, 1964–1968*, Volume 5: *Vietnam, 1967*, ed. Kent Sieg (Washington, DC: Government Printing Office, 2002), 270–71; George A. Carver Jr., "116. Memorandum for the Record: Working Notes on US Delegation Session of Guam Conference, Agana, Guam, Mar. 21, 1967, 10:30 a.m.–2:15 p.m.," in *Foreign Relations of the United States, 1964–1968*, 278.

109. See, for example, "Before Guam," *Harvard Crimson*, 20 Mar. 1967; "U.S. Intensifies War Expansion after Guam Conference," 1967, Folder 01, Box 09, Douglas Pike Collection: Unit 02—Military Operations, Vietnam Center and Archive, Texas Tech University, http:// www.vietnam.ttu.edu/virtualarchive/items.php?item=2130901028; "The Guam Conference: A Plot to Expand U.S. Aggressive War in Vietnam," 1967, Folder 12, Box 08, Douglas Pike Collection: Unit 02—Military Operations, Vietnam Center and Archive, Texas Tech University, http://www.vietnam.ttu.edu/virtualarchive/items.php?item=2130812082.

110. "London Press Shook By Guam Conference," *GDN*, 22 Mar. 1967, 1.

111. "What Chinese Say about Guam Conference," *GDN*, 21 Mar. 1967, 8.

112. Quoted in "The Guam Conference."

113. "Governor Issues Greetings to Nixon," *GDN*, 25 July 1969, 16.

114. "Governor Issues Greetings to Nixon," 16.

115. Richard Nixon, "Address to the Nation on the War in Vietnam," 3 Nov. 1969, *American Presidency Project*, ed. Gerhard Peters and John T. Woolley, http://www.presidency .ucsb.edu/ws/?pid=2303.

116. Richard M. Nixon, "Informal Remarks in Guam with Newsmen, July 25, 1969," in *Public Papers of the Presidents of the United States: Richard Nixon: 1969–1974* (Washington, DC: US National Archives and Records Administration, 1971), 546.

117. Nixon, 546–47.

118. Nixon, 549.

119. Bui, *Returns of War*, 5 (emphasis in original).

120. Nixon, "Informal Remarks," 548.

121. Simeon Man, *Soldiering through Empire: Race and the Making of the Decolonizing Pacific* (Berkeley: University of California Press, 2018), 8.

122. "Air Force B-52s Will Again Bomb Vietnam from Guam?" *PDN*, 12 Feb. 1972, 1; "Air War Step Up?" *PDN*, 17 Feb. 1972, 5.

123. Charles Denight, "Thousands Greet Nixons," *PDN*, 21 Feb. 1972, 1.

124. "Welcome President and Mrs. Nixon," *Pacific Sunday News* (hereafter *PSN*), 20 Feb. 1972, 1.

125. "From the Governor's Desk . . . Post Script," *PSN*, 20 Feb. 1972, 22.

126. Michael Lujan Bevacqua and Tony Azios, "Episode 1: Christmas Odyssey in Vietnam," *Memoirs Pasifika*, 11 Feb. 2021.

127. "From the Governor's Desk," 22.

128. F. T. Ramirez, "Inside the Legislature," *PSN*, 20 Feb. 1972, 4.

129. Ramirez, 4.

130. Earl H Tilford, *Setup: What the Air Force Did in Vietnam and Why* (Maxwell Air Force Base, AL: Air University Press, 1991), 263.

131. Bernard C Nalty, *Air War over South Vietnam, 1968–1975* (Washington, DC: Air Force History and Museums Program, 2000), 178.

132. "Guam Toll Rises As 3 More Fall," *PDN*, 22 Dec. 1972, 69.

133. "Air Blitz on Hanoi Hit; 2 B-52s Lost," *PDN*, 20 Dec. 1972, 1.

134. Soliven, "Where the Political 'War' is Ending."

135. Jeffrey N. Meyer, "Andersen AFB's Legacy: Operation Linebacker II," Andersen Air Force Base, 18 Dec. 2017, https://www.andersen.af.mil/News/Commentaries/Display/Article/416815/andersen-afbs-legacy-operation-linebacker-ii/.

136. Kaplan, *Our American Israel*, 124.

137. "Meir Calls Viet War 'A Tragedy,'" *PDN*, 23 Dec. 1972, 7.

138. Salama, interview with author.

139. For more on this sense of obligation, or *chenchule'* (a Chamorro form of labor based on reciprocal relations), see Vicente Diaz, "Deliberating 'Liberation Day': Memory, Culture and History in Guam," in *Perilous Memories: The Asia-Pacific War(s)*, ed. Takashi Fujitani, George White, and Lisa Yoneyama (Durham, NC: Duke University Press, 2001), 155–80.

140. Martin Manglona, interview with author, Talofofo, Guam, 13 June 2018.

141. Juan O. Blaz, interview with author, Tamuning, Guam, 13 June 2018.

142. Joseph C. San Nicolas, interview with author, Talofofo, Guam, 11 June 2018.

143. Manglona, interview with author.

144. Frank Cruz San Nicolas, interview with Isa Kelley Bowman, "Hongga Mo'na: For the Future" project, emailed to author on 8 June 2016.

145. Blaz, interview with author.

146. Anonymous 1, interview with author; Murphy, interview with author.

147. Regis Reyes, on behalf of Cristobal Reyes, interview with Michael Lujan Bevacqua, "Hongga Mo'na: For the Future" project, emailed to author on 8 June 2016.

148. Reyes, interview with Bevacqua.

149. John G. Taitano, interview with author, Barrigada, Guam, 9 June 2018.

150. Taitano, interview with author.

151. F. San Nicolas, interview with Bowman.

152. Taitano, interview with author.

153. Taitano, interview with author.

154. Taitano, interview with author.

155. Raymond T. Baza, interview with author, Tamuning, Guam, 10 June 2018.

156. Raymond T. Baza, interview with Nancy Bui, Guam, 12 May 2012, Vietnamese in the Diaspora Digital Archive (ViDDA), accessed 14 Sept. 2019, https://vietdiasporastories .omeka.net/items/show/9.

157. Baza, interview with Bui.

158. J. San Nicolas, interview with author.

159. Manglona, interview with author.

160. Blaz, interview with author.

161. Manglona, interview with author.

162. Taitano, interview with author.

163. J. San Nicolas, interview with author.

164. Taitano, interview with author.

165. Taitano, interview with author.

166. Baza, interview with author.

167. Baza, interview with Bui.

168. Lee T. Baza, interview with author, Tamuning, Guam, 10 June 2018.

169. Raymond T. Baza, interview with author.

170. Allan Ramos, interview with author, Tamuning, Guam, 10 June 2018.

171. Joaquin "Danny" Santos, speech, Guam Congress Building, 11 June 2018.

172. See PL 114–328. Previous National Defense Authorization Acts had sought to combat discrimination against potential Medal of Honor recipients by authorizing the review of files of African American, Hispanic, and Jewish veterans, as well as Asian American and Native American Pacific Islanders who had fought in World War II specifically. It wasn't until the 2017 National Defense Authorization Act that the Department of Defense mandated the review of service records of Asian American and Native American Pacific Islander war veterans who had fought during the Korean and Vietnam wars for possible upgrade to the Medal of Honor.

173. Nicolas D. Francisco, interview with author, Mangilao, Guam, 8 June 2018.

174. F. San Nicolas, interview with Bowman.

175. Judith Won Pat, interview with author, Hagåtña, Guam, 7 June 2016.

176. Mariscal, Aztlán and Viet Nam, 41.

177. See F. San Nicolas, interview with Bowman.

178. Ramos, interview with author.

179. John (Juan) Benavente, interview with Laurel A. Monnig, Hagatña, Guam, Nov. 2000, quoted in Camacho and Monnig, "Uncomfortable Fatigues," 147.

180. Juan C. Benavente, interview with author, Tamuning, Guam, 10 June 2018.

181. Benavente, interview with author.

182. Benavente, interview with author.

183. Saidiya Hartman, "Venus in Two Acts," Small Axe 26 (June 2008): 11.

184. Craig Santos Perez, "Between the Pacific and Palestine (2018)," Twitter, July 22, 2019.

185. Perez.

186. Le, Unsettled Solidarities, 24.

## 2. THE "NEW FRONTIER"

1. Craig Santos Perez, "Interwoven," in *Native Voices: Indigenous American Poetry, Craft and Conversations*, ed. CMarie Fuhrman and Dean Rader (North Adams, MA: Tupelo Press, 2019), 443.

2. Perez, 443.

3. Perez, 444.

4. Erica Violet Lee, "Untitled," *Moontime Warrior* (blog), 19 Aug. 2014, https://moon timewarrior.com/2014/08/19/our-revolution-first-nations-women-in-solidarity-with -palestine/.

5. Lee.

6. Gerald Vizenor, *Manifest Manners: Narratives on Postindian Survivance* (Lincoln: University of Nebraska Press, 1999), vii.

7. Salaita, *Inter/Nationalism*, ix.

8. Byrd, *The Transit of Empire*, xv; Jodi Kim, "Settler Modernity, Debt Imperialism, and the Necropolitics of the Promise," *Social Text* 36, no. 2 (June 2018): 42. See also Dunbar-Ortiz, *Indigenous Peoples' History*, 83, 85, 108, 118, 162, 178.

9. For more on "railroad colonialism," see Karuka, *Empire's Tracks*, 40–57. For more on the Mexican-American War, see Dunbar-Ortiz, *Indigenous Peoples' History*, 117–32.

10. Tom Engelhardt, *The End of Victory Culture: Cold War America and the Disillusion-ing of a Generation* (New York: BasicBooks, 1995), 5, 14.

11. Thomas X. Sarmiento, "The Promise of Queer Filipinx Midwestern Domesticity in Edith Can Shoot Things and Hit Them," paper presented at the Association of Asian American Studies Conference, Portland, OR, 14 Apr. 2017.

12. Tuck and Yang, "Decolonization Is Not a Metaphor," 31; Richard Slotkin, *Gunfighter Nation: The Myth of the Frontier in Twentieth-Century America* (New York: Atheneum, 1992), 3; Byrd, *The Transit of Empire*, xxi.

13. Dunbar-Ortiz, *Indigenous Peoples' History*, 193.

14. Karuka, *Empire's Tracks*, xii.

15. Arnaldo Dumindin, "Philippine-American War, 1899–1902," 2006, http://philippine americanwar.webs.com.

16. Robert D. Kaplan, *Imperial Grunts: The American Military on the Ground* (New York: Random House, 2005), 138.

17. Dunbar-Ortiz, *Indigenous Peoples' History*, 164.

18. Dunbar-Ortiz, 164.

19. Dunbar-Ortiz, 165.

20. David J. Silbey, *A War of Frontier and Empire: The Philippine-American War, 1899–1902* (New York: Hill & Wang, 2008), 211.

21. John F. Kennedy, "Acceptance of Democratic Nomination for President," Demo-cratic National Convention, Memorial Coliseum, Los Angeles, CA, 15 July 1960, John F. Kennedy Presidential Library and Museum, https://www.jfklibrary.org/learn/about-jfk /historic-speeches/acceptance-of-democratic-nomination-for-president.

22. Kennedy; See also Slotkin, *Gunfighter Nation*, 1–3, 489–504.

23. Slotkin, *Gunfighter Nation*, 492–94.

24. Slotkin, 3.

25.  Slotkin, 496; Richard Drinnon, *Facing West: The Metaphysics of Indian-Hating and Empire Building* (Minneapolis: University of Minnesota Press, 1981), 369.

26.  Slotkin, *Gunfighter Nation*, 496, 504; John Hellman, *American Myth and the Legacy of Vietnam* (New York: Columbia University Press, 1986), 44; Terrence Maitland, Stephen Weiss, and Robert Manning, *The Vietnam Experience: Raising the Stakes* (Boston: Boston Publishing Company, 1982), 12.

27.  Slotkin, *Gunfighter Nation*, 492–93.

28.  Michael Herr, *Dispatches* (New York: Alfred A. Knopf, 1977), 45.

29.  Howard Zinn, *A People's History of the United States, 1492–Present* (New York: HarperCollins, 1995), 521.

30.  Dunbar-Ortiz, *Indigenous Peoples' History*, 179.

31.  B. D'Arcus, "Contested Boundaries: Native Sovereignty and State Power at Wounded Knee, 1973," *Political Geography* 22 (2003): 415–37; Russell Means and Marvin J. Wolf, *Where White Men Fear to Tread: The Autobiography of Russell Means* (New York: St. Martin's Press, 1995), 271.

32.  Wounded Knee Legal Defense/Offense Committee, "Press release," 22 Mar. 1973, FBI Files on the American Indian Movement and Wounded Knee, file number 176-2404-316.

33.  Dunbar-Ortiz, *Indigenous Peoples' History*, 192–93.

34.  Macon Phillips, "President Barack Obama's Inaugural Address," 20 Jan. 2009, *The White House: President Barack Obama* (blog), 21 Jan. 2009, https://obamawhitehouse.archives.gov/blog/2009/01/21/president-barack-obamas-inaugural-address.

35.  Byrd, *The Transit of Empire*, xix.

36.  Phillips "President Barack Obama's Inaugural Address."

37.  See, for example, Dao Strom, *Grass Roof, Tin Roof* (Boston: Houghton Mifflin, 2003); Qui Nguyen, *Vietgone* (New York: Samuel French, 2018); Thanhhà Lai, *Butterfly Yellow* (New York: HarperCollins, 2020).

38.  Sharon Tran, "Review of *Pioneer Girl: A Novel*," *Amerasia Journal* 40, no. 1 (2014): 116.

39.  Margaret Noodin, "Language Revitalization, Anishinaabemowin, and Erdrich's *The Birchbark House* Series," in *Frontiers in American Children's Literature*, ed. Dorothy Clark and Linda Salem (Newcastle upon Tyne, UK: Cambridge Scholars, 2016), 131.

40.  Emily Anderson, *Little: Novels* (Kenmore, NY: BlazeVOX Books, 2015), 39.

41.  Laura Ingalls Wilder, *Little House on the Prairie* (New York: Harper Trophy, 1971), 236–37.

42.  For more on Lane's ghostwriting, see William V. Holtz, *The Ghost in the Little House: A Life of Rose Wilder Lane* (Columbia: University of Missouri Press, 1995).

43.  "Ông Hai" more accurately translates to "great-uncle." In the novel, however, Lee refers to her maternal grandfather as "Ong Hai" instead of "Ông Ngoại."

44.  For more on the pin as a "gift," see Bich Minh Nguyen, *Pioneer Girl* (New York: Viking, 2014), 5, 46. The description of the pin can be found in Laura Ingalls Wilder, *These Happy Golden Years* (New York: Harper Trophy, 2007), 308; the passage is quoted in Nguyen, *Pioneer Girl*, 4.

45.  Nguyen, *Pioneer Girl*, 46.

46.  Nguyen, 4, 46, 292.

47.  Nguyen, 46–47.

48.  Nguyen, 46.

49. Nguyen, 213.

50. Nguyen, 126.

51. Wilder, *Little House on the Prairie*, 284.

52. Dennis McAuliffe, *Bloodland: A Family Story of Oil, Greed, and Murder on the Osage Reservation* (San Francisco: Council Oak Books, 1999), 113.

53. Nguyen, *Pioneer Girl*, 248.

54. Karuka, *Empire's Tracks*, 40–57.

55. Bich Minh Nguyen, *Stealing Buddha's Dinner: A Memoir* (New York: Viking, 2007), 153, 158.

56. Nguyen, 159.

57. Nguyen, 159.

58. Nguyen, 160.

59. Lauren Berlant, *Cruel Optimism* (Durham, NC: Duke University Press, 2011).

60. Nguyen, *Stealing Buddha's Dinner*, 163.

61. Sigrid Anderson Cordell, "Between Refugee and 'Normalized' Citizen: National Narratives of Exclusion in the Novels of Bich Minh Nguyen," *Studies of the Novel* 49, no. 3 (Fall 2017): 383–99; Sarah Kahn, "Book Reviewed by Sarah Kahn: Bich Minh Nguyen (2014), *Pioneer Girl*," *Journal of Southeast Asian American Education and Advancement* 11, no. 1 (2016): article 6; Anita Clair Fellman, *Little House, Long Shadow: Laura Ingalls Wilder's Impact on American Culture* (Columbia: University of Missouri Press, 2008); Tran, "Review of *Pioneer Girl: A Novel*"; Belén Martín-Lucas, "Burning Down the Little House on the Prairie: Asian Pioneers in Contemporary North America," *Journal of the Spanish Association of Anglo-American Studies* 33, no. 2 (Dec. 2011): 27–41; Emily Anderson, "Adapting the Transnational Prairie: Little House, Little Mosque, and Little Laos," *Journal of Popular Culture* 49, no. 5 (2016): 1003–22.

62. Nguyen, *Pioneer Girl*, 84.

63. Nguyen, *Stealing Buddha's Dinner*, 156–57.

64. Nguyen, *Pioneer Girl*, 84.

65. Nguyen, 138, 78.

66. Nguyen, 90.

67. Nguyen, 292.

68. Nguyen, 293.

69. Margaret Noodin, *Bawaajimo: A Dialect of Dreams in Anishinaabe Language and Literature* (East Lansing: Michigan State University Press, 2014), 40–41; Lorena L. Stookey, *Louise Erdrich: A Critical Companion* (Westport, CT: Greenwood Press, 1999), 2.

70. Noodin, *Bawaajimo*, 40.

71. Noodin, 46.

72. Noodin, 76.

73. Noodin, "Language Revitalization," 124.

74. Noodin, 128, 123.

75. Noodin, *Bawaajimo*, 38.

76. Noodin, "Language Revitalization," 127.

77. Louise Erdrich, *The Birchbark House* (New York: Hyperion Paperbacks for Children, 2002), 1.

78. Erdrich, 166.

79. Erdrich, 5.

80. Nguyen, *Pioneer Girl*, 90.

81. Noodin, "Language Revitalization," 124.

82. Erdrich, *The Birchbark House*, 220.

83. Philip Joseph Deloria, *Playing Indian* (New Haven, CT: Yale University Press, 2007).

84. Simpson, "The Place Where We All Live and Work Together," 18.

85. Ly Thuy Nguyen, "Queer Dis/Inheritance and Refugee Futures," *WSQ: Women's Studies Quarterly* 48, nos. 1–2 (Spring/Summer 2020): 218–35.

86. Tiffany Wang-Su Tran and Demiliza Saramosing, "(Re)Producing Refugees: Chinese-Vietnamese Refugee Resettlement on Indian Land," paper presented at Native American Indigenous Studies Association (NAISA) conference, Hamilton, New Zealand (Aotearoa), 29 June 2019.

87. Quyên Nguyen-Le, *Nước (Water/Homeland)* (film, 2016).

88. Nguyen-Le.

89. Nguyen-Le.

90. Lenard Monkman, "'No Ban on Stolen Land,' Say Indigenous Activists in U.S.," *CBC News*, 2 Feb. 2017, https://www.cbc.ca/news/indigenous/indigenous-activists-immigration ban-1.3960814.

91. Quyên Nguyen-Le, *Hoài (Ongoing, Memory)* (film, 2018).

92. Hirsch, "Past Lives," 659.

93. Nguyen, "Queer Dis/Inheritance and Refugee Futures," 228.

94. Erdrich, *The Birchbark House*, 220.

95. Nguyen, *Pioneer Girl*, 292.

96. Nguyen, "Queer Dis/Inheritance and Refugee Futures," 229.

97. Lan Duong, "Archives of Memory: Vietnamese American Films, Past and Present," *Film Quarterly* 73, no. 3 (1 Mar. 2020): 57.

98. Nguyen-Le, *Hoài (Ongoing, Memory)*.

99. Nguyen-Le.

100. Nguyen-Le.

101. Scott Lauria Morgensen, "Settler Homonationalism: Theorizing Settler Colonialism within Queer Modernities," *GLQ: A Journal of Lesbian and Gay Studies* 16, no. 1–2 (2010); Mark Rifkin, *When Did Indians Become Straight? Kinship, the History of Sexuality, and Native Sovereignty* (New York: Oxford University Press, 2011).

102. José Esteban Muñoz, *Disidentifications: Queers of Color and the Performance of Politics* (Minneapolis: University of Minnesota Press, 1999); Nguyen, "Queer Dis/Inheritance and Refugee Futures."

103. Nguyen-Le, *Hoài (Ongoing, Memory)*.

104. Nguyen-Le.

105. Chris Francescani and Bill Hutchinson, "Viral Video of Catholic School Teens in 'MAGA' Caps Taunting Native Americans Draws Widespread Condemnation; Prompts a School Investigation," *ABC News*, 20 Jan. 2019, https://abcnews.go.com/US/viral-video -catholic-school-teens-taunting-native-americans/story?id=60498772.

106. Quyên Nguyen-Le, "*Hoài (Ongoing, Memory)* film screening," Native American Indigenous Studies (NAISA) Conference, Hamilton, New Zealand (Aotearoa), 29 June 2019.

107. Perez, "Interwoven," 445.

108. Lee, "Untitled."

109. Lowe, *The Intimacies of Four Continents*, 175 (emphasis in original).

110. Wilder, *Little House on the Prairie*, 335.

## 3. OPERATION NEW LIFE

1. Micronesian Area Research Center (MARC) Working Papers 68, Inventory of the Papers of Governor Ricardo Jerome Bordallo, compiled by William L. Wuerch, Magdelar S. Taitano, Carmen F. Quintanilla, and Darien R. Siguera, Box 31, "Correspondence: Operation New Life, 1975." Other secondary sources date the latter part of this telex to 27 March or 18 April 1975, suggesting that this language was perhaps used on multiple occasions. Operation Babylift (3–26 April 1975), which preceded Operation New Life, facilitated the mass evacuation of children from South Vietnam.

2. Citing the 1952 McCarran-Walter Act, the Ford administration authorized the parole of some 150,000 Vietnamese in 1975. These "parolees" would remain nonresident aliens until legislation reclassified them as aliens admitted for permanent residence. "After Action Report: Operations New Life/New Arrivals: U.S. Army Support to the Indochinese Refugee Program, 1 Apr. 1975–1 June 1976," I-A-5.

3. Jana K. Lipman, "'A Precedent Worth Setting . . .': Military Humanitarianism—The U.S. Military and the 1975 Vietnamese Evacuation," *Journal of Military History* 79 (Jan. 2015): 151–79. The 1975 population of Guam is taken from "Guam, 1975," *PopulationPyramid .net*, accessed 7 Oct. 2021, https://populationpyramid.net/guam/1975/.

4. Nebolon, "'Life Given Straight from the Heart,'" 25.

5. Neda Atanasoski, *Humanitarian Violence: The U.S. Deployment of Diversity* (Minneapolis: University of Minnesota Press, 2013); Barbara J. Keys, *Reclaiming American Virtue: The Human Rights Revolution of the 1970s* (Cambridge, MA: Harvard University Press, 2014).

6. Catherine Lutz, "Empire Is in the Details," *American Ethnologist* 33, no. 4 (Nov. 2006): 593–94. See also Sigmund Freud, *Civilization and Its Discontents* (New York: W. W. Norton, 1961).

7. Lilli Perez-Iyechad, "Inafa'maolek: Striving for Harmony," *Guampedia*, accessed 27 May 2021, https://www.guampedia.com/inafamaolek/#:~:text=The%20phrase%20inafa' %20maolek%20(pronounced,'good'%20(maolek).

8. Brown, interview with author.

9. Phillips, "Land," 11. For an Indigenous feminist analysis of Chamorro land politics, see Christine Taitano DeLisle, "A History of Chamorro Nurse-Midwives in Guam and a 'Placental Politics' for Indigenous Feminism," *Intersections: Gender and Sexuality in Asia and the Pacific*, no. 37 (Mar. 2015), http://intersections.anu.edu.au/issue37/delisle.htm.

10. Governor Ricardo J. Bordallo, quoted in Phillips, "Land," 2.

11. Phillips, 11.

12. Carmen Artero Kasperbauer, "The Chamorro Culture," in *Kinalamten Pulitikåt*, 36–37. For a similar argument in the North American context, see Rifkin, *When Did Indians Become Straight?*

13. Phillips, "Land," 5.

14. Kasperbauer, "The Chamorro Culture," 29; Phillips, "Land," 6.

15. Anthony Leon Guerrero, "The Economic Development of Guam," in *Kinalamten Pulitikåt*, 85–86. For more about *lāncho*, see Michael Lujan Bevacqua, "Låncho: Ranch," *Guampedia*, accessed 21 June 2017, http://www.guampedia.com/lancho-ranch/.

16. *Hale'-Ta: I Ma Gobetna-Na Guam / Governing Guam: Before and After the Wars* (Mangilao, Guam: Political Status and Education Coordinating Commission, 1994), 109.

17. Guerrero, "The Economic Development of Guam," 90.

18. For those works that refer to the US's return to Guam in 1944 as a "reoccupation," see, for example, Anne Perez Hattori, "Righting Civil Wrongs: Guam Congress Walkout of 1949," in *Kinalamten Pulitikåt*, 59; Cecilia C. T. Perez, "A Chamorro Re-telling of 'Liberation,'" in *Kinalamten Pulitikåt*, 74, 76; and Guerrero, "The Economic Development of Guam," 90.

19. Rent was calculated using prewar 1941 values, which accounted neither for inflation nor for the fact that the US Navy had isolated the island via a closed-door policy that stagnated the economy and artificially depressed land values. Phillips, "Land," 10.

20. Quoted in Phillips, 9 (emphasis added).

21. Won Pat, interview with author.

22. Forbes, "Military," 42.

23. Hattori, "Righting Civil Wrongs," 59.

24. Guerrero, "The Economic Development of Guam," 91; Alfred Peredo Flores, "'No Walk in the Park': US Empire and the Racialization of Civilian Military Labor in Guam, 1944–1962," *American Quarterly* 67, no. 3 (2015): 813–35; Leland Bettis, "Colonial Immigration in Guam," in *Kinalamten Pulitikåt*, 106.

25. Robert F. Rogers, *Destiny's Landfall: A History of Guam* (Honolulu: University of Hawai'i Press, 1995), 230.

26. Rogers, 230.

27. Quoted in Phillips, "Land," 9–10 (emphasis added).

28. Espiritu, *Body Counts*, 30.

29. Murrey Marder, "Refugees to Guam," *Washington Post*, 24 Apr. 1975, A1, A10.

30. "Guam Prepares for 50,000 as U.S. Shifts Refugee Base," *Pacific Stars and Stripes*, 25 Apr. 1975, A-1. The Philippines would not host Southeast Asian refugees again until 1979 when, following the International Conference on Indochinese Refugees in Geneva, the Marcos regime, in conjunction with the UNHCR, opened the Philippine Refugee Processing Center in Bataan and the Philippine First Asylum Center in Palawan.

31. Madeleine Bordallo, interview with author, Zoom, 18 Mar. 2021.

32. Bordallo, interview with author.

33. Joaquin "Kin" Perez, interview with author, Mangilao, Guam, 9 June 2016.

34. Perez, interview with author.

35. C. S. Morrison and Felix Moos, "The Vietnamese Refugees at Our Doorstep: Political Ambiguity and Successful Improvisation," *Review of Policy Research* 1, no. 1 (Aug. 1981): 34; "Refugee Aid Bill Clears One House Hurdle," *Honolulu Advertiser*, 8 May 1975.

36. William Greider, "Our Last Burst of Ugly Passion," *PDN*, 9 May 1975, 30.

37. Espiritu, *Body Counts*; Greider, "Our Last Burst of Ugly Passion," 30; Talcott quoted in Joe Murphey, "Editorial: The U.S. and Refugees . . ." *PDN*, 7 May 1975, 15.

38. Arlene Lum, "Refugees Face Racial Hostility," *PDN*, 5 June 1975, 12.

39. "Operation New Life Timeline," *PDN*, 19 July 2005, 7.

40. Morrison and Moos, "The Vietnamese Refugees at Our Doorstep," 33.; "One Year Later . . ." *Islander*, 30 May 1976, 4; "50,430 Evacuees On-Island," *PDN*, 15 May 1975, 3.

41. Sanchez, *Guahan/Guam*, 380; Jim Eggensperger, "15,000 Arrive Here Ragged and Dazed," *PDN*, 8 May 1975, 1; Jim Eggensperger, "Evacuee Capacity Reached with 15,000 Sea Arrivals," *PDN*, 13 May 1975, 1, 6.

42. Jim Eggensperger, "Water Cutoffs Considered," *PDN*, 14 May 1975, 1.

43. James T. Hutcherson, "The Impact of the Vietnamese Refugees on the Guam Economy: Special Research Project Submitted as a Requirement of BA 690, Special Project," University of Guam, Mar. 1976, MARC HV 640.5 V5 H8 c. 1, 40.

44. Rogers, *Destiny's Landfall*, 252.

45. "Where They Are," *PDN*, 28 Apr. 1975, 4; "Tokyu Hotel on Guam Busy Again," *Hawaii Times*, 29 Apr. 1975; "One Year Later . . ." 6; "The Camp Sites," *PDN*, 19 July 2005, 6. The military leased the Tokyu Hotel. In contrast, the other three local construction companies were paid roughly $32 per week per refugee by the military, as well as promised reimbursement for any restoration or repairs necessitated by the housing of refugees. See Susan Guffey, "New Life Spends $1.7 Million Here," *PDN*, 21 May 1975, 1.

46. Jim Eggensperger, "Camps Here Almost Full: Some Arrivals Flown to Wake to Ease Local Crowding," *PDN*, 10 May 1975, 1, 3.

47. James A. Hebert, "Job Center Finding Evacuees Homes," *PDN*, 24 Apr. 1975, 3A; David L. Teibel, "Fear, Hostility, Concern Greet Arrivals to Guam," *PDN*, 24 Apr. 1975, 3A.

48. "Guam Legislators Stall on Refugee Aid," *Hawaii-Hochi*, 25 Apr. 1975.

49. Ricky Salas, quoted in "Guam Expects Diseases Outbreak," *Honolulu Star Bulletin*, 21 May 1975.

50. Ricky Salas, quoted in Leanne McLaughlin, "Senators Deny Help from Guam," *PDN*, 26 Apr. 1975, 4.

51. Jerry Rivera, quoted in "Guam Expects Diseases Outbreak"; and in Jim Eggensperger, "Slowdown Worries Leaders," *PDN*, 21 May 1975, 3.

52. Jenna M. Loyd, Emily Mitchell-Eaton, and Alison Mountz, "The Militarization of Islands and Migration: Tracing Human Mobility through US Bases in the Caribbean and the Pacific," *Political Geography* 52 (2016): 69.

53. Colonel John D. O'Donahue, quoted in Staff Sergeant Frank Madison, "'Compassion' Motivates Helpers," *Military Sun*, 21 May 1975; "'Operation New Life': People Helping People," *Military Sun*, 21 May 1975.

54. Lyle Nelson, "Seabees and Vietnam," *Honolulu Star Bulletin*, 10 May 1975; Sanchez, *Guahan/Guam*, 380.

55. Paul Miller, "Guam Actions 'A Great Story': Vietnam Issue Won't Die Quickly," *PDN*, 10 May 1975, 35.

56. "'Operation New Life': People Helping People," *Military Sun*, 21 May 1975.

57. Lipman, "'Give Us a Ship'"; Lipman, "'A Precedent Worth Setting'"; Ayako Sahara, "Operations New Life/Arrivals: U.S. National Project to Forget the Vietnam War" (MA thesis, University of California, San Diego, 2009); Heather Marie Stur, "'Hiding behind the Humanitarian Label': Refugees, Repatriates, and the Rebuilding of America's Benevolent Image after the Vietnam War," *Diplomatic History* 39, no. 2 (2015): 223–44; Espiritu, *Body Counts*, 35.

58. Man, *Soldiering through Empire*, 12.

59. Thuy Dinh, "Of Luggage and Shoes," *Amerasia* 17, no. 1 (1991): 159.

60. Suzanne Naputi, "One Bag, $1,000 Start New Life," *Islander*, 16 Oct. 1983, 4.

61. Naputi, 4.

62. Espiritu, *Body Counts*, 39.

63. Ada, "The Quest for Commonwealth"; James Perez Viernes, "OPI-R: Organization of People for Indigenous Rights," *Guampedia*, accessed 3 July 2020, https://www.guampedia .com/opi-r-organization-of-people-for-indigenous-rights/.

64. Thompson, *Imperial Archipelago*, 11.

65. Wolfe, *Traces of History*, 272.

66. Madison, "'Compassion' Motivates Helpers."

67. Rogers, *Destiny's Landfall*, 250–51.

68. Quoted in Sanchez, *Guahan/Guam*, 379.

69. Lamb's article reprinted in "U.S. & Guam," *Honolulu Advertiser*, 30 Apr. 1975.

70. Sanchez, *Guahan/Guam*, 380–81; Perez, interview with author; Brown, interview with author; Vicky Ritter, interview with author, Zoom, 19 Mar. 2021.

71. Sweet, quoted in Dave Hendrick, "Guam's Refugee Role 'Pleases' Capital," *PDN*, 1 June 1975, 3.

72. Gerald R. Ford, "Letter to Governor Bordallo," MARC, Box 31, 13 May 1975.

73. Raymond T. Baza, interview with Bui.

74. Lee T. Baza, interview with author.

75. Raymond T. Baza, interview with Bui.

76. Raymond T. Baza, interview with author.

77. Raymond T. Baza, interview with Bui.

78. Perez, interview with author.

79. Perez, interview with author.

80. Perez, interview with author.

81. Perez, interview with author.

82. Susan Guffey, "Customs Men Find Stuffed Dog with Art," *PDN*, 26 May 1975, 1, 3.

83. Perez, interview with author.

84. Perez, interview with author.

85. Hutcherson, "The Impact of the Vietnamese Refugees on the Guam Economy," 38.

86. "Funds Spent on Refugees to be Repaid Fully: Ricky," *PDN*, 26 Apr. 1975, 3.

87. Perez, interview with author.

88. David I. A. Quitugua, interview with author, Ordot, Guam, 7 June 2016.

89. "War Survivor: Monsignor David Ignacio Arceo Quitugua," *Guampedia*, accessed 8 Sept. 2019, https://www.guampedia.com/monsignor-david-quitugua/.

90. Quitugua, interview with author.

91. Quitugua, interview with author.

92. Won Pat, interview with author.

93. Jesus Quitugua Charfauros, interview with author, San Diego, CA, 22 Apr. 2017.

94. Vivian Dames, "Agent Orange in Guam, Part 1: Sprayed and Betrayed," *Beyond the Fence*, Ep. 149, 1 June 2013, http://kprg.podbean.com/2013/06/01/ep-149-%25E2%2580%259 Cagent-orange-in-guam-part-1-sprayed-and-betrayed%25E2%2580%259D/; Kyla P. Mora, "Air Force Veteran, 72, Alleges Agent Orange Use on Andersen Air Force Base," *PDN*, 7 Jan. 2017; Rogers, *Destiny's Landfall*, 253; James A. Hebert, "Feeding Tent City Refugees: $1.6

Million," *PDN*, 24 May 1975, 3; R. L. Haddock, R. A. Mackie, and K. Cruz, "Dengue Control on Guam," *South Pacific Bulletin* (2nd Qtr., 1979): 16–24.

95. Won Pat, interview with author.

96. Alvin Lee Young, "Removal from Vietnam and Final Disposition of Agent Orange," in *The History, Use, Disposition, and Environmental Fate of Agent Orange* (New York: Springer, 2009), 121–60. Guam lies 3,049 miles from Johnston Island.

97. Tony Hodges, quoted in Jerry Tune, "New Plans Proposed for Saving Defoliant," *Honolulu Star Bulletin*, 26 Apr. 1975.

98. Giorgio Agamben, *Homo Sacer: Sovereign Power and Bare Life*, trans. Daniel Heller-Roazen (Stanford, CA: Stanford University Press, 1998); Richard Harding and John Looney, "Problems of Southeast Asian Children in a Refugee Camp," *American Journal of Psychiatry* 134 (1977): 407–11; Gail Paradise Kelly, *From Vietnam to America: A Chronicle of the Vietnamese Immigration to the United States* (Boulder, CO: Westview Press, 1977); Kwok Bun Chan and Kenneth Loveridge, "Refugees in 'Transit': Vietnamese in a Refugee Camp in Hong Kong," *International Migration Review* 21 (1987): 745–59; E. F. Kunz, "The Refugee in Flight: Kinetic Models and Forms of Displacement," *International Migration Review* 7, no. 2 (1973): 125–46; C. S. Morrison and Felix Moos, "Halfway to Nowhere: Vietnamese Refugees on Guam," in *Involuntary Migration and Resettlement: The Problems and Responses of Dislocated People*, ed. Art Hansen and Anthony Oliver-Smith (Boulder, CO: Westview Press, 1982), 49–68; Espiritu, *Body Counts*, 49.

99. Nguyen, *The Gift of Freedom*.

100. See Espiritu, *Body Counts*, 76.

101. Matt Franjola, "Vietnamese, All Well-Dressed, Try to Get Evacuated," *PDN*, 25 Apr. 1975, 2; Dave Hendrick, "Vietnam's 'Richest' in 'Tin City'?" *PDN*, 27 Apr. 1975, 4.

102. Franjola, "Vietnamese, All Well-Dressed," 2; Hendrick, "Vietnam's 'Richest' in 'Tin City'?" 4; Perez, interview with author; Ritter, interview with author.

103. Martha Ruth, "Gold Aplenty at 'Tent City,'" *PDN*, 13 May 1975, 14.

104. Garry Marchant, "Incredible Taels of Tent City Gold Rush," *South China Morning Post* (Hong Kong), 27 May 1975, 6.

105. "Gold Rush in Guam," *South China Morning Post*, 23 May 1975, 1; "Bilking of Refugees Claimed," *Honolulu Star Bulletin*, 28 May 1975.

106. Betty L. Johnson, "Voice of the People," *PDN*, 1 May 1975, 26 (emphasis added).

107. Espiritu, *Body Counts*, 55.

108. Johnson, "Voice of the People," 26.

109. Johnson, 26.

110. James A. Hebert, "Feeding Tent City Refugees: $1.6 Million," *PDN*, 24 May 1975, 3.

111. Hebert, 3.

112. David Nally, "The Biopolitics of Food Provisioning," *Transactions of the Institute of British Geographers* 36, no. 1 (2011): 37–53; Taylor Chloe, "Foucault and Food," in *Encyclopedia of Food and Agricultural Ethics*, ed. Paul B. Thompson and David M. Kaplan (Dordrecht, Netherlands: Springer, 2014), 1042–49; John Coveney, *Food, Morals, and Meaning: The Pleasure and Anxiety of Eating* (New York: Routledge, 2000).

113. Chau Nguyen, interview by Thuy Vo Dang, 12 Feb. 2013, UCI Libraries, University of California, Irvine, http://hdl.handle.net/10575/11973.

114. Minh quoted in Gannett News Service, "Refugees Find Pennsylvania Camp 'Nicer,'" *PDN*, 5 June 1975, 4.

115. Morrison quoted in John M. Achterkirchen, "Arrivals Here Steady," *PDN*, 30 Apr. 1975, 1.

116. Ronald Klimek, "The Refugee Success Formula: Group Effort and Hard Work," *Islander*, 30 May 1976, 6; Perez, interview with author.

117. Jim Eggensperger, "Island Was Safe Haven for 1,000s," *PDN*, 14 Jan. 1976, 3A; "Refugees May Be Here through Summer," *PDN*, 31 May 1975, 10.

118. Klimek, "The Refugee Success Formula," 6.

119. Guerrero, "The Economic Development of Guam"; Anne Hattori, "Guardians of Our Soil: Indigenous Responses to Post–World War II Military Land Appropriation on Guam," in *Farms, Firms, and Runways: Perspectives on U.S. Military Bases in the Western Pacific*, ed. L. Eve Armetrout Ma (Chicago: Imprint, 2001), 186–202.

120. Dave Hendrick, "The Black Market Is Everywhere," *PDN*, 15 June 1975, 1, 4.

121. Hendrick, 4.

122. Anonymous 2, interview with author, Mangilao, Guam, 3 June 2016.

123. Wendy Tuyet Tougher, interview with Nancy Bui, 13 May 2012, Guam, ViDDA, accessed 14 Sept. 2019, https://vietdiasporastories.omeka.net/items/show/8.

124. Anonymous, interview with author, Dededo, Guam, 29 May 2016; Lipman, *In Camps*, 30.

125. Perez, interview with author.

126. Perez, interview with author.

127. Guffey, "Evacuee Flood Flows On," 3.

128. Guffey, 3.

129. Jim Eggensperger, "Flow of Refugees from Island Now Below 1,000 Daily," *PDN*, 15 May 1975, 3.

130. Edward F. O'Connor, associate commissioner of examinations for the Immigration and Naturalization Service, quoted in Leanne McLaughlin, "Processing Speeded Up," *PDN*, 30 Apr. 1975, 9A.

131. O'Connor quoted in McLaughlin, 9A. My Bà Ngoại was also allowed to bring her maid to the United States from Vietnam.

132. James A. Hebert, "Man, Fiancee [*sic*] Reunited Here," *PDN*, 9 May 1975, 1; James A. Hebert, "New York Man, Viet Bride Have Guam Wedding License," *PDN*, 10 May 1975, 3; "A 3-Year Wait Ends Today," *Sunday News*, 11 May 1975, 1; James A. Hebert, "Pair Recite Vows," *PDN*, 12 May 1975, 1, 3; Ed Kelleher, "Love Story—In Full," *PDN*, 14 Jan. 1976, 16A.

133. Kelleher, "Love Story," 16A.

134. Dave Hendrick, "At Barrigada, Refugees Form Own Cleaning, Cooking Crews," *PDN*, 28 Apr. 1975, 5.

135. Hendrick, "At Barrigada," 5.

136. Hendrick, "At Barrigada," 5.

137. Susan Guffey, "Asan Camp Picks Own Commander," *PDN*, 26 Apr. 1975, 3; Susan Guffey, "Four Weeks Later, Tony Still Manages Asan Camp," *PDN*, 26 May 1975, 1, 6–7.

138. "Refugees Celebrate July 4 under a Flag of Freedom," *PDN*, 5 July 1975, 1, 5.

139. Quoted in "Refugees Celebrate July 4," 5.

140. Susan Guffey, "There's Nothing to Do but Wait," *PDN*, 18 May 1975, 3.

141. Susan Guffey, "Asan Loses Leader," *PDN*, 24 July 1975, 3; John M. Achterkirchen, "Beach Provides a Way to Beat Camp 'Security,'" *PDN*, 30 Apr. 1975, 7A.

142. Achterkirchen, "Beach Provides a Way," 7A.

143. Achterkirchen, 7A.

144. Susan Guffey, "Camp Asan Celebrates First Mass," *PDN*, 28 Apr. 1975, 3; "Clean and Cool in Mud and Heat," *PDN*, 30 Apr. 1975, 12A; "Fun and Food Playing Roles in 'New Life,'" *PDN*, 1 May 1975, 1; P. J. Ryan, "Photo of Refugees at Black Construction Co. Playing Basketball," *PDN*, 19 May 1975, 1; David V. Crisostomo, "Guam Hosts Refugees in 1975," *PDN*, 18 July 2005, 1; Josephine Mallo, "His Art, Himself Are All He Has," *PDN*, 4 Aug. 1975, 22; Joe Murphey, "Pipe Dreams," *PDN*, 2 July 1975, 18; P. J. Ryan, "Furry . . . but Bearable," *PDN*, 13 June 1975, 3.

145. Dinh, "Of Luggage and Shoes," 163; Dave Hendrick, "Sinbad Soothes the Long Wait," *PDN*, 4 May 1975.

146. Lipman, "'Give Us a Ship,'" 6; "Some Refugees Badly Homesick; Others Worried, Nearing Suicide," *PDN*, 14 May 1975, 21.

147. Jennifer Ada, interview with author, phone, 4 June 2018.

148. Ada, interview with author.

149. Ada, interview with author.

150. Quitugua, interview with author.

151. Dinh, "Of Luggage and Shoes," 163.


## 4. REFUGEES IN A STATE OF REFUGE

1. This war is alternatively known as the June War, the 1967 Arab-Israeli War, or the Third Arab-Israeli War.

2. Most sources identify the *Yuvali* as an Israeli cargo ship. Documents in the Israel State Archive (hereafter ISA) provide more details: the ship was owned by the Israeli firm Ofer and steered by an Israeli captain and crew but flew a Liberian flag of convenience. See Ministry of Foreign Affairs, "Telegram 151 to Washington DC," 10 June 1977, ISA, Vietnamese Refugees File, 5733/29—שה, trans. Kobi Fischer (hereafter KF); Ministry of Foreign Affairs, "Secret Telegram 943," 12 June 1977, ISA, Vietnamese Refugees File, 5733/29—שה, trans. KF; Israeli Embassy in Japan, "Telegram 62," 17 June 1977, ISA, Vietnamese Refugees File, 5733/29—שה, trans. KF; Ministry of Foreign Affairs, "Secret Telegram," 19 June 1977, ISA, Vietnamese Refugees File, 5733/29—שה, trans. KF; Cuong Nguyen Tuan, interview with author, Tel Aviv, Israel-Palestine, 1 July 2016. When Cuong resettled in Israel-Palestine at the age of eighteen, he adopted the name "Jimmy Caldron" in honor of President Jimmy Carter.

3. "66 Vietnam Refugees Find Asylum in Israel," *Victoria (TX) Advocate*, 26 June 1977, 2A.

4. Cuong, interview with author.

5. Initially, Israel hoped the United States would resettle the refugees. When this plan fell through, Israel realized it would have to absorb the refugees or risk bad publicity. There was also some concern that once Israel absorbed the refugees, they would be ineligible for parole to the United States. See Ben Zur, "Secret Telegram 373," 24 June 1977, ISA, Vietnamese Refugees File, 5733/29—שה, trans. KF; Ben Zur, "Top Secret, Urgent Telegram 297," 23 June 1977, ISA, Vietnamese Refugees File, 5733/29—שה, trans. KF.

6. The exact numbers of Vietnamese refugees who were resettled in Israel remains inconsistent across government documents and media reports. Most sources report that 370 refugees total were absorbed. Some documents report that the second wave consisted of 103 refugees, and some report 102. Although Israel set out to accept 200 refugees for the third

wave, they actually accepted 197. The number 366 comes from my calculation of 66 refugees in the first wave, 103 in the second, and 197 in the third.

7. "66 Vietnam Refugees Find Asylum in Israel."

8. Menachem Begin, in "Visit of Prime Minister Menahem Begin of Israel Remarks of the President and the Prime Minister at the Welcoming Ceremony," White House Lawn, 19 July 1977, American Presidency Project, https://www.presidency.ucsb.edu/node/243233.

9. Jimmy Carter, in "Visit of Prime Minister Menahem Begin of Israel."

10. Shabtai Rosenne, "Letter to the Ministry of Foreign Affairs," 5 Jan. 1979, ISA, 105.5, Appendix D, 7248/29—יח, trans. KF; Dr. Ovadia Sofer, "Telegram 507," 6 Sept. 1979, ISA, 105.5, Appendix C, 7248/28—יח, trans. KF; Yoel Alon, "Telegram," 24 Aug. 1979, ISA, 105.5, Appendix C, 7248/28—יח, trans. KF; Moti Levi, "Letter from Bonn, Germany to the Journalism Department regarding Israeli Humanitarian Aid to the Vietnam Refugees," 31 Oct. 1979, ISA, 105.5, Appendix C, 7248/28—יח, trans. KF; Yoel Alon, UN Delegation in New York, "Telegram 8635," 22 June 1979, ISA, 105.5, Appendix C, 7248/28—יח, trans. KF; Ruth Raeli, "Telegram 6286," 13 Sept. 1979, ISA, 105.5, Appendix C, 7248/28—יח, trans. KF; M. Mendes, "Letter to Mr. A. Efrati, Director of the Department for Communications, and Mr. M. Sasson, Special Ambassador of Journalism and Public Relations, regarding the reception of refugees from Vietnam," 29 Jan. 1979, ISA, 105.5, Appendix D, 7248/29—יח, trans. KF; David Ben-Dov, "Letter regarding Australia Sun's coverage of Vietnam Refugees to Israel," 26 Jan. 1979, ISA, 105.5, Appendix D, 7248/29—יח, trans. KF; Yoel Alon, "Telegram 548," 24 Jan. 1979, ISA, 105.5, Appendix D, 7248/29—יח, trans. KF; Yaish, "Telegram 79," Athens, 23 Jan. 1979, ISA, 105.5, Appendix D, 7248/29—יח, trans. KF; Dubi, "Handwritten note regarding publicity of refugees in Ofakim," 10 Jan. 1979, ISA, 105.5, Appendix D, 7248/29—יח, trans. KF.

11. Israel absorbed Vietnamese refugees in order to represent itself as "a nation fully engaging liberal discourses of diversity"—a rhetorical move that can be described using Candace Fujikane's term "yellowwashing," since the resettlement of 366 Vietnamese refugees did not necessarily "advance justice" but rather "appropriate[d] their histories to camouflage Israel's own status as an apartheid state." See Candace Fujikane, "Against the Yellowwashing of Israel: The BDS Movement and Liberatory Solidarities across Settler States," in *Flashpoints for Asian American Studies*, ed. Cathy J. Schlund-Vials (New York: Fordham University Press, 2017), 151. For a critique of Israel's manipulation of humanitarian rhetoric in the context of its attack on Palestinians during the Gaza War of 2008-9, see Rebecca L. Stein, "Impossible Witness: Israeli Visuality, Palestinian Testimony, and the Gaza War," *Journal for Cultural Research* 16, nos. 2–3 (2012): 135–53. The term "humanitarian alibi" refers to the ways the Israeli media drowned out Palestinian voices while focusing on the figure of the humanitarian Israeli who mourned the loss of the "good Palestinian" caught up in the violence allegedly initiated by Hamas.

12. Smadar Lavie, *Wrapped in the Flag of Israel: Mizrahi Single Mothers and Bureaucratic Torture* (New York: Berghahn Books, 2014), 1–4, 42–46.

13. "Begin Mandates the Absorption of Vietnamese Refugees," *Ha'aretz*, 24 June 1977; English translation quoted from Adriana X. Jacobs, "Where You Are From: The Poetry of Vaan Nguyen," *Shofar* 33, no. 4 (2015): 84.

14. Kurt Rene Radley, "The Palestinian Refugees: The Right of Return in International Law," *American Journal of International Law* 72, no. 3 (July 1978): 609; United Nations General Assembly Resolution 3236, 29 GAOR, Supp. (No. 31) 4, UN Doc. A/9631 (1974).

15. Ilana Feldman, "The Challenge of Categories: UNRWA and the Definition of a 'Palestine Refugee,'" *Journal of Refugee Studies* 25, no. 3 (2012): 392.

16. Feldman, 392.

17. In 1948, Egypt, Iraq, Lebanon, Saudi Arabia, Syria, and Yemen voted against UN General Assembly Resolution 194. For more on the UNRWA and its relation to the 1951 Refugee Convention, see Lex Takkenberg and Riccardo Bocco, eds., "UNRWA and the Palestinian Refugees 60 Years Later," special issue, *Refugee Survey Quarterly* 28, no. 2–3 (2009): 227–661.

18. Office of the High Commissioner for Refugees, "Press Release REF/1358: High Commissioner Stresses Universality of Refugee Problems in Speech to Executive Committee," 9 Oct. 1978, ISA, 105.5, Appendix D, 7248/29—חע.

19. Office of the High Commissioner for Refugees, "Press Release REF/1365: UNHCR Executive Committee Takes Decision Concerning Refugees in Southern Africa and South East Asia as well as Displaced Persons in Lebanon," 17 Oct. 1978, ISA, 105.5, Appendix D, 7248/29—חע. See also UN General Assembly, "Report on the Twenty-Ninth Session of the Executive Committee of the High Commissioner's Programme," 20 Oct. 1978, "Section IV—UNHCR Assistance Activities," 20, ISA, 105.5, Appendix D, 7248/29—חע.

20. Eviatar Manor, "Report on the Thirtieth Session of the Executive Committee of the UNCHR," 17 Oct. 1979, ISA, 105.5, Appendix C, 7248/28—חע, trans. KF.

21. Manor.

22. Hueber quoted in "66 Vietnam Refugees Find Asylum In Israel," 2A.

23. Levi quoted in Shoshana Bryen, "Israel and the Boat People," *Times of Israel* (Jerusalem), 6 Jan. 2012, http://blogs.timesofisrael.com/israel-and-the-boat-people.

24. Department of Information for Olim, Office of the Spokesman, "The Absorption of Vietnamese Refugees: The Israel Experience / L'Integration des Refugies Vietnamiens: L'expérience d'Israël," July 1979, ISA, 105.5, Appendix C, 7248/28—עח.

25. Ministry of Immigrant Absorption, Office of the Spokesman, "The Story of the Absorption of the Vietnam Refugees," 1 Jan. 1980, ISA, 105.5, Appendix C, 7248/28—עח.

26. Micha Shagrir, Kastel Films, "Letter to Yigal Efrati, the Israel Film Service," 20 Dec. 1978, ISA, 105.5, Appendix D, 7248/29—עח, trans. KF.

27. Ze'ev Yeffet, "'China Town' in Afula," *Ha'aretz*, 26 Oct. 1979, clipping found in ISA, 105.5, Appendix C, 7248/28—עח, trans. KF.

28. Daniel Bloch, "The Government Decided to Permit the Entry of a 100 Refugees from Vietnam," *Davar*, 8 Jan. 1979, in ISA, 105.5, Appendix D, 7248/29—עח, trans. KF.

29. "Transcript of Knesset Debate on Vietnamese Refugees on the Ship *Hai Hong*," 11 Nov. 1978, trans. KF; "Deciding which Committee will Deal with the Procedural Motion of MKs Nof and Shilansky about the Subject of the Problem of the Vietnamese Refugees who are in the Middle of the Sea," 21 Nov. 1978, private archive, trans. KF; "The Conclusions of the Committee of Interior Ecology about the Subject of the Vietnamese Refugees in the Middle of the Sea," 30 Jan. 1979, ISA, trans. KF; Dara Marcus, "The *Hai Hong* Incident: One Boat's Effect on Canada's Policy towards Indochinese Refugees," 2013 Gunn Prize Paper, International Migration Research Centre (Wilfrid Laurier University), accessed 9 Nov. 2021, 1–21, https://srdjanvucetic.files.wordpress.com/2015/01/sample-paper-20pgs.pdf.

30. Ruth Raeli, "Letter to Mr. S. Z. Katz," 13 Dec. 1978, ISA, 105.5, Appendix D, 7248/29—עח, trans. KF; "Statement by Ambassador Joel Barromi" and "Consultative Meeting with

Interested Governments on Refugees and Displaced Persons in South East Asia (Geneva, 11–12 December 1978)," 19 Dec. 1978, ISA, 105.5, Appendix D, 7248/29—חע.

31. Joel Barromi, "Telegram 35," 7 Dec. 1978, ISA, 105.5, Appendix D, 7248/29—חע, trans. KF.

32. Joel Barromi, "Telegram 82," 20 Nov. 1978, ISA, 105.5, Appendix D, 7248/29—חע, trans. KF.

33. UNHCR, "Refugees from Indochina: Situation on 31.1.79," 31 Jan. 1979, ISA, 105.5, Appendix D, 7248/29—חע.

34. It was initially rumored that Israel would accept 400, not 100, refugees. See Ruth Raeli, "Telegram 10," 3 Jan. 1979, ISA, 105.5, Appendix D, 7248/29—חע, trans. KF. For more on the acceptance of the second wave of refugees, see Poul Hartling, "Letter to Dr. Joel Barromi, Permanent Representative of Israel to the UN Office at Geneva," 12 Jan. 1979, ISA, 105.5, Appendix D, 7248/29—חע; Hanoch Zimmering, Ministry of Immigrant Absorption, "Summary of the Protocol of Meeting No. 2 Regarding Bringing Over the Vietnamese Refugees, Held on the 9th of January 1979," 11 Jan. 1979, ISA, 105.5, Appendix D, 7248/29—חע, trans. KF; Ministry of Immigrant Absorption, Director General's Office, "Decision-Making Procedures and Treatment of the 100 Refugees from Vietnam, Operation Paper No. 1," 14 Jan. 1979, ISA, 105.5, Appendix D, 7248/29—חע, trans. KF; Masok, "Telegram 842," 9 Jan. 1979, ISA, 105.5, Appendix D, 7248/29—חע, trans. KF; Youssef Waxman, "The Government Will Decide Today to Absorb Vietnamese," Ma'ariv, 7 Jan. 1979, ISA, 105.5, Appendix D, 7248/29—חע, trans. KF.

35. "Cabinet Agrees to Admit-100 [sic] Vietnamese Refugees to Israel, Also Discusses Problem of the Falashas," JTA: The Global Jewish News Source (New York), 8 Jan. 1979. See also Uzi Benziman, "The Government Decided to Absorb a 100 Refugees from Vietnam," Ha'aretz, 8 Jan. 1979, ISA, 105.5, Appendix D, 7248/29—חע, trans. KF.

36. Eytan Bentsur, Israeli Embassy in Washington, DC, "Telegram 386 to the North American Department in Jerusalem," 22 Nov. 1978, ISA, 105.5, Appendix D, 7248/29—חע, trans. KF; David Lazar, Israeli Embassy in Paris, "Letter to the Department of Public Affairs, Foreign Ministry, Jerusalem," 22 Nov. 1978, ISA, 105.5, Appendix D, 7248/29—חע, trans. KF; Members of Kibbutz Lohamei Hagetaot ("Ghetto Warriors"), "The Fate of the Vietnam Refugees is Ours (handwritten note)," Jan. 1979, ISA, "Committee for the Absorption of Refugees from Vietnam," 9474/19—לג, trans. KF; Faculty of Architecture at Technion, Haifa, "Letter in support of Absorption of Vietnamese Refugees," 2 Jan. 1979, ISA, "Committee for the Absorption of Refugees from Vietnam," 9474/19—לג, trans. KF. For a rare letter of protest against absorbing more Vietnamese refugees, see Asher Levkovitz, "Letter to the Minister of Building and Housing, Mr. Yaffe (typewritten)," 8 Jan. 1979, ISA, "Committee for the Absorption of Refugees from Vietnam," 9474/19—לג, trans. KF.

37. "The Conclusions of the Committee of Interior Ecology."

38. "Cabinet Agrees to Admit-100 Vietnamese Refugees to Israel."

39. "The Conclusions of the Committee of Interior Ecology."

40. Avi Pazner, "Telegram 98," 9 Jan. 1979, ISA, 105.5, Appendix D, 7248/29—חע, trans. KF.

41. Asia-Pacific Section of the Department of Foreign Affairs (MASOK), "Telegram 510," 8 Jan. 1979, ISA, 105.5, Appendix D, 7248/29—חע, trans. KF. Israel was not unique in having selection preferences. The United States, for example, selected refugees for

resettlement based on anticommunist ideology and prior connections to Americans during the Vietnam War.

42. Sarah Ihmoud, "Policing the Intimate: Israel's Anti-miscegenation Movement," *Jerusalem Quarterly* 75 (2018): 91–103.

43. Tran Tai Dong, interview with author, Tel Aviv, Israel-Palestine, 21 July 2016.

44. Tran, interview with author.

45. Weissberger quoted in Colin Bicker, "Reuter Telegram from Manila Bay, Philippines," 15 Jan. 1979, ISA, 105.5, Appendix D, 7248/29—חע.

46. Weissberger quoted in Bicker, "Reuter Telegram."

47. "Cabinet Agrees to Admit-100 Vietnamese Refugees to Israel."

48. Moshe Dayan, "Telegram 2596," 1 Feb. 1979, ISA, 105.5, Appendix D, 7248/29—חע.

49. Justin Leroy, "Black History in Occupied Territory: On the Entanglements of Slavery and Settler Colonialism," *Theory & Event* 19, no. 4 (2016), https://muse.jhu.edu/article/633276.

50. Homi Bhabha and Jonathan Rutherford, "The Third Space: Interview with Homi Bhabha," in *Identity: Community, Culture, Difference*, ed. Jonathan Rutherford (London: Lawrence & Wishart, 1990), 211; Claire Jean Kim, "The Racial Triangulation of Asian Americans," *Politics & Society* 27, no. 1 (Mar. 1999): 105–38; Ella Shohat, "Taboo Memories, Diasporic Visions: Columbus, Palestine, and Arab-Jews," in *Taboo Memories, Diasporic Voices* (Durham, NC: Duke University Press, 2006), 201–32.

51. MASOK, "Telegram 510"; Ministry of Immigrant Absorption, Office of the Spokesman, "Protocol of the Public Relations Committee's Meeting Regarding the Vietnam Refugees Reception Procedures in Case of a Landing in Athens," 16 Jan. 1979, ISA, 105.5, Appendix D, 7248/29—חע, trans. KF; Ministry of Immigrant Absorption and Department of Absorption Services, "Treatment of the Refugee Group from the Moment of Landing: Responsibility and Implementation by the Ministry of Absorption and the Jewish Agency," 17 Jan. 1979, ISA, 105.5, Appendix D, 7248/29—חע, trans. KF; Department of Information for Olim, Office of the Spokesman, "The Absorption of Vietnamese Refugees." The KLM actually landed in Dubai before traveling on to Athens; therefore, Israeli representatives such as Weissberger had to travel separately to Athens. See Ambassador in Manila, "Telegram 56 to MASOK," 18 Jan. 1979, ISA, 105.5, Appendix D, 7248/29—חע, trans. KF.

52. Tran, interview with author.

53. Yeffet, "'China Town' in Afula." See also Avshalom Ginnat, "Vietnam Refugees—A Month in Afula," *Al HaMishmar*, 15 Feb. 1979, ISA, 105.5, Appendix D, 7248/29—חע, trans. KF.

54. Dayan, "Telegram 2596."

55. "Joint Communique: Twelfth ASEAN Ministerial Meeting," Bali, Indonesia, 30 June 1979, ISA, 105.5, Appendix B, 7248/27—חע.

56. Kurt Waldheim, "Telegram to Menachem Begin," 25 May 1979, ISA, 105.5, Appendix A, 7248/26—חע.

57. Menachem Begin, "Letter to Secretary General Kurt Waldheim," 5 June 1979, Jerusalem, ISA, 105.5, Appendix A, 7248/26—חע (emphasis added).

58. Begin, "Letter to Secretary General Kurt Waldheim."

59. Prime Minister of Malaysia, "Press Release SG/SM/2735," 18 June 1979, ISA, 105.5, Appendix A, 7248/26—חע.

60. Prime Minister of Malaysia, "Press Release SG/SM/2735."

61. "'Shoot on Sight': Malaysia Will Evict 76,000 Boat People," *Los Angeles Times*, 15 June 1979; M. G. G. Pillai and Patrick Keatley, "Malaysia Threatens to Shoot Refugees," *Guardian*, 16 June 1979; Henry Kamm, "Malaysia Is Said to Drop Plan to Fire on Refugees," *New York Times*, 17 June 1979.

62. Menachem Begin, "Telegram to Heads of State," 19 June 1979, ISA, 105.5, Appendix A, 7248/26—עח.

63. Begin, "Telegram to Heads of State."

64. Relations with the Palestinian Liberation Organization, 19 July 1979, UNHCR Fonds II, Series 2, 391.46, International Conference on Indochina, 1979, Vol. 4, Box 597, quoted in Lipman, *In Camps*, 81.

65. See ISA, 105.5, Appendix B, 7248/27—עח, and Begin's letters, 4346/12—א.

66. Aryeh Rubinstein, "Knesset Asks Worlds' Parliaments: Take in Vietnamese Refugees," unidentified newspaper, 21 June 1979, clipping in ISA, 105.5, Appendix A, 7248/26—עח. At Begin's request, a summation of the Knesset debate on Vietnamese refugees was sent to heads of state around the world. Israel received letters of reply from countries such as Great Britain, Thailand, and Switzerland. See ISA, 105.5, Appendix B, 7248/27—עח.

67. Joel Barromi, "Telegram 7083," 20 June 1979, ISA, 105.5, Appendix A, 7248/26—עח; Poul Hartling, "Telegram 3710," 27 June 1979, ISA, 105.5, Appendix A, 7248/26—עח; Kurt Waldheim, "Letter to Menachem Begin," 30 June 1979, ISA, 105.5, Appendix A, 7248/26—עח.

68. Menachem Begin, "Telegram 6828 (Letter to Kurt Waldheim)," 4 July 1979, ISA, 105.5, Appendix A, 7248/26—עח; Kurt Waldheim, "Telegram 7575 (Details of Geneva Conference on 20–21 July 1979)," 5 July 1979, ISA, 105.5, Appendix A, 7248/26—עח; United Nations Press Release, "Statement by United Nations Spokesman on Indochinese Refugees," 30 June 1979, ISA, 105.5, Appendix A, 7248/26—עח.

69. David Levi, "Letter to Government Secretary Aryeh Naor regarding Vietnam Refugees—Government Decision (no. 854) from 1 July 1979," 21 Oct. 1979, ISA, "Committee for the Absorption of Refugees from Vietnam," 9474/19—גל, trans. KF; Ministry of Immigrant Absorption, Office of the Spokesman, "The Story of the Absorption of the Vietnam Refugees."

70. Office of the Vice President's Press Secretary, "Press Release of Vice President Walter F. Mondale's speech to the UN Conference on Indochinese Refugees," 21 July 1979, ISA, 105.5, Appendix B, 7248/27—עח. See also Lipman, *In Camps*, 79.

71. Office of the Vice President's Press Secretary, "Press Release of Vice President Walter F. Mondale's speech."

72. Stephen J. Solarz, "Letter to Zvi Rafiah," 9 Nov. 1978, ISA, 105.5, Appendix D, 7248/29—עח.

73. Solarz, "Letter to Zvi Rafiah." In his speech to the US House of Representatives in September 1978, Solarz also refers to the Southeast Asian refugee crisis as an "Asian Holocaust." See "Aiding the Victims of an Asian Holocaust," *Congressional Record*, Vol. 124, No. 155, Washington DC, 29 Sept. 1978, ISA, 105.5, Appendix D, 7248/29—עח.

74. Letter from Vietnamese Groups of Orange County to UNHCR, 20 July 1979, UNHCR Fonds II, Series 2, 391.46, International Conference on Indochina, 1979, Vol. 4, Box 597.

75. Asia and Oceania Department, "Telegram 197," 19 Sept. 1979, ISA, 105.5, Appendix C, 7248/28—עח, trans. KF; Israeli Embassy in Singapore, "Telegram 134," 20 Sept. 1979, ISA, 105.5, Appendix C, 7248/28—עח, trans. KF; Asia and Oceania Department, "Telegram 1641," 21 Sept. 1979, ISA, 105.5, Appendix C, 7248/28—עח, trans. KF; Israeli Embassy in Singapore,

"Telegram 4964," 28 Sept. 1979, ISA, 105.5, Appendix C, 7248/28—עח, trans. KF; Asia and Oceania Department, "Telegram 47," 1 Aug. 1979, ISA, 105.5, Appendix C, 7248/28—חע, trans. KF; Asia and Oceania Department, "Telegram 3410," 8 Aug. 1979, ISA, 105.5, Appendix C, 7248/28—עח, trans. KF; Ministry of Immigrant Absorption, Office of the Spokesman, "The Story of the Absorption of the Vietnam Refugees."

76.  Asia and Oceania Department, "Telegram 3217 to Geneva, Manila," 1 Aug. 1979, ISA, 105.5, Appendix D, 7248/29—עח, trans. KF; Asia and Oceania Department, "Telegram 4788 to Bangkok," 20 Aug. 1979, ISA, 105.5, Appendix C, 7248/28—עח, trans. KF; A. Ben Yohanan, "Letter to the Ambassador at Bangkok," 22 Aug. 1979, ISA, 105.5, Appendix D, 7248/29—עח, trans. KF.

77.  Moshe Raviv and Yehuda Weissberger, "Telegram 2335," 14 Sept. 1979, ISA, 105.5, Appendix C, 7248/28—עח, trans. KF.

78.  Yehuda Weissberger, "Letter to Azriel Veldman, the Ministry for Immigrant (Aliya) Absorption," 26 Oct. 1979, ISA, 105.5, Appendix C, 7248/29—עח, trans. KF; Ministry of Immigrant Absorption, Spokesman's Office, "The Story of the Absorption of the Vietnam Refugees." For more on Weissberger's time in the Philippines, see Raviv and Weissberger, "Telegram 2335."

79.  Hoài Mỹ Nguyễn, interview with author, Jaffa, Israel-Palestine, 24 May 2015. Nguyễn's wife prefers to remain unnamed.

80.  See, for example, Moshe Raviv, "Telegram 3374," 25 Sept. 1979, ISA, 105.5, Appendix C, 7248/28—עח, trans. KF.

81.  See also Mordechai Lador, "Letter to Director of the Asia and Oceania Department," Bangkok, 15 Oct. 1979, ISA, 105.5, Appendix C, 7248/28—עח, trans. KF.

82.  Yehuda Weissberger, "Letter to Azriel Veldman, the Ministry for Immigrant (Aliya) Absorption," 26 Oct. 1979, ISA, 105.5, Appendix D, 7248/29—עח, trans. KF.

83.  Weissberger, "Letter to Azriel Veldman."

84.  "An American Plane Signaled with Smoke Bombs; Refugee Boat in the Area," Al HaMishmar, 16 Sept. 1979, ISA, 105.5, Appendix C, 7248/28—עח, trans. KF; Israeli Embassy in Singapore, "Telegram 6917," 30 Aug. 1979, ISA, 105.5, Appendix C, 7248/28—עח, trans. KF.

85.  Asia and Oceania Department, "Telegram," 4 Sept. 1979, ISA, 105.5, Appendix C, 7248/28—עח, trans. KF; Asia and Oceania Department, "Telegram 7425," 14 Sept. 1979, ISA, 105.5, Appendix C, 7248/28—עח, trans. KF. In the second telegram, the Asia and Oceania Department notes that a baby on the ZIM ship *Sydney* died in transit, bringing the number of refugees down to 40. It is unclear whether the final total of refugees absorbed from Singapore was 40 or 41.

86.  Weissberger, "Letter to Azriel Veldman."

87.  Minister of Absorption Housing and Building, "Letter regarding 'The Vietnam Refugees—Government Decision (No. 854) of the 1st of July 1979,'" 28 Oct. 1979, ISA, 105.5, Appendix C, 7248/28—עח, trans. KF; Ministry of Immigrant Absorption, Office of the Spokesman, "The Story of the Absorption of the Vietnam Refugees"; "200 Refugees from Vietnam Will Arrive Next Week," Davar, 16 Oct. 1979, ISA, 105.5, Appendix C, 7248/28—עח, trans. KF; "200 Refugees Will Arrive Tomorrow in Israel," Yedioth Ahronoth, 22 Oct. 1979, ISA, 105.5, Appendix C, 7248/28—עח, trans. KF.

88.  Ministry of Immigrant Absorption, Office of the Spokesman, "The Story of the Absorption of the Vietnam Refugees."

89. Dan Arkin and Ezra Yaniv, "'New Refugees' from Vietnam Will Learn Hebrew at the Town Sderot before Absorption in Israel," *Ma'ariv*, 24 Oct. 1979, ISA, 105.5, Appendix C, 7248/28—עח, trans. KF.

90. Arkin and Yaniv, "'New Refugees' from Vietnam Will Learn Hebrew."

91. Knesset Member Mordechai Vershovsky, "Letter to the Honorable Dr. Yosef Burg, Minister of the Interior," 25 Dec. 1979, ISA, "Committee for the Absorption of Refugees from Vietnam," 9474/19—גל, trans. KF.

92. "A Refugee Horror Story," *Jerusalem Post*, 18 June 1979, reprinted in *Jerusalem Post International Edition*, No. 973, 24 June 1979, clipping in ISA, 105.5, Appendix B, 7248/27—עח.

93. Mordechai Lador, "Letter regarding *Bangkok Post* Editorial—Indochina Refugees—The Arab OPEC States," 1 Aug. 1979, ISA, 105.5, Appendix C, 7248/28—עח, trans. KF.

94. "Refugee Viet Adopt Israel," *Features from Jerusalem*, 6 July 1979, clipping in ISA, 105.5, Appendix B, 7248/27—עח.

95. "Refugee Viet Adopt Israel."

96. David Levi, in Department of Information for Olim, Office of the Spokesman, "The Absorption of Vietnamese Refugees."

97. Levi, in Department of Information for Olim, Office of the Spokesman, "The Absorption of Vietnamese Refugees."

98. Tran Quang Hoa, in Department of Information for Olim, Office of the Spokesman, "The Absorption of Vietnamese Refugees," 9 July 1979.

99. Tran.

100. Long Li Tin Lau, in Department of Information for Olim, Office of the Spokesman, "The Absorption of Vietnamese Refugees."

101. Tran Thuan, in Department of Information for Olim, Office of the Spokesman, "The Absorption of Vietnamese Refugees."

102. Jonathan Immanuel, "Today's Focus: Vietnamese Refugees Adjust to Life in the Jewish State," *Associated Press*, 3 Jan. 1986.

103. Immanuel, "Today's Focus."

104. Immanuel, "Today's Focus."

105. Immanuel, "Today's Focus." Today, Vietnamese Israelis are drafted into the IDF.

106. Immanuel, "Today's Focus."

107. Tran, interview with author; Cuong, interview with author.

108. Nguyễn, interview with author.

109. E. Tamir, "Letter regarding Vietnam Refugees—Family Reunions," 3 June 1980, ISA, 105.5, Appendix E, 7248/30—עח, trans. KF; Manfred Paeffgen, Representative in the Philippines, "Letter to Moshe Raviv, Ref: HCR/ML/244," 10 Mar. 1980, ISA, 105.5, Appendix E, 7248/30—עח; Eviatar Manor, "Letter regarding Vietnam Refugee," 13 May 1980, ISA, 105.5, Appendix E, 7248/30—עח, trans. KF; Asia and Oceania Department, "Telegram 9179, Response to Manor regarding Vietnam Refugee," 23 May 1980, ISA, 105.5, Appendix E, 7248/30—עח, trans. KF; A. Amit, "Letter regarding Family Voong Venh Chieng—8 souls—from Honk-Kong," 1 Jan. 1980, Appendix E, 7248/30—עח, trans. KF.

110. Anat Ben-Dor and Rami Adut, "Israel—A Safe Haven? Problems in the Treatment Offered by the State of Israel to Refugees and Asylum Seekers," Report and Position Paper, Buchmann Faculty of Law: Public Interest Law Resource Center (Tel Aviv University),

Physicians for Human Rights, Sept. 2003, 21–23; Sarah Helm, "Bosnian Muslims Find Haven in Israel," *Independent*, 17 Feb. 1993, http://www.independent.co.uk/news/world /bosnian-muslims-find-haven-in-israel-1473480.html; Fran Markowitz, "Living in Limbo: Bosnian Muslim Refugees in Israel," *Human Organization* 55, no. 2 (Summer 1996): 127–32; Karin Fathimath Afeef, "A Promised Land for Refugees? Asylum and Migration in Israel," Research Paper 183, Policy Development and Evaluation Service, UNHCR: The UN Refugee Agency, Dec. 2009, http://www.unhcr.org/en-us/research/working/4b2213a59/promised -land-refugees-asylum-migration-israel-karin-fatimath-afeef.html.

111. In the United States, refugee resettlement was also carried out by executive action as authorized by the 1952 McCarran-Walter Act, until the 1980 Refugee Act created permanent and systematic procedures for refugee admission and absorption.

112. As an intermediary step before the RSD, in 2002 Israel's attorney general established an interministerial committee for determining eligibility for political asylum. The committee evaluated individual requests and made recommendations to the minister of interior. See Galia Sabar and Elizabeth Tsurkov, "Israel's Policies toward Asylum-Seekers, 2002–2014," *Istituto Affari Internazionali* (20 May 2015): 1–18; "Refugee Law and Policy: Israel," Law Library of Congress, accessed 6 Dec. 2019, https://www.loc.gov/law/help /refugee-law/israel.php.

113. Ben-Dor and Adut, "Israel—A Safe Haven?" 24.

114. Ruth Eglash, "Israel Scraps Contested Plan to Deport Tens of Thousands of African Migrants," *Washington Post*, 25 Apr. 2018, https://www.washingtonpost.com/world/israel -scraps-contested-plan-to-deport-tens-of-thousands-of-african-migrants/2018/04/24/8fb9 3924–47f0–11e8–8082–105a446d19b8_story.html.

115. Afeef, "A Promised Land for Refugees?" 1–25.

116. Le, *Unsettled Solidarities*, 4.

117. Batsheva Sobelman, "One Country That Won't Be Taking Syrian Refugees: Israel," *Los Angeles Times*, 6 Sept. 2015, http://www.latimes.com/world/middleeast/la-fg-syrian -refugees-israel-20150906-story.html; Andrew Green, "Inside Israel's Secret Program to Get Rid of African Refugees," *Foreign Policy*, 27 June 2017, https://foreignpolicy.com/2017/06/27 /inside-israels-secret-program-to-get-rid-of-african_refugees_uganda_rwanda/.

118. Bryen, "Israel and the Boat People"; Menucha Chana Levin, "Vietnamese Boat People in the Promised Land: Memories of Holocaust Refugees, but with a Different Ending," *aish* (Jerusalem), 19 Nov. 2011, http://www.aish.com/jw/id/Vietnamese_Boat_People_in _the_Promised_Land.html.

119. Bryen, "Israel and the Boat People."

120. Fujikane, "Against the Yellowwashing of Israel," 151.

121. Sarit Catz, "On Refugees and Racism, a Double Standard against Israel," *CAMERA*, 3 July 2012, http://www.camera.org/index.asp?x_context=2&x_outlet=147&x_article=2265 (emphasis in original).

122. Fujikane, "Against the Yellowwashing of Israel," 151; Leroy, "Black History in Occupied Territory."

123. Lisa Goldman, "I Remember When Israel Rescued Non-Jewish Refugees," +972 *Magazine*, 6 Sept. 2012, http://972mag.com/i-remember-when-israel-rescued-non-jewish -refugees/55387/.

124. Hillel Halkin, "A Shame on Israel," *New York Sun*, 10 July 2007, https://www.nysun .com/opinion/shame-on-israel/58111/.

125. Halkin, "A Shame on Israel."

126. Hirsh Goodman, "Losing the Propaganda War," *New York Times*, 31 Jan. 2014.

127. Goodman, "Losing the Propaganda War."

128. See Naomi Scheinerman, "Immigration to Israel: Vietnamese Boat People in Israel," *Jewish Virtual Library*, accessed 15 Dec. 2013, http://www.jewishvirtuallibrary.org /jsource/Immigration/VietBoatPeople.html; "Truth about Israel: Vietnam," American Zionist Movement, accessed 15 Dec. 2013, http://www.azm.org/truth-about-israel-vietnam/.

129. BlueStar, "Which Middle Eastern Country Provided Refuge and Citizenship to 350 Homeless Vietnamese Desperately Seeking Political Asylum?" *flikr*, accessed 15 Dec. 2013, http://www.flickr.com/photos/wznc/2825835025/in/photostream/.

130. BlueStar.

131. Shelby Grad, "As Trump Bans Syrian refugees, a Look Back at When California Welcomed 50,000 Displaced People," *Los Angeles Times*, 28 Jan. 2017, https://www.latimes .com/local/lanow/la-me-trump-refugees-camp-pendleton-retrospective-20170128-story .html; Michelle Chen, "Trump's Assault on Refugees Is Even Worse Than It Looks," *Nation*, 14 Oct. 2019, https://www.thenation.com/article/refugee-cap/.

132. Idean Salehyan, "How Trump Politicized Refugees," Niskanen Center, 23 Oct. 2019, https://www.niskanencenter.org/how-trump-politicized-refugees/.

133. Nguyen, "Refugeetude," 114.

134. Hirsch, "Past Lives," 659.

135. Simona Weinglass, "35 Years On, Where Are Israel's Vietnamese Refugees?" *Times of Israel*, 20 Sept. 2015, https://www.timesofisrael.com/35-years-on-where-are-israels -vietnamese-refugees/.

136. Weinglass.

137. Weinglass.

138. Nguyen, quoted in Weinglass.

139. Nguyen, quoted in Weinglass.

140. Nguyen, quoted in Weinglass.

141. Tran, interview with author.

142. Cuc Huynh Sears, interview with author, Petah Tikvah, Israel-Palestine, 22 and 26 July 2016.

143. Le, *Unsettled Solidarities*, 5.

## 5. THE POLITICS OF STAYING

1. Andrew H. Malcolm, "Tent City Life Goes On," *Honolulu Star Bulletin*, 22 May 1975, C-10.

2. Malcolm, C-10.

3. Malcolm, C-10.

4. I encourage scholars to analyze whether this permanent/transient temporality applies to other militarized islands, such as Okinawa or Cuba.

5. Bettis, "Colonial Immigration in Guam," 111.

6. Bettis, 108; Flores, "'No Walk in the Park.'"

7. Bettis, "Colonial Immigration in Guam," 108.

8. Bettis, 117.

9. This immigrant transience also has economic implications: Chamorros in Guam are "expected to absorb the costs of providing for [the immigrants'] needs, even though many are transient and will eventually move on" and will "probably never return as productive or contributing members of the community." Bettis, 113.

10. In 2006, the US military initially proposed the transfer of 8,000 marines and 9,000 dependents to Guam. The plans also included "the removal of 71 acres of coral reef from Apra Harbor to allow the entry and berthing of nuclear aircraft carriers, the acquisition of land including the oldest and revered Chamorro village on the island at Pågat for a live-fire training range, and an estimated 47 percent increase in the island's population, already past its water-supply carrying capacity." See Lutz, "US Military Bases on Guam in a Global Perspective"; Na'puti and Bevacqua, "Militarization and Resistance from Guåhan." Since then, protesters have convinced the military to decrease the buildup from 8,000 to 2,500, slow the process of transfer, and refrain from destroying Pågat.

11. Loyd, Mitchell-Eaton, and Mountz, "The Militarization of Islands and Migration," 70.

12. Loyd, Mitchell-Eaton, and Mountz, 70 (emphasis added).

13. Loyd, Mitchell-Eaton, and Mountz, 70.

14. Minh-Hanh Nguyen, oral history by Rachel Mock, 17 May 2012, UCI Libraries, University of California, Irvine, http://ucispace.lib.uci.edu/handle/10575/5223.

15. Williams, *Marxism and Literature*, 132; Le, *Unsettled Solidarities*, 24.

16. Edith Iriate, "Concert for Orote Point Refugees," *Banana Leaf*, 16 May 1975, 8–9. Although Iriate does not reveal her ethnicity in this article, two facts make it safe to assume that she is at least partly Chamorro. First, George Washington Senior High has a predominantly Chamorro population. Second, "Iriate" is either a misspelling or deliberate variation on the name "Iriarte," a common Chamorro last name.

17. Robyn Walls, "Chorus Sings at Asan," *Banana Leaf*, 16 May 1975, 1.

18. Iriate, "Concert for Orote Point Refugees," 8.

19. Iriate, 9.

20. For more on carcerality as a vector by which to connect Asian American and Indigenous studies, see Leong and Carpio, "Carceral States."

21. Iriate, "Concert for Orote Point Refugees," 9.

22. Iriate, 9.

23. Of the soldiers who served in Vietnam, 88.4 percent were white. Vietnam Veterans of America, Chapter 310, "Vietnam War Statistics," accessed 9 Nov. 2021, https://www.vva310.org/vietnam-war-statistics.

24. Iriate, "Concert for Orote Point Refugees," 9.

25. Iriate, 9.

26. Iriate, 9.

27. Iriate, 9.

28. Iriate, 9.

29. Iriate, 9 (emphasis added).

30. Lipman, "'Give Us a Ship,'" 9.

31. Vicky Ritter, interview with author.

32. Gordon Ritter, interview with author, Zoom, 19 Mar. 2021.

33. Lipman, "'Give Us a Ship,'" 15.

34. Lipman, 10.

35. "Give Repatriates a Ship, Bordallo," *PDN*, 20 July 1975; "The Ship Solution . . ." *PDN*, 25 Aug. 1975; Bordallo, interview with author.

36. Trần Đình Trụ, *Ship of Fate: Memoir of a Vietnamese Repatriate*, trans. Bac Hoai Tran and Jana K. Lipman (Honolulu: University of Hawai'i Press, 2017), 137–43. The other 500 or so repatriates decided at the last minute to proceed to the continental United States.

37. Lipman, "'Give Us a Ship,'" 2, 4; Trần, *Ship of Fate*, 112.

38. Trần, *Ship of Fate*, 165–81.

39. The HO program facilitated the immigration of former reeducation camp prisoners from Vietnam directly to the United States.

40. Lipman, "Introduction," 3.

41. Trần, *Ship of Fate*, 38–47.

42. Trần, 46, 54, 123.

43. Trần, 58.

44. Lipman, "Introduction," 3.

45. Trần, *Ship of Fate*, 110, 69, 206, 153, 137, 171.

46. Trần, 137.

47. Trần, 200.

48. Trần, 57–58.

49. Trần, 90–91.

50. Stephen R. Porter, *Benevolent Empire: U.S. Power, Humanitarianism, and the World's Dispossessed* (Philadelphia: University of Pennsylvania Press, 2017).

51. Trần, *Ship of Fate*, 110.

52. Trần, 110.

53. Trần, 74.

54. Nguyễn-võ Thu-hương, "Articulated Sorrows: Intercolonial Imaginings and the National Singular," *Canadian Review of American Studies* 48, no. 3 (2018): 331; Raymond Scupin, "Historical, Ethnographic, and Contemporary Political Analyses of the Muslims of Kampuchea and Vietnam," *Sojourn* 10, no. 2 (1995): 301–28; "Freedom-Justice-Peace," The Council of Indigenous Peoples in Today's Vietnam, accessed 10 Oct. 2021, http://ciptvn.org/.

55. Ronn Ronck, "Evacuee-Employe [*sic*] Hunt Is On," *PDN*, 23 May 1975, 1, 3; Dave Hendrick, "Firms Sponsor Most Cleared Refugees," *PDN*, 28 May 1975, 4; Susan Guffey, "Refugee 'at Home' on Guam," *PDN*, 29 May 1975, 3; Susan Guffey, "Refugees Begin Job Searches," *PDN*, 7 June 1975, 3; "Well Done," *Honolulu Star-Bulletin*, 8 July 1975, A-16; Martha Ruth, "Refugees Want to Stay and Fish around Guam," *PDN*, 12 July 1975, 20; Gloria Lujan, "Seven Refugees Daily Released on Island," *PDN*, 21 July 1975, 4–5; Gloria Lujan, "Vietnamese Refugees Growing into Guam's Culture," *PDN*, 13 Aug. 1975, 22.

56. Lujan, "Vietnamese Refugees Growing into Guam's Culture," 22. Lujan does not report the refugees' last names.

57. Quoted in Lujan, 22.

58. Anonymous 2, interview with author.

59. Anonymous, interview with author, Tamuning, Guam, 23 May 2016.

60. Bottcher quoted in Karen Jowers, "Vietnamese Close in Guam," *PDN*, 2 Feb. 1988, 3.

61. Hoa V. Nguyen, interview with author, Tamuning, Guam, 2 June 2016; "Hoa V. Nguyen," American Medical Center, accessed 5 Nov. 2019, http://www.amc.clinic/providers/hoa-nguyen/.

62. Hoa V. Nguyen, email to author, 7 July 2020.

63. Jennifer Berry, interview with author, Tamuning, Guam, 8 June 2016.

64. Berry, interview with author.

65. Anonymous, email to author, 25 May 2016.

66. Anonymous, email to author, 25 May 2016.

67. Anonymous, email to author, 25 May 2016

68. Anonymous, email to author, 25 May 2016; Anonymous, interview with author, 23 May 2016.

69. Alana Chargualaf, "Guam Lone Sailor Statue Plaques Dedicated," *Pacific Island Times*, 30 Apr. 2019, https://www.pacificislandtimes.com/single-post/2019/04/30/Guam-Lone -Sailor-Statue-plaques-dedicated.

70. Pham quoted in Chargualaf.

71. Anonymous, email to author, 25 May 2016.

72. Dean Itsuji Saranillio, "Colliding Histories: Hawai'i Statehood at the Intersections of Asians 'Ineligible to Citizenship' and Hawaiians 'Unfit for Self-Government,'" *Journal of Asian American Studies* 13, no. 3 (Oct. 2010): 287.

73. Saranillio, 287.

74. Williams, *Marxism and Literature*, 132.

75. Henry Jenkins, "Blog This!" in *Fans, Bloggers, and Gamers: Exploring Participatory Culture* (New York: New York University Press, 2006), 180–81.

76. Anna Poletti and Julie Rak, "The Blog as Experimental Setting: An Interview with Lauren Berlant," in *Identity Technologies: Constructing the Self Online*, ed. Anna Poletti and Julie Rak (Madison: University of Wisconsin Press, 2014), 264–65.

77. Yarimar Bonilla and Jonathan Rosa, "#Ferguson: Digital Protest, Hashtag Ethnography, and the Racial Politics of Social Media in the United States," *American Ethnologist* 42, no. 1 (2015): 4–17.

78. Evyn Lê Espiritu, "'Who Was Colonel Hồ Ngọc Cẩn?': Queer and Feminist Practices for Exhibiting South Vietnamese History on the Internet," *Amerasia* 43, no. 2 (2017): 3.

79. Bianca Nguyen, interview with author, Zoom, 15 Mar. 2021. I thank Joseph Orser for helping me to locate Nguyen.

80. Bianca Nguyen, interview with author.

81. Bianca Nguyen, interview with author, Zoom, 24 Nov. and 18 Dec. 2020.

82. Beau Hodai, "Chamorro Summit Draws Good Crowd among Youth," *Peace and Justice for Guam and the Pacific* (blog), 27 Oct. 2008, http://decolonizeguam.blogspot .com/2008/10/chamorro-summit-draws-good-crowd-among.html.

83. Public Law 23-147; Public Law 23-130.

84. Public Law 23-130, quoted in Victoria-Lola Leon Guerrero, "Chamorro Registry and the Decolonization Registry," *Guampedia*, accessed 26 June 2017, http://www.guampedia .com/chamorro-registry-and-the-decolonization-registry/.

85. Public Law 23-130; Public Law 25-106.

86. Public Law 25-106.

87. Public Law 25-106.

88. General Assembly Official Records, Sixty-Second Session, Supplement No. 23 (A/62/23), 2007.

89. United Nations Special Committee of 24, "Report of the Special Committee on the Situation with regard to the Implementation of the Declaration on the Granting of

Independence to Colonial Countries and Peoples," 2007, 68, https://digitallibrary.un.org/record/605290?ln=en.

90. United Nations, "Report of the Special Committee," 73–74.

91. Bianca Nguyen, "Initiating the Conversation," *The Decolonization Conversation* (blog), 25 Oct. 2008, http://decolonizationconversation.blogspot.com/.

92. Walter Benjamin, "Theses on the Philosophy of History," in *Illuminations* (New York: Schocken Books, 1995), 255.

93. Bianca Nguyen, "8,000: How Will It Change Our Lives?" *The Decolonization Conversation*, 24 May 2009, http://decolonizationconversation.blogspot.com/.

94. Nguyen.

95. Nguyen.

96. Saranillio, "Why Asian Settler Colonialism Matters," 283.

97. Huang, "Between Sovereignties," 33.

98. Saranillio, "Colliding Histories," 304.

99. See, for example, the *Memoirs Pasifika* podcast, to which I contributed an episode on Operation New Life: https://www.memoirspasifika.com/.

100. Tydingco-Gatewood quoted in Jasmine Stole and Jerick Sablan, "Judge: Plebiscite Law Unconstitutional; AG May Appeal," *PDN*, 9 Mar. 2017, https://www.guampdn.com/story/news/2017/03/08/judge-arnold-davis-plebiscite-law-unconsitical/98888880/.

101. Wolfe, "Settler Colonialism and the Elimination of the Native," 388.

102. "61/295, United Nations Declaration on the Rights of Indigenous Peoples," United Nations, 13 Sept. 2007, https://www.un.org/development/desa/indigenouspeoples/wp-content/uploads/sites/19/2018/11/UNDRIP_E_web.pdf; Chris Barnett, "Guam Loses Davis Appeal," *Kuam News*, 30 July 2019, https://www.kuam.com/story/40850000/guam-loses-davis-appeal.

103. Bianca Nguyen, interview with author, 15 Mar. 21.

104. Glen Sean Coulthard, "Fanonian Antimonies," paper presented at a conference at Simon Fraser University, Vancouver, BC, Canada, 2017.

105. Michelle Daigle and Margaret Marietta Ramírez, "Decolonial Geographies," in *Keywords in Radical Geography: Antipode at 50*, ed. Antipode Editorial Collective (Hoboken, NJ: John Wiley & Sons, Inc., 2019), 78–84. See also Brian Batchelor, Hannah Rackow, and Denise Rogers Valenzuela, "Editorial," *Canada Theater Review* 177 (Winter 2019): 5–9.

106. Craig Santos Perez, "Crosscurrents (Three Poems)," *Atlantic Studies* 15, no. 2 (2018): 176.

107. Perez, 177.

108. Perez, 177.

## 6. THE POLITICS OF TRANSLATION

1. Vaan Nguyen, *The Truffle Eye*, trans. Adriana X. Jacobs (Brookline, MA: Zephyr Press, 2021), 99.

2. Nguyen, 99.

3. Gayatri Chakravorty Spivak, "Translation as Culture," *Parallax* 6, no. 1 (2000): 14.

4. Walter Benjamin, "The Task of the Translator," in *Walter Benjamin: Selected Writings*, Vol. 1: *1913–1926*, ed. Marcus Bullock and Michael W. Jennings (Cambridge, MA: Belknap Press of Harvard University Press, 2002), 261.

5. Spivak, "Translation as Culture," 13.

6. Some Palestinians in this neighborhood alternatively self-identify as Israeli Arabs, Christian Arabs, or Muslim Arabs.

7. For more on "Guerilla Culture," see "Guerrilla Tarbut," *Wikipedia*, updated 28 Sept. 2020, https://en.wikipedia.org/wiki/Guerrilla_Tarbut. The group disbanded in mid-2017. Vaan Nguyen, interview with author, Facebook Messenger, 27 Dec. 2017.

8. Trinh T. Minh-ha (writer, director), *Surname Viet Given Name Nam* (film, 1989).

9. Fujikane, "Against the Yellowwashing of Israel," 150–71.

10. For more on "model refugees," see chapter 4.

11. Noura Erakat, *Justice for Some: Law and the Question of Palestine* (Stanford, CA: Stanford University Press, 2019), 238.

12. Williams, *Marxism and Literature*, 132.

13. Atef Alshaer, *Poetry and Politics in the Modern Arab World* (London: Hurst, 2016), 131; Farag, *Politics and Palestinian Literature in Exile*, 12.

14. Erakat, *Justice for Some*, 238.

15. Barghouti, *I Saw Ramallah*, 41. In this chapter, all citations of the original text, transcribed here in standard Romanized Arabic, are drawn from Murīd Barghūthī, *Ra'aytu Rām Allāh* (Bayrūt: al-Markaz al-Thaqāfī al-'Arabī, 1998). Shireen Hamza helped transcribe the Arabic translations.

16. Barghouti, 4.

17. Erakat, *Justice for Some*, 218.

18. Anna Bernard, *Rhetorics of Belonging: Nation, Narration, and Israel/Palestine* (Liverpool: Liverpool University Press, 2013), 69.

19. Edward W. Said, "Foreword," in Barghouti, *I Saw Ramallah*, vii.

20. Bernard, *Rhetorics of Belonging*, 6.

21. Bernard, 70.

22. Norbert Bugeja, *Postcolonial Memoir in the Middle East: Rethinking the Liminal in Mashriqi Writing* (New York: Routledge, 2012), 39–40.

23. Jacobs, "Where You Are From," 93.

24. Jacobs, 99.

25. In *The Journey of Vaan Nguyen*, Nguyen comments that growing up in Israel has meant "identifying with the forced exile so familiar with the Jewish people." Duki Dror, *The Journey of Vaan Nguyen* (documentary film) (DVD, Zygote Films, 2005).

26. Jacobs, "Where You Are From," 83.

27. This observation is based on interviews conducted in 2015–16.

28. Nguyen, *The Truffle Eye*, 59.

29. Nguyen, 7.

30. Nguyen, 93.

31. Nguyen, 97.

32. Farag, *Politics and Palestinian Literature in Exile*, 87.

33. Barghouti, *I Saw Ramallah*, 40–41.

34. Erakat, *Justice for Some*, 234; Qutami and Zahzah, "The War of Words," 84.

35. Shohat, "Taboo Memories, Diasporic Visions."

36. Erakat, *Justice for Some*, 237.

37. Bryan Cheyette, *Diasporas of the Mind: Jewish and Postcolonial Writing and the Nightmare of History* (New Haven, CT: Yale University Press, 2013), 28.

38. Said, "Reflections on Exile," 144, 148–49.

39. Zahi Zalloua, *Continental Philosophy and the Palestinian Question: Beyond the Jew and the Greek* (New York: Bloomsbury, 2017), 100–101.

40. Zalloua, 97.

41. Barghouti, *I Saw Ramallah*, 13.

42. Said, "Reflections on Exile," 148.

43. Judith Butler, *Parting Ways: Jewishness and the Critique of Zionism* (New York: Columbia University Press, 2012), 206.

44. For more on binationalism and the "one-state solution," see Ali Abunimah, "Only a Single-State Solution Will Bring Peace," *New York Times*, 24 Apr. 2014, https://www.nytimes.com/roomfordebate/2014/04/24/can-hamas-fatah-unity-lead-to-mideast-peace/only-a-single-state-solution-will-bring-peace; Haidar Eid, "Interview with Dr. Haidar Eid: 'The Palestinian Struggle Is Not about Independence—It Is about Liberation,'" *Mondoweiss*, 2 Dec. 2013, http://www.palestinechronicle.com/palestinian-struggle-is-not-about-independence-it-is-about-liberation-interview-with-dr-haidar-eid/; Haidar Eid, "Gaza and BDS!" in *Against Apartheid: The Case For Boycotting Israeli Universities*, ed. Ashley Dawson and Bill V. Mullen (Chicago: Haymarket Books, 2015), 31–35; Edward W. Said, "My Right of Return," in *Power, Politics, and Culture: Interviews with Edward W. Said*, ed. Gauri Viswanathan (New York: Vintage, 2001), 443–58; Zalloua, *Continental Philosophy and the Palestinian Question*.

45. Erakat, *Justice for Some*, 235.

46. Erakat, 220.

47. Agamben, "We Refugees," 119.

48. Arendt, "We Refugees," 119.

49. Bhabha and Rutherford, "The Third Space," 211.

50. Vaan Nguyen, "The Boat People: The Next Generation?" *Ynet*, 8 Sept. 2015, trans. and quoted in Adriana X. Jacobs, "Translating Roots: Introducing the Poetry of Vaan Nguyen," in Nguyen, *The Truffle Eye*, xi.

51. Coby Ben-Simhon, "In Her Own Words," *Haaretz*, 27 Mar. 2008, http://www.haaretz.com/in-her-words-1.242793.

52. Sabine Huynh, "The Vietnamese Community in Israel: A Profile," paper presented at 12th Biennial Jerusalem Conference in Canadian Studies (June 2008); "Responding to the Challenge of Diversity in Canada, Israel, and Beyond," https://hal.archives-ouvertes.fr/hal-02914986; Weinglass, "35 Years On, Where Are Israel's Vietnamese Refugees?"; Anonymous, interview with author, Tel Aviv, Israel-Palestine, 13 May 2015.

53. Xing Long (Shalma Rd 134, Tel Aviv-Yafo, Israel) and Yan Yan (Derekh Yafo 26, Haifa, Israel) are two Chinese restaurants owned by ethnic Chinese refugees from Vietnam.

54. This observation is based on interviews I conducted in 2015–16; Huynh, "The Vietnamese Community in Israel."

55. David V. Bartram, "Foreign Workers in Israel: History and Theory," *International Migration Review* 32, no. 2 (Summer 1998): 303–25; Michael Ellman and Smain Laacher, *Migrant Workers in Israel: A Contemporary Form of Slavery*, ed. Sarah Han and Katherine Vanfassen (Copenhagen: Euro-Mediterranean Human Rights Network and International Federation for Human Rights, 2003); Mya Guarnieri Jaradat, *The Unchosen: The Lives of Israel's New Others* (London: Pluto Press, 2017); Sarah S. Willen, "Toward a Critical Phenomenology of 'Illegality': State Power, Criminalization, and Abjectivity among Undocumented Migrant Workers in Tel Aviv, Israel," *International Migration* 45, no. 3 (2007): 8–36.

56. August, *The Refugee Aesthetic*, 55–77.

57. Malkki, "Refugees and Exile."

58. Nguyen, "Refugeetude," 110.

59. Nguyen, *The Truffle Eye*, 3.

60. Said, "Reflections on Exile," 140.

61. Nguyen, *The Truffle Eye*, 3.

62. Nguyen, 21, 9.

63. Nguyen, 3.

64. Kaplan, *Our American Israel*.

65. Nguyen, *The Truffle Eye*, 55, 127.

66. Nguyen, 55, 127.

67. Nguyen, 55.

68. Nguyen, 3.

69. Nguyen, 3.

70. Arendt, *The Origins of Totalitarianism*, 267–302; Agamben, "We Refugees."

71. Nguyen, *The Truffle Eye*, 10 (emphasis added).

72. Jacobs, "Translating Roots," xiv.

73. Nguyen, *The Truffle Eye*, 27.

74. Sharif, "Vanishing Palestine," 18.

75. Nguyen, *The Truffle Eye*, 27.

76. Jacobs, "Where You Are From," 98.

77. Barghouti, *I Saw Ramallah*, 41.

78. David Farrier, "Washing Words: The Politics of Water in Mourid Barghouti's *I Saw Ramallah*," *Journal of Commonwealth Literature* 48, no. 2 (2012): 188; Barghouti, *I Saw Ramallah*, 41.

79. Barghouti, *I Saw Ramallah*, 41.

80. Erakat, *Justice for Some*, 238.

81. Barghouti, *I Saw Ramallah*, 157 (emphasis added).

82. Barghouti, 157.

83. Nguyen, *The Truffle Eye*, 3.

84. Barghouti, *I Saw Ramallah*, 38.

85. Erakat, *Justice for Some*, 229.

86. Yael Munk, "Duki Dror's Journey of the Displaced," *Cinematheque* 138 (Jan. 2006): 45–49.

87. Qutami and Zahzah, "The War of Words," 84.

88. In this section, I refer to Hoài Mỹ Nguyễn by his first name, Hoài Mỹ, in order to distinguish him from his daughter, Vaan Nguyen.

89. Dror, *The Journey of Vaan Nguyen*.

90. Võ Hồng Chương-Đài, "When Memories Collide: Revisiting War in Vietnam and in the Diaspora," in *Film in Contemporary Southeast Asia: Cultural Interpretation and Social Intervention*, ed. David C. L. Lim and Hiroyuki Yamamoto (New York: Routledge, 2012), 78.

91. Translation provided by Adriana X. Jacobs, with the exception of "Vân (Vaan) is a synonym for cloud," which Jacobs mistakenly translates as "Nguyen is a synonym for cloud." I have also changed "Philippine" to "Filipino." Otherwise, this translation is more accurate

than the English subtitles provided in the film for this scene. See Jacobs, "Where You Are From," 100–101.

92. Benjamin, "Theses on the Philosophy of History," 255.

93. Nguyen's mother prefers to remain unnamed.

94. Dror, *The Journey of Vaan Nguyen*.

95. Jacobs, "Where You Are From," 90.

96. This chapter refers to her as "Hong Wa Nguyen" because that is how she is credited in the film and how she self-identifies on Facebook.

97. For more on the "gendered process of racism" underlying this scene, see Võ, "When Memories Collide," 80–81.

98. Dror, *The Journey of Vaan Nguyen* (translation of Hebrew taken from the English subtitles).

99. For a discussion of the *Wizard of Oz* truism "There's no place like home" in relation to Jewish diaspora theory, see Jonathan Boyarin, "Tropes of Home," in *Jewishness and the Human Dimension* (New York: Fordham University Press, 2008), 74–88.

100. Dror, *The Journey of Vaan Nguyen*.

101. Translation of the film's Vietnamese dialogue is taken from Võ, "When Memories Collide," 82.

102. Võ, 83.

103. Võ, 82.

104. "Freedom-Justice-Peace"; Evyn Lê Espiritu Gandhi, "Queer Love across Queer Time: Nonaligned Solidarity, Indigenous Incommensurability, and the Temporal Drag of the Vietnam War," *Critical Ethnic Studies* 5, no. 1 (Spring 2019): 116–17.

105. Dror, *The Journey of Vaan Nguyen* (English translation provided by author).

106. Dror.

107. Dror (English translation provided by author).

108. Qutami and Zahzah, "The War of Words," 84.

109. Nadera Shalhoub-Kevorkian and Sarah Ihmoud, "Exiled at Home: Writing Return and the Palestinian Home," *Biography* 37, no. 2 (Spring 2014): 394–95.

110. Perez, "Off-Island Chamorros."

111. Shalhoub-Kevorkian and Ihmoud, "Exiled at Home," 377.


AFTERWORD. FLOATING ISLANDS

1. Joe Quirk and Patri Friedman, *Seasteading: How Floating Nations Will Restore the Environment, Enrich the Poor, Cure the Sick, and Liberate Humanity from Politicians* (New York: Simon & Schuster, 2017), 5.

2. Quirk and Friedman, 7, 8, 10.

3. Quirk and Friedman, dust jacket.

4. Maile Arvin, *Possessing Polynesians: The Science of Settler Colonial Whiteness in Hawai'i and Oceania* (Durham, NC: Duke University Press, 2019), 3.

5. Malkki, "Refugees and Exile."

6. Nguyen, "Refugeetude."

7. Quirk and Friedman, *Seasteading*, 6.

8. Linh Dinh, "A Floating Community," in *Blood and Soap: Stories* (New York: Seven Stories Press, 2004), 59.

9. Dinh, 59.

10. Nguyen, "Nước/Water," 72.

11. Rachel Yacaaʔał George and Sarah Marie Wiebe, "Fluid Decolonial Futures: Water as a Life, Ocean Citizenship, and Seascape Relationality," *New Political Science* 42, no. 4 (2020): 505.

12. Dinh, "A Floating Community," 59.

13. *The Island, Tuan Andrew Nguyen*, accessed 21 Oct. 2021, https://www.tuanandrewn guyen.com/theisland.

14. Han Hai Van, quoted in Lesleyanne Hawthorne, ed., *Refugee: The Vietnamese Experience* (Melbourne: Oxford University Press, 1982), 270–71.

15. Tuan Andrew Nguyen, *The Island*, video installation, Whitney Museum of American Art, 2017. For more on the memorial at Palau Bidong, see Quan Tue Tran, "Remembering the Boat People Exodus: A Tale of Two Memorials," *Journal of Vietnamese Studies* 7, no. 3 (2012): 80–121.

16. Nguyen, *The Island*.

17. Nguyen.

18. Nguyen.

19. Hau'ofa, "Our Sea of Islands," 148–61.

20. Nguyen, *The Island*.

21. Nguyen.

22. Nguyen.

23. Nguyen.

24. Nguyen, "Nước/Water," 66.

25. Nguyen, *The Island*.

# BIBLIOGRAPHY

## ARCHIVAL SOURCES

Institute of Palestine Studies. Ramallah, Palestine.
Israel State Archives. Jerusalem, Israel-Palestine.
Nieves M. Flores Memorial Library. Hagåtña, Guam.
Richard F. Taitano Micronesian Area Resource Center. University of Guam.
Vietnam Center and Archive. Texas Tech University.

## ONLINE SOURCES

Guampedia.com
MemoirsPasifika.com
Newspapers.com

## ORAL HISTORY SOURCES

Hongga Mo'na: For the Future
Vietnamese American Oral History Project. University of California, Irvine.
Vietnamese in the Diaspora Digital Archive (ViDDA)

## ORAL HISTORIES BY AUTHOR

Ada, Jennifer. Phone, 4 June 2018.
Anonymous. Dededo, Guam, 29 May 2016.
Anonymous. Email, 25 May 2016.
Anonymous. Tamuning, Guam, 23 May 2016.

Anonymous. Tel Aviv, Israel-Palestine, 13 May 2015.

Anonymous 1. Mangilao, Guam, 3 June 2016.

Anonymous 2. Mangilao, Guam, 3 June 2016.

Baza, Lee T. Tamuning, Guam, 10 June 2018.

Baza, Raymond T. Tamuning, Guam, 10 June 2018.

Benavente, Juan C. Tamuning, Guam, 10 June 2018.

Berry, Jennifer. Tamuning, Guam, 8 June 2016.

Blaz, Juan O. Tamuning, Guam, 13 June 2018.

Bordallo, Madeleine. Zoom, 18 Mar. 2021.

Brown, Rose Franquez. Zoom, 3 May 2021.

Charfauros, Jesus Quitugua. San Diego, CA, 22 Apr. 2017.

Cuong Nguyen Tuan. Tel Aviv, Israel-Palestine, 1 July 2016.

Francisco, Nicolas D. Mangilao, Guam, 8 June 2018.

Manglona, Martin Ada. Talofofo, Guam, 13 June 2018.

Murphy, Shannon. Mangilao, Guam, 27 May 2016.

Nguyen, Bianca. Zoom, 24 Nov. and 18 Dec. 2020, 15 Mar. 2021.

Nguyễn, Hoài Mỹ. Jaffa, Israel-Palestine, 24 May 2015.

Nguyen, Hoa V. Tamuning, Guam, 2 June 2016 and email, 7 July 2020.

Nguyen, Vaan. Facebook Messenger, 27 Dec. 2017.

Perez, Joaquin "Kin." Mangilao, Guam, 9 June 2016.

Quitugua, David I. A. Ordot, Guam, 7 June 2016.

Ramos, Allan. Tamuning, Guam, 10 June 2018.

Ritter, Gordon. Zoom, 19 Mar. 2021.

Ritter, Vicky. Zoom, 19 Mar. 2021.

Salama, Saadi. Hà Nội, Vietnam, 22 July 2015.

San Nicolas, Joseph C. Talofofo, Guam, 11 June 2018.

Sears, Cuc Huynh. Petah Tikvah, Israel-Palestine, 22 and 26 July 2016.

Taitano, John G. Barrigada, Guam, 9 June 2018.

Talhami, Daoud. Ramallah, Palestine, 7 July 2016.

Tran Tai Dong, Tel Aviv, Israel-Palestine, 21 July 2016.

Won Pat, Judith. Hagåtña, Guam, 7 June 2016.

## NEWSPAPERS AND PERIODICALS

*+972 Magazine*

*Aish.com*

*Al HaMishmar*

*Alexandria (VA) Gazette*

*Allentown (PA) Daily Leader*

*Arizona Republic* (Phoenix)

*Ashbury Park Press*

Associated Press

*Baltimore Sun*

*Banana Leaf* (Guam)

*Big Spring (TX) Daily Herald*

*Buffalo (NY) Enquirer*

*CAMERA*
*Chân Trời Mới*
*Charlotte Observer*
*Cincinnati Enquirer*
*Courier* (Waterloo, IA)
*Daily American* (Nashville, TN)
*Daily Constitution* (Atlanta, GA)
*Daily Democratic Statesman* (Austin, TX)
*Daily Press* (Newport News, VA)
*Dayton Herald*
*Decatur (IL) Sunday Herald and Review*
*Des Moines Register*
*Desert News* (Salt Lake City)
*Detroit Free Press*
*Elmira (NY) Gazette*
*Evening Star* (Washington, DC)
*Foreign Policy*
*Greenley News*
*Guardian*
*Ha'aretz*
*Hawaii Times*
*Hawaii-Hochi*
*Helena (MT) Weekly Herald*
*Honolulu Advertiser*
*Honolulu Star Bulletin*
*Independent* (London, UK)
*Indianapolis News*
*Indianapolis Star*
*Islander* (Guam)
*Jerusalem Post*
*JTA: The Global Jewish News Source*
*Kuam News*
*Leader-Telegram* (Eau Claire, WI)
*Los Angeles Times*
*Ma'ariv*
*Marion (OH) Star*
*Military Sun*
*Mondoweiss*
*Monitor* (McAllen, TX)
*Montgomery Advertiser*
*Morning Star* (London)
*Nation*
*Neue Deutsch Zeitung*
*New York Sun*
*New York Times*
*News Journal* (Wilmington, DE)

*Observer* (Raleigh, NC)
*Osage County Chronicle* (Burlingame, KS)
*Pacific Daily News*, née *Guam Daily News*
*Pacific Island Times*
*Pacific Stars and Stripes*
*Pantagraph* (Bloomington, IL)
*Peking People's Daily*
*Petaluma Weekly Argus*
*Philadelphia Inquirer*
*PhilStar Global*
*Pike Country Press* (Milford, PA)
*Pittsburg Press*
*Poughkeepsie Eagle-News*
*Poughkeepsie Sunday New Yorker*
*Public Ledge* (Memphis, TN)
*Raleigh News*
*Randall (KS) Enterprise*
*Reading Times*
*Salt Lake Tribune*
*San Francisco Good Times*
*Shreveport Times*
*South China Morning Post* (Hong Kong)
*Summit County Beacon* (Akron, OH)
*Sunday News*
*Sunday Times* (New Brunswick, NJ)
*Tennessean* (Nashville)
*Times* (Philadelphia)
*Times of Israel*
*Times-Picayune* (New Orleans)
*Tri-Weekly Herald* (Marshall, TX)
*Valley Spirit* (Chambersburg, PA)
*Victoria (TX) Advocate*
*Washington Post*
*Weekly Observer* (Raleigh, NC)
*Wilkes-Barre (PA) Record*
*Wilkes-Barre (PA) Semi-Weekly Record*
*Wilmington Morning Star*
*Yedioth Ahronoth*
*Ynet*

## UNPUBLISHED TALKS AND MANUSCRIPTS

"After Action Report: Operations New Life/New Arrivals: U.S. Army Support to the Indo-chinese Refugee Program, 1 April 1975–1 June 1976."
Coulthard, Glen Sean. "Fanonian Antimonies." Paper presented at a conference at Simon Fraser University, Vancouver, BC, Canada, 2017.

Huang, Yu-ting. "Between Sovereignties: Chinese Minor Settler Literature Across the Pacific." PhD diss., Department of Comparative Literature, University of California, Los Angeles, 2015. UCLA Electronic Theses and Dissertations.

Hutcherson, James T. "The Impact of the Vietnamese Refugees on the Guam Economy: Special Research Project Submitted as a Requirement of BA 690, Special Project," University of Guam, Mar. 1976, MARC HV 640.5 V5 H8 c. 1.

Juhasz-Wood, Christina. "Contesting Historical Enchantment: Militarized Settler Colonialism and Refugee Resettlement in New Mexico." PhD diss., University of New Mexico, 2020. UNM Electronic Theses and Dissertations.

Sahara, Ayako. "Operations New Life/Arrivals: U.S. National Project to Forget the Vietnam War." MA thesis, University of California, San Diego, 2009.

Sarmiento, Thomas X. "The Promise of Queer Filipinx Midwestern Domesticity in Edith Can Shoot Things and Hit Them." Paper presented at the Association of Asian American Studies Conference, Portland, OR, 14 Apr. 2017.

Tran, Tiffany Wang-Su, and Demiliza Saramosing. "(Re)Producing Refugees: Chinese-Vietnamese Refugee Resettlement on Indian Land." Paper presented at Native American Indigenous Studies Association (NAISA) conference, Hamilton, New Zealand (Aotearoa), 29 June 2019.


## PUBLISHED BOOKS AND ARTICLES

Ada, Joseph F. "The Quest for Commonwealth, the Quest for Change." In *Kinalamten Pulitikåt: Siñenten I Chamorro / Issues in Guam's Political Development: The Chamorro Perspective*, 125–203. Agaña, Guam: Political Status and Education Coordinating Commission, 1996.

Agamben, Giorgio. *Homo Sacer: Sovereign Power and Bare Life*. Translated by Daniel Heller-Roazen. Stanford, CA: Stanford University Press, 1998.

———. "We Refugees." Translated by Michael Rocke. *Symposium* 49, no. 2 (Summer 1995): 114–19.

Afeef, Karin Fathimath. "A Promised Land for Refugees? Asylum and Migration in Israel." Research Paper No. 183, *Policy Development and Evaluation Service, UNHCR: The UN Refugee Agency* (Dec. 2009): 1–25. http://www.unhcr.org/en-us/research/working/4b2213a59/promised-land-refugees-asylum-migration-israel-karin-fatimath-afeef.html.

Allen, Chadwick. *Trans-Indigenous: Methodologies for Global Native Literary Studies*. Minneapolis: University of Minnesota Press, 2012.

Alshaer, Atef. *Poetry and Politics in the Modern Arab World*. London: Hurst, 2016.

Amar, Paul. *The Security Archipelago: Human-Security States, Sexuality Politics, and the End of Neoliberalism*. Durham, NC: Duke University Press, 2013.

Anderson, Emily. "Adapting the Transnational Prairie: Little House, Little Mosque, and Little Laos." *Journal of Popular Culture* 49, no. 5 (2016): 1003–22.

———. *Little: Novels*. Kenmore, NY: BlazeVOX Books, 2015.

Arendt, Hannah. *The Origins of Totalitarianism*. New York: Harcourt, 1973.

———. "We Refugees." In *Altogether Elsewhere: Writers on Exile*, edited by Marc Robinson, 110–19. Boston: Faber and Faber, 1994.

Aruri, Naseer H. "AAUG: A Memoir." *Arab Studies Quarterly* 29 (Summer–Fall 2007): 33–46.

Arvin, Maile. *Possessing Polynesians: The Science of Settler Colonial Whiteness in Hawai'i and Oceania.* Durham, NC: Duke University Press, 2019.

Asaka, Ikuko. *Tropical Freedom: Climate, Settler Colonialism, and Black Exclusion in the Age of Emancipation.* Durham, NC: Duke University Press, 2017.

Atanasoski, Neda. *Humanitarian Violence: The U.S. Deployment of Diversity.* Minneapolis: University of Minnesota Press, 2013.

August, Timothy K. *The Refugee Aesthetic: Reimagining Southeast Asian America.* Philadelphia: Temple University Press, 2021.

Barghouti, Mourid. *I Saw Ramallah.* Translated by Ahdaf Soueif. New York: Anchor Books, 2003.

———. *Ra'aytu Rām Allāh.* Bayrūt: al-Markaz al-Thaqāfī al-'Arabī, 1998.

Bartram, David V. "Foreign Workers in Israel: History and Theory." *International Migration Review* 32, no. 2 (Summer 1998): 303–25.

Batchelor, Brian, Hannah Rackow, and Denise Rogers Valenzuela. "Editorial." *Canada Theater Review* 177 (Winter 2019): 5–9.

Ben-Dor, Anat, and Rami Adut. "Israel—A Safe Haven?: Problems in the Treatment Offered by the State of Israel to Refugees and Asylum Seekers." *Report and Position Paper*, Buchmann Faculty of Law: The Public Interest Law Resource Center (Tel Aviv University), Physicians for Human Rights, Sept. 2003, 21–23.

Benjamin, Walter. "Theses on the Philosophy of History." In *Illuminations*, 253–64. New York: Schocken Books, 1995.

———. "The Task of the Translator." In *Walter Benjamin: Selected Writings*, Volume 1: *1913–1926*, ed. Marcus Bullock and Michael W. Jennings, 253–63. Cambridge, MA: Belknap Press of Harvard University Press, 2002.

Berlant, Lauren. *Cruel Optimism.* Durham, NC: Duke University Press, 2011.

Bernard, Anna. *Rhetorics of Belonging: Nation, Narration, and Israel/Palestine.* Liverpool: Liverpool University Press, 2013.

Bettis, Leland. "Colonial Immigration in Guam." In *Kinalamten Pulitikåt: Siñenten I Chamorro / Issues in Guam's Political Development: The Chamorro Perspective*, 102–18. Agaña, Guam: Political Status and Education Coordinating Commission, 1996.

Bevacqua, Michael Lujan. "The Exceptional Life and Death of a Chamorro Soldier: Tracing the Militarization of Desire in Guam, USA." In *Militarized Currents: Toward a Decolonized Future in Asia and the Pacific*, edited by Setsu Shigematsu and Keith L. Camacho, 33–61. Minneapolis: University of Minnesota Press, 2010.

Bhabha, Homi, and Jonathan Rutherford. "The Third Space: Interview with Homi Bhabha." In *Identity: Community, Culture, Difference*, edited by Jonathan Rutherford, 207–21. London: Lawrence & Wishart, 1990.

Blum, Hester, Mary Eyring, Iping Liang, and Brian Russell Roberts, eds. "Archipelagoes/Oceans/American Visuality." *Journal of Transnational American Studies* 10, no. 1 (2019): 1–222.

Bonilla, Yarimar, and Jonathan Rosa. "#Ferguson: Digital Protest, Hashtag Ethnography, and the Racial Politics of Social Media in the United States." *American Ethnologist* 42, no. 1 (2015): 4–17.

Boyarin, Jonathan. "Tropes of Home." In *Jewishness and the Human Dimension*, 74–88. New York: Fordham University Press, 2008.

Brenner, Michael. *Zionism: A Brief History*. Translated by Shelley L. Frisch. Princeton, NJ: Markus Wiener, 2006.

Bugeja, Norbert. *Postcolonial Memoir in the Middle East: Rethinking the Liminal in Mashriqi Writing*. New York: Routledge, 2012.

Bui, Long T. *Returns of War: South Vietnam and the Price of Refugee Memory*. New York: New York University Press, 2018.

Butler, Judith. *Parting Ways: Jewishness and the Critique of Zionism*. New York: Columbia University Press, 2012.

Byrd, Jodi A. "American Indian Transnationalisms." In *The Cambridge Companion to Transnational American Literature*, edited by Yogita Goyal, 174–89. Cambridge: Cambridge University Press, 2017.

———. *The Transit of Empire: Indigenous Critiques of Colonialism*. Minneapolis: University of Minnesota Press, 2011.

Camacho, Keith L. *Cultures of Commemoration: The Politics of War, Memory, and History in the Mariana Islands*. Honolulu: University of Hawai'i Press, 2011.

———. *Sacred Men: Law, Torture, and Retribution in Guam*. Durham, NC: Duke University Press, 2019.

Camacho, Keith L., and Laurel A. Monnig. "Uncomfortable Fatigues: Chamorro Soldiers, Gendered Identities, and the Question of Decolonization in Guam." In *Militarized Currents: Toward a Decolonized Future in Asia and the Pacific*, edited by Setsu Shigematsu and Keith L. Camacho, 147–79. Minneapolis: University of Minnesota Press, 2010.

Chamberlin, Paul Thomas. *The Global Offensive: The United States, the Palestine Liberation Organization, and the Making of the Post–Cold War Order*. Oxford: Oxford University Press, 2012.

Chan, Kwok Bun, and Kenneth Loveridge. "Refugees in 'Transit': Vietnamese in a Refugee Camp in Hong Kong." *International Migration Review* 21 (1987): 745–59.

Cheyette, Bryan. *Diasporas of the Mind: Jewish and Postcolonial Writing and the Nightmare of History*. New Haven, CT: Yale University Press, 2013.

Chloe, Taylor. "Foucault and Food." In *Encyclopedia of Food and Agricultural Ethics*, edited by Paul B. Thompson and David M. Kaplan, 1042–49. Dordrecht, Netherlands: Springer, 2014.

Cogan, Doloris Coulter. *We Fought the Navy and Won*. Honolulu: University of Hawai'i Press, 2008.

Collins, John. "Global Palestine: A Collision for Our Time." *Critique: Critical Middle Eastern Studies* 16, no. 1 (Spring 2007): 3–18.

Cordell, Sigrid Anderson. "Between Refugee and 'Normalized' Citizen: National Narratives of Exclusion in the Novels of Bich Minh Nguyen." *Studies of the Novel* 49, no. 3 (Fall 2017): 383–99.

Coulthard, Glen, and Leanne Betasamosake Simpson. "Grounded Normativity/Place-Based Solidarity." *American Quarterly* 68, no. 2 (2016): 249–55.

Coveney, John. *Food, Morals, and Meaning: The Pleasure and Anxiety of Eating*. New York: Routledge, 2000.

Cumings, Bruce. *Dominion from Sea to Sea: Pacific Ascendancy and American Power*. New Haven, CT: Yale University Press, 2009.

Daigle, Michelle, and Margaret Marietta Ramírez. "Decolonial Geographies." In *Keywords in Radical Geography: Antipode at 50*, edited by Antipode Editorial Collective, 78–84. Hoboken, NJ: John Wiley & Sons, 2019.

D'Arcus, B. "Contested Boundaries: Native Sovereignty and State Power at Wounded Knee, 1973." *Political Geography* 22 (2003): 415–37.

Darwish, Mahmoud. *Memory for Forgetfulness: August, Beirut, 1982*. Translated by Ibrahim Muhawi. Berkeley: University of California Press, 1995.

Davis, Rochelle. *Palestinian Village Histories: Geographies of the Displaced*. Stanford, CA: Stanford University Press, 2011.

Day, Iyko. *Alien Capital: Asian Racialization and the Logic of Settler Colonial Capitalism*. Durham, NC: Duke University Press, 2016.

DeLisle, Christine Taitano. "A History of Chamorro Nurse-Midwives in Guam and a 'Placental Politics' for Indigenous Feminism." *Intersections: Gender and Sexuality in Asia and the Pacific*, no. 37 (Mar. 2015). http://intersections.anu.edu.au/issue37/delisle.htm.

Deloria, Philip Joseph. *Playing Indian*. New Haven, CT: Yale University Press, 2007.

Derrida, Jacques. *Archive Fever: A Freudian Impression*. Translated by Eric Prenowitz. Chicago: University of Chicago Press, 1998.

Diab, Zuhair, ed. *International Documents on Palestine 1968*. Beirut: Institute for Palestine Studies, 1971.

Diaz, Vicente M. "Deliberating 'Liberation Day': Memory, Culture and History in Guam." In *Perilous Memories: The Asia-Pacific War(s)*, edited by Takashi Fujitani, George White, and Lisa Yoneyama, 155–80. Durham, NC: Duke University Press, 2001.

———. "No Island Is an Island." In *Native Studies Keywords*, edited by Stephanie Nohelani Teves, Andrea Smith, and Michelle H. Raheja, 90–108. Tucson: University of Arizona Press, 2015.

———. "'To "P" or Not to "P"?': Marking the Territory between Pacific Islander and Asian American Studies." *Journal of Asian American Studies* 7, no. 3 (Oct. 2004): 183–208.

Diaz, Vicente M., and J. Kehaulani Kauanui. "Native Pacific Cultural Studies on the Edge." *Contemporary Pacific* 13, no. 2 (2001): 315–42.

Dinh, Linh. "A Floating Community." In *Blood and Soap: Stories*, 59. New York: Seven Stories Press, 2004.

Dinh, Thuy. "Of Luggage and Shoes." *Amerasia* 17, no. 1 (1991): 159–63.

Drinnon, Richard. *Facing West: The Metaphysics of Indian-Hating and Empire Building*. Minneapolis: University of Minnesota Press, 1981.

Dror, Duki. *The Journey of Vaan Nguyen*. DVD, Zygote Films, 2005. Documentary film.

Dunbar-Ortiz, Roxanne. *An Indigenous Peoples' History of the United States*. Boston: Beacon Press, 2014.

Duong, Lan. "Archives of Memory: Vietnamese American Films, Past and Present." *Film Quarterly* 73, no. 3 (Mar. 1, 2020): 54–58.

Eid, Haidar. "Gaza and BDS!" In *Against Apartheid: The Case For Boycotting Israeli Universities*, edited by Ashley Dawson and Bill V. Mullen, 31–35. Chicago: Haymarket Books, 2015.

Ellman, Michael, and Smain Laacher. *Migrant Workers in Israel: A Contemporary Form of Slavery*. Edited by Sarah Han and Katherine Vanfassen. Copenhagen: Euro-Mediterranean Human Rights Network and International Federation for Human Rights, 2003.

Engelhardt, Tom. *The End of Victory Culture: Cold War America and the Disillusioning of a Generation*. New York: BasicBooks, 1995.

Erakat, Noura. *Justice for Some: Law and the Question of Palestine*. Stanford, CA: Stanford University Press, 2019.

Erdrich, Louise. *The Birchbark House*. New York: Hyperion Paperbacks for Children, 2002.

Espiritu, Yến Lê. *Body Counts: The Vietnam War and Militarized Refuge(es)*. Berkeley: University of California Press, 2014.

———. "The 'We-Win-Even-When-We-Lose' Syndrome: US Press Coverage of the Twenty-Fifth Anniversary of the 'Fall of Saigon.'" *American Quarterly* 58, no. 2 (2006): 329–52.

Espiritu, Yến Lê, and J. A. Ruanto-Ramirez. "The Philippine Refugee Processing Center: The Relational Displacements of Vietnamese Refugees and the Indigenous Aetas." *Verge* 6, no. 1 (Spring 2020): 118–41.

Estes, Nick. *Our History Is the Future: Standing Rock versus the Dakota Access Pipeline, and the Long Tradition of Indigenous Resistance*. London: Verso, 2019.

Farag, Joseph R. *Politics and Palestinian Literature in Exile: Gender, Aesthetics, and Resistance in the Short Story*. London: I. B. Tauris, 2017.

Farrier, David. "Washing Words: The Politics of Water in Mourid Barghouti's *I Saw Ramallah*." *Journal of Commonwealth Literature* 48, no. 2 (2012): 187–99.

Feldman, Ilana. "The Challenge of Categories: UNRWA and the Definition of a 'Palestine Refugee.'" *Journal of Refugee Studies* 25, no. 3 (2012): 387–406.

Feldman, Keith P. "Representing Permanent War: Black Power's Palestine and the End(s) of Civil Rights." *CR: New Centennial Review* 8, no. 2 (Fall 2008): 193–231.

———. *A Shadow over Palestine: The Imperial Life of Race in America*. Minneapolis: University of Minnesota Press, 2015.

Fellman, Anita Clair. *Little House, Long Shadow: Laura Ingalls Wilder's Impact on American Culture*. Columbia: University of Missouri Press, 2008.

Flores, Alfred Peredo. "'No Walk in the Park': US Empire and the Racialization of Civilian Military Labor in Guam, 1944–1962." *American Quarterly* 67, no. 3 (2015): 813–35.

Forbes, Mark. "Military." In *Kinalamten Pulitikåt: Siñenten I Chamorro/Issues in Guam's Political Development: The Chamorro Perspective*, 39–44. Agaña, Guam: Political Status and Education Coordinating Commission, 1996.

Foucault, Michel. *Discipline and Punish: The Birth of the Prison*. Translated by Alan Sheridan. New York: Vintage Books, 1995.

Freud, Sigmund. *Civilization and Its Discontents*. New York: W. W. Norton, 1961.

Fujikane, Candace. "Against the Yellowwashing of Israel: The BDS Movement and Liberatory Solidarities across Settler States." In *Flashpoints for Asian American Studies*, edited by Cathy J. Schlund-Vials, 150–71. New York: Fordham University Press, 2017.

———. *Mapping Abundance for a Planetary Future: Kanaka Maoli and Critical Settler Cartographies in Hawai'i*. Durham, NC: Duke University Press, 2021.

Fujikane, Candace, and Jonathan Y. Okamura, eds. *Asian Settler Colonialism: From Local Governance to the Habits of Everyday Life in Hawai'i*. Honolulu: University of Hawai'i Press, 2008.

Gandhi, Evyn Lê Espiritu. "Historicizing the Transpacific Settler Colonial Condition: Asian–Indigenous Relations in Shawn Wong's *Homebase* and Viet Thanh Nguyen's *The Sympathizer*." *MELUS* 45, no. 4 (Winter 2020): 49–71.

———. "Queer Love across Queer Time: Nonaligned Solidarity, Indigenous Incommensurability, and the Temporal Drag of the Vietnam War." *Critical Ethnic Studies* 5, no. 1 (Spring 2019): 99–123.

George, Alan. "'Making the Desert Bloom': A Myth Examined." *Journal of Palestine Studies* 8, no. 2 (Winter 1979): 88–100.

George, Rachel Yacaa?ał, and Sarah Marie Wiebe. "Fluid Decolonial Futures: Water as a Life, Ocean Citizenship and Seascape Relationality." *New Political Science* 42, no. 4 (2020): 498–520.

Ghanayem, Eman. "Colonial Loops of Displacement in the United States and Israel: The Case of Rasmea Odeh." *WSQ: Women's Studies Quarterly* 47, no. 3–4 (2019): 71–91.

Glissant, Édouard. *Poetics of Relation.* Ann Arbor: University of Michigan Press, 1997.

Goeman, Mishuana. "Land as Life: Unsettling the Logics of Containment." In *Native Studies Keywords*, edited by Stephanie Nohelani Teves, Andrea Smith, and Michelle H. Raheja, 71–89. Tucson: University of Arizona Press, 2015.

Guerrero, Anthony Leon. "The Economic Development of Guam." In *Kinalamten Pulitikåt: Siñenten I Chamorro / Issues in Guam's Political Development: The Chamorro Perspective*, 83–101. Agaña, Guam: Political Status and Education Coordinating Commission, 1996.

Haddock, R. L., R. A. Mackie, and K. Cruz. "Dengue Control on Guam." *South Pacific Bulletin* (2nd Qtr., 1979): 16–24.

*Hale'-Ta: I Ma Gobetna-Na Guam / Governing Guam: Before and After the Wars.* Mangilao, Guam: Political Status and Education Coordinating Commission, 1994.

Hall, Lisa Kahaleole. "Which of These Things Is Not like the Other? Hawaiians and Other Pacific Islanders Are Not Asian Americans, and All Pacific Islanders Are Not Hawaiian." *American Quarterly* 67, no. 3 (2015): 727–47.

Harding, Richard, and John Looney. "Problems of Southeast Asian Children in a Refugee Camp." *American Journal of Psychiatry* 134 (1977): 407–11.

Hartman, Saidiya. "Venus in Two Acts." *Small Axe* 26 (June 2008): 1–14.

Hattori, Anne. "Guardians of Our Soil: Indigenous Responses to Post–World War II Military Land Appropriation on Guam." In *Farms, Firms, and Runways: Perspectives on U.S. Military Bases in the Western Pacific*, edited by L. Eve Armetrout Ma, 186–202. Chicago: Imprint, 2001.

———. "Righting Civil Wrongs: Guam Congress Walkout of 1949." In *Kinalamten Pulitikåt: Siñenten I Chamorro / Issues in Guam's Political Development: The Chamorro Perspective*, 57–69. Agaña, Guam: Political Status and Education Coordinating Commission, 1996.

Hau'ofa, Epeli. "Our Sea of Islands." *Contemporary Pacific* 6, no. 1 (Spring 1994): 148–61.

Hauptman, Laurence M. "Refugee Havens: The Iroquois Villages of the Eighteenth Century." In *American Indian Environments: Ecological Issues in Native American History*, edited by Christopher Vecsey and Robert W. Venables, 128–39. Syracuse: Syracuse University Press, 1980.

Hawthorne, Lesleyanne, ed. *Refugee: The Vietnamese Experience.* Melbourne: Oxford University Press, 1982.

Hellman, John. *American Myth and the Legacy of Vietnam.* New York: Columbia University Press, 1986.

Herman, R. D. K. "Inscribing Empire: Guam and the War in the Pacific National Historical Park." *Political Geography* 27 (2008): 630–51.

Herr, Michael. *Dispatches.* New York: Alfred A. Knopf, 1977.

Herzl, Theodor. *The Jewish State.* Translated by Harry Zohn. New York: Herzl Press, 1970.

Hirsch, Marianne. "Past Lives: Postmemories in Exile." *Poetics Today* 17, no. 4 (Winter 1996): 659–86.

Holtz, William V. *The Ghost in the Little House: A Life of Rose Wilder Lane*. Columbia: University of Missouri Press, 1995.

Hu Pegues, Juliana. "Empire, Race, and Settler Colonialism: BDS and Contingent Solidarities." *Theory & Event* 19, no. 4 (2016). http://muse.jhu.edu/article/633272.

———. *Space-Time Colonialism: Alaska's Indigenous and Asian Entanglements*. Chapel Hill: University of North Carolina Press, 2021.

Huynh, Sabine. "The Vietnamese Community in Israel: A Profile." 12th Biennial Jerusalem Conference in Canadian Studies (June 2008), "Responding to the Challenge of Diversity in Canada, Israel, and Beyond." https://hal.archives-ouvertes.fr/hal-02914986.

Huỳnh Sanh Thông. "Live by Water, Die for Water: Metaphors of Vietnamese Culture and History." *Vietnam Review* 1 (Autumn–Winter 1996): 121–53.

Ihmoud, Sarah. "Policing the Intimate: Israel's Anti-miscegenation Movement." *Jerusalem Quarterly* 75 (2018): 91–103.

Iriye, Akira. *Global and Transnational History: The Past, Present, and Future*. London: Palgrave Macmillan, 2013.

Jacobs, Adriana X. "Where You Are From: The Poetry of Vaan Nguyen." *Shofar* 33, no. 4 (2015): 83–110.

———. "Translating Roots: Introducing the Poetry of Vaan Nguyen." In Vaan Nguyen, *The Truffle Eye*, translated by Adriana X. Jacobs, ix-xix. Brookline, MA: Zephyr Press, 2021.

Jaradat, Mya Guarnieri. *The Unchosen: The Lives of Israel's New Others*. London: Pluto Press, 2017.

Jenkins, Henry. "Blog This!" In *Fans, Bloggers, and Gamers: Exploring Participatory Culture*, 178–81. New York: New York University Press, 2006.

Kahn, Sarah. "Book Reviewed by Sarah Kahn: Bich Minh Nguyen (2014), *Pioneer Girl*." *Journal of Southeast Asian American Education and Advancement* 11, no. 1 (2016): article 6.

Kaplan, Amy. *Our American Israel: The Story of an Entangled Alliance*. Cambridge, MA: Harvard University Press, 2018.

———. "Violent Belongings and the Question of Empire Today: Presidential Address to the American Studies Association, Hartford, Connecticut, October 17, 2003." *American Quarterly* 56, no. 1 (2004): 1–18.

Kaplan, Robert D. *Imperial Grunts: The American Military on the Ground*. New York: Random House, 2005.

Karuka, Manu. *Empire's Tracks: Indigenous Nations, Chinese Workers, and the Transcontinental Railroad*. Berkeley: University of California Press, 2019.

Kasperbauer, Carmen Artero. "The Chamorro Culture." In *Kinalamten Pulitikât: Siñenten I Chamorro / Issues in Guam's Political Development: The Chamorro Perspective*. Agaña, Guam: Political Status and Education Coordinating Commission, 1996.

Kelly, Gail Paradise. *From Vietnam to America: A Chronicle of the Vietnamese Immigration to the United States*. Boulder, CO: Westview Press, 1977.

Kelly, Jennifer Lynn. "Asymmetrical Itineraries: Militarism, Tourism, and Solidarity in Occupied Palestine." *American Quarterly* 68, no. 3 (Sept. 2016): 723–45.

Kennedy, John F. "Acceptance of Democratic Nomination for President." Democratic National Convention, Memorial Coliseum, Los Angeles, California, 15 July 1960. John F. Kennedy Presidential Library and Museum. https://www.jfklibrary.org/learn/about-jfk/historic-speeches/acceptance-of-democratic-nomination-for-president.

Keys, Barbara J. *Reclaiming American Virtue: The Human Rights Revolution of the 1970s.* Cambridge, MA: Harvard University Press, 2014.

Khadduri, Walid, Walid Qaziha, George Dib, George K. Nasrallah, Husain Sirriya ed. *International Documents of Palestine 1969.* Beirut: Institute for Palestine Studies, 1972.

Khadduri, Walid, Anne R. Zahlan, Hussein Sirriyyah, and George K. Nasrallah, ed. *International Documents of Palestine 1970.* Beirut: Institute of Palestine Studies, 1973.

Khalidi, Walid, ed. *All That Remains: The Palestinian Villages Occupied and Depopulated by Israel in 1948.* Washington, DC: Institute for Palestine Studies, 2006.

Kim, Claire Jean. "The Racial Triangulation of Asian Americans." *Politics & Society* 27, no. 1 (Mar. 1999): 105–38.

Kim, Jodi. *Ends of Empire: Asian American Critique and the Cold War.* Minneapolis: University of Minnesota Press, 2010.

———. "Settler Modernity, Debt Imperialism, and the Necropolitics of the Promise." *Social Text* 36, no. 2 (June 2018): 42.

Kimmerling, Baruch, and Joel S. Migdal. *The Palestinian People: A History.* Cambridge, MA: Harvard University Press, 2003.

King, Tiffany Lethabo. *The Black Shoals: Offshore Formations of Black and Native Studies.* Durham, NC: Duke University Press, 2019.

Klinghoffer, Judith Apter. *Vietnam, Jews, and the Middle East: Unintended Consequences.* New York: St. Martin's Press, 1999.

Kunz, E. F. "The Refugee in Flight: Kinetic Models and Forms of Displacement." *International Migration Review* 7, no. 2 (1973): 125–46.

Kwon, Heonik. *The Other Cold War.* New York: Columbia University Press, 2010.

Lai, Thanhhà. *Butterfly Yellow.* New York: HarperCollins, 2020.

Lavie, Smadar. *Wrapped in the Flag of Israel: Mizrahi Single Mothers and Bureaucratic Torture.* New York: Berghahn Books, 2014.

Lê Espiritu, Evyn. "Cold War Entanglements, Third World Solidarities: Vietnam and Palestine, 1967–75." *Canadian Review of American Studies* 48, no. 3 (Nov. 2018): 352–86.

———. "'Who Was Colonel Hồ Ngọc Cẩn?': Queer and Feminist Practices for Exhibiting South Vietnamese History on the Internet." *Amerasia Journal* 43, no. 2 (Fall 2017): 3–24.

———. "Vexed Solidarities: Vietnamese Israelis and the Question of Palestine." *LIT: Literature, Interpretation, Theory* 29, no. 1 (2018): 8–28.

lê thi diem thúy. *The Gangster We Are All Looking For.* New York: Anchor Books, 2003.

Le, Quynh Nhu. "The Colonial Choreographies of Refugee Resettlement in Lan Cao's *Monkey Bridge*." *Journal of Asian American Studies* 21, no. 3 (Oct. 2018): 395–420.

———. *Unsettled Solidarities: Asian and Indigenous Cross-Representations in the Américas.* Philadelphia: Temple University Press, 2019.

Lee, Erica Violet. "Untitled." *Moontime Warrior* (blog), 19 Aug. 2014. https://moontimewarrior .com/2014/08/19/our-revolution-first-nations-women-in-solidarity-with-palestine/.

Leong, Karen J., and Myla Vicenti Carpio, eds. "Carceral States." *Amerasia Journal* 42, no. 1 (2016): vi–152.

Leroy, Justin. "Black History in Occupied Territory: On the Entanglements of Slavery and Settler Colonialism." *Theory & Event* 19, no. 4 (2016). https://muse.jhu.edu/article /633276.

Lieu, Nhi T. *The American Dream in Vietnamese.* Minneapolis: University of Minnesota Press, 2011.

Lionnet, Françoise, and Shu-mei Shih, eds. *Minor Transnationalism*. Durham, NC: Duke University Press, 2005.

Lipman, Jana K. "'A Precedent Worth Setting . . .': Military Humanitarianism—The U.S. Military and the 1975 Vietnamese Evacuation." *Journal of Military History* 79 (Jan. 2015): 151–79.

———. "'Give Us a Ship': The Vietnamese Repatriate Movement on Guam, 1975." *American Quarterly* 64, no. 1 (2012): 1–31.

———. *In Camps: Vietnamese Refugees, Asylum Seekers, and Repatriates*. Oakland: University of California Press, 2020.

———. "Introduction." In *Ship of Fate: Memoir of a Vietnamese Repatriate*, 1–30. Honolulu: University of Hawai'i Press, 2017.

Lloyd, David, and Laura Pulido. "In the Long Shadow of the Settler: On Israeli and U.S. Colonialisms." *American Quarterly* 62, no. 4 (Dec. 2010): 795–809.

Lowe, Lisa. *The Intimacies of Four Continents*. Durham, NC: Duke University Press, 2015.

Loyd, Jenna M., Emily Mitchell-Eaton, and Alison Mountz. "The Militarization of Islands and Migration: Tracing Human Mobility through US Bases in the Caribbean and the Pacific." *Political Geography* 52 (2016): 65–75.

Lubin, Alex. *Geographies of Liberation: The Making of an Afro-Arab Political Imaginary*. Chapel Hill: University of North Carolina Press, 2014.

Lutz, Catherine. "Empire Is in the Details." *American Ethnologist* 33, no. 4 (Nov. 2006): 593–611.

———. "US Military Bases on Guam in a Global Perspective." *Asia-Pacific Journal* 30, no. 3 (26 July 2010). http://apjjf.org/-Catherine-Lutz/3389/article.html.

Maga, Timothy P. "The Citizenship Movement in Guam, 1946–1950." *Pacific Historical Review* 53, no. 1 (1984): 59–77.

Maira, Sunaina, and Magid Shihade. "Meeting Asian/Arab Studies: Thinking Race, Empire, and Zionism in the U.S." *Journal of Asian American Studies* 9, no. 2 (2006): 117–40.

Maitland, Terrence, Stephen Weiss, and Robert Manning. *The Vietnam Experience: Raising the Stakes*. Boston: Boston Publishing Company, 1982.

Malkki, Liisa H. "Refugees and Exile: From 'Refugee Studies' to the National Order of Things." *Annual Review of Anthropology* 24 (1995): 495–523.

Man, Simeon. *Soldiering through Empire: Race and the Making of the Decolonizing Pacific*. Berkeley: University of California Press, 2018.

Manjapra, Kris. *Age of Entanglement: German and Indian Intellectuals across Empire*. Cambridge, MA: Harvard University Press, 2014.

Mariscal, George, ed. *Aztlán and Viet Nam: Chicano and Chicana Experiences of the War*. Berkeley: University of California Press, 1999.

Markowitz, Fran. "Living in Limbo: Bosnian Muslim Refugees in Israel." *Human Organization* 55, no. 2 (Summer 1996): 127–32.

Martín-Lucas, Belén. "Burning Down the Little House on the Prairie: Asian Pioneers in Contemporary North America." *Journal of the Spanish Association of Anglo-American Studies* 33, no. 2 (Dec. 2011): 27–41.

McAlister, Melani. *Epic Encounters: Culture, Media, and U.S. Interests in the Middle East since 1945*. Berkeley: University of California Press, 2005.

McAuliffe, Dennis. *Bloodland: A Family Story of Oil, Greed and Murder on the Osage Reservation*. San Francisco: Council Oak Books, 1999.

Means, Russell, and Marvin J. Wolf. *Where White Men Fear to Tread: The Autobiography of Russell Means*. New York: St. Martin's Press, 1995.

Morgensen, Scott Lauria. "Settler Homonationalism: Theorizing Settler Colonialism within Queer Modernities." *GLQ: A Journal of Lesbian and Gay Studies* 16, nos. 1–2 (2010).

Morrison, C. S., and Felix Moos. "Halfway to Nowhere: Vietnamese Refugees on Guam." In *Involuntary Migration and Resettlement: The Problems and Responses of Dislocated People*, edited by Art Hansen and Anthony Oliver-Smith, 49–68. Boulder, CO: Westview Press, 1982.

———. "The Vietnamese Refugees at Our Doorstep: Political Ambiguity and Successful Improvisation." *Review of Policy Research* 1, no. 1 (Aug. 1981): 28–46.

Mountz, Alison. "Political Geography II: Islands and Archipelagos." *Progress in Human Geography* 39, no. 5 (2015): 636–46.

Muhawi, Ibrahim. "Introduction." In *Memory for Forgetfulness: August, Beirut, 1982*, xi–xxx. Berkeley: University of California Press, 1995.

Munk, Yael. "Duki Dror's Journey of the Displaced." *Cinematheque* 138 (Jan. 2006): 45–49.

Muñoz, José Esteban. *Disidentifications: Queers of Color and the Performance of Politics*. Minneapolis: University of Minnesota Press, 1999.

Nally, David. "The Biopolitics of Food Provisioning." *Transactions of the Institute of British Geographers* 36, no. 1 (2011): 37–53.

Nalty, Bernard C. *Air War over South Vietnam, 1968–1975*. Washington, DC: Air Force History and Museums Program, 2000.

Na'puti, Tiara R. "Archipelagic Rhetoric: Remapping the Marianas and Challenging Militarization from 'A Stirring Place.'" *Communication and Critical/Cultural Studies* 16, no. 1 (2019): 4–25.

———. "Oceanic Possibilities for Communication Studies." *Communication and Critical/ Cultural Studies* 17, no. 1 (2020): 95–103.

Na'puti, Tiara R., and Michael Lujan Bevacqua. "Militarization and Resistance from Guåhan: Protecting and Defending Pågat." *American Quarterly* 67, no. 3 (Sept. 2015): 837–58.

Nassar, Maha. "'My Struggle Embraces Every Struggle': Palestinians in Israel and Solidarity with Afro-Asian Liberation Movements." *Arab Studies Journal* 22, no. 1 (Spring 2014): 74–101.

Nebolon, Juliet. "'Life Given Straight from the Heart': Settler Militarism, Biopolitics, and Public Health in Hawai'i during World War II." *American Quarterly* 69, no. 1 (Mar. 2017): 23–45.

Nielsen, Jorgen S., and George K. Nasrallah, ed. *International Documents on Palestine 1972*. Beirut: Institute of Palestine Studies, 1975.

———. *International Documents on Palestine 1974*. Beirut: Institute of Palestine Studies, 1977.

Nguyen, Bianca, *The Decolonization Conversation* (blog), http://decolonizationconversation.blogspot.com/.

Nguyen, Bich Minh. *Pioneer Girl*. New York: Viking, 2014.

———. *Stealing Buddha's Dinner: A Memoir*. New York: Viking, 2007.

Nguyen, Ly Thuy. "Queer Dis/Inheritance and Refugee Futures." *WSQ: Women's Studies Quarterly* 48, nos. 1–2 (Spring/Summer 2020): 218–35.

Nguyen, Marguerite. *America's Vietnam: The Longue Durée of U.S. Literature and Empire*. Philadelphia: Temple University Press, 2018.

Nguyen, Mimi Thi. *The Gift of Freedom: War, Debt, and Other Refugee Passages*. Durham, NC: Duke University Press, 2012.

Nguyen, Phuong Tran. *Becoming Refugee American: The Politics of Rescue in Little Saigon*. Urbana: University of Illinois Press, 2017.

Nguyen, Qui. *Vietgone*. New York: Samuel French, 2018.

Nguyen, Tuan Andrew. *The Island*. Video Installation, 2017.

Nguyen, Vaan. *The Truffle Eye*. Translated by Adriana X. Jacobs. Brookline, MA: Zephyr Press, 2021.

Nguyen, Viet Thanh. *Nothing Ever Dies: Vietnam and the Memory of War*. Cambridge, MA: Harvard University Press, 2016.

Nguyen, Vinh. "Nước/Water: Oceanic Spatiality and the Vietnamese Diaspora." In *Migration by Boat: Discourses of Trauma, Exclusion, and Survival*, edited by Lynda Mannik, 65–79. New York: Berghahn Books, 2016.

———. "Refugeetude: When Does a Refugee Stop Being a Refugee?" *Social Text* 139, no. 2 (June 2019): 109–31.

Nguyen-Le, Quyên. *Hoài (Ongoing, Memory)*. 2018. Film.

———. *Nước (Water/Homeland)*. 2016. Film.

Nguyễn-võ Thu-hương. "Articulated Sorrows: Intercolonial Imaginings and the National Singular." *Canadian Review of American Studies* 48, no. 3 (2018): 327–51.

Noodin, Margaret. *Bawaajimo: A Dialect of Dreams in Anishinaabe Language and Literature*. East Lansing: Michigan State University Press, 2014.

———. "Language Revitalization, Anishinaabemowin, and Erdrich's *The Birchbark House* Series." In *Frontiers in American Children's Literature*, edited by Dorothy Clark and Linda Salem, 123–32. Newcastle upon Tyne, UK: Cambridge Scholars, 2016.

Pappé, Ilan. *A History of Modern Palestine: One Land, Two Peoples*. Cambridge: Cambridge University Press, 2004.

Pelaud, Isabelle Thuy. *This Is All I Choose to Tell: History and Hybridity in Vietnamese American Literature*. Philadelphia: Temple University Press, 2011.

Pennock, Pamela E. *The Rise of the Arab American Left: Activists, Allies, and Their Fight against Imperialism and Racism, 1960s–1980s*. Chapel Hill: University of North Carolina Press, 2017.

Perez, Cecilia C. T. "A Chamorro Re-telling of 'Liberation.'" In *Kinalamten Pulitikåt: Siñenten I Chamorro / Issues in Guam's Political Development: The Chamorro Perspective*, 70–77. Agaña, Guam: Political Status and Education Coordinating Commission, 1996.

Perez, Craig Santos. "Between the Pacific and Palestine (2018)." Twitter, July 22, 2019.

———. "Crosscurrents (Three Poems)." *Atlantic Studies* 15, no. 2 (2018): 176–82.

———. *from Unincorporated Territory [lukao]*. Oakland, CA: Omnidawn, 2017.

———. "Interwoven." In *Native Voices: Indigenous American Poetry, Craft and Conversations*, edited by CMarie Fuhrman and Dean Rader, 443–45. North Adams, MA: Tupelo Press, 2019.

———. "Off-Island Chamorros." *Craig Santos Perez*, 25 July 2017. https://craigsantosperez.wordpress.com/2017/07/25/off-island-chamorros/.

Phillips, Michael F. "Land." In *Kinalamten Pulitikåt: Siñenten I Chamorro / Issues in Guam's Political Development: The Chamorro Perspective*. Agaña, Guam: Political Status and Education Coordinating Commission, 1996.

Poletti, Anna, and Julie Rak. "The Blog as Experimental Setting: An Interview with Lauren Berlant." In *Identity Technologies: Constructing the Self Online,* edited by Anna Poletti and Julie Rak, 259–72. Madison: University of Wisconsin Press, 2014.

Porter, Stephen R. *Benevolent Empire: U.S. Power, Humanitarianism, and the World's Dispossessed.* Philadelphia: University of Pennsylvania Press, 2017.

*Public Papers of the Presidents of the United States: Richard Nixon: 1969–1974.* Washington, DC: US National Archives and Records Administration, 1971.

Quirk, Joe, and Patri Friedman. *Seasteading: How Floating Nations Will Restore the Environment, Enrich the Poor, Cure the Sick, and Liberate Humanity from Politicians.* New York: Simon & Schuster, 2017.

Qutami, Loubna, and Omar Zahzah. "The War of Words: Language as an Instrument of Palestinian National Struggle." *Arab Studies Quarterly* 42, nos. 1–2 (Winter/Spring 2020): 66–90.

Radley, Kurt Rene. "The Palestinian Refugees: The Right of Return in International Law." *American Journal of International Law* 72, no. 3 (July 1978): 586–614.

Rana, Junaid, and Diane C. Fujino. "Taking Risks, or The Question of Palestine Solidarity and Asian American Studies." *American Quarterly* 67, no. 4 (2015): 1027–37.

Raygorodetsky, Gleb. *The Archipelago of Hope: Wisdom and Resilience from the Edge of Climate Change.* New York: Pegasus Books, 2017.

Rifkin, Mark. *When Did Indians Become Straight? Kinship, the History of Sexuality, and Native Sovereignty.* New York: Oxford University Press, 2011.

Roberts, Brian Russell. *Borderwaters: Amid the Archipelagic States of America.* Durham, NC: Duke University Press, 2021.

Roberts, Brian Russell, and Michelle Ann Stephens, eds. *Archipelagic American Studies.* Durham, NC: Duke University Press, 2017.

Rogers, Robert F. *Destiny's Landfall: A History of Guam.* Honolulu: University of Hawai'i Press, 1995.

Rothberg, Michael. *The Implicated Subject: Beyond Victims and Perpetrators.* Stanford, CA: Stanford University Press, 2019.

Sabar, Galia, and Elizabeth Tsurkov. "Israel's Policies toward Asylum-Seekers, 2002–2014." *Istituto Affari Internazionali* (20 May 2015): 1–18.

Sa'di, Ahmad H., and Lila Abu-Lughod, eds. *Nakba: Palestine, 1948, and the Claims of Memory.* New York: Columbia University Press, 2007.

Said, Edward W. "Chomsky and the Question of Palestine." *Journal of Palestine Studies* 4, no. 3 (Spring 1975): 91–104.

———. "Foreword." In *I Saw Ramallah,* vii–xi. New York: Anchor Books, 2003.

———. "My Right of Return." In *Power, Politics, and Culture: Interviews with Edward W. Said,* edited by Gauri Viswanathan, 443–58. New York: Vintage, 2001.

———. "Reflections on Exile." In *Reflections on Exile and Other Essays,* 137–49. Cambridge, MA: Harvard University Press, 2000.

Salaita, Steven. *The Holy Land in Transit: Colonialism and the Quest for Canaan.* Syracuse: Syracuse University Press, 2006.

———. *Inter/Nationalism: Decolonizing Native America and Palestine.* Minneapolis: University of Minnesota Press, 2016.

Sanchez, Pedro C. *Guahan/Guam: The History of Our Island.* Agaña, Guam: Sanchez, 1991.

Saranillio, Dean Itsuji. "Colliding Histories: Hawai'i Statehood at the Intersections of Asians 'Ineligible to Citizenship' and Hawaiians 'Unfit for Self-Government.'" *Journal of Asian American Studies* 13, no. 3 (Oct. 2010): 283–309.

———. *Unsustainable Empire: Alternative Histories of Hawai'i Statehood.* Durham, NC: Duke University Press, 2018.

———. "Why Asian Settler Colonialism Matters: A Thought Piece on Critiques, Debates, and Indigenous Difference." *Settler Colonial Studies* 3, no. 3–4 (2013): 280–94.

Scupin, Raymond. "Historical, Ethnographic, and Contemporary Political Analyses of the Muslims of Kampuchea and Vietnam." *Sojourn* 10, no. 2 (1995): 301–28.

Shalhoub-Kevorkian, Nadera, and Sarah Ihmoud. "Exiled at Home: Writing Return and the Palestinian Home." *Biography* 37, no. 2 (Spring 2014): 377–97.

Sharif, Lila. "Vanishing Palestine." *Critical Ethnic Studies* 2, no. 1 (Spring 2016): 17–39.

Shemesh, Moshe. "Did Shuqayri Call for 'Throwing the Jews into the Sea'?" *Israel Studies* 8, no. 2 (Summer 2003): 70–81.

Shigematsu, Setsu, and Keith L. Camacho, eds. *Militarized Currents: Toward a Decolonized Future in Asia and the Pacific.* Minneapolis: University of Minnesota Press, 2010.

Shohat, Ella. "Taboo Memories, Diasporic Visions: Columbus, Palestine, and Arab-Jews." In *Taboo Memories, Diasporic Voices*, 201–32. Durham, NC: Duke University Press, 2006.

Sieg, Kent ed. *Foreign Relations of the United States, 1964–1968*, Volume 5: *Vietnam, 1967*. Washington, DC: Government Printing Office, 2002.

Silbey, David J. *A War of Frontier and Empire: The Philippine-American War, 1899–1902.* New York: Hill & Wang, 2008.

Simpson, Leanne Betasamosake. "Indigenous Resurgence and Co-resistance." *Critical Ethnic Studies* 2, no. 2 (Fall 2016): 19–34.

———. "The Place Where We All Live and Work Together: A Gendered Analysis of 'Sovereignty.'" In *Native Studies Keywords*, edited by Stephanie Nohelani Teves, Andrea Smith, and Michelle H. Raheja, 18–24. Tucson: University of Arizona Press, 2015.

Slotkin, Richard. *Gunfighter Nation: The Myth of the Frontier in Twentieth-Century America.* New York: Atheneum, 1992.

Smith, Linda Tuhiwai. *Decolonizing Methodologies: Research and Indigenous Peoples.* 2nd edition. London: Zed Books, 2012.

Spady, James. "As if in a Great Darkness: Native American Refugees of the Middle Connecticut River Valley in the Aftermath of King Philip's War." *Historical Journal of Massachusetts* 23, no. 2 (Summer 1995): 183.

Spivak, Gayatri Chakravorty. "Translation as Culture." *Parallax* 6, no. 1 (2000): 13–24.

Stein, Rebecca L. "Impossible Witness: Israeli Visuality, Palestinian Testimony, and the Gaza War." *Journal for Cultural Research* 16, nos. 2–3 (2012): 135–53.

Stookey, Lorena L. *Louise Erdrich: A Critical Companion.* Westport, CT: Greenwood Press, 1999.

Strom, Dao. *Grass Roof, Tin Roof.* Boston: Houghton Mifflin, 2003.

Stur, Heather Marie. "'Hiding behind the Humanitarian Label': Refugees, Repatriates, and the Rebuilding of America's Benevolent Image after the Vietnam War." *Diplomatic History* 39, no. 2 (2015): 223–44.

Suarez, Harrod J. "Archipelagoes and Oceania in Asian American and Pacific Islander Literary Studies." *Oxford Research Encyclopedia of Literature*, July 2018.

Suzuki, Erin. *Ocean Passages: Navigating Pacific Islander and Asian American Literatures.* Philadelphia: Temple University Press, 2021.

Takkenberg Lex and Riccardo Bocco, eds. "UNRWA and the Palestinian Refugees 60 Years Later." *Refugee Survey Quarterly* 28, no. 2–3 (2009): 227–661.

Taparata, Evan. "'Refugees As You Call Them': The Politics of Refugee Recognition in the Nineteenth-Century United States." *Journal of American Ethnic History* 38, no. 2 (Winter 2019): 10.

Teves, Stephanie Nohelani, Andrea Smith, and Michelle H. Raheja. "Indigeneity." In *Native Studies Keywords*, edited by Stephanie Nohelani Teves, Andrea Smith, and Michelle H. Raheja, 109–18. Tucson: University of Arizona Press, 2015.

Thompson, Lanny. "Heuristic Geographies: Territories and Area, Islands and Archipelagoes." In *Archipelagic American Studies*, edited by Brian Russell Roberts and Michelle Ann Stephens, 57–73. Durham, NC: Duke University Press, 2017.

———. *Imperial Archipelago: Representation and Rule in the Insular Territories under U.S. Dominion after 1898.* Honolulu: University of Hawai'i Press, 2010.

Tilford, Earl H. *Setup: What the Air Force Did in Vietnam and Why.* Maxwell Air Force Base, AL: Air University Press, 1991.

Tran, Quan Tue. "Remembering the Boat People Exodus: A Tale of Two Memorials." *Journal of Vietnamese Studies* 7, no. 3 (2012): 80–121.

Tran, Sharon. "Review of *Pioneer Girl: A Novel*." *Amerasia Journal* 40, no. 1 (2014): 116–18.

Trần Đình Trụ. *Ship of Fate: Memoir of a Vietnamese Repatriate.* Translated by Bac Hoai Tran and Jana K. Lipman. Honolulu: University of Hawai'i Press, 2017.

Trask, Haunani-Kay. "Settlers, Not Immigrants." In *Asian Settler Colonialism: From Local Governance to the Habits of Everyday Life in Hawai'i*, edited by Candace Fujikane and Jonathan Y. Okamura, vii. Honolulu: University of Hawai'i Press, 2008.

———. "Settlers of Color and 'Immigrant' Hegemony." In *Asian Settler Colonialism: From Local Governance to the Habits of Everyday Life in Hawai'i*, edited by Candace Fujikane and Jonathan Y. Okamura, 45–65. Honolulu: University of Hawai'i Press, 2008.

Trinh T. Minh-ha. "An Acoustic Journey." In *Rethinking Borders*, ed. J. Welchman. London: Macmillan Press Ltd; Minneapolis: University of Minnesota Press, 1996.

———. *Surname Viet Given Name Nam.* 1989. Film.

Tuck, Eve, and K. Wayne Yang. "Decolonization Is Not a Metaphor." *Decolonization: Indigeneity, Education & Society* 1, no. 1 (2012): 1–40.

Um, Khatharya. *From the Land of Shadows: War, Revolution, and the Making of the Cambodian Diaspora.* New York: New York University Press, 2015.

Vecsey, Christopher, and Robert W. Venables, eds. *American Indian Environments: Ecological Issues in Native American History.* Syracuse: Syracuse University Press, 1980.

Veracini, Lorenzo. *The Settler Colonial Present.* New York: Palgrave Macmillan, 2015.

Vizenor, Gerald. *Manifest Manners: Narratives on Postindian Survivance.* Lincoln: University of Nebraska Press, 1999.

Võ Hồng Chương-Đài. "When Memories Collide: Revisiting War in Vietnam and in the Diaspora." In *Film in Contemporary Southeast Asia: Cultural Interpretation and Social Intervention*, edited by David C. L. Lim and Hiroyuki Yamamoto, 73–92. New York: Routledge, 2012.

Watson, Irene. "Settled and Unsettled Spaces: Are We Free to Roam?" In *Sovereign Subjects: Indigenous Sovereignty Matters*, edited by Aileen Moreton-Robinson, 15–32. Crows Nest, New South Wales: Allen & Unwin, 2007.

Wendt, Albert. "Towards a New Oceania." *Mana Review* 1, no. 1 (1976): 49–60.

Wilder, Laura Ingalls. *Little House on the Prairie*. New York: Harper Trophy, 1971.

———. *These Happy Golden Years*. New York: Harper Trophy, 2007.

Willen, Sarah S. "Toward a Critical Phenomenology of 'Illegality': State Power, Criminalization, and Abjectivity among Undocumented Migrant Workers in Tel Aviv, Israel." *International Migration* 45, no. 3 (2007): 8–36.

Williams, Raymond. *Marxism and Literature*. Oxford: Oxford University Press, 1978.

Wolf, Daniel, and Shep Lowman. "Toward a New Consensus of the Vietnamese Boat People." *SAIS Review* 10, no. 2 (1990): 101–19.

Wolfe, Patrick. "Purchase by Other Means: Dispossessing the Natives in Palestine." In *Traces of History: Elementary Structures of Race*, 203–38. London: Verso, 2016.

———. "Settler Colonialism and the Elimination of the Native." *Journal of Genocide Research* 8, no. 4 (Dec. 2006): 387–409.

———. *Traces of History: Elementary Structures of Race*. London: Verso, 2016.

Wynter, Sylvia. "Unsettling the Coloniality of Being/Power/Truth/Freedom: Towards the Human, After Man, Its Overrepresentation—An Argument." *CR: New Centennial Review* 3, no. 3 (Fall 2003): 257–337.

"Yasser Arafat in Berlin." *Journal of Palestine Studies* 3, no. 1 (Autumn 1973): 166–68.

Young, Alvin Lee. "Removal from Vietnam and Final Disposition of Agent Orange." In *The History, Use, Disposition and Environmental Fate of Agent Orange*, 121–60. New York: Springer, 2009.

Young, Robert J. C. *Postcolonialism: An Historical Introduction*. Oxford: Blackwell, 2001.

Zalloua, Zahi. *Continental Philosophy and the Palestinian Question: Beyond the Jew and the Greek*. New York: Bloomsbury, 2017.

Zinn, Howard. *A People's History of the United States, 1492–Present*. New York: HarperCollins, 1995.

# INDEX

Baza, Lee T., 45–47, 89, 100
Baza, Raymond T., 44, 45–47, 89
Begin, Menachem, 7, 102–5, 107–10, 114–17, 125–26, 176, 188, 223n66
Benavente, Juan C., 48–49
Ben-Gurion, David, 9, 26
Benjamin, Walter, 152, 158, 177
Berlant, Lauren, 62
Berry, Jennifer, 147
Bettis, Leland R., 134
binationalism, 165–66, 233n44
biopolitics, 93, 95
*The Birchbark House* (Erdrich), 53, 64–66, 71
Black Panther Party, 29
Black, refugee settlers, 4; Third World solidarities, 28–29
blackwashing, 126
Blaz, Juan O., 42–44, 47
blogs, 149–52
Blue Frontier, 185–86
boat people, 103, 125; "A Floating Community" (Dinh) and, 186; SOS Boat People, 147. *See also* boat refugees.
boat refugees: "Packing Poem" (Nguyen) and, 157–158; second wave of Vietnamese refugees as, 7–8, 93, 114–15; Syrian, 11. See also *Tung An* (refugee ship)
Bordallo, Ricardo J., 8, 79–81, 83, 85, 87, 89, 92, 140–41, 141fig., 144
Bordallo, Madeleine, 83, 141fig.
borders, erosion of, 11; inclusion/exclusion through, 3; liquid, 75; of empire, 23
Bosnian Muslim refugees, 122
Bosnian War, 122
Boumediene, Houari, 28
Bousac, Julien, 12fig., 13
Brathwaite, Kamau, 4
Bui, Long T., 39
Butler, Judith, 165–66
Byrd, Jodi, 4, 5, 9, 52, 54

Calvo, Eddie, 154
Camacho, Carlos G., 38–40, 40fig.
Camacho, Keith L., 8
Cambodia, 27, 29, 37, 114, 116, 117
Camp Asan: Iriate, Edith, 137; life at, 86, 97–99; Nguyen, Hoa Van, 146; refugees at, 84, 94fig.; Tran Dinh Tru, 142
Camp Palawan, 117, 167
Canville Treaty, 58
carcerality, 137–40, 144, 228n20; Foucault on, 11
"Care" (Perez), 155–56

Carter, Jimmy, 103–4, 115
Central American, refugees and asylum seekers, 68, 70–71, 155
Chamorro Registry, 150–51
Chamorro(s), 42–49; decolonization movement of, 6–7; on Guam, 23; Guamanian (term) and, 198n94; on Guam's colonial status, 34–42; immigrant transience and, 228n9; Iriate and, 228n16; Marianas, 13; Operation New Life and, 87–93; on Pågat, 228n10; Perez, Craig Santos, 1, 10, 49–50, 51–52, 155–156; population in Guam, 8; soldiers, 23, 42–49, 199n11; term usage, 14–15, 198n94; US citizenship, 8
CHamoru, 14, 150
*Chân Trời Mới* (periodical), 98
"Chaos" (Nguyen), 163
*chenchule'* (sense of obligation), 206n139
Cheyette, Bryan, 164
Chicano soldiers, 199n11
Chickasaw, 4, 6, 56
China, 27, 36, 39–40, 167, 201n42
Chomsky, Noam, 33
co-colonizer, 4
Cold War, 22–23; Indian tropes and, 54–57; US foreign policy and, 24–26; Vietnam/Palestine connections during, 26
colonial nativity myth, 2–3
colonial violence, 2, 5, 52; humanitarian resettlement of refugees and, 3
Commonwealth of the Northern Mariana Islands (CNMI). *See* Northern Marianas Islands
contested land, 5; in Guam, 136; home-making and, 184; in Israel-Palestine, 15, 50, 166, 181; in post-war Vietnam, 181. *See also* land
continental imperialism, 9, 54–57, 70, 185
Coulthard, Glen, 10, 155
critical juxtaposing, 5
critical refugee studies, about, 2–3
"Crosscurrents" (Perez), 155–56
cross-racial identification, 23
cross-racial relationships, 42–49, 87–93, 178
Cuba, 9, 27, 31, 103, 227n4
"Culture Stain" (Nguyen), 171–72
Cumings, Bruce, 11
Cuong Nguyen Tuan, 218n2

Darwish, Mahmoud, 1, 32, 163
Davis, Arnold "Dave," 154
Day, Iyko, 4
Dayan, Moshe, 26, 110, 114

Phillips, Nathan, 73
*Pioneer Girl* (Nguyen), 53, 57–67, 70
poetics of relation, 11. *See also* Glissant, Édouard
politics of staying, 17, 136
politics of translation, 158–161; in *The Island* (Nguyen), 187
Popular Front for the Liberation of Palestine (PFLP), 28, 165
postmemory, 15, 70, 128. *See also* Hirsch, Marianne
problematic families category, 117
Puerto Rico, US acquisition of, 9
Pulau Bidong, 187–90

al-Qasim, Samih, 30–31
queer dis/inheritance, 67, 72
Quitugua, David I. A., 91, 101
Qutami, Loubna, 13–14, 174, 183

racial capitalism, 50, 87; intersectionality with, 3–4; violence of, 155
racialization: of Asian subjects in North America, 4, 111, 124; by US military, 6, 138–39; of Palestinians, 160
racism: interpersonal versus structural, 62; Zionism and, 109; gendered process of, 235n97
railroad colonialism, 4, 52, 61
Ramirez, Florencio T., 40–41
Ramos, Allan, 48
Raygorodetsky, Gleb, 11
reeducation camp, 142, 229n39
Refugee Act of 1980, 226n111
refugee futurity, 17, 64, 185–90
refugee home-making: defined, 5; ethical forms of, 53, 67–73, 156, 184; narratives of, 57–67; of Vietnamese Israelis, 158
refugees: representations of, 2–3; as a solution for settler colonial states, 3; term usage, 15
refugee settler condition: about, 2, 3
refugee settler desire, 53; home-making narratives and, 57–67; queer interrogations of, 67–73; term usage, 59; in Israel-Palestine, 160
refugee settlers: about, 3; as implicated subjects, 5; term usage, 4–5
Refugee Status Determination Unit (RSD), 123, 226n112
refugeetude, 15, 128, 168–173, 186
repatriates, 21, 140–45
Republic of Vietnam, 7, 141
resettlement, about, 2, 5, 16

Rhodesia, 27, 29
Right of Return, 9, 17, 49, 106–7, 119, 124, 159, 165, 174, 178, 180, 181–82
Ritter, Vicky, 140
Roberts, Brian Russell, 11, 13
Rothberg, Michael, 5

Sablan, Johnny, 39–40, 149
Said, Edward, 9, 162, 164–65, 168
Sài Gòn (Saigon): climate of, 145; Fall of, 7, 16, 22, 41, 60, 79, 90, 103, 111, 141–42; Saigon Sally, 45; spelling of, 15
Salama, Saadi, 33–34, 41
Sāmoa, US acquisition of, 9; settler imperialism and, 53
San Nicolas, Frank Cruz, 42–43, 47
San Nicolas, Joseph C., 42, 44–45
Santos, Joaquin "Danny," 47
Saraha, Ayako, 86
Saranillio, Dean Itsuji, 4, 148–49
Saudi Arabia, on UN Resolution 194, 220n17
sea of islands, 2, 188. *See also* Hau'ofa, Epeli
Sears, Cuc Huynh, 129–30
seasteading, 185–86
Selassie, Haile, 112
settler allies, in Hawai'i, 4
settler aloha 'āina, in Hawai'i, 4
settler colonialism: about, 2–3; challenges to, 186; connections to settler militarism and settler imperialism, 8; in Guam, 8; imperialism and, 6; in Israel-Palestine, 8–9; refugee futurity and, 187; in United States, 10, 51–52; of Vietnam War, 52; violence of, 8, 11, 17, 49, 60–61, 65, 67, 128, 129, 159, 163
settler colonial studies, 2–3
settler imperialism: about, 9, 52–53; archipelago of, 74; connections to settler militarism and settler colonialism, 8; humanitarian rhetoric and, 86; Indigenous critiques of, 69; in the Pacific, 52–53; refugee settler desire and, 53; rhetoric of, 56–57; Vietnam War and, 54–57, 149; violence of, 4, 54, 61–63, 72, 75; white settler narrative of refugeehood and, 4
settler militarism: about, 8, 79; carcerality and, 137–40; connections to settler colonialism and settler imperialism, 8; humanitarianism and, 85–87, 93; Juliet Nebolon, 8, 79; land expropriation in Guam and, 80–82; Nixon on, 38; racial identifications and, 137–40; repatriates and, 140–45; temporality of, 133–36; Vietnamese refugee settlers and, 145–153; violence of, 93, 136

Founded in 1893,
UNIVERSITY OF CALIFORNIA PRESS
publishes bold, progressive books and journals
on topics in the arts, humanities, social sciences,
and natural sciences—with a focus on social
justice issues—that inspire thought and action
among readers worldwide.

The UC PRESS FOUNDATION
raises funds to uphold the press's vital role
as an independent, nonprofit publisher, and
receives philanthropic support from a wide
range of individuals and institutions—and from
committed readers like you. To learn more, visit
ucpress.edu/supportus.

CPSIA information can be obtained
at www.ICGtesting.com
Printed in the USA
JSHW051725190123
36535JS00005B/33

9 780520 379657